APOSTLE
TO THE
CONQUERED

PAUL IN CRITICAL CONTEXTS

The Paul in Critical Contexts series offers cutting-edge reexaminations of Paul through the lenses of power, gender, and ideology.

The Arrogance of Nations: Reading Romans in the Shadow of Empire
Neil Elliott

The Politics of Heaven: Women, Gender, and Empire in the Study of Paul
Joseph A. Marchal

Christ's Body in Corinth: The Politics of a Metaphor
Yung Suk Kim

APOSTLE
TO THE
CONQUERED

REIMAGINING PAUL'S MISSION

DAVINA C. LOPEZ

Fortress Press
Minneapolis

APOSTLE TO THE CONQUERED
Reimagining Paul's Mission

Cover design: Laurie Ingram
Cover image: The emperor Claudius subdues Britannia, personified as a woman. Photo © New York University/Institute of Fine Arts Excavations at Aphrodisias.
Book design and typesetting: The HK Scriptorium, Inc.

Library of Congress Cataloging-in-Publication Data

Lopez, Davina C., 1975-
Apostle to the conquered : reimagining Paul's mission / Davina C. Lopez.
p. cm.
Includes bibliographical references and index.
ISBN 978-0-8006-6281-3 (alk. paper)
1. Paul, the Apostle, Saint. I. Title.
BS2651.L67 2008
225.9'2—dc22

2007044122

The paper used in this publication meets the minimum requirements of American National Standard for Information Sciences—Permanence of Paper for Printed Library Materials, ANSI Z329.48-1984.

Manufactured in the U.S.A.

12 11 10 09 08 1 2 3 4 5 6 7 8 9 10

Contents

Illustrations

Preface

For issues surrounding religion, morality, and politics, Paul of Tarsus is one of the most widely quoted and influential figures in Western civilization—inside and outside of professional theological circles, academic biblical studies, and so-called organized religion. Half of the canonical New Testament is attributed to this ancient man, dead for almost two millennia. Anything but dead, his texts have been deployed forcefully, in different historical moments, to tell Christians to submit to the government at all costs, slaves to obey their masters, Jews that they no longer are God's chosen people, women that they should be subordinate to men, and those with partners of the same sex that their relationships are unnatural. Paul is a model for religious conversion and zealous exclusion. He has provided the premier scriptural prooftexts for sexual abstinence, and portions of his letters ("love is patient, love is kind . . .") are commonly used in American heterosexual marriage rituals. Some love Paul, some hate him, and hardly anyone is neutral about him. Misogynist, homophobic, racist, anti-Semitic, xenophobic, elitist—Paul seems to serve as a mirror for our own anxieties about religion, politics, domination, and justice.

In light of such a controversial and deeply embedded cultural legacy, this book seeks to re-imagine Paul's consciousness and communities as critically liberationist in orientation and transformative in potential. Given the particular context in which I currently write—that is, a post-9/11 United States fighting a war in Iraq and on terror with explicit imperial overtones, a United States whose cultural machinery celebrates diversity while creating and managing diverse social identities that are safe for mass consumption, a United States whose public equates religion largely with certain stripes of fundamentalist-leaning, Bible-believing Christianity, a United States wherein deep divisions about sex and power inevitably refer to "what the Bible says"—I submit that it is crucial to re-read, re-situate, and re-imagine the Apostle Paul, his life, his work, and his world. Readings of Paul sit at the center of many contemporary debates appealing to biblical texts. Often he serves as a proverbial stumbling block in a variety of situations. It may be the case that many perspectives can be articulated, but authority rests with Paul, and whoever is thought to be on Paul's good side occupies a preferable moral stance. However, those in marginalized social positions usually lose, as the perceived victims and casualties of what are asserted as Paul's static rhetorical pronouncements and platitudes. If this is indeed the case, is re-imagining Paul even possible or desirable, given all of the ideological energy and weight given to his supposed pro-hierarchical, status-quo-obsessed, anti-liberation stance on any number of issues? Why not just forget about him or at least refuse to engage those who infuse his texts with seemingly irresistible clout? Why not just admit defeat about Paul and move on?

This book does not admit defeat about Paul, even as it asserts that Paul labored among those who were considered defeated. One critical consideration is: Who can claim Paul as authoritative? Another is: With whom does Paul side? I re-imagine Paul as occupying a vulnerable, subversive social position of solidarity among others and as part of a useable past for historically dominated and marginalized peoples in the present. Such attention to the past is not in the service of what some might dismiss as a rehabilitation of Paul and old Pauline hierarchies. I contend that it is a critical re-reading of Paul, and not the refusal to read Paul, that is actually a more potent tool for holding dominant and oppressive interpretations of Paul accountable for injustices. Blaming Paul for various tenacious damages takes some of the weight off of our shoulders for unfortunate histories of Pauline interpretation, particularly around contemporary political issues, where marginalized peoples are made more so. Building what seems unimaginable at this contemporary juncture—a more just human and earth community—is largely why I attempt to re-imagine Paul.

Rethinking Paul as a political figure interested in a more just world order has been a much-deliberated topic among New Testament scholars for some time. In the broadest possible sense, I place this work alongside recent scholarship that has rediscovered the Roman Empire as a world to which Paul responds. However, I depart from this stream of scholarship in two significant ways. First, emergent empire-critical scholarly engagement of Paul has, as far as I know, done very little to take related controversies about gender, race, and sexuality seriously. Though Paul could be called a hero of anti-imperial approaches, ideas about how such an approach changes the way we see his concerns as related to gender, race, and sexuality have been generally overlooked beyond affirmations of perceived misogyny and homophobia and the affirmation that it is unfortunate he thought in these terms. This recent paradigm shift in New Testament scholarship from uncritical religion to the study of empire and politics has really missed the mark on the gendered, sexualized, and racialized texture of dominant ideology. The present work seeks to begin to fill this significant gap.

The second way that I depart from empire-critical approaches is in my reading of visual representation as part of what I call a gender-critical re-imagination. More than illustrations of texts, I position images as that which can be read and critically engaged. I am not involved in the formal identification and classification of art; I am interested in visual communication as a part of the world Paul inhabited, part of the readable evidence available to us. Moreover, images reveal the complex interconnectivity of status, race, gender, and sexuality in a way that some of the ancient texts with which scholars are familiar do not. However, as I hope my book shows, a realignment of the primary sources available to us, and reading literary representations through the lens of these complex images, reveals patterns and suggestions that previously we have not noticed or fully understood.

Throughout this book I ask numerous questions in the service of re-imagining Paul. At the center is what seems like an innocent exegetical inquiry. Who are the Gentiles to whom Paul claims he is sent? It is the case that the Gentiles are the "others" of the New Testament's Jewish orientation and of the traumatic memory of Israel's history as a minority people forever under threat of danger from foreign empires. However, is the binary opposition maintained between Jews and Gentiles still tenable when Paul's Roman imperial context is brought to bear on these categories? In some ways, yes, but I argue that the Gentiles are also the others to the Romans, whose ideological metanarrative structured the world at Paul's time and within which the texts that eventually became the New Testament were fully embedded. They are not the theological non-Jews or Christians defined solely by their non-Israelite status or religion but the theo-political others who should inevitably be defeated and subordinated—according to the will of the gods—as a matter of Roman destiny.

The identity and semiotic properties of the Gentiles, as well as Paul's relationship to them in his Roman imperial context, constitutes a thoroughgoing challenge to, as well as path toward, re-imagining Paul. As a social and theological category, the Gentiles are neither self-evident nor simplistic. In this book's opening chapter I situate the problem of Paul and the Gentiles as well as outline an alternative, non-idealist, methodological shift that I call gender-critical re-imagination. The remaining chapters proceed as follows:

Chapters 2 and 3 are concerned with a realignment of the primary sources of Paul's context; both concern an analysis of what I call the fate of the nations in Roman imperial ideology. Chapter 2 considers Roman imperial visual representation as the most graphic way to see how power relationships and hierarchy operate in the Roman imperial world. I elaborate on Roman imperial visual representation as a complementary semantic system to New Testament texts, in this case Pauline literature. Attention to Roman imperial visual representation contributes profoundly to a gender-critical re-imagination of Paul as apostle to the defeated nations. In particular, the hierarchical construct "Roman is to nation as male is to female" is strikingly vivid. I choose one pattern that has been underestimated in New Testament studies: the personification of defeated peoples as racially distinct female bodies that are displayed publicly in series and called nations. I choose only a few examples to discuss. What is clear from the visual representation that is not so clear in the texts is that the Jews/Judeans are represented as occupying the same ideological space as other conquered enemy peoples and also are the most likely to be personified as a woman's body.

The primary visual sources I discuss in chapter 2 are linked to the textual sources in chapter 3. This chapter concerns literary representation of the nations in relation to Romans. Through analysis of texts displaying what I call the predestination, justification, and eternalization of Roman conquest and universal domination, I provide a richer context as part of a gender-critical re-imagination of Paul as apostle to the defeated nations. I show that in literary representation, the Romans express a construct of inevitable conquest in terms of the same hierarchical power relationships as in visual representation: Roman is to nation as male is to female. Conquest is portrayed as a penetrative, sexual act that sows the seeds of a fertile Roman future. As such, Romans "write" themselves as the masculine master race and the conquered as the feminine inferior races. From a Roman perspective, the nation of the Jews is a particularly pernicious people among many, if not all, of the defeated nations. Therefore, a power differential of interest to New Testament studies should shift from *Jews* over against *other nations* to *Romans* over against *all the nations including Jews*.

Chapter 4 begins a gender-critical re-imagination of Paul as apostle to the defeated nations, focusing on a re-reading of Galatians. I propose that Paul changes both his self-presentation (from conqueror to conquered, from strong penetrating male to weak penetrated female, and to anguished, painful, creative mother) and self-in-relation to all the nations under Roman rule. The gendered and racial implications of this maneuver are that Paul operates on the ground, from a non-elite perspective. His mission is to unite the peoples defined and delimited by Roman conquest through transgressing and subverting the boundaries of identity and association established for them by Roman imperial ideology and often replicated in the self-definition of the conquered. Both transgression and subversion among the nations are accomplished through reconciliatory solidarity and unity under the umbrella of the God of Israel, who promises that all nations will be blessed in Abraham and ultimately gathered together in Zion. Such a rhetoric, which somehow genealogically pits Mother Zion (Sarah) against *pater patriae* (Caesar), is amplified by a transformed "mother Paul" in the only allegory present in the New Testament canon: the Sarah and Hagar allegory in Galatians 4:21—5:1. I argue that, in light of my consideration of Roman imperial ideology of conquest of all the nations, this allegory is among the most transparent literary evidence we have of Paul's embeddedness in both Jewish and Roman contexts. Stemming from this dual embeddedness is an alternative fate of the nations according to Pauline imagination.

Chapter 5 includes concluding observations and raises possible implications and trajectories for this study, in particular, as well as more generally for the methodological shift I propose. I give special attention to the possibilities for re-reading and re-imagining Paul from the margins around contemporary political issues. Here, I again consider the questions of solidarity and universalism that have been the site of contestation in Pauline studies.

The search for a critical re-imagination of Paul is also the search, then, for a viable future, a future that does not stop with acceptance and tolerance for the marginalized. It is the hope for another world and the excavation of a New Testament that gives a glimpse at hope for that world. Consciousness-raising and subversive action among the defeated are processes at the core of Paul's agenda. In this sense, the Gentiles/nations are the most significant others in the New Testament, in fact in the Bible as a whole. Theologically, embracing the nations in a different relationship—solidarity, not assimilation—is not a measure of obedience to certain law constructs. It is a reactivation of the good news of and with the impoverished, the poor, the others: those who are the subjects, not objects, of biblical consciousness. By going to the defeated nations and meeting them where they are—in the dominated places all over Roman territory—Paul recognizes their humanity in a context that has chronic dehumanization as divine mandate. In our own context of chronic dehumanization orchestrated by divinely ordained empire, and in our own acceptance of its terms in many subtle and often undetected ways, I ask us to be challenged again and again by Pauline imagination.

Acknowledgments

Re-imagining Paul as an apostle to the conquered has been an adventure, a mission with many listeners and colaborers. The present work is a revision of my doctoral dissertation in New Testament studies, submitted to Union Theological Seminary in the City of New York. I owe much to the Burke Library, where Betty Bolden and Eun Ja Lee provided every assistance to me. Additionally, the collections in art history and architecture at Columbia's Avery Library were invaluable for my research and writing.

I am fortunate to have enjoyed rich resources for collaboration during graduate studies and the subsequent completion of this project. Rachel A. R. Bundang is an abiding renaissance woman who is the late-night worker (and baker) to my early-morning efforts. Melanie L. Harris has reminded me constantly that our work is conducted in the name of justice and care for all of creation. Maggie Monroe Richter has showered me with plain brilliance. Jenny Phillips has been a diligent coconspirator in staring at Roman buildings around New York and elsewhere. Lillian I. Larsen has been a tenacious sojourner in texts, contexts, interpretations, and cheese fries. The monthly Doctoral Seminar on New Testament, Christian Origins, and Early Christianity at Union, Columbia University, and Barnard College provided a critical intellectual atmosphere for testing some of the ideas that made it into the present work, and many that did not. I am grateful for comments and questions from Vincent L. Wimbush, John McGuckin, Elizabeth Castelli, Steed Davidson, Rosamond Rodman, and Delman Coates. My students at Union were a captive audience and a group of critics for many of my thoughts and interpretations. Teaching a course with Luise Schottroff on Paul gave me much-needed energy for refining my approach.

As a New Testament scholar with interests and training in ethics, social theory, and visual representation, I am indebted to the insights of those who are (by disciplinary convention) outside the field of New Testament studies but no less interested. Beverly Wildung Harrison admonished me to take my feminist scholarly voice seriously. She modeled a rigorous and joyful intellectualism in the classroom that continues to encourage me; in Bev, I began to see how participation in the academy constitutes a certain form of political activism in its own right. Similarly, Larry Rasmussen and Emilie M. Townes encouraged my questions concerning the intersections of ethical methodologies and biblical hermeneutics. Jan Rehmann's inquiries and conversations have constantly reminded me that left-leaning research, writing, and argumentation require careful attention to primary sources. Natalie Boymel Kampen responded to a very early version of my work on Roman imperial visual representation and has been most encouraging about my explorations of art history and things Roman. In particular, her comments helped me give chapters 2 and 3 the shape presented here.

My dissertation committee deserves untold amounts of recognition for their support during that phase of this project. Halvor Moxnes became an essential conversation partner while he was on study leave at Union; his work in queer and space theories has been crucial for this project. Hal Taussig's commitment and collegiality are limitless. He consistently has encouraged me to make bold connections where traditional approaches to biblical studies would never dare to venture. Hal has patiently reminded me just to be myself in my work and has enabled me to begin to (re-)claim art and performance as critical, not peripheral, modes of interpretive agency.

My mentor, Brigitte Kahl, unwaveringly walked with me the entire time I was at Union and now occasionally walks with me on Florida sand. Brigitte's courage, counsel, and great capacity for critical dialogue have indelibly formed me as a scholar and teacher. Re-imagining Paul as apostle to the conquered would not have been possible without her truly Pauline sense of faith, spirit, and grace—which, of course, we should "translate" into solidarity, mutuality, and hope for justice.

Portions of this work benefited from public presentation and critical conversation. Large seeds for this project were sown as a result of my coordination of and participation in Union's 2004 conference "New Testament and Roman Empire: Shifting Paradigms for Interpretation." The Society of Biblical Literature's Paul and Politics group discussed several initial drafts of my work on the Gentiles as conquered nations in Roman imperial visual representation. Richard Horsley provided a space for me to present some of my work on Roman images and ideology and has offered important feedback and critical observation. Todd Penner has been a most cordial conversation partner over portions of this work that eventually were published in a volume he co-edited. Melanie Johnson-DeBaufre, Virginia Burrus, and their graduate students at Drew University offered valuable discussion of Roman sculpture of the conquered and overlapping ideological concerns with Paul's letters.

Eckerd College has been a delightfully ideal environment in which to finish this project. Countless people in the Eckerd community have supported me along the way. Lloyd Chapin, Dean of Faculty, provided me with funding for a research assistant and professional development that have proved invaluable. Julienne Empric, chair of the Letters Collegium, has generously shared her wisdom on critical teaching and negotiating religion in the undergraduate classroom. My students at Eckerd are a joy to teach all things Bible- and Paul-related. My Religious Studies colleagues, Constantina Rhodes Bailly and David Bryant, have been very patient, welcoming, and jovial. Among Letters colleagues, Heather Vincent has talked with me at length concerning the study of the ancient world in our contemporary context. I am grateful to Jared Stark for his intellectual and pedagogical companionship;

I have learned much from his innovative work on literary representations of death and suicide among marginalized peoples.

At Fortress Press, Neil Elliott is an editor extraordinaire and a very wise and welcome conversation partner on Paul, the nations, and liberation. Josh Messner and Marshall Johnson also read the whole manuscript, guided the project to a smooth completion, and enabled me to see gaps and fissures clearly. Any remaining errors are all mine.

My partner, Grace Lewis, has been the most patient listener and relentless skeptic during the writing of this project. Her expertise in reading visual propaganda, moreover, is almost as striking as her knowledge of the New Testament. For this and so much more, I dedicate this work to her.

CHAPTER ONE

The Nations in Nero's Nightmare

Nero, who executed Paul of Tarsus,[1] was in quite a difficult situation before he took his own life. He was unpopular and publicly mocked. Revolts by subject peoples were happening all over his empire around the year 68 C.E. According to his biographer Suetonius, those who were supposed to have faith (*fides*) in Rome's *imperium*—notably peoples in the hard-won Gallic provinces and Spain—were in a state of unrest. We also know that at this time trouble was brewing in the south among the Judeans, who called Jerusalem their capital and refused to worship an image of the emperor as deity. This particular emperor is reported to have persecuted the "Christians," who were a "race of men given to a new and mischievous superstition" (Suetonius, *Nero* 16.2),[2] that is, they had a "hatred of humanity" (Tacitus, *Ann.* 15.44)—meaning, of course, humanity as the Romans promoted it. Nero lamented to his nurse that he was suffering the "unheard of and unparalleled fate" of losing "supreme power" (*summum imperium*) while still alive. He also was given to frightening dreams, portents, and omens about his coming fate. Among the dreams is that he was steering a ship and the helm was taken from his hands; that his wife Octavia dragged him into the darkness; that he was covered with a swarm of flying ants; and that the images of the nations dedicated in Pompey's theater surrounded him and kept him from moving (Suetonius, *Nero* 46.1). Each one of these nightmares is tied to Nero's impending fall from the heights of political power.

The question of what, precisely, the *simulacra gentium*—images of the nations—that came to life in Pompey's theater might have looked like can be addressed by a quick glance at the recently re-discovered Julio-Claudian Sebasteion at Aphrodisias in Asia Minor. Here, at the largest Roman imperial cult complex found to date, one particular image of the nations stands out (figure 1).[3] A man and a woman are carved in high relief. The man is almost naked except for a cloak and military helmet. He is holding the woman down with his knee, and it looks as if he is about to violate her sexually or kill her. No matter the action, the scene depicted is clearly violent. The female figure also is scantily clad, her right breast is bared, and she looks out since her head is being held up by the man's left hand. The couple is identified by an inscription: the man is the emperor Claudius; the woman is Britannia. She represents the territory and people of Britain—the islands north of the European mainland. She is an image of the nation called Britannia.

Figure 1. The emperor Claudius subdues Britannia, personified as a woman; from the Sebasteion (temple to Augustus) at Aphrodisias. Photo © New York University/Institute of Fine Arts Excavations of Aphrodisias.

Lest we think the Aphrodisian Britannia is an island in her position vis-à-vis Rome, perhaps we should try to envision what she could see from underneath Claudius's leg. Across the processional way from her pinned-down body was found a series of what archaeologists believe could have been approximately fifty nation images, each of them a woman, each of them labeled according to their Greek name and territorial designation, for example *ETHNOUS PIROUSTŌN* to signify a vaguely Gallic nation somewhere in the Alps.[4] The nations, who had been defeated and enslaved by Roman military power, were displayed as part of the sculptural program of a public space honoring the emperors as gods. If these *simulacra gentium* were similar to those in Pompey's theater at Rome, then we could imagine a group of captive women coming to life, climbing down from their pedestals, surrounding the embattled Nero, and working together to keep him from moving.

New Testament scholars and other interpreters have not been able to imagine what Nero's fearful dream about the images of the nations has to do with Paul—the Jewish man he had beheaded, according to legend—or the letters Paul wrote to communities all over the Roman Empire that now are canonized as scripture. Yet Paul wrote to Gallic peoples whose uprisings concerned Nero—the assemblies of Galatia—and he also expressed a wish to visit those rebellious Spaniards in his letter to the emperor's home city. And like Nero, Paul also had a vision of being surrounded by the nations. Only Paul did not wait for them to come to life out of Pompey's theater; he went to resurrect them, to pull them out from under Claudius's triumphant body, out from their decorative position in public spaces. Paul sat the nations down to eat. If we examine Paul's rhetoric in light of such images, we can see that his "good news" to the nations is that they no longer are captive and enslaved to a victorious general or raped and killed by divine emperors, but are (re-) born as children of Abraham and belong to the God who brought the Israelites (and others) out of Egypt.

> God was pleased to reveal his son in me, that I might proclaim him among the nations (*en tois ethnesin,* Gal 1:16).

> The one who worked Peter into an apostle of the circumcision worked me also into the nations (*eis tois ethnesin*, Gal 2:8).

> Know, then, that these ones [born] out of faith are sons of Abraham. And having seen that the God would justify the nations (*ta ethnē*) out of faith, the scripture brought the good news to Abraham, that "in you all of the nations (*panta ta ethnē*) will be blessed" (Gal 3:7–8).

> Is God of Judaeans alone? Not also of nations (*ethnōn*)? Yes, also of nations (Rom 3:29).

The collective idea represented visually by Britannia and other women's bodies in the Sebasteion at Aphrodisias and, presumably, in Pompey's theater at Rome is linked to the term in Paul's letters quoted above: in Greek *ta ethnē* (Latin *gentes, nationes*). Could it be that Paul is saying that his God—the God of Israel, of the Judeans—is also the God of Britannia being forced to the ground by another "god"? Is Paul saying that the nations of the earth, in Pompey's theater and the Sebasteion at Aphrodisias, are "justified" through loyalty to his God and blessed in Abraham who exhibited that same faith? If so, what exactly would that mean? Could we imagine? Should we?

In the dominant historical imaginary represented by the guild of New Testament scholarship and interpretation, we cannot and should not connect these images and texts to the Bible. There is no meaning possible in such a connection. Paul is not engaged in going toward the nations—the colonized territories, the collectively defeated peoples, the woman about to be vanquished—in order to announce their liberation from the enslavement characteristic of Roman rule. This would be a political agenda, and Paul's conversion and mission should not be about politics.[5] Paul is on a theological mission, inaugurated in the sky and sent blindingly to earth, to evangelize the non-Jewish Gentiles and bring them the good news of individual faith without works in Jesus Christ. In that sense, Nero's dream about the resurrected *simulacra gentium*, and the complex material and political realities of the Roman Empire it represents, have absolutely nothing to do with Paul's Gentiles.

The Problem with the Nations

Could it really be that Paul's letters were all and only about the spread of a new form of personal faith to individuals who erroneously thought they would be justified by works of the law?[6] Is it true that anything else is a wild dream, wishful thinking, or a figment of the imagination? It seems as if the history of New Testament interpretation would have it this way. After all, scholars of the New Testament and early Christianity know that *ta ethnē*, as used in the New Testament, is the technical theological term for the Gentiles. And the Gentiles, we know, are at the epicenter of Christianity. In major New Testament lexica and reference works, the term *ethnos, ethnē* is defined as a religious signifier for non-adherents to the Jewish cult.[7] Even if, at its core, the term symbolizes a collective of people who share kinship, customs, and traditions,[8] in the field of biblical scholarship *ta ethnē* are usually defined and translated as the peoples who are foreign[9] only to the Jews. *Ta ethnē* are also the non-Israelite Christians and unbelievers, even heathens.[10] According to traditional exegetical perspectives, the word for Gentiles, both in the LXX and New Testament, enjoys a small range of meaning "non-sociologically to describe all the peoples who do not belong to the chosen people"[11] and where politics is not at stake, but "the decisive point is the ethico-religious distinction in relation to salvation history."[12]

Indeed, religious terminology and oppositions drive the definition and interpretation of the Gentiles. In the LXX, the term often translates the Hebrew *goyim*, in supposed contrast to the holy people of Israel, who are called *ʿam*.[13] Staying with this construct appears to strengthen a characterization of the Gentiles as marked by a quality of un-chosenness. Opposed to the Israelites who are chosen by God, the term "conveys a negative judgment from the Jewish standpoint."[14] The radicalness of Paul's gospel, then, is that after he leaves the judgmental constrictions of Judaism behind for the illumination of Christianity, he goes to those who have received harsh negativity and exclusion from his former religious group. By going to the Gentiles, the "unchosen," Paul completes a split from the chosen people of the God of Israel.

Sometimes the terms *ethnos, ethnē* are exegetically linked to the term *Hellēn*, for example,[15] based on a cursory review of Paul's use of what scholars think are terms to designate non-Jews. The differences between these terms and the people they represent—Greeks, barbarians, Gentiles, Scythians—does not seem to matter as *Gentiles* is the New Testament's catch-all category for "difference." Even with a slightly broader nationalistic and geographical signification, the Greeks are positioned alongside or equated with the Gentiles because "for the Jews . . . this Greek sphere is a religious rather than political matter . . . already in Jewish

Greek of the period 'Greek' has the accompanying sense of 'hostile to the Jews,' and it thus approximates the term 'Gentile.'"[16] "Gentiles" are "namely, the mass of peoples not previously drawn into salvation history."[17] Once again, Jewishness and non-Jewishness constitute a binary distinction based on religious orientation. So if we were to ask questions only about soteriology and belief in God and, ultimately, Christ, we should be satisfied with the answer: the Gentiles are the "others," the pagans, the morally inferior, the sinners. Theologically and practically, they are the whole point of Christian missionary work, beginning with Paul himself, in order to propogate the right beliefs. Gentiles do not have a real definition or substance of their own, except in relation to Jews and Israel.

That the Gentiles are usually defined in terms of what they are not—Jewish—points to the fact that dichotomy and opposition characterize our understanding of who they are. In this sense they really do differ very little from the ancient "barbarians" who are defined largely by their non-Greekness through stereotypes.[18] But a quite large problem for the study of the New Testament is that Paul's entire mission rests on the Gentiles. They are the peoples to whom he declares himself sent and among whom he negotiates his famous dogmatic life-sentence of "justification by faith." In fact, nothing in Pauline theology can be understood adequately without attention to the positioning of the Gentiles in his rhetoric and vision. Yet this attention has been limited to rehearsal of the theological Jewish-Gentile divide and, in Christian terminology, distinction on the basis of the type of affiliation with Christianity, for example, "Jewish Christian" and "Gentile Christian." Gentile Christians, of course, are definitively associated with the development of Christianity as an entity separate from Judaism. Even relatively recent New Testament scholarship that affirms Paul's thoroughgoing Jewishness does not ask the question of who, precisely, the Gentiles are outside of a construct dependent on differences from Jews.[19] They exist only in an ideal theological other-world, where they are urged to become religious in the right way.

In such an ideal theological world, where the Bible is its own closed semantic system, images such as those depicting Claudius and Britannia, especially, symbolize nothing but the pre-Christian pagan background to the New Testament. Moreover, images cannot have anything to do with the New Testament because they are not literary texts and, therefore cannot communicate in the same way. In real biblical scholarship images always must be subordinated to words. But what if the images of the nations in Pompey's theater that surround Nero in his dream did have something to do with Paul's world? What if the images I began to describe, and others like them, and the structures that produced them, could tell us something about how to imagine the real world of the Pauline letters? What if images of the nations were not in the background as objects but in the foreground as subjects? What if the images of the nations in visual and literary representation—defeated, enslaved, and female—could tell us something about the New Testament's constructions of gender and the mission to the Gentiles? What if the images could help us engender the others the Gentiles represent?

If we remain in the stratosphere with traditional, "rational" biblical scholarship and interpretation, there is no room for exploring and imagining the complexities and political realities of this larger world and, therefore, no opportunity to ask the question that often is not asked: who exactly are the Gentiles, and why is it so important to Paul that they relate to Jews in a different way? Would the Gentiles have understood themselves as non-Jewish and heathens? In an ideal theological world, where there is no real context for Paul's rhetoric besides personal religious piety and struggles over dogmatic correctness, perhaps they would have. However, if we bring the theological world down to earth, that is, to the inhabited earth dominated—in fact, constructed—by the Roman Empire in the first century C.E., we can see that a whole range of issues are currently unsettled concerning Paul's Gentiles. It is the aim of this study to address such issues.

A Gender-Critical Approach to the Problem

A politically undifferentiated, uncritically theological, and dichotomous view of the Gentiles is a major stumbling block to a reinterpretation of Pauline theology. In this study I make the case for a recontextualization and redescription, or "gender-critical re-imagination," of Paul's relationship with the Gentiles through an examination of the ideology of conquest and universal domination in the Roman Empire. The Roman Empire constitutes the world itself in the period encompassing Paul's life and mission, and the Romans represented themselves as destined to rule over that world and bring peace to it by defeating and incorporating not only their perceived enemies but *all* the Gentiles, otherwise known as the nations. The shift toward a gender-critical re-imagination that I propose involves seeing the Gentiles, particularly in Paul's letters, as precisely the enemies—even all the nations including the Jews—destined to be defeated by and incorporated into Roman imperial territorial rule. A gender-critical re-imagination, then, is as much about the figure of Paul himself as it is about the Gentiles. In fact, it is about reconfiguring Paul as apostle to the defeated nations, as subversive to Roman imperial ideology.

When we open our imagination to the Roman Empire as the context for Paul's letters, we must include a reconsideration of this core term of Pauline theology. The signifier Gentiles, when investigated in a Roman imperial context, takes on a more politically multivalent meaning. Besides meaning non-Jews in an individualized and uncritical religious sense, it also refers to peoples conquered by the Romans and incorporated into (i.e., made to serve) their territorial empire. We must realize that when Paul uses the term *ethnē,* there is more to this emergent picture than religious and theological difference from Israel and Judaism. Paul's use of this term has significance within his Jewish framework, to be sure, but a Jewish framework undoubtedly and unavoidably shaped by the Roman imperial metanarrative ordering the whole world at his time. Additionally, Roman imperial visual representation—Claudius and Britannia and similar images—helps us see both the gendered and sexual connotations of the term *nations*, as well as its broader political relevance.

When brought back to this world, the Gentiles, or nations, are positioned at the busy intersection of empire, colonization, gender, sexuality, and ethnicity. Each of these collective identity-signifiers speaks, however polyvalently, in the language of the others. A gender-critical re-imagination of Paul as apostle to the defeated nations that I propose is indebted to several critical and theoretical perspectives in order to arrive at such intersectionality. In the following, I further describe the methodological approach I employ in the following chapters.

So far, I have argued that in most "idealist" scholarly approaches to Paul and the Gentiles the latter term is treated as a purely theological category, where Nero and his nightmares have nothing to do with Paul and his visions. In this section, I situate my own "non-idealist" methodological approach to this interpretive problem. By situate I mean that methodological considerations are not born of nothing or in isolation; the task is to identify specific contemporary hermeneutical concerns that inform my own work, as well as to provide a set of interpretive patterns with which I am in conversation and from which I depart. To that end, I propose a gender-critical re-imagination of Paul as apostle to the defeated nations as part of a non-idealist framework that draws on elements from contemporary empire-critical, postcolonial, feminist, and queer theoretical contributions.

A Non-Idealist Framework

All of the perspectives I consider below as informative to a gender-critical re-imagination—empire-critical, postcolonial, feminist, queer—rely on exposing the situatedness, biases, and veiled objectivism of traditional scholarly exegetical approaches to the New Testament, as well as in many cases a mandate to change social relations in this world in the name of justice for the marginalized. Quests to pull otherworldliness from the sky and situate it in alignment with or in contrast to any world at all, however, are connected to non-idealist, or materialist, approaches to the Bible. Non-idealist approaches engender a re-examination of the historical-critical method of biblical exegesis—which has been co-opted in some sense and turned from its radical roots to decontextualized adherence into a historical scientific positivism[20]—and challenge it once again to become more critical through readdressing its general lack of consideration for "concrete realities of life, such as economic and political power structures, social struggles against oppression, exploitation, discrimination, and so forth."[21]

In a non-idealist framework for biblical interpretation, three interrelated alterations are made to the traditional exegetical task, constituting a significant departure from it. First, historical-critical approaches are manipulated to take into account the concrete social contexts of biblical texts, including political and economic structures, patterns of domination and subordination, and marginalization. Non-idealist readings insist that ideas and texts "do not fall from the sky"[22] but are products of culture, specifically political and economic structures. Second, authors and readers, in every historical context, reflect embeddedness in and interaction with political and economic structures and social positioning. Because texts (and authors and readers) are products of culture, they must be treated as part of its social texture, which means that for the Bible, a wider variety of cultural artifacts must be considered to describe adequately the "textile" constituting a social context.

Third and perhaps most urgently, a non-idealist reading has social transformation and justice as its agenda. By turning away from idealist readings of the Bible and attending to the first two tasks mentioned above, non-idealist approaches aim to liberate the Bible from appropriations and interpretations aligned with privilege, elitism, and imperialism that masquerade as value-neutral. Such are interpretations that obscure an overall consistent biblical message of liberation from slavery,[23] the "gospel of the poor" at the center of both Testaments.[24] In this sense, the Bible is not seen as necessarily affirming the social texture of which it is a part, but is re-positioned and reclaimed as a counter-narrative that proclaims counter-practices from the margins.

A gender-critical re-imagination of Paul as apostle to the defeated nations is, at its core, a non-idealist mode of reading and seeing New Testament texts. First, I endeavor to bring the Gentiles down to earth and locate them in the material and social realities of the Roman Empire that serves as the historical context for Paul's letters. Second, this re-imagination and recontextualization of the theological Gentiles as the nations destined to be both defeated by Roman rule and restored to the God of Israel is accomplished through analyzing Roman imperial visual and literary representation as part of the social fabric into which Paul is threaded and to which he responds. Third, through this critical re-imagination, I submit that the "gospel for the poor" is reactivated in Paul's "gospel for the defeated nations." This is the case because the nations are not an apolitical category, but signify the marginalized peoples and colonized lands to whom Paul is sent. They are not disembodied, but ideologically located in space and time underneath the emperor's weighty, ever-expanding body. The apostle to the defeated nations advocates their liberation from the slavery of Roman domination via solidarity with Israel, whose forebears were brought out of Egypt and Babylon and whose capital city became a "light to the nations" according to prophetic rhetoric. Paul's letters, then, can be re-read as a "rhetoric of resistance,"[25] promoting alternatives to imperial oppression. The "glue" holding this approach together is the capacity to use re-imagination in the service of making a different future.

Empire-Critical and Postcolonial Frameworks

A gender-critical re-imagination notices the tensions and resistant dynamics in Paul's rhetoric, repositioning them as expressing some form of resistance. When resituated in the Roman Empire, Paul's advice, as well as his manhood and the communities among whom he dwells, are all thrown into drastic relief as anti-imperial. Paul emerges as a Jewish person negotiating his political world and responding not to dogmatic charges of theological errancy, but to the economic realities of Roman imperial domination. The realization, or really the rediscovery,[26] that the world of Paul, the Jewish person, is the Roman imperial world has led to a major new, increasingly productive, area of scholarship in New Testament studies that seeks to relocate Pauline concepts and strategies in terms of their relation to political and economic relationships, ancient and present. In this sense, "empire-critical"[27] scholarship echoes a non-idealist agenda by its commitment to renewed and reconfigured historical analysis, recognition of the need to pay attention to imperialism ancient and modern, and a concern for transformation of social conditions.

Empire-critical New Testament scholarship on Paul has the advantage of several major methodological maneuvers. Proponents acknowledge that "whether or not to look at the connections between cultural texts and imperialism is therefore to take a position in fact taken—either to study the connection in order to criticize it and think of alternatives for it, or not to study it in order to let it stand."[28] Having decided that imperialism in the modern context is too pernicious to "let it stand," empire-critical approaches bring political sensitivity toward imperial designs to bear on the most influential of ancient cultural texts. First, the New Testament is seen as a collection of documents demonstrating negotiation of and resistance to Roman imperial rule. There is a clear confrontation with what is asserted as a false dichotomy between politics and religion. The anchor of much empire-critical work regarding the New Testament is the Roman imperial cult, considered to be the primary religio-political system operative at Paul's time and to which the letters respond.[29] With a major dualism challenged and the Roman Empire identified as a religious *and* political context, empire-critical approaches draw on non-idealist endeavors to relocate the history of ideas approach toward a history of people and movements over time, especially people who have been and/or are dominated and marginalized and associated movements. Judaism and Christianity, in these perspectives, constitute two such movements in the ancient world.[30]

The interest in explicitly contesting imperialism as a means of seeing the New Testament differently is where empire-critical approaches intersect with postcolonial interpretation. The term postcolonial "describe[s] the modern history of imperialism, beginning with the process of colonialism, through the struggles for political independence, the attainment of independence, and to the contemporary neocolonialist realities."[31] This term "emphasizes the connection and continuity between the past and the present, between the colonizer and the colonized."[32] Yet the very designation "postcolonial" itself implies a commitment to transformation of the present[33] by acknowledging the imperialist misdeeds of history, as well as how imperialism and colonialism have indelibly shaped present discourses, identities, and political and economic structures.[34] Postcolonial subjects[35] are those "whose perception of each other and of economic, political, and cultural relationships cannot be separated from the global impact and constructions of Western/modern imperialism, which still remain potent in forms of neocolonialism, military arrogance, and globalization."[36] In postcolonial studies, the intersecting issues of land, race, military power, international connectivity, and gender are considered essential to the interpretive enterprise.

Postcolonial modes of dealing with the Bible cannot precisely be called exegesis in the traditional way. This is by choice, because to many adherents of postcolonial biblical interpretation, the point is not to perpetuate usage of the tools promoted by a discipline that is itself inextricably bound to imperialism and colonialism.[37] A major tenet of postcolonial biblical studies is that the academic discourse of biblical exegesis is thoroughly implicated in the perpetuation of imperialism and colonialism.[38] In this sense, a postcolonial approach to the Bible is in alignment with non-idealist methodologies.

However, a significant departure of postcolonial biblical interpretation from non-idealist perspectives is that postcolonial biblical critics treat the traditional tasks and results of exegesis with suspicion. This treatment is partly because of trenchant postcolonial claims that imperial language is contained in the Bible itself, across both Testaments, that mandates and legitimates a colonial project on behalf of both Israel (First Testament) and then Christianity (New Testament) to dominate the ends of the earth.[39] This is a different set of claims and methodological foci than recognizing that the Bible has been used as a tool of and icon for Western imperialism and colonization. Though critics who engage in postcolonial biblical studies endeavor for a "reading of the Bible in which imperialistic strategies are confronted, exposed, and arrested by postcolonial subjects,"[40] often what results is a condemnation of the Bible itself, so that its texts and contradictions are rendered impotent for social transformation from the margins in the present. Thus, a re-reading of the Bible as a cultural artifact and production with the marginalized as its center, with all the problems that brings, is not often promoted in postcolonial biblical interpretation.

The conflation of the colonialism and imperialism thought to be *in* the Bible with that which is *mapped onto* it through the historical usage of the Bible, and a refusal to engage in a practice of counter-reading, do not resolve the thoroughgoing methodological issues that postcolonial biblical study raises. The Bible itself, according to a non-idealist view, has been put "in chains"[41] and colonized; the text is among the victims and casualties of imperialism. One of the main agenda items of non-idealist approaches is the liberation of the Bible. This means a recovery of the option for the poor/marginalized/colonized, through a radical recontextualization and "re-fabric-ation" (placing the Bible in its place as part of the textile of life). In fact, it could be said that postcolonial biblical interpretation, by dismissing such re-discovery as a viable possibility, participates in the continued obfuscation of the Bible's core message of "release of the captives," where the captives are the real subject (not the object) of biblical discourses.[42]

Empire-critical and postcolonial approaches to interpretation of the New Testament are heavy on criticism of established and traditional reading practices, and both propose alternatives to (academic) biblical studies in the name of liberation and self-definition of the marginalized victims of colonization and imperialism. Subject to debate is whether the Bible itself can be of any use in the formulation of such alternatives or as a tool in the process of liberation, and whether the Bible can really re-emerge as a counter-impression of imperial culture, given its full co-optation and employment in the name of world-wide missionary-style domination.[43]

Significant blind-spots exist in both the empire-critical and postcolonial biblical interpretation that I address throughout this work and are at the intersection of gender analysis and Paul. In terms of gender studies, empire-critical and postcolonial approaches are at times sensitive to the inclusion of women,[44] but are undertheorized concerning the gendered texture of imperialist and colonialist discourses as a whole—even if the entire project of studying empire requires attention to the intersections of gender, race, class, and military power within a context of globalization and alienation. Although Paul is a current hero of empire-critical approaches, I know of no full-length postcolonial treatment of Paul's life and work, including his mission to the nations.[45] Empire-critical and postcolonial studies of the Bible also still place primary emphasis on philology and literary expression, whose prominence as tools for reading is unquestioned, despite art historian Paul Zanker's contribution to *Paul and Empire.*[46]

In contrast to an exclusively literary and philological approach, or an approach that sees visual representation as secondary or illustrative to literary claims, a gender-critical re-imagination seeks to follow up on a distinct lack of attention to visual representation as a crystallization of the basic ideological framework of the Roman Empire through which the Bible, with the defeated nations or colonized others at its center, does in fact emerge as a counter-narrative to colonialism. Inattention to gender and images leaves interpretive gaps and open questions when we look at Britannia underneath Claudius. Her femininity and status as a defeated other land at the margins of the Roman Empire begs for analysis and connection that is currently absent in empire-critical and postcolonial biblical interpretation.[47]

A gender-critical re-imagination seeks to do just this kind of analysis from a non-idealist vantage point of thoroughgoing interest not only in anti-imperial or political formulations of Paul, but such formulations of Paul informed by feminist, queer, and other liberationist agendas and struggles for a different, re-imagined world in the past *and* in the present. In that sense I hear the call for shifting the agenda of biblical studies from sifting the past for the universal and linear history of ideas to searching for a past that is usable for historically dominated and underrepresented peoples, a past that also requires us to ask different questions about the present.[48]

Feminist and Queer Approaches

The gender-critical emphasis of a gender-critical re-imagination is directly connected to feminist and, more recently, queer theories and readings of New

Testament studies and texts. Feminist New Testament studies, in particular, is a massive enterprise that only three decades ago was not very well known or populated. In recent years, major reference works, book series, issues of journals, and academic conferences are devoted to this increasingly diversified path of scholarly inquiry. Queer studies, which has gained more momentum outside of the theological disciplines than within, due at least in part to institutionalized homophobia and heterosexism, also is finding a somewhat more marginal place as that which provides a critical appraisal and, hopefully, transformation of traditional idealist exegetical methods. Both approaches to the Bible consciously assume gender as a lens through which to analyze and criticize naturalized power relationships and differences in hierarchy.

Feminist New Testament interpretation has numerous iterations, all taking women's experiences as a foundational impetus for understanding, revising, and transforming the exegetical task.[49] At its center are three interdependent components that connect such hermeneutics to broader non-idealist proposals for biblical studies. Related to the non-idealist impulse for contextual reading, feminist biblical interpretation has sought to remember women as historical subjects. This is accomplished by insisting not only that women are part of the texture of the biblical text itself, but also part of any social context in which the production of a text is embedded. Putting women back into history, however, is only a piece of this reflective maneuver; "complicating" the picture with the presence of women in the past and present makes it necessary for biblical interpreters to ask difficult but obvious questions about the application of androcentrically produced and supported ancient texts to modern situations where women's authority and agency are at stake.

Using women's experience as a resource for biblical scholarship and teaching reveals, as with another general principle of non-idealist approaches, the reality that ideas do not fall out of the theological sky but are created and supported by people who enjoy specific social and economic positioning. Authors, texts, and readers are always socially located; for feminist interpretation, this has meant a critical appraisal of the reality that biblical texts and interpretations have been overwhelmingly filtered through men and others aligned with patriarchal interests as authors, readers, and interpreters.[50] Through doing so, a main contribution of feminist interpretation is exposure of the unquestionable androcentricism of biblical texts and the situatedness of all interpreters and interpretations. Likewise, according to certain strands of feminist interpretation, economic and social structures that make possible the production of texts also are recognized as hierarchical creations that promote and naturalize the subordination of women to men.[51]

Feminist New Testament scholarship has historically been concerned with recovering, as much as is possible, women's voices in the texts, as well as positioning women as readers and interpreters with agency. This complex of concerns has been directly influenced by contemporary questions regarding women's placement in church and society, such as whether or not they should be ordained and what kind of authority the Bible legitimates. These specific questions fit into larger discourses promoting women's liberation. In this sense, as in non-idealist approaches, the first and third tasks are co-dependent. The re-discovery of an original "women-church" or "discipleship of equals"[52] betrayed by the New Testament that can be useful for the emancipation of women today has at times led to an impasse: is the New Testament liberating for women or not?[53] While some New Testament passages are thought to be recoverable as useful to the contemporary project of women's emancipation (Galatians 3:28 comes to mind),[54] others are dismissed as impossible to reconcile with the project of feminist-oriented liberation.[55] How do we negotiate the passages that seem to be anti-woman—is it enough to emphasize the androcentricism of the context in which they were produced as a way to deal with such texts? The question of how women's voices can be recovered without re-inscribing and affirming traditional patriarchal historical-critical approaches is a major area of contention in feminist New Testament studies. For some, insofar as biblical interpretation has been associated with male privilege veiled as objectivity or value-neutrality, women would do well to turn away and find alternate paths.[56]

A major contribution of feminist New Testament interpretation is the assertion that patriarchal power relationships are not natural or created by God. Patriarchy is historically located and situated and therefore can be overcome in favor of different structures and social arrangements.[57] Even if this is a lasting achievement, it also should be clear that gender constructs that constitute patriarchy are not natural or given, or even the same across time and space. Such variability points to a major hermeneutical debate connected to questions in gender theory common to both feminist and queer biblical interpretation: that between essentialism and social construction. Are the categories and identities called women and men to be taken for granted, or do social and economic structures help create them?[58] What is the correlation between sex (believed to be tied to biology) and gender (the making of sex into a natural category and social position)? Should we limit our interpretive task to women alone or to instances in the New Testament where women appear or are explicitly named? It would make a difference to broaden gender analysis to focus on the gendered texture of texts and ideology as a whole.

Like feminist readings, "queer" approaches to the Bible also enter conversations about the social construction of gender roles and categories. Such modes of reading have originated partially out of necessity as a way for lesbian, gay, bisexual, and transgender (LGBT)-identified people to negotiate inquiries and anxieties concerning sexual orientation and participation in social institutions (including churches and marriage). Contemporary public debates about sexual orientation are engaged rather simplistically at crucial moments by uncritical appeals to the Bible.[59] Biblical scholars are thought to provide definitive solutions to questions about LGBT inclusion by demonstrating, for example, whether Paul was pro- or anti-gay, or whether the biblical witness condones homosexual activity. In a best-case scenario, Bible readings that inform such debates are limited to the nominal passages that have historically been read as having to do with same-sex activity or homosexual individuals (e.g., Lev 18:22, Rom 1:18-32, 1 Cor 6:9).[60] Interpreters have been forced into a conversation concerning homosexuality and the Bible on terms that have already been determined—namely, how can homosexuality be acceptable in a predominantly heterosexual world? Acceptance or rejection of homosexuality is a priority. As a result, the dominant heterosexual imaginary is not overcome.[61]

In such debates, homosexual and heterosexual are taken for granted as essential, ahistorical, and static identities within individuals and across cultures. But queer, rather than solely a descriptive term, a stand-in for "homosexual," or abbreviated way to say "lesbian, gay, bisexual, or transgender," is a challenge to the heterosexual/homosexual hierarchy promoted as natural but in fact is elaborately built into economic and social structures in different historical and social contexts. Being and acting queer necessitates structural analysis and a shift in focus from how to deal with *what is* to how to imagine *what is possible*. Queer signifies a stance against comfort and against the ordinary order of the world. When confronted with the question of whether or not homosexuals are acceptable, a queer position does not automatically engage it, but asks why acceptability is the only, or best, option available. Queer hermeneutics moves from simple answers and prescriptions to complex questions and considerations. The interest in exposing the privileged character of the sexual binary, as well as the ability to imagine a different future, cements queer positionality as a non-idealist orientation.

Informed both by materialist, feminist, and gay liberationist struggles and by selected postmodern theoretical orientations, queer theoretical investigation aims to disrupt seemingly fixed paradigms of sexual orientation and gender formation.[62] Its proponents interrogate what counts as normal or natural sexual roles and identities in a given historical and social context. At its best, queer theory insists that sexuality is political and not separate from the complexities of social life.[63] To "queer" a text is to locate spaces where the so-called normative bodily narratives—monogamy, the heterosexual nuclear family, manly men, and feminine women—are destabilized. As ancient historian David Halperin notes, what should be challenging about queer theory is its capacity to "surprise and startle," to make how the world operates visible so we can imagine where to go from here.[64]

I claim the non-idealist orientation of queer theory as that which can be employed as a tool, as part of a gender-critical re-imagination, to confront and interrupt dominant political rhetoric that is expressed using gendered and sexual imagery. This requires moving beyond simple presentation of gender and sexuality as categories for analysis or positing the expression or existence of homosexuality in antiquity as a reason to (dis)regard the New Testament as authoritative for contemporary public decision making on matters sexual. Categorically, becoming queer encourages movement from center to margins, from high to low, from already to not-yet, from self to other. It seeks to subvert dominant normal categories and transform them in the service of building a different world, an-other world. For non-idealist purposes as outlined in this project, queer subjectivity is at the core of the biblical message of liberation; leaving the ordinary slavery-perpetuating structures of the world behind in pursuit of the "promised land" is most certainly an anti-patriarchal, unnatural movement.

Such subversive impulses are not yet fully integrated into queer New Testament studies, because queer interpreters are still, understandably, responding to the pro-gay/anti-gay debates, especially in light of increased visibility of LGBT people and recent movements for gay marriage in the United States.[65] However, there are crucial implications for further analysis in the recent work of Halvor Moxnes on Jesus that integrates spatial and queer theories.[66] Overcoming the (irrelevant) question of Jesus' personal sexual orientation or that of his followers, Moxnes positions Jesus' queerness as exemplary dislocation from dominant institutional social order and categories (such as the household) and not as a theory that he had sex with other men. In this sense a queer reading is more thoroughgoing and promising than examination of selected passages or citing prooftexts for debates over the legitimacy of homosexuality; queerness is an expression of that which challenges the projected normalcy of the world. The Kingdom of God is a re-imagined, queer space properly stationed as a not-yet-place that transforms dominant social and cultural configurations.

Feminist and queer biblical interpretation have evolved into multifaceted methodological tools for addressing biblical texts and contexts from the margins in the service of liberation.[67] In both cases, however, Paul has been considered a major obstacle to true emancipatory re-readings of the New Testament due to his perceived insurmountable hatred of women and gay people, as well as his overall domineering masculine self-presentation and expectation of his communities. This is at least partly due to the reality that famous and enduring prooftexts for misogyny and homophobia are in Paul's letters. While I would not argue that Paul is perfect or even a feminist or gay man himself, I submit that characterizations of Paul as excessively dominating and irretrievably harmful suffer from a lack of complexity. Ancient Paul is not simply for or against contemporary women and LGBT people. As is the case with empire-critical and postcolonial interpretation, conflation of what is perceived to be *in* the text with the prejudices that have been *mapped onto it* in its "captured" form throughout time,[68] primarily by those who seek to maintain privilege, has prevented a thorough re-evaluation and re-imagination of Paul from feminist, gender-critical, and/or queer perspectives.

In a non-idealist framework, the discipline of biblical exegesis is responsible not only for participating in the exclusion and oppression of large groups of people, but also for hiding the basic radicalness of the Bible itself. A gender-critical re-imagination of Paul as apostle to the defeated nations seeks to emphasize such radicalism. To do so, I rely on several threads of critical evaluation stemming from feminist and queer theory and hermeneutics. Central is the articulation that gender and sexuality are not about what an individual essentially has or is, but about how one behaves in relation to others within a larger framework that is expressive of power and privilege. In other words, gender and sexuality are useful optics for seeing more adequately the hierarchical relations of power operative in the Roman Empire of Paul's time—and how his correspondence is situated in that context. It is precisely the possibility that Paul unhinges the naturalness and inevitability of the Roman Empire that is important to this project. The apostle to the defeated nations attempts such unhinging through imagining a counter-discourse to the gender expression central to the creation of imperial power. Likewise, repositioning the nations at the margins of Roman rule makes Paul's call for solidarity between Jews and Gentiles look entirely different, even transformative, when gender and sexuality are better recognized as speaking for and about hierarchical difference and structural domination.

Summary and Outlook

Each of the methodological perspectives I have outlined above has several components in common. First, the New Testament (and the Bible as a whole) is shaped by the culture in which its texts were written and also by its history of interpretation and the cultures that have read and used it throughout time. Second, all biblical interpretation is situated and comes from a socially and historically located perspective; a primary step in interpretation is to be suspicious of readings that declare themselves neutral. Third, histories of dominated and marginalized peoples should matter to the discipline of New Testament studies. It is painfully and unavoidably true that the New Testament has been appropriated, domesticated, and used as a weapon by those who have had power throughout time. Students of the New Testament and early Christianity must continue to come to terms with that reality; we must never forget it. However, this reality renders an imperative for progressive and radical re-readings. Even as the New Testament is a document of massive cultural influence, it is also a document of resistance to imperial domination. It makes a difference to understand, through attention to the intersectional dynamics of Roman imperial ideology, that Paul in particular is concerned with the core issue of social transformation.

The theoretical perspectives discussed above also share undertheorization concerning interconnection and interdependency between issues of marginalization, as well as how such marginalization is expressed using gendered and sexual imagery in an imperial context. New Testament scholars of many interpretive stripes, including those dyed with liberationist hues, have been blind to the possibility that the image of Britannia, a defeated nation, pinned under Claudius, is in any way linked to the Gentiles to whom Paul is sent. But since her likeness is part of the social fabric into which Paul threaded his letters, it is also imperative to explore such a link in the service of re-reading and re-engaging Paul's texts.

Cursory examination of the image of Claudius conquering Britannia reveals that no single form of interpretation outlined above is adequate enough to properly "read" her position. If we (can) read for gender alone, we see a female body violently situated under a male body. If for queerness, we see both a female body in forced hierarchical relationship to maleness, as well as an unruly Amazonian type of gender transgression held in check by the forces of male power and, perhaps, an anxiety about penetration. If we think about empire and religion, we see a divine emperor "sacrificing" and taming an inferior woman's body; we also see this relief as part of an imperial cult complex, where provincials would go to worship. And if postcolonial analysis is brought to bear on this relief, perhaps we see a representative of the central colonizing power defeating a colonized borderland, forcing her into "civilization."

Each of these perspectives demonstrates a different aspect of this same image, revealing its complexity. However, none of the relationships suggested by Claudius and Britannia's proximity to one another is intelligible without attention to the other facets. The significance of the New Testament's nations, then, cannot be simply that they are theologically not Jewish. The relief of Britannia and Claudius, and therefore the representation of the nations, shows them as lying at the intersection of gender and sexuality, religion and politics, and ethnicity and colonization. I submit that there is not a way to successfully separate out these factors within the material reality of Paul's context. A gender-critical re-imagination hopes to explore this intersection as creatively, as imaginatively, as possible. Below I outline some tools that will assist in the reconceptualization of Paul and the nations that I propose.

Re-Imagining Paul and the Nations

Reconsideration of the Roman imperial context of the New Testament writings reveals a complexity to the concept of Gentiles as representing nations conquered by and assimilated into Roman territorial and cosmic rule. Multiple primary sources attest to this political reality. However, the power differential between Romans and other nations is perhaps most clearly expressed in Roman imperial visual representation, which employs gendered imagery, notably personifications of conquered nations as women's racially specific bodies, sometimes in poses of deference toward Roman emperors or soldiers. A gender-critical re-imagination requires a realignment of the primary materials available to us concerning the world in which Paul lived and wrote as well as tools for a re-interpretation of these materials as counter-impressions of one another. Interdisciplinary work is not always methodologically obvious; in this section, I provide a wide-angle view of some helpful concepts to situate this project further.

Ideology, Imaginary, Imagination, Re-Imagination

As each of the interpretive perspectives I have outlined indicates, I am primarily interested in departing from traditional New Testament exegesis. One of the problems with proposing alternatives, as a non-idealist orientation makes visible, is that idealist New Testament interpretation creates, maintains, and affirms particular patterns of seeing texts and the world. A gender-critical re-imagination seeks to disrupt such patterns by strongly repositioning a reading of Roman imperial ideology as central to conducting Pauline studies.

The designation *ideology* is vital for understanding the structure of Paul's context. Ideology, according to Louis Althusser's well-known formulation, is "the imaginary relationship of individuals to their real conditions of existence."[69] For Althusser, imaginary does not necessarily mean pretend. The *imaginary* designates what is created out of the presentation of knowledge as inevitable and universal. It is a relentless display of reality as unmediated and neutral and renders such reality invisible to criticism. Marginalized peoples know the imaginary only all too well: it is the "way it is and always has been"; that is, it is a world just fine as it is,[70] a world that does not welcome voices in the wilderness. Within the landscape of the imaginary, it is sufficient to just tweak, alter, and add; a wholesale transformation is neither desirable nor possible. Yet the imaginary is also seductive to the marginalized. Continuous co-optation of the borders and historically dominated in the name of celebrating diversity is promoted as dominant culture's concept of social justice, causing fractious debates within marginalized communities themselves.[71] Insofar as the imaginary suppresses transformative impulses, it is not emancipatory.

An important aspect of the imaginary as crucial to ideology, as far as can be applied in both ancient and contemporary contexts, is the discouragement and suppression of counter-voices through the threat of, and actual, violence. This is certainly the case in the Roman example, as I assert throughout this project. However, counter-voices and counter-practices can be detected speaking out of what can be called *imagination*. Imagination serves as a powerful tool, when coming from the marginalized, not only to confront the imaginary as deceptive, dominant, and harmful, but also to identify voices that have been repressed and articulate new discourses and ways of being that overcome its power.[72] In other words, through the identification of imagination, the imaginary is revealed as false, perhaps as pretend indeed. Imagination arises from a position of hope among the disenfranchised; it is the ability to envision a different world when that task seems overwhelming, implausible, and forbidden. Imagination is, in a sense, an often-coded revenge of the margins and the borders; it is often only vaguely familiar or intelligible to the imaginary while at the same time shattering its totalizing grip. I contend that, when examined in light of Roman imperial ideology, Paul's mission to the nations emerges not as a direct parallel, or even as an oppositional rhetoric, but as a counter-hegemonic discourse exemplary of imagination.

Yet *imaginary* and *imagination* occupy a double context: I use imaginary to designate the naturalness inherent in Roman imperial ideology, and imagination for Paul's response. However, I am not unaware that the term imaginary could also designate the contemporary context, including the ideology of idealist interpretive constructs characteristic of biblical studies and imagination, a non-ideal hermeneutical response from the margins. The role of imagination from the margins as a response to what is promoted as natural (read: exegetically proper) in biblical studies "urges the development and use of new methods of biblical interpretation" by questioning and seeing a different future "through transformative imagination as a counter-hegemonic subversive practice."[73]

In a gender-critical re-imagination, one major step of subversion and development of new methods is an in-gathering of primary sources and fields of study, usually considered unimaginable or irrelevant to Pauline studies. This is necessary in order to show the subversive imagination of Paul's letters in their Roman imperial ideological context. It requires (ad)ventures outside the traditional idealist discipline of New Testament studies toward the theoretical perspectives I have reviewed. It also means a (re-)engagement with disciplines working on various aspects of Paul's context: ancient history, art history, archaeology, and classical studies.[74]

Imagination is a critical subversive practice; *re-imagination* is involved in the process of re-alignment, recontextualization, and re-reading. Re-imagination seeks to re-install Paul in his place as exhibiting critical subversive practice in his Roman imperial ideological context. I endeavor to re-read Paul among the nations as the subject of marginalized consciousness and imagination; I re-imagine Paul as a comrade, and not commander, of those at the borders and on the bottom. Critical re-imagination, then, promotes an alternative image of Paul. To do this, re-imagination as methodological process also posits a different relationship with non-textual sources. Visual representation in particular constitutes a primary, and not secondary, site where meaning is made and mapped. Re-imagination means to replace the image as central to Paul's imagination. Hopefully, through such a process, we are able to see the nations come to life.

Mapping Roman Imperial Ideology

I allege that the nations in Pompey's theater who come to life and surround Nero, as well as the nations like Britannia underneath Claudius in the Sebasteion relief, are among those to whom Paul claims he is sent as apostle. I also take the gendered expression of imperial power relationships seriously and imagine Paul as commenting on such power structures. By doing so I place Paul and images of the nations defeated by Rome in the same symbolic space, together on a map toward meaning-making. Such placement necessarily involves taking the structure that produced the representative images of the nations seriously as well as seeing the images themselves as reflective of Roman imperial ideology.

While images are reflective of ideology, they also construct it and participate in its dissemination. Roman imperial visual representation constitutes a mode of communication, or a semantic system[75] essential to expressing ideology to as wide an audience as possible, elite and non-elite. Roman imperial visual representation, rather than consisting of numerous individual objects that are unintelligible, exhibits a consistency of themes and elements that indicate a language of its own.[76] Images play a large role in cementing the imaginary quality of reality that for the Romans had much to do with the reinforcement of perception concerning state achievements. More than an illustration of a text, images provide a window onto culture and power relationships; they also render such relationships, and the institutions that keep them going, natural. Key categories useful to understanding social structure and hierarchy are rendered effortlessly yet complexly through visual culture.

Using the relief of Claudius and Britannia as an example, several significant and opposing concepts emerge, the analysis of which will assist in mapping Roman imperial ideology more transparently. Some of these already were mentioned: self and other, male and female, active and passive, high and low, conqueror and conquered, order and threat, law and lawlessness, civilization and barbarism, city and country, colonizer and colonized, Greek and Amazon, Roman and nation, god and land, cosmos and chaos. As Claudius is defined by his relationship to Britannia and vice versa, none of these concepts can take on meaning independent of a relationship to one another. And each of these oppositions operates in a wider framework, where they help to define "the way it is." The relief itself might be a portrait of an emperor vanquishing a barbarian people represented as a woman, but structurally the relationship between Claudius and Britannia also communicates more than that. Roman imperial ideology, through images like this one as well as texts, represents these relationships at once as inevitable, natural, and universal. The task of a gender-critical re-imagination, by reading such images and Paul together, is to analyze such representation and locate Paul's imaginative responses.

Semiotics, or analysis of systems of signs, is a tool that assists in understanding such representation. Semiotic analysis begins with the assumption that language, or what enables representation, consists of interlocking patterns of signs. The value of signs depends on their relations to other signs within the system; a sign has no value independent of its context or semantic field.[77] A sign has two parts: that which it is and that which it is not.[78] In other words, according to structuralist semiotics, signs are given meaning by what they are not; meaning is relational, and mostly differential.

Language, however, is not an innocent product of reality; it constructs reality. The task of non-idealist semiotic analysis is to show how ideology works and is maintained as natural through an understanding that reality is not unmediated or objective, but is composed of interlocking patterns of signs and codes that make meaning in specific historical and cultural contexts. Semiotic analysis is, then, ideological analysis, as "whenever a sign is present, ideology is present."[79] Representation and reality construction occur at sites of (class) struggle, where those who gain control of the codes gain control of ideology. Therefore, certain signs and codes contribute to reproducing specifically bourgeois ideology, making it seem universal and natural.[80] Semiotics also recognizes a fuller range of systems of signification than just words. The overall task of semiotics is to determine how, and in whose interests, reality is constructed, precisely so it can be denaturalized through the location of contradictions, inconsistencies, and gaps that form the basis of social change. For the New Testament, the construction of reality under consideration is the Roman Empire, the ideology of which is easily accessible through its public art.

As discussed above, Claudius and Britannia represent several significant differential categories through their visually represented relationship to one another, revealing a language of oppositions structuring the reality of the Roman imperial context of the relief. Such oppositions can be mapped using a semiotic diagram, developed by Algirdas Greimas, by arranging them in differential relationship to one another:[81]

Figure 2. Semiotic Diagram: Structural Oppositions Constructing Reality. This Semiotic diagram maps power relationships as hierarchy. The A and B positions signify the dominant position. A and B, however, define and are defined by non-A and non-B, which represent not only the "opposite" of A and B but also a subordinate position. Spatially, Claudius overwhelming Britannia is a succinct expression of hierarchical relationships.

Here elements common to this image and the "table of oppositions" originally developed by Aristotle (quoting Pythagoras)[82] are mapped to show tensions. Following Brigitte Kahl, I alter the Greimasean diagram by turning it on its side. This maneuver affords a clearer picture of the hierarchical dimensions of the oppositions constructing ideology, rather than representing them neutrally as side-by-side.[83] Male, for example, is in a hierarchical relationship to female even as male cannot be understood apart from female. The signs in the A and B positions represent the top of a power structure, the values; non-A and non-B represent the bottom anti-values.

Through this mapping of Roman imperial ideology, we can readily identify the nations as semantically associated with the non-A and non-B anti-values of other, female, passive, low, conquered, threat, lawlessness, barbarism, country, colonized, land, and chaos. The Romans, personified by Claudius, are associated with the A and B values of self, male, active, high, conqueror, order, law, civilization, city, colonizer, god, and cosmos. The interlocking systems of signification, then, reveal a construction of reality created and maintained by the Roman imperial house and elite to protect privilege and power at the expense of the multivalent nations who are defeated. This is the structure in which Paul also works.[84]

For a gender-critical re-imagination of Paul, texts and images are not just read alongside each other, but emerge as counter-impressions of one another. Images may speak at times in a louder and clearer voice concerning dominant ideology than do texts, and may more obviously suggest points of resistance. I submit that this is certainly the case with the nations (see chapter 2). Working with Roman imperial visual representation as a semantic system reveals gender constructs as essential to the deep structure of Roman imperial ideology. A Roman imperial ideology of divinely ordained conquest and rule without end over all the nations is coded using gendered signifiers, exemplified by the Claudius and Britannia relief briefly discussed here. The manliness of the Romans overcomes the perceived (and often exaggerated) femaleness of foreigners. This is shown most graphically by the visual evidence: the Romans personified the nations using female bodies in public viewing contexts, thus solidifying a hierarchical differentiation central to constructing the reality of their domination as natural, inevitable, and universal.

Re-Mapping the Nations in Paul's Letters

A main point of this study is to recontextualize, in a non-idealist way, the Gentiles and nations and position them as occupying the same semantic field as the poor and marginalized. Such a shift re-imagines Paul as an apostle to the marginalized through his mission to the defeated, linking Paul's mission to the nations with the preferential option for the poor and marginalized at the core of the Bible. This requires attention to the whole of his historical and social context, including visual and literary representation from those in charge, the Romans. Therefore, in light of such attention, an expanded and re-imagined grammar of the nations is in order.

Paul's use of *ethnē*[85] is always in the plural, save for one instance where he quotes Deut 32:21 (Rom 10:19) referring to the "not-nation" and (the nation of) Israel.[86] This indicates that he does not conceive of Gentile as a designation for a singular person (a Gentile person, for example). Paul's use of the term for Gentiles can be viewed, therefore, not so much as a marker of individual but collective identity. Paul refers to himself multiple times as the apostle to the nations.[87] In several instances Paul's letters,[88] when mentioning the nations, are interested in a relationship to Jews.[89] He also uses the term relative to *peritomē*, "circumcision" (e.g., Gal 2:8, 9).[90] The term *peritomē* is used alongside *akrobustia*, "foreskin" (usually translated: "uncircumcised"). Paul's use of *peritomē* and *ethnē* as oppositions places nations and uncircumcised in the same semantic position.[91] This does indicate a semantic opposition between Israel and nations, but it is also important to locate Paul's discussion of this term in its immediate literary context and ask the question of what he does with such opposition.

Paul employs these oppositions as a part of his discourse on reconciliation. His use of nations, circumcision, and foreskin is highly concentrated in his rhetoric concerning "justification by faith" in Galatians and Romans. These are places where Paul builds his case that the Gentiles and the Jews are *both* justified, and therefore must relate to one another differently as part of "one body."[92] The term *ethnē* appears frequently in Romans 9–11 (the "tree-grafting" of Jews and nations)[93] and 14–15 (the "weak and strong" sharing at table),[94] both main passages explicitly concerned with an integrative relationship between Jews and other nations that overcomes, not reinforces, the dichotomy and hierarchy implied in Jews/Gentiles. In Romans 4, Paul locates both circumcision and foreskin in the same genealogical position by making Abraham the father of both groups. Putting Jews and nations in the same space, by having them eat in the same place, is also a preoccupation of Paul's in Galatians 2 and Romans 15.[95] Peter's fear of the "circumcision faction" and his subsequent withdrawal from the "table of nations" is what Paul says is his reason for "opposing him to his face" in Antioch, according to Gal 2:11. Jews and Gentiles, then, appear to be oppositions within which Paul operates and with which Paul struggles to build different relationships.

James Scott has identified the "Table of Nations" tradition of Genesis 10 as a motivator in Paul's use of the term in his letters, particularly Galatians.[96] According to this tradition, all of the nations of the earth were descended from Noah after the flood. They blanket the whole world and can trace their origins back to a common father, further back even than Noah to the creator God of Israel. The world according to Jewish conceptualization, therefore, is composed of all of the nations who share a common ancestry. Scott indicates that Paul references this Jewish historical and geographical tradition to justify his travels to the specific peoples to whom he wrote.[97] However, it is not clear that "sacred geography" is the only impetus for Paul's mission. Even if that is the case, however, geography is not politically neutral. Paul's possible use of Jewish geographical constructs must be positioned in light of the dominant, Roman geographical imaginary of his context.[98]

Paul genealogically links "all of the nations" to Abraham. This means Israel *and* Gentiles. Abraham is presented as the father of Jews and other nations, circumcised and uncircumcised, since he himself "trusted" (*pisteuō*) God before he received the covenant of circumcision (Rom 4, Gal 3:8–9). In other words, according to Paul's rhetoric, Abraham was identified both with the foreskin (nations) and circumcision (Jews), making him the father of both groups. In Galatians, Paul draws on the Genesis tradition that "all the nations" will be blessed in Abraham (Gal 3:8). His fatherhood of the one promised "seed" (*sperma*) is activated in Christ; through trusting Christ, "all" (the nations) are "sons of God" (Gal 3:26), the "seed of Abraham," and "heirs according to the promise" (Gal 3:29; see also the transformation from slaves to sons to heirs in 4:1–7). In Paul's imagination as it relates to his Jewish framework, all of the nations are (re-)connected through common descent from the God of Israel.[99]

It is the case that one of Paul's reference points for his use of *ethnē* must be his Jewish context, exemplified by "his scripture" and other Jewish texts available to us. Scott has provided extensive cataloging and analysis of the use of *ethnos*, *ethnē* in the LXX and other Hellenistic Jewish literature. I do not endeavor to duplicate that work, even if sustained reconsideration of Paul's Roman imperial context leads to a different conclusion about how Paul interacts with that material. Similarly, Paul's Jewish identity and scriptural context has been well established, and I assume

Paul operates fully in reference to that identity and context. I seek to broaden the semantic field available to Pauline significations. Therefore, how Paul's Jewishness signifies in light of Roman imperial ideology is a specific concern of this project.

While all of the nations, including Israel, might belong to the same human family in Paul's Jewish framework, in this study I entertain the notion that Paul relates to a different framework as well. The Romans also have a tradition of locating all of the nations in space and time through visual and literary representation.[100] The theme of "original relatedness" is not the case in the Roman imperial ideology of Paul's time.[101] The fate of all of the nations, according to the Roman imaginary, is to be ferreted out and found, conquered, and incorporated into the Roman family through military violence and diplomacy, as well as subsequent enslavement and death. Such is the divine mandate of the master nation chosen by Jupiter and given "empire without end, without limits on space or time" (Virgil, *Aen.* 1.279). Rome, the chosen nation, celebrated chosenness through violence against others. In this sense, Rome constitutes a nation herself, though designated as the "nation of the toga" and the nation endowed with "civilization" and a mandate to supply order and peace to the chaotic outsiders at the borders.

In Roman foundation myths and stories, geographical and historical texts, accounts of events such as triumphal processions, and visual representation, other nations are foreign to Rome and threatening, and must be defeated and displayed as such. Cataloging and defeating foreign nations builds up Rome's power as universal dominators and slaveholders. The great men of the genealogy of Roman rule, from the gods to the father Augustus as displayed in his Forum, have in common achievements like military victory over non-Romans. In the Roman imperial framework, all of the nations are linked to the *pater patriae* through conquest and capture, not creation and brotherhood. The nations who blanket the earth, in this schema, belong to Rome and should be subjugated to a god who is also a human state ruler. Therefore, the nations have political, geographical, gendered, and racial dimensions to their semantic field. They cannot be defined without attention to power relationships. Such a recontextualization needs to inform Paul's self-presentation and view of the nations.

A re-imagined grammar of the nations especially notices that the difference in hierarchy between Romans and nations is communicated in gendered terms; the semantic field of *ethnē* ἔθνη, then, is necessarily also about constructions of gender and power. The Romans in the early principate conceived of relations of power as "power over," in excessively masculine terms,[102] and this is evident in constructions of the Roman male body: he is to be always a penetrative sexual partner, literally or figuratively. A "real man" is not to be penetrated in any way.[103] Any hint of penetrability rendered the body "un-male," or female, and thus on the "bottom." Yet this conception extends far beyond the individual body to Roman corporate, national ideology. Femaleness—foreignness—is always to be conquered by force or to be complicit in the impenetrability of imperial maleness.

Romans' stories about themselves and their conquered world in the imperial period, in conversation with visual representation, reveal that the hierarchical dichotomy and opposition to examine in Paul's letters, particularly Galatians, should shift from Jews/Gentiles to Romans/nations. The Jews belong to the underside of a Romans/nations hierarchy as one of many defeated and incorporated peoples, and Paul's self-presentation and mission as outlined in his letters should be seen in that light. I use these chapters to provide examples for positioning the Romans/nations difference in hierarchy as a primary ideological constellation at the center of a reconceptualization of Paul's self-presentation and mission to the nations.

The Romans/nations hierarchy is a power differential expressed through gender constructs and has a sexual connotation: conquest is rendered as male penetration of femaleness (women's bodies and land) on a grand, international scale. This is especially apparent in visual representation, where victorious Romans are personified by a single male body in relationship to a nation personified by a female body, but the literary examples are clear enough as well. Roman imperial conquest "was a brutal affair, and, like later Western imperialism, probably produced a similar reservoir of phallic oppression on the frontiers, where 'women became conquests' and 'conquests became women.'"[104] Likewise, in literary representation, gender and sexual constructs played a rather large role in how Roman imperial ideology communicated the idea of what it meant to be Roman, and what it meant to belong to the empire/fatherland and its leader, who was imaged as father and god at the same time.

A re-imagined grammar of the nations through inclusion of sources usually dismissed as ornamental to New Testament studies reveals the term as politically charged and symbolic of conquest and defeat. The nations lie at a complex intersection of gender, race, sexuality, nationality, geography, military power, and economic structures. As a signifier, they occupy a site of struggle.

CHAPTER TWO

The Fate of the Nations in Roman Imperial Representation

The inclusion of Gentiles in Paul's rhetoric is a theme that benefits from attention to gender and Roman imperial power dynamics. This means endeavoring to understand the concept of Gentiles in a more nuanced, non-idealist, and power-conscious way, taking into account what Gentiles signified, not just in Paul's Jewish context but also in his Roman imperial context. As a recontextualized symbol, *ethnē* means the non-Roman peoples of the Roman Empire; it maps the terrain of Roman *imperium* in terms of its "others." As a result of such a broader, non-idealist analysis bolstered by attention to gender, sexuality, ethnicity, and militarism, the meaningful hierarchy for Pauline studies emerges as not Jews/Gentiles, but Romans/nations.

To better view the Romans/nations hierarchy, a gender-critical re-imagination of Paul as apostle to the defeated nations employs visual representation as a complementary semantic system to literary materials. Rather than posit images as merely illustrative of or subordinate to texts, I treat Roman imperial visual representation as a type of communication, controlled and propagated by the Roman imperial house and elite, who maintained "peace." Therefore, this chapter is concerned with *seeing* conquered peoples and nations in relationship to conquering Romans, or rather, how the Romans depicted the machinery of their relationship to non-Romans as their rulers. In particular, this chapter is interested in visual representation as an integral component expressive of Roman imperial ideology. Through visually representing conquered peoples as the necessary casualties of peace and those to whom the Romans had a divine mission to civilize, world domination was naturalized and justified. Through representing personifications of conquered nations in series in the context of an imperial cult complex, the Romans affirmed "peace through victory" as predestined and eternal, a matter of civic religiosity. The gendered dimensions of conquest are also more obvious and striking through images, which serve to help create and maintain gender and social hierarchy as natural, inevitable, and unalterable.

In this chapter I present and discuss relevant material examples of ancient visual representation of conquered nations from the early Roman imperial period. Although the Romans depicted their historical enemies in a variety of media, as well as in the flesh and in different settings, here I am interested in the consolidation of conquered peoples into ethnically specific singular female bodies, designating both people and land, who are then depicted alone or together, labeled nations, and shown in deference to Roman rule in public contexts. It is this pattern of visual representation in particular that contributes most strongly to a re-picturing of the Gentiles as a political category in Paul's letters, and in the New Testament more generally, as part of a gender-critical re-imagination. Understanding the dominant ideology, as much as is possible, assists in a more confident identification of counter-voices.

Visual Representation of Roman Imperial Ideology

Although scholarly attention to Paul as a respondent to his Roman imperial context is growing, few efforts have been made to fully understand the visual dimensions of the Roman imperial context Paul navigates.[1] Sustained attention to visual representation is an overlooked but fruitful way to analyze constructions of gender and power in Paul's Roman imperial context. As articulated by feminist art historian Natalie Boymel Kampen, a particular ideological task of representation is to express institutions and cultural configurations as "natural," so "inevitable and universal" that the viewer accepts them as such without question.[2] In other words, visual representation plays a crucial, and not peripheral, role in the construction of Roman imperial reality.[3]

The Romans literally *constructed* an imaginary reality communicating a rather consistent reality through what C. R. Whittaker has called the two imperial "instruments of power": the city and the army, both powerful indicators of a colonizing presence outside the capital city.[4] Both city and army were completely re-envisioned and energetically implemented, particularly outside Italy, by Augustus. Roman imperial emphasis on the "production of space"[5] enabled the development of a self-referential Roman elite identity that also allowed for local indigenous elite to participate. Through the standardization of spatial production, the Roman Empire modeled connectivity, encouraged similar behaviors, and projected "the unity and stability of the imperial system while, at the same time, allowing for the display of local identity"[6] throughout its territory.

But the kind of local identity permissible to display in the Roman imperial system was limited to what the Romans found acceptable from their subjects. On the underside of promoting elite cooperation with Roman constructions of reality in the colonies and provinces, the production of outsider identities based on stereotypes was no less vigorous or consistent. In fact, Roman imperial identity was directly linked to specific representations of "others," particularly others in the provinces and frontiers into which the Romans expanded through territorial conquest. This is observable through reading the story of Roman imperial identity and culture through attention to visual representation in the context of imperially produced and managed spaces; "in a society that had no regular newspapers, radio, or television, the official means of communication were mostly visual: coins, statues, paintings, relief sculpture."[7] Visual communication made the naturalization of ideas about institutions, cultural configurations, and hierarchies intelligible to a wider range of people than just textually literate elite:[8] all who could see and walk past a victory monument would probably be able to "read" it. Public art in public space proclaimed the corporeality, coherence, and universality of the Roman state. The iconography of Roman imperial art thus forms a symbolic system, or a multivalent "grammar,"[9] that articulates and naturalizes power relationships.

Such visual representation offers a revealing path to comprehending perceptions and constructions of gender and power in Roman society, as well as to perceiving how gendered imagery communicates the Roman imperial ideology that the New Testament writers navigate. Therefore, reading these images in conversation with New Testament texts can be productive. Methodologically, attention to visual representation of the Roman/nations hierarchy as a thoroughgoing current in imperial ideology also assists in asking different questions of Pauline rhetoric. In a gender-critical re-imagination, Roman visual representation is used as what I call a *complementary semantic system* through which New Testament texts can be interpreted. Analyzing what Paul Zanker has called "the power of images"[10] together with text works toward fostering a deeper understanding of gender constructs and therefore power relations in the New Testament.

Visual representation offered the Romans a striking way to publicly depict the nations as conquered outsiders incorporated into their territorial empire. The Romans used visual symbols and allegory[11] to portray conquered lands and were especially innovative in this regard. Moreover, Roman visual representation of nations was usually accomplished using gendered personifications. While personifications were also used in more positive ways (e.g., for Roma or Tellus), the Romans consistently represented conquered territories and provinces in the form of women's bodies, often displaying several women together in order to depict a collective of conquered territories. The use of ethnic personifications was part of a pattern in Roman visual representation that affirmed imperial ideology in distinctly gendered ways. But gender understood as "difference in hierarchy"[12] is only comprehensible in terms of a relationship of one sort or another. The Romans/nations hierarchy (or: "Romans on top") was thus communicated by showing female personifications of conquered lands in contrast to their male Roman conquerors. Land is to conqueror, as nation is to Roman, as female is to male; such analogies visually represented as "the way it is" in the Roman imaginary.

Visual Traditions and the Language of Roman Conquest

This section describes visual traditions informing the Roman imperial pattern of using women's bodies to denote conquered nations in public visual representation. This pattern is used consistently in promoting a Roman imperial ideology of conquest over all the nations. Although a pattern of personifying lands, peoples, and virtues is not a Roman innovation, the Romans accomplished their particular pattern of personifying defeated lands and peoples by combining historical commemoration with depictions of mythological enemies and "real" barbarians that they inherited from Hellenistic Greek visual traditions.[13]

Yet, unlike in Hellenistic representation, Roman personifications appear as a part of a relatively consistent pattern of Roman triumphal or victory art.[14] Stereotypical attributes and clothing were employed in representation of the nations that help to identify them to the viewer and differentiate them from one another and the Romans. The Romans also developed a practice of depicting several (or a whole series of) nations together, conveying an idea of collective deference to predetermined Roman rule. Such images also provided a consistent platform from which to project messages about the Romans' emergent consciousness as the rightful rulers of the known world.

Personifications of Conquered Enemies in Hellenism

Allegorical personifications—of cities, lands, rivers and oceans, and concepts like virtues—enjoy a long history in the ancient world. In the Hellenistic Greek period, there was "created and extensively employed a great number of political and geographical personifications in art."[15] These personifications usually took the form of a female body (lands, virtues) or male body (bodies of water).[16] Though the same shape as later Roman figures, allegorical personifications functioned differently in a Hellenistic Greek context. Political personifications included the "spirit" of a Greek city, Tyche, as well as various civic virtues. Evidence for geographical personifications includes those denoting cities and larger areas.[17]

Hellenistic Greek cities and "favored foreign groups"[18] also transmitted a tradition of personifying lands and peoples with women's bodies to the city of Rome by sponsoring the erection of monuments to express gratitude toward a Roman patron. Several extant examples from Rome display this kind of relationship: a monument to Tiberius from fourteen cities of Asia Minor to thank him for aid received after an earthquake displayed in the Forum Iulium, as well as a gold statue of Augustus "probably accompanied by personifications"[19] donated by Hispania Ulterior Baetica. It is probably the case that monuments featuring allegorical personifications seen by Romans on their travels, as well as those brought to and displayed at the city of Rome, most likely informed Roman imperial visual representation of conquered lands and peoples, as well as the personification of their own city, Roma, though she retains an unconquered, victorious-warrior quality for fairly obvious reasons.

In addition to manufacturing the personification of conquered peoples from the Hellenistic pattern of personifying cities and virtues, the Romans also drew their visual language of conquest over foreigners from a Hellenistic tradition of victors depicting their enemies, real and mythological, in order to assert and affirm power over them.[20] This pattern betrays, by consequence of royal victory, an interest in representing territorial expansion. In the Hellenistic period, most expressly exemplified by the rise of Pergamene visual representation,[21] the art of conquest was elevated to allegorical terms through mythological battles. Through portrayal of "dying enemy" figures,[22] the strength of the victor was emphasized through the expiration of a noble savage opponent.[23]

Of particular interest to this project regarding the depiction of historical enemies is the consistency with which ethnic characteristics specific to enemy types like the Celts/Gauls were included. Hellenistic Gauls were represented as having the stereotypical limed hair of textual description and are often accompanied by their characteristic shield, torque, and trumpet (figure 3). Likewise, eastern peoples, such as the Dacians and Armenians, were shown in dress specific to their tribes and

Figure 3. Dying Gaul. Roman marble copy of a Hellenistic original of 230–220 B.C.E. Location: Musei Capitolini, Rome, Italy. Photo © Erich Lessing / Art Resource, N.Y.

intelligible to their conquerors and aligned elite. These detailed clues to ethnicity are central to identifying the subjects as enemy or other to their conquerors and to each other. Hellenistic representation of mythological and historical victims took on new meaning in a Roman context.

Hellenistic allegorical monuments were reinterpreted within a Roman framework: myth and history were collapsed, and the distance between the mythological threat of Giants and the material threat of barbarians like the Celts/Gauls (who also terrorized the Romans) became smaller. The defeat of earlier enemies, then, took on a specifically Roman connotation. The mythological battles against others to defend world-order became explicitly historical commemorations celebrating mythologically and historically inevitable Roman expansion and defense of its borders in the name of law. The elements and overall message were similar, but the difference is that the Romans both vanquished and resurrected their historical enemies into participants in empire. This is noticeable through examination of the Roman pattern of representing conquered barbarian enemies, including personifications, in historical triumphal art in the Republican and especially imperial periods. The real enemies are depicted as being conquered in much the same way as Giants, Amazons, and Centaurs. However, behind the mythological clothing lie historical barbarians who serve their conquerors.

Representations of Captured Barbarians in the Roman Republic

Even if the Romans adopted patterns in Hellenistic personifications and victory art, partially in response to and imitation of Greek culture as civilization, they manipulated such patterns to fit an ideology of conquest. In Roman visual representation, the expression of this ideology came in representation of the diversity of the world under Roman rule and "a greater emphasis on the superiority of the victors, shown in an upper register, leaping over an enemy on the ground."[24] The enemies lying on the ground were usually captured non-Romans, depicted as barbarians. The Roman Empire depicted barbarian enemies in imperial public art as part of the commemoration of historical battles, military triumphs, and other encounters.

The construction of the enemy as barbarian was something the Romans inherited and appropriated from their Greek predecessors (with the help of elite in eastern cities), similar to their inheritance of representations of dying figure types and allegorical personifications. Visual expression of difference was informed by perceptions of cultural difference that were elaborated into natural deficiency. Greeks, and later Romans, characterized barbarians in this way largely in order to serve the project of articulating and naturalizing self-definition, that is, the deficiency of the barbarians enhanced the greatness of the victors. Cultural differences between Romans and non-Romans were articulated using gendered signs: the outlandishness of the barbarians was expressed in literary sources most tangibly by accounts of basic gender transgression, usually rendered as male effeminacy or female masculinity (see chapter 3).[25]

Whatever the case actually may have been, ethnic stereotyping through gender constructs served the purpose of historicizing and legitimating hierarchical relations of conquest and assimilation on patriarchal terms. Roman visual representation of captured barbarians communicated as much through showing realistic, ethnic, and gendered features as being different from and inferior to Roman features. Such features—clothing, hairstyles, attributes—were consistent enough to constitute elements of the visual language of difference in hierarchy.[26]

Roman imperial ethnic/provincial personifications also drew on a Roman tradition of showing defeated barbarian enemies. Such a tradition can be traced to the Republican period, where certainly the images and rhetoric had a different meaning and purpose.[27] Though much less public art survives from the Roman pre-Augustan era, it is clear from literary sources that Roman generals took up a Greek tradition of erecting trophies on the battlefield to commemorate their victories.[28] Such monuments were built out of the defeated enemy's armor and weapons. The Romans then translated these less permanent monuments into stone and coins and included the likeness of non-Roman prisoners, winged Victories, and in the case of public monuments, inscriptions listing the names of peoples conquered.[29] Surviving examples of the conquered on coins include those commemorating Caesar's conquest of Gaul. These coins feature trophies and barbarian heads, male and female, along with the Gallic *carnyx*/war trumpet.[30] The trophies and prisoners were also manipulated and standardized in appearance for the purpose of parading them in triumphal processions.

During the early principate, the Romans portrayed their conquered barbarians in various media alone and also with their vanquishers, who are mostly anonymous representatives of the Roman army and discernible emperors. No doubt the travels of the Romans to the lands that they captured, as well as the performance of the Roman triumph with its parading of the captives through the streets of Rome, served as inspiration for such depictions.[31] Surviving visual representation of captured barbarians includes mostly public sculpture and a few private (i.e., household) items. From the visual evidence, it is evident that captured and bound barbarians constitute a consistent representational pattern in Roman imperial art, public and private alike.[32]

Aside from ethnic particularity, Romans gave their defeated barbarian enemies either male or female likeness (by showing a male and female pair, for example). Male barbarians are often bound with hands behind the back, and females are shown in a mourning pose.[33] In the case of several imperial panels from the Aphrodisias Sebasteion's south portico (figures 4 and 5), male and female northern barbarians are represented as bound, near trophies and (heroically nude) victorious emperors, and smaller than their vanquishers. The Romans also showed their defeated enemies in what looks like the moments immediately following victory in battle, such as on the Gemma Augustea (figure 6). In such cases the barbarians are bound and shown chained to a tree or pole decorated with their distinctive weapons and armor.[34] On the Gemma's bottom register, the Romans are shown erecting a trophy

Figure 4. Germanicus with Captive. The Sebasteion in Aphrodisias. Photo © New York University/Institute of Fine Arts Excavations at Aphrodisias.

Figure 5. Augustus with Nike and Trophy. The Sebasteion in Aphrodisias. Photo © New York University/Institute of Fine Arts Excavations at Aphrodisias.

Figure 6. Gemma Augustea, made for Emperor Augustus, seen seated in the pose of Jupiter with scepter, laurel wreath, and lituus, the staff of the augurs. In the center Roma, left Germanicus and Tiberius descending from a chariot. Sardonyx, 10 C.E. 19 × 23 cm, mounting 17th. Inv. IX A 79. Kunsthistorisches Museum, Vienna, Austria. Photo © Erich Lessing / Art Resource, N.Y.

with barbarians underneath and soldiers dragging a foreign woman by her hair toward the scene on the left. The trophy erection and barbarian subjugation marks the end of the battle and Roman success. Roman success, as we shall see in more detail in the examples I discuss below, is rendered as a masculine act predicated on the violent subjugation of femaleness and the redirection of reproduction.

Personifications of Peoples and Provinces in the Roman Republic

Evidence of ethnic personifications exists from the Republican and early imperial periods.[35] The commonality between the two lies partially in an emergent ideology concerning the Romans as the master race or the people most naturally fit to rule over others. In the Republican period, Roman visual reference to other places and peoples was done in order to show a particular general's superiority over others. Such peoples were consolidated into women's bodies represented mostly (so we have) on coins and said to belong to the victorious general. Republican personifications could "designate the sphere of authority held by a given official."[36] Such coins, issued not by the state but by those who wished to celebrate their own acquisitions, often feature warriors and personifications of lands.

Unlike the Republican portrayals that designated a particular location of authority for a particular victorious general, Roman imperial ethnic/provincial personifications consolidated the diverse peoples of the world into one purposefully diverse geo-political unity under *one* victor, the emperor. A Roman imperial innovation in the visual representation of conquered peoples was to visually link their historical territorial conquests with personifications, rendered as ethnically delimited women's bodies in specific poses and dress and reminiscent of allegorical imagery and portrayals of captured barbarians. Like anonymous barbarians, personifications represent casualties of and hostages from war in the name of territorial expansion and world domination. Personifications of conquered lands and peoples constitute one particular method for Roman representation of foreign relations—but for my purposes—the most ideologically charged, explicitly gendered, and relevant for a re-imagination of Paul. Below I examine the Romans/nations hierarchy through specific examples of visual representation featuring personifications.

The Visual Representation of the Romans/Nations Hierarchy

A Judaea Capta *Coin*

Scholars have long noted the importance of ancient coins as important primary sources for the study of the New Testament. The sheer number and variety of coins makes them especially useful for filling out the architectural and material record of the New Testament world, in some cases even confirming the historical *realia* of New Testament writings. Ancient coins also feature images that provide insight into the politics and social issues of their context. The obverse sides of Roman coins, followed next by imperial portraiture, constituted the most important and wide-reaching medium for official dissemination of the emperor's likeness.[37] Aside from images of the emperor and other political figures, coins feature pictures of buildings, gods and goddesses, historical events, daily use objects, plants, animals, and personifications of lands and bodies of water.

Images on Roman coins are not only important for identifying historical events and archaeological sites. These coins also served as an official medium for communication of state-sanctioned concepts, including proclamation and celebration of victories over enemies.[38] They were a product of Roman political power, especially in conquered territories.[39] While the images may have been chosen by a few, "the fact of the coin, its existence as a product of political power, had a compelling impact on the beholder. . . . The image conveyed the message"[40] to its holders. The regularity with which images of imperial victory appear on Roman coins speaks to such images as expressive of Roman imperial ideology. As a form of state-sanctioned public communication, coin iconography naturalized the universality and inevitability of Roman state domination.

The *Judaea Capta* coin series is among the most famous that Rome issued in the imperial period, and to New Testament scholars is one of the most familiar depictions of conquered peoples during this time.[41] Because of the relationship of the coins to a most decisive event in Jewish history, the destruction of the Jerusalem Temple in 70 C.E., scholars of the New Testament and early Judaism have tended to emphasize this series as an appropriate area of material culture to engage. It is easy to assume that the Roman conquest of the Jews is the most (if not the only) important conquest of interest to the study of the New Testament and early Christianity. Such an assumption, however, underscores an inattention to power relationships and politics in the Roman imperial context of the New Testament.

Judaea Capta coins depict Roman victory and domination over the Jewish people and territory. An extensive series, the majority of the coin types show captured, bound, draped and seated female bodies, as well as some captured, seated and/or standing, scantily-clad male bodies.[42] All of the captive bodies, male and female, are thought to be Judean due to their hairstyles, costuming and specific identifiable attributes (such as weaponry). Roman figures are also present on some types, as are palm trees and military trophies. One version of this reverse type is typical and will be used for the present study. On this coin (figure 7), a palm tree stands in the middle, between a soldier on the left and a sitting woman on the right. This coin commemorates the end of the Jewish war, illustrated by the depicted Jewish woman shown mourning the fate of her people.

Figure 7. "Judaea Capta" *Sestertius of Vespasian, issued following the destruction of Jerusalem. Illustration by author, after LIMC "Iudaea" no. 14 (also BMCRE 117).*

Elements of *Judaea Capta*'s iconographic program tell a coherent story about imperial power relationships beyond simple historical commemoration. The palm tree, for example, symbolizes abundance in the Middle Eastern desert and thus acts as a signifier of the people now under Roman control. The tree also serves as a further designation for the province of Judea *herself*, which may emphasize the point that only the Jews living in Jerusalem and its environs, and not those in the Diaspora, were responsible for their own defeat at Roman hands.[43] The female body sitting dejectedly at the tree's base has often been called a Jewess, intimating that she is an individual female.[44] But feminist New Testament scholar Luise Schottroff has noted that, though the Romans probably had other intentions with the visual program, Jewish persons might have seen this woman as "the mother of Zion," whom the Romans defeated but God will raise up again.[45] This point underscores the notion that in biblical imagery, women are similarly often used to personify land,[46] suggesting that such visual representation was widespread in the ancient world.

Art historians support this point, as they also understand that it is not unusual in visual representation of the Roman imperial period to use women's bodies as personifications of territories and defeated peoples. The woman here need not be an individual or specific Jewish woman. She is representative, rather, of a geographically specific *ethnos*, Judea. She is the smallest figure in this composition, sitting in the dress of her people and appearing draped. She holds her head in one hand and looks downward. The man on this coin is a Roman soldier symbolizing military victory. Some have posited this figure to be Emperor Vespasian himself,[47] although most important is his designation as an undefeated representative of Roman military power. As such, his body is the largest figure in the composition, almost as tall as the tree. He holds a staff upright with his right arm, and a *parazonium* (a dagger designed to be held at the girdle) with his left. He steps with his left foot on a helmet. Even though he is in close spatial relationship to Judea, he does not appear to be directly watching the woman. Yet his strength is linked to her dejection; he is not victorious without an enemy. Such a relationship reminds the holder of this coin that the Romans will ensure, after Judea's defeat, that she will never again revolt with any success.

The image program articulated by this *Judaea Capta* coin constitutes a tiny, everyday portrait of basic imperial power relations: dominant and subordinate, active and passive (or, in this case, pacified). The empire is dominant, the land captured and subordinate. These power relations are visually expressed using gendered bodies both to show the differences between the conquerors and conquered and to communicate social superiority and inferiority. The coin captures the point well enough: Roman forces have defeated and *feminized* (i.e., placed in the subordinate female role) the people of Judea. Such feminization articulates a position of lowliness and humiliation in a Roman-defined, male-dominated hierarchy. The people are a passive, penetrated object; they are rendered harmless by defeat and disarmament.[48] The nation's collective femininity is not only humiliating, but contributes to the definition and reinforcement of Roman masculinity. The soldier appears as a real man. Allusions to penetration and domination emphasize and reinforce his prowess. In this respect, the positioning of his dagger in his groin area appears to be no accident. This representation of territorial conquest thus renders as naturalized a potent pattern of gender relations.

The Cuirassed Statue of Augustus

Sculptural representations of the Roman emperor constitute a form of officially disseminated imperial portraiture whose visual grammar is also important for understanding the New Testament's context. While larger and of a different medium than a coin, a portrait statue of Augustus from Prima Porta (figure 8)[49] also makes a statement about Roman imperial ideology by employing gendered and ethnic differences to express victory and peacemaking. This depiction of Augustus is one of the earliest examples of Roman imperial cuirassed (breastplated) statues featuring an emperor.[50] Such statues were erected throughout the Roman world to honor reigning and deceased emperors, imperial family members, victorious military generals, local heroes, and the war god Mars.[51] The Roman cuirassed statue functioned as an important form of honorific dedication that would have been recognized as such in Rome and its provinces.[52] Provincial territories received officially sanctioned

Figure 8. The emperor Augustus depicted in a military cuirass. Prima Porta, first century C.E. Marble, 204 cm. Vatican Museums, Vatican State. Photo © Erich Lessing/Art Resource, N.Y.

imperial portraits about every two years, and these often affirmed the imperial cult or commemorated battles won.[53] These portraits belonged to a pattern of triumphal art identifiable in most areas of the Roman Empire, making the cuirassed statue another vehicle for expressing Roman imperial ideology.[54]

Cuirassed portrait statues utilized iconographic programs to communicate to the viewer the message of imperial victory, Roman identity, and non-Roman subjugation. Often such programs visually documented Roman territorial expansion and invasion, communicating that such conquest ensured peace. On the Prima Porta Augustus, as on the *Judaea Capta* coin, these ideas are depicted using gendered imagery. The emperor's strong, sturdy frame expresses victorious manliness. This portrait's bodily representation, from square head to heroically and divinely unclad feet,[55] depicts ideal Roman masculinity and impenetrable stability. Augustus the victor sports features common to portraits of important Roman men: short-cropped and tame hair, a penetrating gaze on his straightly aligned face and muscular legs. Military dress emphasizes winning status and shows off a well-proportioned manly physique. This Augustus is eternally youthful and vigorous, just as biographer Suetonius half-heartedly reports.[56] Here there is no hint of the eyebrows meeting, the limp, the spots, or itchiness supposedly plaguing the *pater patriae*'s older body. The remembered god-man image is flawless, without contradictions. Such is the imaginary representing Roman imperial ideology at work.

Although in the Prima Porta rendering of Augustus the whole man is visually arresting, his cuirass (figure 9) has preoccupied scholars of the Roman Empire, especially in terms of its visual representation. This breastplate is considered the most ideologically sophisticated and elaborate of the cuirassed statues.[57] Its visual display marks the form of Augustus as a stand-in for the masculine triumphalism of the Roman Empire itself. The emperor bears a gospel of imperial salvation worn on his perfectly chiseled chest.[58] The central scene on the *imperator*'s abdominal muscles provides an entry point for interpreting the cuirass composition and the statue as a whole. It features two prominent figures positioned around the first navel, flanked by gods, goddesses, and various personifications.

On the viewer's left, a Roman soldier[59] stands with his arm outstretched toward a non-Roman man on the right, who hands an eagle-topped military standard to him. This exchange represents a decisive historical event during the reign of Augustus: Roman victory over and pacification of the rival Parthian empire. In 53 B.C.E., the Parthians took the Roman standards after a battle with Crassus's army. Capturing standards was a humiliation of the first order for the Romans, and the Parthians' actions marked one of the most embarrassing events of Roman history where "[t]he chorus of those urging revenge never stopped."[60] Despite repeated attempts to recover the standards through military action (e.g., Antony in 40 and 36 B.C.E.), the Romans were not able to defeat the Parthians, and Julius Caesar was assassinated while planning a campaign against them. In 20 B.C.E., Armenia became a client kingdom by way of diplomacy. This nation served as a Roman-aligned threat to the Parthians, who then returned the standards to Augustus in exchange for

Figure 9. Breastplate of Augustus of Prima Porta (detail). Braccio Nuovo, Vatican Museums, Vatican State. Photo © Alinari/Art Resource, N.Y.

Roman support against the Armenians. Even though the standards' return was non-violent, and the Romans had never properly defeated the Parthians, Augustus inscribes in the *Res Gestae* that he "forced" them to return the standards and to ask, "as suppliants," for Roman "friendship" (Augustus, *Res Gestae* 29).

The ideological construction of Roman conquest over others receives support in this central scene on Augustus's cuirass, where the appearance of the Roman and Parthian men express differences in the hierarchical relations of power between them. The Roman male models masculinity just as his big host, Augustus, does. He wears a helmet and cuirass, wearing a *paludamentum* clasped to his shoulder and a dagger at his side. The Parthian,[61] by contrast, has unruly, uncut hair and a big beard. He wears a loose-fitting, short tunic with trousers that the Romans associated with exotic eastern barbarian peoples who had not achieved their level of masculinity.[62] He is clearly not a part of the nation of the toga, and he bears no armor, showing him to be an evident outsider. Indeed, the Parthian needs both hands to hold the imperial eagle. The Parthian's stance, dress, and passivity betray *effeminacy*. He is a "girlyman," representing an entire nation of the same, who cannot literally handle the weight (both literal and symbolic) of the Roman standard—further implying that they are failures in military exploits despite historical attestation to the contrary.

Roman recovery of their standards from the Parthians was considered pivotal to the Augustan development of the *saeculum aureum* (golden age) and its related visual representation. In such idealized imagery, the event of the Parthian surrender of the standards was manipulated from an embarrassing series of Roman military failures into a triumph that portrayed the east being brought to its knees.[63] This act of diplomacy was celebrated as a glorious vanquishing in several texts of the period, and the image of a Parthian man on his knees was an especially popular one in coinage and other forms of visual communication.[64] Thus, regardless of what actually happened, these images on Augustus's cuirass tell the story of masculine Romans saving the world from the exotic barbarian (and here passively constructed with male effeminacy) east. This representation is consistent with numerous textual accounts portraying the Romans as being the race most fit to rule the world, especially the east, on account of their special manliness or *virtus*.[65]

Such good news is portrayed on Augustus's chest as taking place in the presence, or according to the will, of the gods. They (Sol, Luna, Apollo, Diana), along with a personified Dawn pouring dew over Augustus's left pectoral muscle, encircle the victorious event.[66] The opening of a new day of Roman peace, signified by the sun god drawing his chariot across the sky, commences with this event at the imperial savior's navel, his rock-hard abdominal and pectoral muscles forming a frame. The Parthian defeat is portrayed here as resulting from, and further enabling the continuance of, Roman imperial masculinity as central to the reinstatement of cosmic order. The body of the emperor represents all that is right and good with the world.

I have been preoccupied above with the male imagery in the representation, because it is a necessary foil for understanding female visual representation, as effeminizing imagery functions on the basis of recognized cultural constructions of the female body in relationship to an impenetrable male body. Indeed, Roman masculinity as portrayed in this scene on Augustus's torso also provides the stability needed for a fertile future. A draped female figure appearing to be Tellus (Mother Earth)[67] reclines near the emperor's genitals, which are safely ensconced beneath the form-fitting armor and cloak. She holds an overflowing cornucopia upward and looks beyond it at the Roman soldier. This fertile groin is the locus of a peaceful and abundant future. That pacification of the east results in Roman fertility and prosperity is further indicated by two infant children clawing at the woman's loose-fitting gown. Likewise, baby Eros sits on a dolphin and clings to the much larger Augustus's military skirt. In addition to this feature supporting the statue, the dolphin signifies *imperium* over the sea, and Eros, along for the ride, illustrates that the future is bright.

Visually, the manliness expressed by and on Augustus would not be as strong or intelligible without the contrasting feminized non-Roman conquests. Two women sitting across from each other under the emperor's nipples, almost in his armpits, provide this contrast. The figures represent conquered *ethnē* at, physically and geographically, the borderlands of the Roman Empire.[68] Each woman sits in traditional dress with attributes of the ethnic group she personifies. The woman under the left armpit is thought to be Gallia/Gaul. She is fully clothed and wears the tight-fitting *bracae*/trousers typical of northern barbarians.[69] Her sheath is empty, indicating disarmament. She holds an indigenous horn with a dragon's head, probably a Celtic *carnyx*.[70] A Gaulish military standard fashioned as a wild boar sits on the ground in front of her.[71] Her "sister" under the right armpit differs in dress, position, and attribute. Her cloak has a fringe detail, and she does not wear trousers. Scholars have called her Hispania, referring to Augustus's conquests of Spanish territory and peoples shortly before the statue's estimated date of commission.[72] She sits near a military trophy,[73] and her sheath has a sword in it. The weaponry she bears indicate her status as an assimilated or client nation,[74] but her crouching stance under the trophy decorated with the weapons and armor of her people designates her as a nation brought to the ground by Roman forces.

Though the two female personifications on Augustus's cuirass differ from one another, they are, like the Parthian exchange, crucial elements of the imperial order his body communicates. They function as characters at the margins, indicating that the borders are under control. The recapture of standards from the barbarian Parthian east, the feminization of northern and western territories, and the approval of the gods all mark the opening of the golden age of Roman peace. This peace is dependent on relations of domination and subordination, communicated visually as naturalized power relations between male and female (including passive, penetrated male) bodies. These representations of femininity, like Judea juxtaposed with the Roman soldier on the *Judaea Capta* coin, enhance the domineering masculinity and submissive femininity at the core of Roman imperial consciousness and ideology.

Reliefs from the Sebasteion at Aphrodisias

Both the *Judaea Capta* coin and statue of Augustus from Prima Porta feature images of Roman victory, portraying the conquest of nations at symbolic and geographical frontiers. There are also racial and sexual overtones to this imperial ideology, which is not so subtly expressed through the rendering of military men as dominating native women. Such dimensions of Roman victory over foreign peoples are more overtly displayed in selected reliefs from the Sebasteion at Aphrodisias in Asia Minor, part of the largest imperial cult complex found to date.[75] The Aphrodisias complex was privately funded by local elite, dedicated to the imperial family, and stressed the relationship of that provincial city with Rome. It was started and completed during the Julio-Claudian period, with slight modifications afterward.[76] The complex had a temple of Aphrodite—who also was known as Venus Genetrix, the mother of Aeneas, and the ancestral mother of the divine Augusti[77]—at one end and a *propylon* (a colonnaded entry-porch) at the other. Its two approximately 90-meter-long buildings faced each other and featured portico façades with two upper stories of life-size relief panels above a ground-floor level of what were probably shops. The buildings' proximity to each other and boundedness by the *propylon* formed a "processional way"[78] between the porch and temple.

Though not all of it survives, the Sebasteion's recovered sculptural program provides a narrative window into how free, eastern Greek cities interpreted ideas about Roman imperial social structure and power relations. The complex appears to have set an example for later Roman imperial visual representation in Asia Minor,[79] yet was probably based on extant programs at Rome.[80] Each portico level seems to have had its own theme. The upper story of the south portico included scenes showing emperors and members of the imperial family, personifications, military trophies, and several barbarians in various postures of defeat.[81] The lower story displayed a standard cache of mythological scenes (Leda and the Swan, Achilles and Penthesilea, the Three Graces), including some with a more specifically Roman connotation (e.g., Aeneas carrying Anchises and the *penates* out of a burning Troy) as one moved closer toward the temple.[82]

The panel of most interest for the present discussion depicts the vanquishing of a personified Britannia by a heroically and divinely nude Claudius (figure 1, introduced in chapter 1). This scene probably originally stood next to a similar relief of Nero hauling away a defeated Armenia[83] (figure 10) with a triumphant, winged Nike/Victoria figure fixed between them. These reliefs were among several others showing captured male and female barbarian figures alongside victorious emperors.[84] Here Claudius stands over Britannia,[85] cape flying behind him. His left leg is behind his victim, and his right leg, knee on her thigh, holds her legs down. He grasps her head by her hair and pulls it back, leaving her no place to look but out. The emperor's right arm is missing, but it seems as though he is poised for the final

Figure 10. Nero defeats a personified Armenia. The Sebasteion in Aphrodisias. Photo © New York University/Institute of Fine Arts Excavations at Aphrodisias.

blow. The sheath on his left side is empty, and the weapon could be in his absent hand. Britannia, for her part, does not necessarily play the passive part all that willingly. She is dressed in a short *chiton* baring her right breast, a characteristic of Amazon warriors and other female captives. The bare breast is a popular motif in depictions of women as wild (Amazons, dancers) and captured (violence, rape, and supplication, often of Amazons).[86] She has barbarian hair—long, loose, and in the thick plaits common to depictions of Celtic peoples. She reaches up and, though her forearm is missing, her hand is fixed to his chest.

This Aphrodisian relief's representation of Britannia as a nation that will not surrender easily is consistent with the Roman conquest of Celtic Britain in the historical sources. Yet the image of a manly Claudius throwing Britannia down is inconsistent with his reputation as an incompetent ruler and with descriptions of persistent British uprisings after the emperor's suppression of the island's native tribes. As with the earlier Parthian encounters, Rome only conquered Britain with great difficulty and largely through diplomacy. Regardless of these details, Claudius is portrayed far away in Asia Minor as a strong Roman man putting a female representation of Celtic Britain in her place, on her knees and on the ground underneath him.

Britannia's Amazonian and captive imagery designates her as a worthy opponent, but one who should predictably lose. In this sense, she is related to other depictions of Hellenistic Amazon warriors and similar figures, such as Gaulish types perhaps most readily identified as "Dying Gauls" and other dying figures in Pergamene iconography. While the Amazon as such does not appear to be as prevalent a motif in Roman visual representation, allusion to defeat of these mythological woman-warriors and gender transgressors is recognizable in Britannia's appearance. As Iain Ferris notes, such imagery makes a powerful statement "about Roman attitudes to imperial actions and politics and to conquered lands and peoples, and finally, of course, about male attitudes to women."[87] The female portrayal of this nation further associates sexual humiliation and violence with military conquest.[88] Britannia seems posed to be sexually conquered by Claudius, illustrating his impenetrability and her vulnerability. Sexual conquest is inferred by the choice of weapon used to subdue this nation—presumably a sword, an instrument of penetration.

Claudius's possible sexual conquering of Britannia also infers a relationship involving Roman state fertility and the resurrection of conquered peoples to serve it. A Roman emperor did not kill nations permanently—he received submission, extended the hand of peace to them, and incorporated them into his large-scale house, the fatherland. Guaranteeing Roman familial fertility and dynastic reproduction through curtailing the fertility of captured barbarians is a common theme in Roman visual representation: the forced barrenness of the barbarians supports Roman peace.[89] The Ara Pacis and Trajan's Column at Rome, for example, feature scenes where Romans take children and women as captives. One of the Boscoreale cups (discussed below) shows male Gaulish captives giving their children to Augustus. Likewise, as Suetonius reports, Augustus tried a new form of hostage taking, that is, he took women from their native lands, as barbarians seemed to respond well to the persistent threat posed therein.[90]

In this scenario, should Britannia live after Claudius is through, her children would be born into Roman slavery, into a colonized existence. Children born of this union are descendants of the attractive and powerful Roman emperor and the debased native nation, now forming part of the extended family inclusive of the entire known world. The emperor continues to manufacture children—heirs to Roman world order—through the defeat and acquisition of nations, thereby ensuring peace and the maintenance of the Roman family and race inaugurated by the first father, Augustus.[91]

The Portico of Nations at Aphrodisias

The Claudius and Britannia relief in the Aphrodisian Sebasteion provides a telling portrait of the gendered and sexual dimensions of Roman imperial ideology.[92] This panel probably faced the north portico, ideologically linking opposite sides of the complex. The north portico featured a series of imperial and allegorical reliefs in the uppermost story, including about fifty personified female *ethnē*. These figures indicated nations that the Romans had conquered and incorporated, from the Callaeci in western Spain to the Judeans and Egyptians in the south. While allegorical images like Day and Ocean perhaps serve to provide time and world-defining elements, the *ethnē* indicate a "distinctively Roman and imperial" way of visually representing the boundaries and conquered nations of the Roman Empire.[93]

The Aphrodisian *ethnē* were rendered as life-size, single, female bodies in high relief, each holding an attribute of her race and placed on a decorated and inscribed base with her name on it. Of the proposed fifty in the series, only fifteen intact panels and bases have been excavated (figures 11 and 12). The names include thirteen *ethnē* designations[94] and three major islands (Crete, Cyprus, and Sicily).[95] On one of the inscribed bases appears the phrase, *ETHNOUS IOUDAIŌN*[96] (figure 12, center), indicating that the Jews stood in line with the rest of the nations conquered by Rome. The women's bodies in these relief panels and pieces are shown in varying shades of [un]civilized femininity. Variation in their dress indicates difference in status, and from the outlandish look of the foreign warrior designated *PIROUSTŌN* (a vaguely Gallic, Alpine tribe) to the bound submission and disheveled look of an unknown captive to the Greek familiarity (read: assimilation or cooperation) of the well-dressed woman, each appears to be different from the others. This is consistent with the Roman preoccupation with ethnically specific details designating their different conquests, such as clothing, hairstyle, attribute, facial expression, and posture. All of the nations, however, are unified in that they have been defeated and now show deference to Roman rule.

Seen together, the *ethnē* map the conquered Roman world.[97] Britannia as represented in the Sebasteion's south portico is a woman who provides a northern

Figure 11. Ethnos Piroustae. *The Sebasteion in Aphrodisias. Photo © New York University/Institute of Fine Arts Excavations at Aphrodisias.*

boundary, and Armenia signifies an eastern border; the *ethnē* in the north portico designate other borderlands. Britannia also points to a continuity between a conquered nation in process (her past and present) and already conquered nations (her supposed future). Claudius holds Britannia's head up by her hair, as if to show her the *ethnē* across the way, representing what she is about to become post-submission. We can imagine that she might get up and stand with her sisters in slavery and that those women similarly experienced what Britannia is now experiencing. The vanquishing emperor possesses an invincible, semi-nude, divine, male body and stands among a family of super-men and supportive Roman women (Livia, Agrippina), forcing the world's most outlandish nations to surrender and position themselves in line.

Roman world conquest is collapsed with mythological destiny in the Sebasteion by the inclusion of historical commemoration alongside recognizable mythological scenes, reinforcing the naturalness and inevitability of Roman rule. Familiar myths of the Greeks fold into those of the Roman state. Aphrodite is also Venus Genetrix, ancestral mother of the Roman imperial family. Personifications of Hemera/Day and Okeanos/Ocean are near the nations, as well as a suggestive portrayal of a draped Augustus over small personifications of land (holding a cornucopia) and sea (holding an oar).[98] Elsewhere, personified Roma stands over a reclining Ge (Gaia) and receives her bounty, indicating that the abundance of the land belongs to the victorious city of Rome.[99] These scenes, along with the imperial reliefs depicting conquest and capture, are near those featuring Apollo, Herakles, Dionysus, and Aeneas. The crucial myth, that of Roman invincibility, serves to engender the cosmos[100] in this imperial cult complex. Power relationships and social order are built into the very structure of the Sebasteion as a vertical hierarchy where impenetrable

Ethnos Base—Bessōn *Ethnos Base—Bosporōn* *Ethnos Base—Dakōn*

Ethnos Base—Iapodōn *Ethnos Base—Ioudaiōn*

Ethnos Base—Piroustōn *Ethnos Base—Krētē*

Ethnos Base—Kypros *Ethnos Base—Ethiopia*

Figure 12. Inscribed Ethne *Bases. The Sebasteion in Aphrodisias. Photo © New York University/Institute of Fine Arts Excavations at Aphrodisias.*

Figure 13. Augustus showing mercy to captured barbarians (the depiction of the captives, kneeling before the emperor, has been damaged). Silver cup from a private estate at Boscoreale, Italy. First century C.E. *The Louvre, Paris. Photo © Erich Lessing / Art Resource, N.Y. Portions of the cup reconstructed in this photo by Michah Thompson, Augsburg Fortress.*

masculinity tops penetrated, humiliated, and acquiescent femininity. The hierarchy is presented as the natural order of the world, the result of which is Roman peace, fertility, and abundance.

Cup 1 of the Boscoreale Treasure

An extant portrayal of a series of conquered nations in procession is also on the so-called Cup 1 of the Boscoreale treasure (figure 13).[101] The scenes compactly illustrate, using allegorical personifications, a Roman imperial ideology of world domination. On the top panel, Augustus is seated *togate* in the middle holding the globe in his right hand. Two processions flank him. On the left, his mother Venus approaches him with a small Victory. Behind her is Amor. Populus (the male personification of the Roman people), holding a cornucopia, and Roma, standing on a helmet of the defeated, appear to be conversing with one another. On the right, father Mars leads a procession of personified conquered nations toward the emperor. Gallia is in front, and of the at least seven women Hispania, Asia, and Africa are also recognizable by dress and headgear. They are the only figures on this cup with their heads down in submissive posture.

On this cup, the foreign nations/women are being led away as prisoners toward the emperor from the scene on the other side of the thumb-handles; recall the taking of female hostages by Augustus. Surrounded by soldiers as if a battle has just been finished, Augustus, again central, extends his right hand in clemency toward the conquered men. They are the only figures on the cup with their heads tilted upward, submitting to Rome like the processing women. At least four non-Roman men are in this scene, their unruly hair and non-Roman dress designating them as certainly of northern origin, and probably Gauls; they match the prominence of Gallia on the cup's other side.

Three of the non-Roman men are bringing children to the emperor. This scene, however, is ambiguous: though it could be the case that the foreign fathers try to ensure that they will live by submitting to Roman power and giving the children away, it also could be that this conquered people is attempting to show deferential friendship with, or loyalty to, Rome.[102] Even with this ambiguity, the anchor of the cup is the emperor, who receives victory and the nations on one side and children of a conquered nation on the other. The outcome is the same: victory's result and reward is the submission of the others. Such submission—leading away a procession of women, giving away children—to exactly one man (Augustus) curtails the fertility of the conquered and redirects their immediate survival and reproduction onto Roman terms.

The spatial setting and use of the cup add to the image program's communicative power. The reliefs in the round make it difficult to read the events portrayed as temporally linear. In other words, it makes no difference what side of the cup is discussed first. Whereas victory over the Gauls and subsequent triumph was a Roman historical reality, here two scenes work together as a cycle of conquest and commemoration because according to Roman destiny's imperative, there are always more peoples to defeat and triumphs to celebrate. Characters flanking the central emperor on both sides are related to the other frieze. The nations are led away from the men and children; we can see the backside of one submissive man behind the procession of women. This cup is one of a pair, indicating communal drinking and discussion in a meal setting. Elite Romans who used such a vessel at their meals would participate in the scene depicted. The Roman hand that grabbed this cup divided the nations from the men and children, for example, and no matter which side faces the holder, the emperor's likeness and presence are noticeable.

What Has Judea to Do with Britannia?

Although the examples of the Roman visual representation I considered above may be different from one another in media and viewing context, they nevertheless show important consistencies and reveal a common theme in visual representations of Roman imperial ideology. The predominant message is that Roman peace comes through conquering the whole world and all of the nations; insisting that all marginalized knees (and heads) shall bow to the centralized single (male) victor. The conditions for peace are visually rendered in gendered terms that are hard to ignore, revealing gender as a fundamental grammatical element in narrative structures of Roman visual representation. Gender makes intelligible power relationships and hierarchies that are further correlated with ethnicity and social status. And, it is especially important to recognize that Roman peace in this representation is patriarchal at its core.

Consistency in Visual Representation of the Romans/Nations Hierarchy

Power relationships are communicated by the images on the coin, cuirassed statue, portrait reliefs, and silver cup. All of these examples depict female personifications of defeated, ethnically specific nations at the geographical borders of an expanding Roman Empire. Although the women differ in ethnic identification by stereotypical elements such as clothing, hairstyle, and attribute, they are similar in their stance and relationship to the empire as subjugated entities. They are embattled, disheveled, dejected, captured and subdued, and shown in deferent line. The Roman male bodies, by contrast, show a remarkable consistency of style and stance: erect, virile, and stable. The Roman soldier on the *Judaea Capta* coin and the Roman on Augustus's cuirass, not to mention the emperor's Prima Porta embodiment as *himself*, all certainly fit within this framework. Further, Aphrodisian Claudius throws and pins Britannia to the ground with little effort, his hair perfectly coiffed while doing so.

Visual representation of conquered peoples is not isolated or unusual but constitutes a visible pattern in Roman imperial visual representation as integrated into public spaces. Such examples should be considered synchronically[103] as part of the same semantic system. The coin, cuirassed statue, and reliefs do not merely commemorate individual conquests, but each is also part of a larger series. Though the *Judaea Capta* coin is well known and documented by scholars, Judea is not the only captured nation depicted on coins. The Flavian dynasty may particularly have favored such a portrayal, and Hadrian later would further domesticate the nations by picturing them as loyal and cooperative subjects of Rome on his own coinage.[104] The *capta* image on this coin and others like it recalls earlier depictions of conquered peoples at the borders, such as the portrayal of Gaul and Spain on coins issued by Caesar.[105] This pose indicates that a Roman enemy was resistant to civilization or was a barbarian threat needing containment. Although Judea had status as a Roman province, and such status was probably understood as being more civilized than some other provinces, she is still pictured as an enemy that must be conquered.[106] As is well known from primary sources, Jewish people in Judea criticized various Roman programs, including the erection of statues of the emperor and imperial cult, before their rebellion against Rome that ended with Jerusalem's destruction. Judea's appearance as an uncivilized, ethnically distinct woman reinforces the Roman view of *her* as a body to be tamed and controlled in order for the civilizing peace to endure.

That the subjugation of women/nations inaugurates manly Roman peace is also evident on the Prima Porta Augustus's body and cuirass composition. The active (large and small) Roman men and passive non-Roman women (including the non-manly Parthian) set the stage for Roman peace and stability. The pacification of these "women" at the borders is necessary for continued peace and abundance. Though this cuirass composition is most sophisticated, it is also but one of many such statues displaying the capture of outlandish, barbarian peoples as essential to victory.

The Sebasteion at Aphrodisias shows that worship of the emperor and imperial dynasty is equated with worship of the imperial victory that generates peace and stability, even (perhaps, especially) for relatively wealthy eastern client cities. Victory here is specific to that result awarded following the defeat of various far-flung nations of the inhabited world. While Britannia is a particularly graphic representation of a woman being vanquished, the portico of *ethnē* signifies the numbers and variety of peoples who might have endured the same fate. At least, in the Roman imperial imaginary, they are presented as such. The women shown standing in line represent diverse points in a whole world dominated by Roman *imperium*. Thus, there is a consistency and continuity to the representation of conquered territories and peoples being displayed in and on these diverse media.

The Nations "United" in Deference to Rome

The universality of Roman rule is a thoroughgoing notion in Roman imperial ideology, consistent in image and text. In visual representation, the personification of nations as women's bodies and conquerors as men's bodies communicates hierarchical power relations between Romans and nations, as well as reinforcing those existing between male and female, masculinity and femininity, free and slave, colonizer and colonized, and cosmos and chaos. Images and lists of nations added to Rome's empire through military conquest are spread throughout public spaces of the early imperial age. The whole world itself is composed of Romans and *omnes gentes*, or *panta ta ethnē*.[107] The nations, as tribes and peoples conquered and acquired by the Romans, have in common that they comprise the inhabited world.

The coherence and implications of the victorious-Romans-over-defeated-nations message should not be underestimated. Representation of this imaginary amounts to a mapping of empire's boundaries through attention to gender and ethnic interconnectedness. In this framework, the world is composed of individual, racially distinct parts, as evidenced by attention given to clothing and the diversity of attributes.[108] By representing the world in this manner, Roman imperial ideology creates and maintains the notion that the whole world is within reach. The nations together, then, are united in their status and relationship to Roman rule, whatever the perceived or real differences from each other may be.

The Aphrodisians probably did not invent their "united nations" of conquered peoples but most likely relied on an extant series from, and approved by, the empire's capital.[109] It is documented that Pompey's theater in Rome's Campus Martius, which was restored by Augustus (*Res Gestae* 20; Summary 3), included a portico with fourteen *nationes*, the same *simulacra gentium* who surround Nero and keep him from leaving in his dream.[110] Servius's commentary on the *Aeneid* reports that Augustus also erected his own portico of nations where he placed "images of all the peoples."[111] This portico was apparently conceived from the procession of future conquered peoples shown on Aeneas's prophetic shield in Virgil's epic, where the bodies "move in long array, as diverse in fashion of dress and arms as in tongues" (*Aen.* 8.721).[112] The diversity of the nations—as different from one another as from Rome's toga-clad race—is emphasized throughout. Such national diversity is intelligible by the use of stereotypically distinct clothing and hairstyles of the sculpted *ethnē* and their attributes such as weapons, instruments, and the like.

In addition to Virgil's procession of conquered nations on the prophetic shield in *Aeneid* 8, he describes a public space he will build and dedicate to his Caesar in Book 3 of his *Georgics*.[113] The complex includes a theater, portico, and temple to Augustus, and images of the conquered abound. On stage, "Britons raise the crimson curtain they are woven into" (*Georg.* 3.24–25). The imagined temple doors are carved "in solid gold and ivory the battle of Ganges' hordes . . . and the Nile in flood and billowing with war" (*Georg.* 3.27–28), that is, the Battle of Actium. A portico displays the dominated cities of Asia and the routed Parthians, as well as "two trophies forcefully taken (*rapta*) from diverse hostile enemies, and two nations (*gentes*) that yielded a triumph from the two shores" (e.g., Spain in the west and Palestine in the east; *Georg.* 3.30–33). In Virgil's design, the battles and vanquished are displayed near another series of images of Jupiter's nation (*ab Iove gentis*), the Romans, including the Trojan forefathers (*Georg.* 3.35). This juxtaposition of conquerors (Jupiter's nation) and conquered (the others) is meant to communicate hierarchical imperial power relationships. Such relationships are inextricably linked to the public spatial context of civic worship; in fact, they are the relationships on which such reverence is predicated.

Velleius Paterculus also records that the Forum of Augustus included *tituli* (inscriptions and images) detailing "Spain and the other *gentes*" (*Hist.* 2.39.2). Inscriptions and images of the various *gentes* under Roman auspices would make for a telling spatial juxtaposition with the *summi viri*, represented by singular male bodies standing in line inside a colonnade.[114] Here men formed a Roman genealogy detailing the achievements of masculinity from the city's founding, reinvented just in time for the designation of Augustus as *pater patriae* in 2 B.C.E. Another gendered aspect of this space is manifest in the *caryatides*, or columns in the shape of captured women's bodies, holding up the roof of the Forum. Such contributes to a statement reflecting power relationships between rulers and subjects.[115] Roman display of personifications of conquered peoples in series is congruent with other methods of visually and publicly recording the logic (creating and preserving world peace) and variety (diversity of nations making up the world) of Roman conquests.

Roman representation of conquered nations was not limited to life-size women's bodies, although the femininity of the defeated was behind the display of trophies, indigenous art, and other booty (sculpted and actual), or anonymous captured barbarians.[116] Inscriptions of those conquered, cataloged, and mounted near arches and/or imperial altars were part of the constructed spatial landscape. Monumental inscriptions were another means of describing various elements of the conquered Roman world, both in Rome and the provinces. Inscriptions were erected publicly as part of Roman architectural projects and were meant to be seen. The *Res Gestae* itself, including the lists of Augustus's conquests in the name of peace, was inscribed on two bronze tablets on his tomb and was located near the large world map of Agrippa featuring the entire Roman world, comprised of Italy and conquered lands.[117] Weapons and other spoils from accomplished conquests were collected and displayed in Roman temples, and images and deities were taken from conquered peoples and planted at Rome in the name of "diversity."[118]

Descriptions of the nations of the Roman world were also mounted outside the capital city. The *Res Gestae* was inscribed at the temple of Augustus and Roma in Ancyra in the Roman province of Galatia (see chapter 3).[119] Its connection to the imperial cult strengthens an interpretation of the Aphrodisias Sebasteion as a visual elaboration upon achievements of the imperial family, descended from Venus and Mars, starting with Augustus "over land and sea" (i.e., the cosmos; see figure 14).

Figure 14. Augustus "over land and sea." The Sebasteion in Aphrodisias. Photo © New York University/Institute of Fine Arts Excavations at Aphrodisias.

Seeing such inscriptions, when paired with images of captives with and without trophies, indigenous weaponry and personifications, served to demonstrate victory in battle and remind Romans and non-Romans alike of their ideal place in naturalized social and political order.

Josephus reports that trophies of the nations Caesar had conquered were displayed in Herod's amphitheater at Jerusalem,[120] which, along with a monumental inscription of his achievements, encompassed the theater structure. The trophies were made of pure gold and silver. The natural Jews apparently disliked all that the theater represented since it was against their customs. However, more than the throwing of people to wild beasts and changing their law to accommodate such impiety, the Jews could not tolerate the trophies of the conquered in the theater because they thought they were images of people "to whom it was not the custom of their nation to pay honors" (*A. J.* 15.276). In fact, the presence of the images in the theater caused a disturbance in the city; though the Jews thought of tolerating the rest of Herod's "offenses . . . they would never bear images of peoples in their city, meaning the trophies, because this was disagreeable to the laws of their nation" (*A. J.* 15.277).

Herod attempted to solve the public outcry about what the Jews thought were images of people by inviting some of their leaders to the theater to closely inspect the trophies and asking what kind of images they thought them to be. When they cried out that they were images of people, Herod had the armor, weapons, and adornments removed from each of the *tropaea* to reveal the wooden poles underneath (*A. J.* 15.279). Josephus resolves this conflict by having the Jews laugh at their error in perception about the trophies (*A. J.* 15.279). Herod narrowly avoided an open rebellion with his solution. Nevertheless, what remains at the end of this episode is Josephus's restatement about the Jewish derision of both images of people *and* Herod's collaboration with Roman structures of power through visual display (*A. J.* 15.280–81). I submit this description as a rather rare view of how non-Romans read these images of Roman conquest, all the more important for the reality that it may reflect a Jewish perception of images of the nations as the Romans portrayed them in public spaces.

To summarize: the *Judaea Capta* coin, the statue of Augustus from Prima Porta, reliefs from the Sebasteion at Aphrodisias, and the Boscoreale cup each feature personifications of nations as defeated and deferential female bodies depicted alongside victorious Roman male bodies. The femininity mapped onto the objects of conquest extends, as well, to defeated male bodies, such as the Parthian man on the Prima Porta Augustus and the Gauls on the Boscoreale cup. Roman conquest is represented in gendered visual language, and Roman imperial world order is expressed as a gendered world order. Roman peace is achieved through patriarchy: feminine submission stabilizes Roman masculinity.

Images of maleness dominating femaleness are consistent, from the small coins changing hands every day to the honorific portraits of emperors—from an imperial forum in Rome to the largest imperial cult complex found and identified to date in western Asia Minor. Visual representation presents this social order as if it were fundamental to cosmic stability, as if it were the natural, inevitable, and best possible arrangement for social relations. And within this framework the nations form a central component—Roman identification of the nations as outsiders, as that which must be penetrated in order to maintain peace, is a critical element in this broader, gendered, imperial imagery of the natural cosmic and colonial order of things.

Conclusion

As I discuss in chapter 1, traditional idealist New Testament scholarship still affirms the term *ethnē* (nations) as a solely Jewish theological designation for non-Jews. Such designation identifies Paul's usage as consonant with his Jewish tradition, but misses the political and imperial dimensions of this term. In Roman imperial ideology, this term has a very specific designation as nations or tribes of people conquered and assimilated into Roman rule. The term is political in these contexts and imposed from the perspective of the Roman conquerors.[121] The widespread dissemination of images to the public depicting Roman men conquering female nations, and conquered nations arranged in deferential line following their conquest, served to justify and naturalize not only Roman territorial expansion and imperial domination, but also patriarchal gender constructs.

The portrayal of the nations conquered and incorporated into the Roman world in the name of peace and empire without end provides a striking visual complement to the New Testament's thoroughgoing concern for the inclusion of the Gentiles into a renewed and restored Israel. In my view, this is attested by Paul's emergent consciousness that Jewish people belong, according to Roman imperial ideology, in the ideological position of the conquered and assimilated. In an attempt to overcome the drive toward assimilation and vertical hierarchy characteristic of Roman imperial ideology, Paul uses the tactics of imagination to construct a counter-hegemonic movement of solidarity across ethnic differences. Exclusive focus on the literary texts of Paul's Roman imperial context gives only an inkling of such a perspective. It is primarily through the narrative language of Roman visual representation, seen through a gender-critical lens, that the fate of all the nations is crystallized and justified. Such images function as a communicative system by which gendered power relationships in New Testament texts can be more adequately illuminated. The next chapter continues a recontextualization of the Gentiles through a discussion of literary accounts demonstrating a Roman imperial ideology of conquest over all the nations.

CHAPTER THREE

The Fate of the Nations and the Naturalization of Conquest

After discussing visual representation concerning the "fate of the nations" in Roman imperial ideology, in this chapter I aim to highlight a selection of literary resources for a gender-critical re-imagination.[1] To that end, I present three interrelated sections of textual examples expressive of gendered hierarchy apparent in the Roman attitude toward "all the nations" in the early imperial period concurrent with the New Testament's textual production.

First, I attend to Roman mytho-historical origin stories that provide a prediction of conquest and world rule over all the nations, or what I call the predestination and historicity of the Romans/nations hierarchy. Such *aitia*, of which there are contested and contradictory versions, were written to defend the majesty of the Romans to the now-dominated Greeks (Dionysius of Halicarnassus), to emphasize the distance between the historical and contemporary Roman moral compass (Livy), and as part of mythologizing imperial renewal projects under Augustus (Virgil). The conception and birth of Rome's founders, Romulus and Remus, the deception and rape of the neighboring Sabine women, and relevant prophetic passages from the *Aeneid* serve as examples of the predestined and historicized quality of Roman world rule emphasized in Augustan literature and visual representation. The *Aeneid* in particular expresses prophecy concerning the Augustan house in genealogical terms, as the culmination of a long line of Roman kings, warriors, and heroes.

Second, I discuss the justification and naturalization of Roman world rule over all the nations during the Augustan and Julio-Claudian reigns. I use the *Res Gestae* of Augustus, itself both "Acts" and public monument (the only copies are from Asia Minor, in the Roman province of Galatia), to frame and focus the section. The *Res Gestae* has Augustus stating the various ways that he has brought peace to the world; he characterizes such peace, in the latter portion of his testimony, as being cemented by "ridding the sea of pirates" as well as extending the boundaries of Roman influence over "many nations," including many that have never been encountered previously. World conquest, domination, and incorporation of all the nations, as Augustus presents it, have an ideological function beyond the seemingly neutral reporting of works accomplished. There is a quality of prophecy fulfillment or enacting Roman destiny as the sole ruler of the known world and tamer of the unknown world. Ethnographical and historiographical descriptions of various nations, barbarians, and enemies, who are often described as feminine or otherwise gender transgressors, support an ideological characterization of the Romans as masculine conquerors and bearers of correct civilization and values, that is, gender roles, to the world. Such material is vast, and I consider only a few outstanding examples. Roman conquest is linked to sexual violence in texts that explicitly discuss wartime rape of non-Roman enemies.

Third, I briefly examine what I call the ritualization and eternalization of Roman rule over all the nations through a consideration of selected accounts of the Roman triumph and imperial funeral processions. Such accounts have a multilayered relevance for this project. As explored in chapter 2, images of the nations, as well as representatives of conquered peoples themselves, were displayed publicly in triumphal and imperial funeral processions. The triumph also places the Jews in the same ideological plane, much like ethnographic description, as other nations such as Gaul or Spain. The fullest extant depiction of a triumphal procession is from an author familiar to New Testament scholars: that of Josephus describing the Flavian triumph over the Jews of Judea following the Roman destruction of Jerusalem in 70 C.E. The politics of display of the Roman triumph is reminiscent of the porticoes of nations, such as that in Pompey's theater in Rome (which Augustus says he restored at his own expense) and in the Aphrodisian Sebasteion. The two types of display contribute to an ideology of Roman rule over all the nations, including the Jews.

This chapter concludes with a summary and delineation, of the implications gleaned from this and the previous chapter on visual representation, for my proposed recontextualization of the Gentiles in the New Testament as the defeated nations in Roman imperial ideology. Such a re-description lies at the center of a gender-critical re-imagination of Paul as apostle to the conquered.

Predestination and the Historicity of Roman Conquest

Rather than provide the story of how it actually happened, Rome's etiological narratives, or creation stories about the founders, Romulus and Aeneas, reflect a basic gendered pattern of male domination and violence where femininity represents that which must be vanquished or used to further Roman virility. The Romulus story begins with the rape of a Vestal Virgin. Rome, the city, is founded through fratricide and the inclusion of outsider men, and the Romans can only guarantee a future for their city and race through the trickery and rape of their neighbors that results in peace and assimilation. The *Aeneid* contains three prophetic passages of critical importance to the logic of Roman imperial ideology concerning the vanquished: Jupiter's prediction in Book 1, Anchises's underworld speech in Book 6, and the description of Aeneas's shield in Book 8, which includes pivotal historical events culminating in the central Battle of Actium, a victory over the east and feminine excess embodied by Cleopatra, as well as a triumphal procession of conquered nations.

Romulus (and Remus) as Founder(s) of Rome[2]

The stories about Romulus and Remus that I include here are couched within histories justifying and often extolling the virtues of the Rome of Augustus's time as providential or predicted by the gods.[3] Livy, for example, aims to record the acts of the world's "first people" and explore their mores and plainly states:

> if any people ought to be allowed to consecrate their origins and refer them to a divine source, so great is the military glory of the Roman People that when they profess the Father of their Founder was none other than Mars, the nations (*gentes*) of the earth may well submit to this also with as good a grace as they submit to Rome's dominion. (1.1.6)

Livy appears to take it as somewhat of a given that the nations have already submitted to Rome's dominion, and so they too should acknowledge that their submission is not the result of random victory, but the consecrated origins of a divinely born people.

Likewise, Dionysius of Halicarnassus[4] attempts to ground Roman rule in the history of Greekness to an ostensibly Greek audience[5] who may not like having been defeated by a formerly barbarian people. To accomplish this, he gives a complicated (and to some, convoluted) genealogical construction tracing Rome back through Greece, and particularly through heroes like Hercules and Greek peoples who had settled in Italy. This genealogical construction frames his narrative concerning Romulus and Remus, and he outlines his purpose for doing such work:

> I shall in this book show who the founders of the city were, at what periods the various groups came together, and through what turns of fortune they left their native countries. By this means I engage to prove that they were Greeks and came together from nations not the smallest nor the least considerable. And beginning with the next book I shall tell of the deeds they performed immediately after the founding of their city and of the customs and institutions by virtue of which their descendants advanced to so great dominion . . . to the end that I may instill in the minds of those who shall then be informed of the truth the fitting conception of this city—unless they have already assumed an utterly violent and hostile attitude toward it—and also that they may neither feel indignation at their present subjection, which is grounded on reason (for by a universal law of nature, which time cannot

> destroy, it is ordained that superiors shall ever rule over the inferior ones), nor rail at Fortune for having wantonly bestowed upon an undeserving city a supremacy so great and already of so long a duration; particularly when they shall have learned from my history that Rome from the very beginning, immediately after its founding, produced infinite examples of virtue in men whose superiors, whether for piety (*eusebesterous*) or for justice (*dikaioterous*) or for life-long self-control (*sōphrosunē*) or for war-like valour no city, Greek or barbarian, has ever produced . . . perhaps if they understand this they will lay aside their resentment at being ruled by Rome. . . . (1.5.2–5)

Here Dionysius links the generation of Rome out of Greece to a "universal law of nature," that is that the superior should always enact dominion over the inferior. The Romans have surpassed the Greeks several times over in terms of world rule and power and thus are justified in their empire according to natural, universal law. It is not just that the Romans are descended from Greeks but that they are better at being Greek than the Greeks were.

The history of supremacy ends with Rome, who has surpassed all previous cities and nations in "extent of its dominion and splendor of its achievements." The history of Rome according to this narrative is a logical culmination of a universal history[6] begun by Greece. Accounts of Rome's origins, written by historians like Dionysius, presuppose that a history of political power culminates with Rome's rule over the known world.[7]

This section concerns three episodes from Roman genesis accounts: the conception of Romulus and Remus, the founding of Rome and murder of Remus, and the trickery and rape of the Sabine women for the perpetuation of the Roman race. Such accounts must be thought of in the context of a world power telling its own story: they are stories that helped the Romans make sense of their position in the world. In that light, the themes of rape and violence stand out. I include the report of Rhea Silvia/Ilia's rape by the god Mars as the point of conception for Rome's twin founders, which shows that the god of war is genealogically responsible for bringing the city's starters into being, as well as links him as a father to the ancestors of Augustus. The murder of Remus just after Rome's walls are built is posed as a source text for understanding the Roman "there can be only one" ideology of rule—and Remus's death serves, according to the story, as a warning to those who would dare breach the sacred city walls. The rape of the neighboring Sabine women betrays an early impulse to intermarry, or really to make sure the Romans can reproduce, as well as a necessity to expand into neighboring lands, seeking cooperation.

The Conception of Romulus and Remus

When we think of Rome's founder Romulus and his brother Remus, the first image that comes to mind is usually that of the she-wolf, teeth bared, standing over two naked boys attached to her teats. This is an important element of Rome's genesis, to be sure, and not precisely where the story of Romulus and Remus begins according to literary representation. Stories of their conception attest to the predestined greatness of Romulus and therefore Rome. The twins' mother, Rhea Silvia/Ilia, has been forced to become a Vestal Virgin so as not to provide offspring for Numitor, the older of two brothers who was dethroned by the younger Amulius.

The passage in Livy reads as follows:

> To Numitor, the elder, he (Procas) bequested the ancient kingship of the Silvian nation (*gentis*). Yet violence proved more potent than a father's wishes or respect for seniority. Amulius beat (*pulso*) his brother and ruled. Adding crime to crime: he killed his brother's male offspring (*stirpem fratris virilem interemit*), and Rhea Silvia, his brother's daughter, he appointed a Vestal under pretense of honoring her, and by consigning her to perpetual virginity, deprived her of the hope of children. But the fates were resolved, as I suppose, upon the founding of this great city, and the beginning of the mightiest of empires, second to that of gods (. . . *secundum deorum opes imperii principum*). The Vestal was forced (*compressa*), and having given birth to twin sons, named Mars as the father of her doubtful offspring, whether actually so believing, or because it seemed less wrong if a god were the author of her fault. (1.3.10–4.3)

And the account of Dionysius:

> In the fourth year after this, Ilia, upon going into a temple grove for Mars to get some pure water that might be used for sacrifices, was forced (*biazetai*) by someone in the temple precinct (*en tō temeni*). Some have the opinion that one of the suitors of the girl came, loving the slave girl (*erōnta tēs paidiskēs*); others that it was Amulius himself, and that, since his purpose was to destroy her as much as to sate his desire, he had arrayed himself in as much armor as would render him most terrible to see and that he also kept his features disguised as safely as possible. But most writers relate a fabulous story to the effect that it was an image of the god (*tou daimonos eidōlon*, of Mars), whose place it was, many others even add that the suffering (*tō pathei*) was accompanied by divine works (*daimonia erga*), including the sudden disappearance of the sun and a darkness that spread over the sky, and that the appearance of the image (*eidōlon*) was more wondrous than that of men (*anthrōpōn*) according to size/stature and beauty (*kata megethos kai kallos*). They say that the forcer/violator (*ton biasamenon*), comforting the pain (*tēn lupēn*), out of which it became clear that he was a god, said to the girl to never mourn for her suffering (*tō pathei*), for the communication of marriage made her toward/with the divinity who entered the place, and would be born to her out of the violation (*ek tou biasmou*) two infant boys (*paidas*) far excelling

> men (*anthrōpōn makrō*) in virtue (*aretēn*) and the arts of war (*ta polemia*). And having said these things he was enveloped in a cloud and, being lifted away from earth, went up through air. (1.77.1–2)

Enmity and deception between two brothers, one older (Numitor) and one younger (Amulius), play a prominent role in the development of the city destined to have dominion over the world. Both Dionysius and Livy relate that the pretense of Ilia/Rhea becoming a Vestal Virgin was to bestow honor to Numitor's family, but really she is to be kept chaste for the purpose of preventing a Numitor dynasty and keeping Amulius in power. She became a Vestal by Amulius's force and his motive to never see his own power upended by his defeated brother's offspring—to whom the throne belonged by law.[8] Such deception and ulterior motive is underscored by Amulius's murder of Numitor's son so that no progeny could come from the firstborn either.[9] The damage is made worse by the fact that Ilia is narrated as being of marriageable age and no longer a girl—thus her sexuality, her ability to bear a son, is threatening to the already-precarious power structure Amulius constructs for himself, even if Livy names her as the one who harbors the hope of having offspring (1.3.11). Numitor, knowing the plot was deceptive, chooses not to act on Ilia's behalf lest serious vengeance be made on what was left of his house, including himself. His daughter, therefore, lives as a hostage of sorts, in exchange so that he can live—even if he lives as an "emasculated" man, stripped of sovereignty.

The centrality of the violence against Ilia/Rhea, presented as what must occur for her to give birth to the founder(s) of Rome, should not be overlooked—this pivotal event in the divinely ordained story of Roman origins is a rape narrative. The twin founders of Rome are born out of a sexual battle instigated by the war god himself. Livy only states that the Vestal was "pressed" (1.4.2), names Mars as the father, and then gives birth to the twins. Here the rape is only insinuated. Ilia/Rhea is a virgin who has not been married and is serving an honorable deity, but the transgression is hers: she names Mars as the father as if divine paternity seems less wrong in light of her ignoring her vow of chastity.[10]

Dionysius's longer exposition is instructive on matters reflective of gender and power. He has typically consulted several available writers on the issue, preferring what he claims "most" write: an elaboration on the circumstances surrounding the paternity of Mars. This account emphasizes the force of Mars and the pain of Ilia. Like Livy, he points out that the virgin was forced (*biazetai*) and reinforces this characterization by using this term twice more: once to describe the one who did the deed (*ton biasamenon*) and once to have Mars declare that it is out of the violation (*ek tou biasmou*) that Romulus and Remus will be born. The encounter is termed a "suffering" (*tō pathei*) accompanied by divine works. The violator comforts the pain (*tēn lupēn*) of his victim by telling her that she should not mourn for her suffering (again, *tō pathei*), because she is now married to the god "who entered" (*ton embateuonta*) the place (and her); out of the violation would be born the twin founders of Rome. In both Livy and Dionysius's telling, the only action the virgin performs is going about her sacred duties. The rest of the activity—speaking, entering, generating—belongs to an animated likeness of Mars, and she serves as an object.

As the force, pain, and violence toward Ilia/Rhea are central to the conception of Romulus and Remus, so are the location of the conception as well as the excessive beauty and divinity of Mars, the violator. Livy does not give a setting for the encounter but does remark, concerning the inevitability of Rome's founding, that "the fates were resolved . . . upon the founding of this great city, and the beginning of the first of empires [*imperii principum*], second to that of the gods [*secundum deorum*]" (1.4.1), highlighting the importance and inevitability of this turn of events for the founding of the "first of empires." Again, Dionysius provides a telling spin on this point: the rape of Ilia/Rhea does not take place just anywhere, but in a temple precinct of Mars and while the Vestal was fetching pure water for a ritual from the consecrated grove there. Twice more in this passage the place is named as belonging to Mars: once when Dionysius initially relates who it was who violated Ilia, and again when Mars tells her not to mourn her suffering, since she was married to "the god who entered the place." This historian also presents the coming of Mars and Ilia's violation as accompanied by supernatural works: when it happened, "the sun disappeared and darkness spread over the sky." The image of the god himself is said to be more wondrous in stature/size and beauty than men; Mars says, as part of his comforting speech that his infant sons through Ilia would surpass men in virtue and the "things of war" (*ta polemia*). Finally, the god of war, wrapped in a cloud and going up to the sky, leaves her in his place with her pregnancy and a subsequent scandal.

The placement of this rape in a temple precinct of Mars[11] is striking, given that Augustus seeks to consolidate the story of his emergent Roman Empire into a clean genealogical line back to Mars and Venus, and part of how he accomplished this visually and spatially was to construct his Forum with a temple to Mars Ultor as its focal building. Although the temple was vowed to avenge the death of Augustus's father Julius Caesar,[12] a temple to this god signifies not just war or the conquest of foreign enemies—where evidence of military potency in the form of booty would be stored inside—but the original conquest itself by the same god. The rape of the Vestal Virgin jump-started the whole genealogy of Rome's founding and development as ruler of the world. In Ovid's famous description of the Forum, Ilia is present in his description of Romulus: "Here he sees the son of Ilia carrying on his shoulders the arms of the conquered leader" (*hinc videt Iliaden umeris ducis arma ferentem*) (*Fasti* 4.565); Romulus is not explicitly named, and the naming of Ilia again alludes to her rape by Mars.[13] Such allusions, built into the structure of the complex itself, certainly fit with Barbara Kellum's characterization of the Forum as a "sexually charged, masculine environment."[14]

Ovid's version of this story emphasizes the predestined quality of Roman rule. Here Ilia is on the way to get water to wash her holy things when she becomes tired and induced to sleep. At this point Mars sees her, is inspired with desire, and "desire was followed by possession." Ilia awakens to a big belly and does not know why. She has a vision, however: her Vestal-bridal hair is undone by the wooden fillet falling from her hair into the ground. Where it falls,

> there rise two palm trees side by side. Of them one was the taller and by its heavy boughs spread a canopy over the whole world, and with its foliage touched the topmost stars. My uncle wielded an axe against the trees; the warning terrified me and my heart did throb with fear. A woodpecker—the bird of Mars—and a she-wolf fought in defense of the twin trunks, and by their help both of the palms were saved. (*Fasti* 3.31–40)

In Ovid's version of Ilia/Silvia's vision, Romulus/the taller palm tree is tall enough to "spread a canopy over the whole world." This vision alludes not only to the founding of Rome but the prophecy that Rome would, in fact, cover the whole world with the sacred canopy of empire.

Romulus Kills Remus and Builds "Creation"

The story of Romulus and Remus continues in a manner that biblical scholars might find slightly reminiscent of the Moses narrative in Exodus. Their mother is bound for her transgression, and the boys sent up the river in a basket.[15] Of course, they are found by the infamous she-wolf, suckled near the holy fig tree,[16] and raised as wild men (Livy 1.4) or herdsmen (Dionysius 1.79.10). On their appearance, Dionysius reports that when they grew to be men

> they showed themselves both in dignity of aspect and elevation of mind not like swineherds, but such as we might expect those to be who are born out of the imperial race (*tous ek basileiou te phuntas genous*) and are looked upon as the offspring of the gods: and as such they are still celebrated by the Romans by hymns in their fatherland. (1.79.10–11)

They lived by working with their hands and building their own houses (*skēnas*, "tents," Dionysius 1.79.11). The dignified twin men were associated with robbers and other herders. In fact, as Livy reports, "having . . . gained both strength and resolution, they would now not only face wild beasts, but would attack robbers laden with their spoils, and divide up what they took from them among the shepherds, with whom they shared their toils and pranks, while their band of young men grew larger every day" (1.4). A failed robbery attempt of Amulius results in the capture and near-death of Remus, which in turn prompts the exposure of the real identity of the twins by their father, Faustulus, who had previously kept it to himself. A final battle with Amulius proves to be his end, as Romulus slays him, frees his brother, and restores power to Numitor.

The death of Amulius and Numitor's rethroning is how, apparently, Rome's plot of land becomes identified. According to Livy, the brothers found it themselves, having been "seized with desire" to make their own city (1.6.3), while Dionysius, in a characteristically long retelling, has Numitor give the land to the brothers out of a fear of overpopulation and wanting to send any remaining enemies away (1.85.1). They go, together with others whom Dionysius calls "great numbers of common people" and "sufficient number of the prominent men of the best class, and of the Trojan element all those who were noblest" (1.85.3), to a place where they were raised.

Rome's founding provides a setting for the enmity between the twins that results in the death of Remus. According to Dionysius:

> After they had led their people out of Alba and intermingled them with the local population that still remained in Pallantium and Saturnia, they divided the whole multitude into two parts. They did this in the hope of arousing a spirit of emulation, so that through their rivalry with each other their tasks might be sooner finished; however it produced the greatest of evils, discord. For each group, exalting its own leader, extolled him as the proper person to command them all; and the youths themselves, being now no longer one in mind or feeling it necessary to have brotherly sentiments toward one another, since each expected to command the other, scorned equality and craved superiority. (1.85.4–5)

In this narrative, the strife between Romulus and Remus begins as soon as they are out of Alba. Now that they have their own place, they realize that only one can be the ruler, and so they should no longer "have brotherly sentiments toward each other" when they do not agree on where to found the new city, and they each choose a place. Numitor's advice results in the "decision of the gods" being called upon to grant rulership. The brothers, stationed on their respective hills, look for the auspicious birds. Romulus, jealous of the possibility that his brother might receive the more profitable augury, tricks him into thinking that he had seen the birds first and won.[17] Remus, picking up on the trickery, complains and refuses to give up his colony. Because of this, even greater animosity is fostered between the brothers, and a battle breaks out between them, where Faustulus and Remus are both killed. Romulus, grieving but comforted by Faustulus's wife Laurentia,[18] builds the city of Rome on the Palatine with the remaining Latin soldiers.

The struggle for sole rulership over the new city between twin brothers is solved through what amounts to a civil war. The first builders with Romulus constitute his loyal army, connecting Rome's construction to military strategy and victory. Another, more common story concerning the nascent wall is related by Livy and Dionysius, and referenced elsewhere.[19] In this account, according to Livy, Remus willingly submits to the sovereignty of Romulus, and while Romulus was building his city, "Remus leaped over the new walls in mockery of his brother, whereupon Romulus in great anger slew him, and in menacing tones added these words withal 'so perish whoever else should leap over my walls!'" (1.7). Dionysius takes the weapon out of Romulus's hand:

> Remus yielded the leadership to Romulus, though not without resentment and anger at the fraud, but that after the wall was built, wishing to demonstrate the weakness of the fortification, cried, 'Well, as for this wall, one of your enemies could cross it as easily as I do,' and immediately leaped over it. Then Celer, one of the men standing on the wall . . . said, 'well, as for this enemy, one of us could easily punish him,' and striking him on the head with a mattock, he killed him right there. (1.87.4)[20]

Whether or not it is Celer or Romulus who murders Remus, it is clear from Rome's foundation stories that the murder plays a pivotal role in the city's development. After the murder, Dionysius relates that there is now not an "obstacle" (*empodōn*, 1.88.1) to the "creation" (*tō ktismati*). There are no words for "city" here. Even if city could be implied, a lack of specificity further gives a cosmic significance to Rome's building. After Remus is murdered and buried, Livy and Dionysius immediately put Romulus back to work appeasing the gods, marking off boundaries, and building Rome/creation.

The material building of Rome/creation is linked to the appeasement of the gods. The Ara Maxima to Herakles, still extant in the time of Livy and Dionysius's writing, is built and offered to the gods closely following Remus's murder (Livy 1.7).[21] Livy also describes Romulus as Rome's lawgiver after creation is up and running.[22]

Once an abnormally manly twin son of a divinely raped Vestal Virgin, then sent up the river and suckled by a she-wolf, and then raised by a lower-class couple mourning their own barrenness, the robber-turned-warrior-turned-ruler Romulus now gives the law to the multitude. Somehow he understands that only the rules of law would foster unity among them, the power to pull all people into a "single body." He also understands, according to this passage, that he must put on the appearance of a ruler to make the law more binding in the eyes of the "rustic" people. Romulus must make himself look as if he belongs at the top of a vertical hierarchy for Roman law to work.

Romulus was invoked as Rome's glorious military founder during the Augustan age in literature and visual representation.[23] Octavian was apparently offered that name as his own in order to further exemplify his status as Rome's new founder following a period of civil wars (Suetonius, *Aug.* 7).[24] A particular significance of one brother's murder, in a battle for supremacy when initially they could not be told apart, lies in allusions to the struggle for power between prominent Roman generals in the late republic, particularly Caesar and Pompey.[25] However, the melancholy necessity of Remus's murder for creation to move forward was seen by at least one Augustan author as a "curse" upon later developments:

> Why are your hands grasping the swords that have once been sheathed? Has too little Roman blood been shed on field and flood—not that the Roman might burn the towers of jealous Carthage, or that the Briton, as yet unscathed, might descend the Sacred Way in fetters, but that, in fulfillment of the Parthians' prayers, this city might perish by its own right hand? Such habit never belonged to wolves or lions, whose fierceness is turned only against beasts of other kinds. Does some frenzy drive us on, or some stronger power, or guilt? Give answer—they speak not; a ghastly pallor spreads over their faces; and dazed are their shattered senses. It is thus: a bitter fate pursues the Romans, and the crime of a brother's murder, ever since blameless Remus's blood was spilled upon the ground, to be a curse for posterity. (Horace, *Epod.* 7)

Horace makes the murder of Remus a direct precedent for the ever-present threat of civil war, war between brothers, even after Caesar and Pompey. Regardless of what kind of peace has been established, it appears to be the fate of the Romans to be tempted to destroy themselves by in-fighting. Thus, fighting and struggle should be directed at outsiders destined to "walk the Sacred Way in fetters"[26] like the Britons and the rest of the conquered nations, and not at family. This attitude is reflected in Roman imperial foreign policy, where the eradication of civil war and the unification of Italy redefined what counted as Roman, and many different national others were brought back in fetters.

The Romulus and Remus narrative insists that Rome's founder is, from childhood, a better warrior—and therefore, man—than all who challenge or even are related to him. He is imaged in the Forum of Augustus as carrying a trophy, indicating his prowess as a victorious military commander. In the narratives I have briefly considered here, this is clear by his conception outside of ordinary reproductive means: the forced union between a virgin and a god. Descent from the war god Mars is visible on account of the twins being more beautiful and stronger than humans. Romulus becomes a model for Roman active masculinity through success in battle, killing his brother and therefore removing the last obstacle to building creation/Rome, and giving the law and taking on the appearance of a more holy enforcer so as to ensure unity among his new subjects.

Rape of the Sabine Women

Among Romulus and Remus legends, the "Rape of the Sabine Women" is a particularly famous account of Roman origins. Often invoked in the imperial period (e.g. , on the *Aeneid*'s shield of Aeneas, discussed below) and visually portrayed in a coin from M. Titurius Sabinus of 89–88 B.C.E. and surviving reliefs from Rome's Basilica Aemilia,[27] it is a telling portrayal of Roman attitudes toward women and gender roles. It is also part of the genesis account of the incorporation of other peoples into the Roman family, using stolen and raped non-Roman women, through violence and then compromise, to ultimately graft peoples/nations into the fatherland in the name of peace.[28]

The "Rape of the Sabine Women" is one of two extant origin stories relating how the population of Rome increases after initial building. First, Romulus built an "asylum" or hut where male refugees and runaway slaves from other nations would find a safe place.[29] Genealogically speaking, many of Rome's early inhabitants were non-Roman men who came to the city from elsewhere, perhaps pointing to the international character of the city later on.

Whatever the city's early greatness, taking in rabble would not provide Rome the means—women's bodies—to make successive generations. In short, there are no original Roman women. After scouring the neighboring countryside for the privilege of intermarriage and insurance of a populous future, Roman lady-scouts come up short as no neighboring nations would provide wives for them. Envoys are mocked: "on being dismissed, if they had opened an asylum for women as well as for men, for in that way only would they obtain suitable wives" (Livy 1.9). Insulted, Roman men keep returning home empty-handed, and "the matter seemed certain to end in violence" (Livy 1.9). The Sabines were among those refusing to give women, thus marking them as enemies, and Romulus decides that the remaining option is to use violence with a dose of trickery to lure the Sabines within the walls for a family-style festival where the abduction takes place:

> Romulus, concealing his resentment, made ready solemn games in honor of the equestrian Neptune, which he called Consualia. He then bade proclaim the spectacle to the surrounding peoples, and his subjects prepared to celebrate it with all the resources within their knowledge and power, that they might cause the occasion to be noised abroad and eagerly expected. Many people—for they were also eager to see the new city—gathered for the festival, especially those who lived nearest, the inhabitants of Caenina, Crustumium, and Antemnae. The Sabines, too, came with all their people, including their children and wives. They were hospitably entertained in every house, and when they had looked at the site of the city, its walls, and its numerous buildings, they marvelled that Rome had so rapidly grown great. When the time came for the show, and people's thoughts and eyes were busy with it, the prearranged attack began. At a given signal the Romans darted this way and that, to seize and carry off the maidens. In most cases these were taken by the men in whose path they chanced to be. Some, of exceptional beauty, had been marked out for the chief senators, and were carried off to their houses by plebeians to whom the office had been entrusted. One, who far excelled the rest in mien and loveliness, was seized, the story relates, by the gang of a certain Thalassius, and this was the origin of the wedding-cry. The sports broke up in a panic, and the parents of the maidens fled sorrowing. They charged the Romans with the crime of violating hospitality, and invoked the gods to whose solemn games they had come, deceived in

> violation of religion and honor. The stolen maidens were no more hopeful of their plight, nor less indignant. But Romulus himself went amongst them and explained that the pride of their parents had caused this deed, when they had refused their neighbors the right to intermarry; nevertheless the daughters should be wedded and become co-partners in all the possessions of the Romans, in their citizenship and, dearest privilege of all to the human race, in their children; only let them moderate their anger, and give their hearts to those whom fortune had given their persons. A sense of injury had often given place to affection, and they would find their husbands the kinder for this reason, that every man would earnestly endeavor not only to be a good husband, but also to console his wife for the home and parents she had lost. His arguments were seconded by the wooing of the men, who excused their act on the score of passion and love, the most moving of all pleas to a woman's heart. (Livy, 1.9)

In Livy's version, the Romans take revenge on the Sabines for spurning them, and obtain the wives they need to make their future, by tricking neighboring families into coming to the apparently well-publicized Consualia. Amazed at Rome's quick growth, they do not expect the women among them to be forcibly taken. But the prearranged attack ensues, the women are stolen, their parents flee in sorrow and charge the Romans with violating hospitality, religion, and honor. The women are upset, but Romulus convinces them that it is in their best interest to partner with the Romans.

The Sabine men then take revenge on the Romans, and a war between them ensues. The Sabines gain an early advantage, taking control of the Roman citadel. According to Livy, the leader of the Roman army, Hostilius Hostius, is defeated, the army swells toward the citadel in his absence, and Romulus is taken up in the crowd. As the Sabines are about to charge and win the battle against the disadvantaged Romans, Romulus lifts his sword and shield to the sky and offers a prayer to Jupiter Optimus Maximus, and their destiny changes. No sooner is the leader of the Sabines, Mettius Curtius, able to utter "we have beaten our inhospitable enemies! They now know how great is the difference between carrying off maidens and fighting with men!" (Livy 1.12) than the Roman men charge and force him to escape through a swamp. Both armies, without the restraint of their respective leaders, rush toward one another.

At this chaotic point the Sabine women, now wives of the Romans, enter the picture with disheveled hair and torn garments, and broker a deal between the fighting fathers and husbands:

> Then the Sabine women . . . dared to go among the flying missiles, and rushing in from the side, to part the hostile forces and disarm them of their anger, beseeching their fathers on this side, on that their husbands, that fathers-in-law and sons-in-law should not stain themselves with impious bloodshed,

> nor pollute with parricide the suppliants' children, grandsons to one party and sons to another. "If you regret," they continued, "the relationship that unites you, if you regret the marriage-tie, turn your anger against us; we are the cause of the war, the cause of wounds, and even death to both our husbands and our parents. It will be better for us to perish than to live, lacking either of you, as widows or orphans." It was a touching plea, not only to the rank and file, but to their leaders as well. A stillness fell on them, and a sudden hush. Then the leaders came forward to make a truce, and not only did they agree on peace, but they made one people out of the two. They shared the sovereignty, but all *imperium* was transferred to Rome. . . . The sudden exchange of so unhappy a war for joyful peace endeared the Sabine women even more to their husbands and parents, and above all to Romulus himself. (Livy, 1.13)

The peace that the Sabine women broker is accomplished by literally putting their bodies in the way of the ensuing battle. That the women interrupt a war between men is consistent in different accounts. Their plea is powerfully made, as they are the genealogical link between the Roman and Sabine men. Livy makes their rape into the action that transforms them from foreigners into Romans, as well as the impetus for the Sabine men's assimilation into Rome. This assimilation comes in the name of peace: one people was made out of two and sovereignty shared, but all rule (*imperium*) transferred to Rome. Because of this, the Sabine women are endeared even more to all on both former sides of the now-unified people.

Dionysius has the premeditated attack deliberated and approved by Romulus's grandfather Numitor and then the senate instead of instigated solely by Romulus.[30] Here the virgins (*parthenoi*) are taken from several different neighboring nations instead of just the Sabines (but note that the greatest number of women come from them, 2.32.3), and Romulus assures the captured women, whose chastity the Romans respect at first, that they have been taken for the purpose of an ancient Greek wedding custom (2.30.5).[31] Dionysius's battles against the men of various nations are also longer and more protracted, and the Sabine men are singled out for delaying their commencement of arms against the Romans. However, most striking is the reasoning Dionysius gives behind taking the women:

> As regards the reason for the seizing of the virgins, some ascribe it to a scarcity of women, others to the seeking of a pretext for war, but those who give the most plausible account—with whom I agree—attribute it to making an alliance through force (*anankaian*) with the neighboring cities, founded on friendship (*philotēta*). (2.31.1)

The prospect of forcing alliance with neighboring peoples in friendship indicates the use of women as a tool for the expansion and welfare of the state. It seems "most plausible" that the Romans seize the virgins in order to take the neighbors.

It is not an accident that the rape of the Sabine women legend became popular during the late republican[32] and early imperial periods. This story has been read as explaining the origins of Roman marriage, denoting the development in private life of the conjugal bond. This is on account of the marriage cry given in Livy's presentation, for example.[33] The Consualia festival was still celebrated in the early imperial period, and Ovid tells that the Sabine women were remembered on the first day of March (according to Mars) "either because, boldly thrusting themselves on the bare blades, they by their tears did end these martial wars; or else mothers duly observe the rites on my day because Ilia was happily made a mother by me" (*Fasti* 3.230–34).

Given the popularity of Augustan treatments of Rome's origins, perhaps in the service of attempts at social renewal through regulation of gender roles and (especially female) sexuality (that were largely unsuccessful), the rape of the Sabine women seems to have served an ideological function concerning relations between men and women. It also has, however, larger collective implications as a reflection of or "metaphor for the relationship between Self and Other."[34] In this sense male and female are representative of the wider dynamics of Roman conquest. The story can be seen as "a paradigm of the character of Roman conquest and expansion . . . through the assignment of new statuses and through grants of citizenship."[35]

The rape narrative as a paradigm for imperial expansion is precisely where I submit this story is truly foundational to Roman imperial ideology as it expresses relationships between self and other on an international scale: Romans over foreign nations. There are no Roman women—there are only Roman men in a creation whose founder is a better man than the rest. For the Roman state to care for itself and provide citizens for its future—that is, to guarantee fertility—Rome must steal and rape the women of other nations under the pretense of a nice family festival. The women become the link between the Romans and foreign men and function as the catalyst for cooperation and assimilation into Rome. They are transformed into allies, as are the men from their nation of origin.

The seizure and rape of women as integral to the process of assimilation, compromise, and peace between Romans and others is, I submit, a key element of the personification of conquered nations as women's bodies in Roman imperial art. The act of imperial expansion through expanding the borders is a sexual act where the Roman men take the women of the nations they defeat and rape them, thus curtailing the natural fertility of the conquered and rechanneling it for the future of the Roman Empire. Personification of the nations (that contain women and men) as female bodies draws the rape narrative into a larger ideological pattern. It is not just individual women being raped, but entire nations—the land and people are violated and feminized. Further, the characterization of the intervening Sabine women with disheveled hair and the clothing of mourning is reminiscent of some of the poses of the nations in the Aphrodisias Sebasteion.

Origin stories serve a purpose of making such activity itself seem like the natural order of the world. In fact, the rape of the Sabine women makes such conquest and peacemaking inevitable for the future of the original core group of men, as well as the empire. The women's cooperation makes the ideology of Roman conquest and assimilation seem more complicated: yes, there is rape, and yes, they are not unilaterally aligned with their fathers and brothers when they suggest peace. Degrees of assimilation and the terms of cooperation are brought into relief by stolen women who become part of the Roman self before they appeal to the remaining others, men of their nations.

The location of the Sabine women narrative so early in Rome's history also emphasizes the preordained quality of the episode. Romulus is, after all, destined to spread his canopy over the world. When Ovid has Mars tell the story of the Sabine women during the calendar explanation of his month, he puts into the god's mouth the suggestive words "I chafed and bestowed on you, Romulus, your father's temper. 'A truce to prayers!' I said. 'What you seek, arms will give'" (*Fasti* 3.197).[36] The god of war himself declares that the best way for Rome to expand is not through prayer, but battle; not negotiation, but arms.

The Romulus and Remus narratives reflect a Roman attempt to integrate an emergent imperial consciousness with divine predestination and historicity, giving the weight of the past to present circumstances and making them seem all the more natural. Such is a function of ideology. When I look at the relief of Claudius over Britannia from Aphrodisias or the *Judaea Capta* coin in light of these Roman origin stories, I see not only the commemoration of those particular and historically located conquests of particular foreigners, but also a reenactment of early rape episodes as central to the creation and re-creation of the Roman Empire, or the world itself. In that sense, these materials are not so distant from each other in terms of what they communicate about ideal relationships between Romans and others, sanctioned by the gods and necessary for Rome's growth and sustainability.

The conquest and assimilation of the nations into one body, with all rule transferred to Rome, is predicted and given a template in the rape of the Sabine women. First, Romans over neighboring women, then the Roman Empire over whole nations. Conquest rendered in these terms reflects a gendered difference in hierarchy: the impenetrable masculinity inherent in Roman rule is chosen to penetrate the femininity of other lands and peoples. This dynamic is central to the Romans/nations hierarchical construct that I am posing as integral to a gender-critical re-imagination of Paul as apostle to the conquered.

Aeneas as Founder of the Roman Empire

Stories of Rome's origins predicting world conquest over all the nations surface again in Virgil's *Aeneid* as part of the epic cycle prophesying the Roman Empire. Romulus is the founder of Rome, but he is descended from Trojan Aeneas. The *Aeneid* details the Trojan claiming of Italy that leads to the founding of Rome, begins with "arms and the man" (1.1), and includes a tension between potential rulers over the nations (Rome and Carthage), where those destined to be the losers have a woman leader (Dido). The epic serves as a foundation story serving—at least in part, though this is contested—to legitimate the Augustan age, putting both Roman Empire and Augustus himself at the very beginning, as the culmination of greatness.[37] The construction of the Romans/nations dichotomy is the ultimate achievement and outcome of Aeneas's life and legacy.

Along Aeneas's divinely-wrought journey, women are eliminated or left behind, including Aeneas's wife Creusa, as "Rome's destiny requires her ancestor to be a widower."[38] The epic ends with a last-man-standing battle over a marriage/colonization of Lavinia/um, the overall goal. Pious Aeneas finally penetrates Turnus with his sword in a rage over dead Pallas,[39] signifying decisive victory and ensuring that all prophecies concerning Rome will come to pass. Not surprisingly, manliness drives this representation of Rome's origins. Outsiders are imaged as women, reflecting the gendered terms on which Romans and non-Romans are defined.[40] The figure of Dido serves as a prime example. Juno, who is rooting for Turnus until the end, is characterized in much the same way: vengeful, angry, misguided for suggesting that things will not turn out in Aeneas's favor, since Jupiter (the father of the gods) has willed it that way.

However, even as female characters must be eliminated, femininity also serves to signify non-Roman customs, dress, and speech. This is especially true of exotic, woman-ruled Carthage. Aeneas and his men are themselves degraded by their Latin opponents as effeminate/eunuch followers of Cybele/Magna Mater, who also acts as a protector throughout the poem.[41] In the end, Aeneas must become Latin, that is, a real man, in Roman consciousness. He must leave behind the stereotypical eastern trappings of his Trojan heritage to become the forefather of the Roman Empire. He becomes such a man, interestingly enough, through combat and the defeat of the Latins. The transformation of Trojans into Latins and, eventually, into Romans is also embodied in Juno's plea that the Latins not take the clothing and customs of the Trojans, which Jupiter grants with a smile:

> Ausonia's sons shall keep their fathers' speech and customs (*mores*) . . . the Teucrians shall but sink down, merged into the mass. I will give them their sacred laws and rites and make them all Latins of one tongue. From them shall rise a race (*genus*), mixed with Ausonian blood, which you will see overpass men, overpass gods in piety, and no nation (*gens*) will celebrate your worship with equal zeal. (12.834–40)

The Trojans will be made into the nation of the toga, surpassing (other, eastern) men and ruling over less well-dressed peoples, such as the Gauls who feature prominently on Aeneas's shield (see below).

As is well known, the *Aeneid* is the Roman foundation myth of the whole world: Aeneas does not found Rome, but is the founder, or forefather, of the Roman Empire encompassing the cosmos. The empire is predestined: gods, not the man, predict Roman rule on a number of occasions. Though the hero has as his immediate objective to conquer, unify, and rule over Italy, this activity has direct implications for Rome's conquest, unification, and rule over the universe.[42] At several key points in the *Aeneid*, Aeneas hears (and the reader learns) about the extensive importance attached to the Romans and their rule over all the nations. Here the text historicizes the rise of empire: genealogies of heroic fathers graft great men onto Rome's history and give a family line of great military leaders and conquerors leading to Augustus. To this effect, the three passages I discuss below include Jupiter's prediction in Book 1, Anchises's underworld speech in Book 6, and the description of Aeneas's prophetic shield of Book 8.

Jupiter's Prediction in *Aeneid*, Book 1

In Book 1, Aeneas feigns hope and shares a meal of roasted meat and old wine with his remaining men on the shores of Libya following his initial, devastating shipwreck. His teary mother Venus approaches her father Jupiter while he peers down on them from above. Asking why it is that all looks lost for her son, she refers to a previous prediction of Jupiter concerning the rise of the Romans:

> [W]hat great crime could my Aeneas—could my Trojans—have wrought against you, to whom, after many disasters borne, the whole world is barred for Italy's sake? Surely it was your promise that from them some time, as the years rolled on, the Romans were to arise; from them, even from Teucer's restored line, should come rulers to hold the sea and all lands beneath their sway (*qui mare, qui terras omnis tenerent*). What thought, father, has turned you? (*Aen*. 1.231–237)

Jupiter responds with a smile and a kiss. "Your fates stand unmoved," he says, and then gives away the story, so to speak:

> You will see the city of Lavinium and its promised walls; and, great-souled Aeneas you will raise on high to the starry heavens . . . This, your son—for, since this care gnaws at your heart, I will speak and, further unrolling the scroll of fate, disclose its secrets—will wage a great war in Italy, shall crush proud peoples, and for his people will set up laws (*mores*) and city walls, until the third summer has seen him ruling in Latium and three winters have passed in cap since the Rutulians have been laid low. But the boy Ascanius, now surnamed Iulus—Ilus he was, while the Ilian state stood firm in sovereignty—shall fulfill in empire (*imperio*) thirty great circles of rolling months, shall shift his throne from Lavinium's seat, and, great in power, shall build the walls of Alba Longa. Here then for three hundred years unbroken shall the kingdom endure under Hector's race, until Ilia, a royal priestess, shall bear to Mars her twin offspring. Then Romulus, proud in the tawny

> hide of the she-wolf, his nurse, shall take up the line, and found the walls of Mars and call the people Romans after his own name. For these I set no bounds in space or time, but have given empire without end. Spiteful Juno, who now in her fear troubles sea and earth and sky, shall change to better counsels and with me cherish the Romans, lords of the world, and nation of the toga (*rerum dominos, gentemque togatam*). Thus it is decreed. There shall come a day, as the sacred seasons glide past, when the house of Assaracus shall bring into bondage Phthia and famed Mycenae, and hold lordship over vanquished Argos. From this noble line shall be born the Trojan Caesar, who shall extend his empire over the ocean, his glory to the stars, a Iulius, name descended from great Iulus! Him, in days to come, shall you, anxious no more, welcome to heaven, laden with Eastern spoils; he too, shall be invoked in vows. Then wars will cease and savage ages soften; white-haired Fides and Vesta, Quirinus with his brother Remus, shall give laws. The gates of war, grim with iron and close-fitting bars, shall be closed; within, impious Furor, sitting on savage arms, his hands fast bound behind with a hundred brazen knots, shall roar in the ghastliness of blood-stained lips. (1.259–96)

In Jupiter's prediction of how the Roman Empire will come into being, history and rule unfold and become ever-more expansive in four genealogical steps that also have geographical, temporal, and gendered components. At the beginning of the genealogy is Venus (who Jupiter is addressing as "you"), mother of the line, and at the end, Augustus ("a Trojan Caesar . . . a Iulius, name descended from the great Iulus!"). In between are three more men propelling the family forward: Aeneas, Ascanius/Iulus, and Romulus. Both Aeneas and Augustus will see heaven: Aeneas will be raised by Venus and Augustus will be "welcomed to heaven, laden with Eastern spoils."

Aeneas's first action, according to this prophecy, is to "wage a great war in Italy" and "crush proud peoples." Then, he is able to give laws and build city walls. The removal of the obstacle that is proud peoples through domination can lead to city-building; this is reminiscent of the account of Romulus giving law after Remus is murdered and the walls built. Ascanius and Romulus also are to build walls, Ascanius for Alba Longa and Romulus for Rome. Each building project represents a shift in the seat of power: Ascanius will shift the throne from Lavinium to Alba Longa, and Romulus will "found the walls of Mars" and shift power to Rome. The "Trojan Caesar" builds no walls, however, as his empire extends beyond cities and lands to the ocean, the stars, and even the underworld (evidenced by the capture and bondage of Furor/Rage, who usually dwells there). In other words, there will be nothing outside of the Roman Empire headed by Augustus.

Jupiter also predicts the boundlessness of the Augustan empire as being without temporal limits, outside of "bounds in space or time." Aeneas and Ascanius have temporal boundaries set on their rule along with the walls. Aeneas can set up his laws and walls in Lavinium until "the third summer has seen him ruling" and "three winters have passed . . . since the Rutulians have been laid low." Ascanius/Iulus will build Alba Longa, the kings of which will rule for a hundred times longer than his father and predecessor ("three hundred years unbroken"). It is when Romulus is born to Mars through Ilia that Jupiter ceases mentioning time and space limits, because everything that comes after Romulus—epitomized in the figure of Augustus—is boundless. So Romulus builds walls, but there is no end to his reign. Instead, there is a vagueness about time between Romulus and Augustus: "there shall come a day" between them, according to Jupiter, when the Romans (descendants of the "house of Assacarus," the Dardanian king) will defeat Greece, putting Phthia and Mycenae into bondage/slavery and vanquishing Argos. Someday, even Juno—who acts as the main divine antagonist to Aeneas throughout Virgil's epic—will join Jupiter in cherishing the Romans, lords of the whole world.

Defeating the others in battle guided by the gods is a driving theme of the *Aeneid* that also frames Jupiter's genealogical summary of what fate has in store for the son of Venus. Even though it appears as though all hope is lost far from Italy on the shores of Libya, Aeneas is destined to fight and win. After Ascanius founds Alba Longa, the kingdom endures under "Hector's race;" the first-born of King Priam and the best Trojan warrior (until he was killed by Achilles) is mentioned in this family tree, again raising the importance of strength in battle. Romulus is born of Mars, himself the god of war. Augustus will put a stop to all of the wars and bring peace to the boundless empire. Victory lingers, however, with the invocation of Fides, the goddess of faith, whose temple enclosed and protected treaties made between the Romans and foreign powers. The gates of war, the temple of Janus at Rome, will be closed. Impious Rage/Furor, however, will be captured and bound with a hundred knots and placed inside on what appears to be a trophy, the arms of the defeated. He will sit inside, screaming through blood-stained lips. Outside those doors, the world will be at peace; inside, a bloody consequence of world conquest will be tied up on top of war booty. Augustus will also have the heavy burden of eastern spoils (of war) on his back as he ascends to heaven and prepares to receive the vows invoked in his name.

The turning points of the Roman genealogical line center on men who serve as warriors, rulers, and fathers. There are three female presences, but no ordinary human mothers or women at all. Venus is the narrative's addressee. Vesta and Fides are goddesses who protect the Roman state. Ilia, here named a royal priestess, is not raped as she is in the historical narratives discussed above, but still bears the children of Mars. It seems as if the only other female is the she-wolf serving as the nurse to Romulus and Remus. The female presence in this genealogical prediction serves largely to bolster what will ultimately become Roman-(male)ness.

There is a female presence that further connects land and Roman conquest to gender constructs. Lavinia is hinted at twice in the city named for her;[43] she is the promised land of the *Aeneid*. As Yasmin Syed has recently discussed, the femininity of land surfaces in the figure of Lavinia/Lavinium. Aeneas will both name and colonize Lavinium, the land, and Lavinia, the woman. Naming and drawing city boundaries are "universally associated with the male."[44] Lavinia is the object of the *Aeneid*—the story marches toward who will colonize and keep her. Aeneas is destined to win that battle, but at the same time she is already occupied by Turnus. The relationship between Lavinia/um stands for and points to the Roman Empire's future relationship with all the nations.

Anchises's Underworld Prediction in *Aeneid*, Book 6

A second well-known prediction of the Roman Empire's rule over all the nations occurs in Book 6 while Aeneas is in the underworld visiting his father. Anchises takes him throughout, and they watch a procession of the souls of the heroes who integrated into the Trojan—eventually Roman—race. The procession takes place partly in chronological order, according to the historical achievements of the Romans, particularly the conquest over non-Romans. The speech has both a genealogical and geographical focus and gives its most extensive prophecy regarding Augustus.

I present Anchises's prediction in its entirety here and discuss it by sections. The first section is a genealogy of the Trojan race through Romulus. The second focuses on Romulus himself, comparing his success to that of Cybele. The third, most famous, section predicts the world-rule of Augustus and the Roman nation. Next in the procession are kings and generals of Rome as well as Caesar and Pompey. The final part of this prediction mentions the triumphators who frame the often-quoted "be sure to rule the people with empire, Roman. . . ." I include the whole prediction because the logic of Roman rule over all the nations is presented as a culmination of great men's deeds, particularly in their military triumphs over others in the service of strengthening the Roman state.

In the first part, Anchises says that he will describe the glory of the Trojan race that is preordained to greatness by fate. He then proceeds to name Aeneas's descendants as they walk by:

> Now then, the glory that will attend the Trojan race (*prolem*), what children of Italian nation (*Itala de gente nepotes*) are held in store by fate, glorious souls waiting to inherit our name, this I shall reveal in speech and inform you of your destiny. The youth you see leaning on an untipped spear holds by lot of life the most immediate place: he first shall rise into the air with Italian blood in his veins, Silvius of Alban name, last-born of your children, whom late in your old age your wife Lavinia will rear in the woodlands, a king and father of kings, with whom our breed (*genus*) shall hold sway in Alba Longa. He next is Procas, pride of the Trojan nation (*Troianae Gloria gentis*), then Capys and Numitor and he who will resurrect you by his name, Aeneas Silvius, no less eminent in goodness and in arms, if ever he come to reign over Alba. What fine men are these! Mark the strength they display and the civic oak that shades their brows! These to your honor will build Nomentum and

> Gabii and Fidena's town, these shall crown hills with Collatia's towers, and Pometii, the Fort of Inuus, Bola and Cora; one day to be famous names, these are now lands without names. (6.760–76)

Aeneas moves the stock of his descendants from Troy to Italy. The youngest of the sons that Lavinia will bear to Aeneas, Silvius, will become a "king and father of kings" in Alba Longa. This series of men will name and build, to the honor of Aeneas, several cities and towers; one day, the lands will be famous. Now, according to Anchises, they are "lands without names." The project of finding and naming places, starting with Aeneas and Lavinia/um, will continue through his descendants. The prediction concerning the future glory of the Trojan race then turns to Romulus:

> Further, a son of Mars will keep his grandfather company, Romulus, who his mother Ilia shall bear of Assacarus's stock. Do you see how twin plumes stand upright on his head and how the Father (of the gods) himself stamps him with honor? Under his auspices, my son, shall that glorious Rome extend her empire to earth's ends, her ambitions to the skies, and shall embrace seven hills with a single city's wall, blessed in a brood of men, even as the Berecyntian mother, turret-crowned, rides in her chariot through Phrygian towns, happy in a progeny of gods, clasping a hundred grandsons, all denizens of heaven, all tenants of celestial heights. (6.777–787)

As Jupiter's prediction in Book 1 also revealed, it is when Romulus, son of Ilia, is introduced that Rome will extend outside of Alba Longa, "to the earth's ends." Under Romulus, ambitions will soar to the skies, and Rome will be a city fortified not of one hill alone, but will encase seven hills within its walls, marking it as a better establishment than those previous. Rome is also compared to the dominion of Cybele, the "Berecyntian Mother" who was brought to Rome in 294 B.C.E. and became a goddess in the service of the Roman state. Cybele is often portrayed with a chariot and a crown made of walls, signifying her role as a teacher in city fortification.[45] She is also the mountain mother of Aeneas's hometown and assists him in the *Aeneid*. As the inhabitants of all those eastern Phrygian towns, who are blessed by her presence and protection, so too will the Romans be blessed as men in the west. Like her progeny, the Romans will be "denizens of heaven, all tenants of celestial heights."[46] The Romans are comparable even to the achievements of the Mother of the Gods.

While Anchises anticipates that the Romans under Romulus will stretch empire to the earth's ends, he also explains that Augustus will in fact extend it even further in space. After the procession of Romulus, the nation of the Romans, starring Augustus, streams in front of Aeneas's eyes:

> Turn here now your two-eyed gaze, and behold this nation (*gentem*), the Romans that are yours. Here is Caesar and all the descendants (*progenies*) destined to pass under heaven's great sphere. This man, he is the one you often hear promised to you, Augustus Caesar, divine offspring (*divi genus*), who will again make a golden age in Latium amid fields once ruled by Saturn; he will extend empire beyond the Garamants and Indians to a land which lies beyond our stars, beyond the paths of year and sun where sky-bearing Atlas wheels on his shoulders the blazing star-studded sphere. Against his coming both Caspian realms and the Maeotic land even now shudder at the oracles of their gods, and the mouths of sevenfold Nile quiver in alarm. Not even Hercules traversed so much of earth's extent, though he pierced the stag of brazen foot, quieted the woods of Erymanthus, and made Lerna tremble at his bow; nor he either, who guides his car with vine-leaf reigns, triumphant Bacchus, driving his tigers down from Nysa's lofty peak. And do we still hesitate to spread our virtue by our works, or hold back in fear from occupying Ausonian land (*et dubitamus adhuc virtutem extendere factis, aut metis Ausonia prohibet consistere terra*)? (6.788–807)

The golden age that the divine seed, Augustus, will shepherd in is more expansive than that of Romulus. Virgil here uses geographical markers to show just how extensive, as in Jupiter's prediction of Book 1. Empire will go *beyond* the farthest reaches of human settlement, denoting the preordained cosmic and universal significance of Augustus. At first the places in the great beyond are named as "fields once ruled by Saturn," which could be Latium, where Saturn supposedly fled after being defeated by his son Jupiter and where he taught the people farming. The Roman Empire also will extend from the "Garamants," in Libya to the south, to the Indians, as far east as anyone in the ancient Mediterranean had gone. Both spots are known in ancient literature as edges of the world, where what Herodotus or Pliny the Elder might call outlandish peoples live.[47]

Empire will not stop at strange border-people, however; Augustus will reach to land beyond the stars and the zodiac. Other border-markers "tremble in fear" and are regions named geographically by their waters in a counter-clockwise fashion: the Caspian realms to the east (Armenians and Parthians), the Maeotic lands to the north (Scythians, perhaps Hyperboreans), and the Nile (Egyptians), indicating again an expansion of geographic dominion over peoples historically resistant to Roman rule. Augustus also has gone further than Hercules or Bacchus in his world-reach and travels. Geographically, the Roman Empire will blanket the world; ethnographically, all of the peoples—including border peoples—will be held under its sway in peace.

The next section of Anchises's prediction continues with further genealogical information concerning the great men of Roman history:

> But who is he apart, crowned with sprays of olive, offering sacrifice? Ah, I recognize the white hair and beard of that king of Rome who will make the infant city safe on the basis of laws, called from the needy land of lowly Cures to sovereign might. Him shall Tullus next succeed, the breaker of his country's peace, who will rouse to war an inactive folk and armies long unused to triumphs. Hard on his heels follows over-boastful Ancus, who even now enjoys too much the breeze of popular favor. Would you also see the Tarquin kings, the proud spirit of Brutus the Avenger, and the fasces regained? He first shall receive a consul's power and the cruel axes, and when his sons would stir up revolt, the father will hale them to execution in fair freedom's name, unhappy man, however later ages will extol that deed, yet shall a patriot's love prevail and unquenched thirst for fame.
>
> Now behold over there the Decii and the Drusi, Torquatus of the cruel axe, and Camillus bringing the standards home! But they whom you see, resplendent in matching arms, souls now in harmony and as long as they are imprisoned in night, alas, if once they attain the light of life, what mutual strife, what battles and bloodshed will they cause, the bride's father swooping from Alpine ramparts and Monoecus's fort, her husband confronting him with forces from the East! Steel not your hearts, my sons, to such wicked war nor vent violent valour on the vitals of your land. And you who draw your lineage from heaven, be you the first to show mercy; cast the sword from your hand, child of my blood. . . . (6.809–35)

Here Anchises describes the Kings of Rome. Conquest and military valor are emphasized again. Of note is Numa, who made the city safe through law, and Brutus, regarded as the "founder of the republic" who drove out the Tarquin family on account of the rape of Lucretia by King Lucius Tarquinius Superbus's son, Sextus Tarquinius. Another major event in the history of Rome—the end of monarchy and the putting of power in the hands of the Senate—is accomplished through a rape story.[48] Brutus also allegedly had his sons executed for attempting to restore Tarquin rule. General Camillus "brought the standards" back to Rome after sacking the Veii in Tuscany and was called in to finish the job against the Gauls in 390 B.C.E.[49]

The next few lines (8.826–35) demonstrate that the main concern of the Roman Empire is not war for war's sake, however, but that conquest over non-Roman enemies is the real objective. Caesar and Pompey, "resplendent in matching arms," are described without being named. Caesar, as a descendant of heaven, is implored to show mercy and put down weapons. One reason this is significant is that during the Augustan period, effort was made to integrate former related enemies into a seamless genealogical construction. This is evident in the proposed *summi viri* series displayed in the Forum of Augustus, for example, where Caesar and Pompey are both displayed: former enemies are part of the same family line in the service of the Roman Empire. Unity between Romans is important for rule over all the other nations to endure.

That the conquest of non-Romans in the name of peace, and not civil war, is what ultimately is preferable is reiterated in the very next section of Anchises's prediction:

> He there, triumphant over Corinth, shall drive a victor's chariot to the lofty Capitol, famed for Achaeans he has slain. That other one shall uproot Argos, Agamemnon's Mycenae, and even an heir of Aeacus, descendant (*genus*) of mighty Achilles: he will avenge his Trojan sires and Minerva's polluted shrine. Who, lordly Cato, could leave you unsung, or you, Cossus, who the Gracchan race or the Scipios twain, two thunderbolts of war and the ruin of Carthage, or Fabricus, in penury a prince, or you, Serranus, sowing seed in the soil? Whither, O Fabii, do you hurry me all breathless? You are he, the mightiest, who could, as no one else, through inaction preserve our state. Others, I doubt not, shall with softer mould beat out the breathing bronze, coax from the marble features to the life, plead cases with greater eloquence and predict the rising of the stars; you be sure to rule the people with empire, Roman, (for these are your arts), to impose peace with law, to show mercy to the subjected and subdue the proud (*tu regere imperio populos, Romane, memento [hae tibi erunt artes], pacique imponere morem, parcere subiectis et debellare superbos*).
>
> Thus Father Anchises, and as they marvel, adds: "Behold how Marcellus advances, graced with the spoils of the chief he slew, and towers triumphant over all! When the Roman state is reeling under a great shock he will steady it, he will ride down Carthaginians and rebellious Gaul, and offer up to Father Quirinus a third set of captured arms." (6.836–59)

This section concerns major triumphators and the decisive Roman battles against main enemies: Greece, Carthage, and "rebellious Gaul." Basically, those mentioned tell us something about the state of Roman power around 146 B.C.E.[50] However, the three entities conquered here are all at one point or another competitors with Rome for rule of all the nations.[51] Anchises predicts the destruction of Corinth, leading to the dissolution of the Achaean League and the incorporation of Greece as a province. The destruction of Carthage is mentioned along with all the major actors in the Punic Wars. Marcellus additionally is bringing home the spoils from Gaul and Carthage, further indicating victory.

Couched in the midst of this procession of triumphators is the famous charge to Aeneas: whereas other peoples could work with bronze or marble or could be better lawyers or astrologers, they will show deference to Rome in the end—"you be sure to rule the people with empire, Roman, (for these are your arts), to impose peace with law, to show mercy to the subjected and subdue the proud" (6.851–53). In other words, the civilizations undergirding Greece and Carthage—the monumental work with bronze and marble, the intellectual prowess of astrology and rhetoric—

might be more advanced or smarter, but the arts of the Romans will put the nations under peace and law. In this sense, the arts of the others matter very little, because they will inevitably show deference to Rome. Whereas Jupiter's prediction in Book 1 has Augustus bringing peace to a boundless empire, Anchises's speech has that peace brought through law and conquest over all the nations.

Aeneas's Prophetic Shield in *Aeneid*, Book 8

Virgil sings of "arms and the man," and these two closely related topics are precisely what concerns the third and final passage I consider from the *Aeneid*. The inevitable relationship between the Romans and the nations has been predicted in Books 1 and 6, and in Book 8, Aeneas sees for himself the story of Rome displayed on the shield his mother Venus commissioned for him. Important for the study of the series of conquered nations in Roman imperial visual representation[52] is the central scene depicting the Battle of Actium and Augustus leading a procession of diverse conquered nations. As in the predictions of Books 1 and 6, the Romans/nations hierarchy is part of a larger discourse on the genealogy of Roman world domination, highlighting its main men and culminating in the figure of Augustus.

I discuss the entire shield rather than the description of the nations because the central procession must be seen as occupying a position in relation to the whole of the shield, that is, the whole of Roman history. First is the genealogical material around the outside of the shield (8.628–51), then the top depicting, among other scenes, the sack of Rome by the Gauls in 390 B.C.E. (8.652–74), and then the central Actium battle and procession (8.675–713 and 714–26).

In Book 8, Aeneas is preparing for battle against the Latins and has enlisted the help of Evander and his son Pallas. Venus interrupts a conversation between Aeneas and Evander to deliver the arms she has ordered. These arms include a helmet, "terrifying with its plumes and sprouting flames" (8.620), the "death-dealing sword," the "stiff bronze corslet, blood-red and mighty" (8.621–22), and the shield, with "the story of Italy and the triumphs of Rome" (8.626). The items were fashioned by Vulcan, who we are told knew the prophecy and of the coming age. On the shield,[53] the whole of Roman history is compactly represented:

> [E]very generation of the stock to spring from Ascanius, and the wars they fought in their sequence . . . the mother wolf lying stretched out in the green cave of Mars; around her teats the twin boys hung playing, and suckled their dam without fear; with shapely neck bent back, she fondled them by turns, and moulded their limbs with her tongue. Not far from here he had set Rome and the Sabine women lawlessly carried off when the great Circus games were held from the theatre's seated throng; then the sudden uprising of a fresh war between the sons of Romulus and aged Tatius and his stern Cures. Next, the same kings, their strife laid at rest, stood armed before Jove's

> altar, cup in hand, and made covenant with each other over sacrifice of swine, and the palace was rough, fresh with the thatch of Romulus. Not far from there, four-horse chariots, driven apart, had torn Mettus asunder (but you, Alban, should have stood by your words!), and Tullus dragged the liar's body through the woods, and the brambles dripped with dew of blood. There, too, was Porsenna, bidding them admit the banished Tarquin, and oppressing the city with mighty siege: the sons of Aeneas rushing on the sword for freedom's sake. You could see him shown as angry, as threatening, because Cocles dared to tear down the bridge, and Cloelia broke her bonds and swam the river. (8.628–51)

Much of this description matches what Anchises relates regarding the procession of heroes in Book 6, though the names are slightly different. All the sons of Ascanius, every generation, are hammered out in relation to the wars that each one of them fight. The next major event, as is to be expected, is the rearing of Romulus and Remus by the she-wolf. She is hanging around the cave of Mars, referring to his paternity. She, and not Ilia or Mars, gives the twins' bodies shape with her tongue. Then the Sabine women episode is shown, cementing this lawless maneuver as important to the foundation of Rome—in fact, the city is first mentioned here by name in relation to the Sabines. Kings at war and in pious poses are near Romulus's hut. Romulus-like King Tullus is shown with his chariots tearing the Alban dictator Mettus apart for not helping the Romans in battle after Tullus had defeated the Albans and made them subject to Roman rule.[54] King Porsenna's attempt at helping the banished Tarquins forcibly enter Rome is depicted, as is its routing by Cocles's heroic effort to destroy the bridge linking the Janiculum (where Porsenna and company were stationed) with Rome. Cloelia's patriotic swimming with other Roman women won her Porsenna's admiration and an equestrian statue in the city.[55] The first cycle on Aeneas's shield shows major events in the victorious Roman defense of freedom.

Virgil describes the top of the shield next, where the sack of Rome by the Gauls in 390 B.C.E. is depicted among other scenes of threats to Rome's freedom:

> At the top of the shield Manlius, warder of the Tarpeian fort, stood before the temple and held the lofty Capitol. And here the silver goose, fluttering through gilded colonnades, cried that the Gauls were close by in the thickets, laying hold of the fort, shielded by darkness, and the boon of shadowy night. Golden are their locks and golden their raiment; they glitter in striped cloaks, and their milk-white necks are gilded with gold; two Alpine pikes each brandishes in hand, and long shields guard their limbs. Here he had wrought the dancing Salii and the naked Luperci, the crests bound with wool, and the shields that fell from heaven, and in cushioned carriages chaste maidens moved through the city in solemn progress. At a distance from

> these he adds also the abodes of Tartarus, the high gates of Dis, the penalties of sin, and you, Catiline, hanging on a frowning cliff, and trembling at the sight of the Furies; and far apart, the loyal (*pios*), with Cato giving them laws. (8.652–70)

Manlius's nighttime defense of Rome against the Gauls, together with the snitching goose, is known as an important event in the historical relationship between Romans and Gauls. However, it is also sculpted as an integral part of Rome's future on Aeneas's shield. The Gauls themselves are given the kind of specific detail marking them as barbarian enemies common to visual representation, as well as historical and ethnographic texts. Particular attention is paid to their "golden locks" of hair, "milk-white" skin, striped cloaks, weapons, and shields. The Salii and Luperci, priests of Mars and Lupercus, respectively, are depicted nearby.[56] Elsewhere, the "penalties of sin" for transgressing Rome are shown: the two components of the underworld for criminals (Tartarus) and the gates of Dis (Pluto). Held in tension on this part of the shield are additionally Catiline, perceived traitor against Rome for his allegiance with the poor,[57] and Cato, who opposed Roman excess and luxury the correct way—by supporting laws opposing the open display of wealth. While the Gauls represent a threat from outside, Catiline represents a threat to Roman order from inside.

The likely spatial arrangement of Augustus on this shield, if we follow the logic of the prophetic passages from Books 1 and 6, is in the center. Indeed, Virgil does not disappoint. Encircling the threats, the sea is sculpted in gold with silver dolphins and white billows on the waves (8.671–74). In a vivid description, the Battle of Actium becomes a cosmic triumph on the scale of a battle between gods and Giants:

> In the center could be seen bronze ships—the battle of Actium; you could see all Leucate aglow with Mars's array, and the waves ablaze with gold. On the one side Augustus Caesar stands on the lofty stern, leading Italians to strife, with Senate and People, the Penates of the state, and all the mighty gods; his auspicious brows shoot forth a double flame, and on his head dawns his father's star. Elsewhere, favored by winds and gods, high-towering Agrippa leads his column; his brows gleam with the beaks of the naval crown, proud token won in war. On the other side comes Antony with barbaric might and motley arms, victorious over the nations of the dawn and the ruddy sea, bringing in his train Egypt and the strength of the East and farthest Bactra; and there follows (shame!) his Egyptian wife. All rush on at once, and the whole sea foams, torn up by the sweeping oars and triple-pointed beaks. To the deep they race; you would think that the Cyclades, uprooted, were floating on the main, or that high mountains were clashing with mountains: in such huge ships the seamen attack the towered sterns. Flaming tow and

> shafts of winged steel are showered from their hands; Neptune's fields redden with strange slaughter. In the midst the queen calls upon her hosts with their native sistrum; not yet does she cast back a glance at the twin snakes behind. Monstrous gods of every form and barking Anubis wield weapons against Neptune and Venus and against Minerva. In the middle of the fray storms Mavors, embossed in steel, with the grim Furies from on high; and in rent robe Discord strides exultant, while Bellona follows her with bloody scourge. Actian Apollo saw the sight, and from above was bending his bow; in terror at this all Egypt and India, all Arabians, all Sabaeans, turned to flee. The queen herself was seen to woo the winds, spread sail, and now, even now, fling loose the slackened sheets. Amid the carnage, the Lord of Fire had fashioned her pale at the coming of death, borne on by waves and the wind of Iapyx; while over against her was the mourning Nile, of massive body, opening his wide folds and with all his rainment welcoming the vanquished to his azure lap and sheltering streams. (8.675–713)

The Battle of Actium is as a reformulated cosmic giant-battle drawing on the same logic as the Great Altar of Pergamon.[58] It is a violent encounter between Augustus on one side, accompanied by Italians, Senate and People, and all the mighty and beautiful gods (8.678–80); divinely approved Agrippa rides in nearby. Former ally Antony and his foreign wife Cleopatra (depicted as pale, like the Gauls above her) are on the opposing side with "barbarian strength and motley arms" as well as the "strength of the east" all the way to Iran (Bactra) and the Hindu Kush ("nations of the dawn") (8.685–86). The "monstrous" gods of every wrong shape and "barking Anubis" fight against Augustus, Neptune, Venus, and Minerva. Mars (Mavors), Discord, and Bellona, fighters supreme, help in the middle of the battle.[59] Great carnage and Cleopatra's death are depicted among the fleeing Egyptians, Indians, Arabians, and Sabeans, all of whom are known in the Roman world as having scary savage appearances, or being giant-like. Their destiny, it has been predicted, is to fall under the auspices of Roman world rule following the defeat of Antony and Cleopatra.

The winner of the battle enjoys a triumph place near the battle-scene:

> But Caesar, entering the walls of Rome in triple triumph, was dedicating to Italy's gods his immortal votive gift—three hundred mighty shrines throughout the city. The streets were ringing with gladness and games and shouting; in all the temples was a band of matrons, in all were altars, and before the altars slain steers covered the ground. He himself, seated at the snowy threshold of shining Phoebus, reviews the gifts of peoples and hangs them on the proud portals. The conquered nations proceed in long line (*incedunt victae longo ordine gentes*), as different custom of dress and arms as in languages. Here Mulciber had portrayed the Nomad race and the ungirt Africans, here

> the Leleges and Carians and quivered Gelonians, Euphrates moved now with humbler waves, and the Morini were there, furthest of mankind, and the Rhine of double-horn, and undominated Dahae, and Araxes chafing at his bridge. (8.713–29)

The last man standing with the gods is Augustus, of course, shown entering the walls of Rome in triple triumph. He leads a parade of conquered nations shown in deference to Rome, who "move in long array" and are "as diverse in fashion of dress and arms as in tongues" (8.722–23). The gods guide not just this most decisive combat against the monstrous east, rehearsed again and again by the Romans in their subsequent historical battles, but also the processional display of the captured to bolster the "rule without end" Jupiter has given to his chosen people, the descendants of Aeneas.

In the genealogical prophecies of *Aeneid* Book 1, 6, and 8, Romulus and Augustus feature prominently. Roman rule, expanding over and beyond all the nations, is a large-scale outcome of the *Aeneid*'s ultimate battle between Aeneas and Turnus. Jupiter reveals the fate about Aeneas to Venus, Anchises shows and tells the history-to-be of the Romans to his son, and Aeneas sees destiny on the weapon he will use in his war against the Latins. In each case the future is clear: the Roman Empire will be universal, it will surpass all other civilizations, and it will extend peace through subjugation of all the nations. Roman victory over and incorporation of all the nations is an inevitable consequence of conquest.

The procession of conquered nations in Book 8 may be, as R. R. R. Smith has argued, a source-text for the public monumental display of the series of conquered peoples, such as the Sebasteion at Aphrodisias—which arguably represents an innovation in Roman visual representation. But the subjugation of all the nations is a consistency in prophecies concerning Roman rule, and the procession of nations on the shield, a reflection of how "all" could be displayed. The role of gender and incorporation into the story of Rome, as in the story of the Sabine women and the passages discussed here, renders the power dynamics of conquest more visible. Femaleness is harnessed and transformed by maleness for the reproduction of state power.

I have considered several key passages from Roman origin stories that depict Roman rule over all the nations as a key outcome of Roman history. The placement of such rule at the beginning of creation and in the mouths of gods serves to further bolster and naturalize Roman claims to universal sovereignty. Romulus and Remus are children of Mars, conceived through rape, that fate has ordained to build the city that will rule the cosmos as its center. Aeneas has a special duty, predicted in at least three often-quoted passages from Virgil's *Aeneid*, to colonize Italy and sire the family tree whose branches will shade the whole world, reaching beyond its borders.

Roman claims to sovereignty over all the nations have geographical, temporal, and gendered implications. That *someone* should rule over all the nations is an assumption or, according to Dionysius, a "universal law," where the ruler is naturally stronger than the ruled, who are weak. Geographically, all the nations include those at the far-flung borderlands, as well as those close-by, the Indians, Spaniards, Egyptians, Gauls, and everyone in-between. Temporally, the origin stories I have considered make it fairly clear that Roman rule is naturally to last forever, it has always been, and it will surpass all other forms of rule.

That Roman rule represents a gendered process of men dominating women—or, even more expansively, maleness dominating femaleness—is also evident in these stories. The characterization of outsiders as feminine and in need of destruction or taming through Roman peace and law, as well as the use of women to broker peace between nations and foster assimilation, serves as a thread running throughout these prophetic texts. Likewise, the transformation of those incorporated into willing collaborators with such masculinity—and in the case of the body of Aeneas, from east/feminine to west/masculine—bolsters the vertical hierarchical difference between male and female, center and outskirts, Romans and nations.

The Justification and Naturalization of Roman Conquest

This section concerns texts that reflect what I call the justification and naturalization of an ideology of Roman rule over the nations. As with the origin stories, I read these texts in light of the gender constructs expressed by the examples of Roman imperial visual representation of the nations discussed in chapter 2. Such gender constructs figure in textual representation to articulate a hierarchical difference between Romans and nations. Two different types of texts help me accomplish this. First, I discuss the *Res Gestae Divi Augusti*, the "Acts" of Augustus. I briefly explore the ideological implications of this text as a monument in the Roman province of Galatia, where all the extant copies have been found. This inscription constitutes yet another means for publicly communicating Roman rule over the nations, yet also provides glimpses of the complexity of Roman/nations relations.

The second type of literary representation I consider here could fall under the category of ethnography, or writing about the nations, which is done from a dominant perspective. I explore the ideological texture of the texts and ask what they reflect about the relationship between selves and others, center and marginalized, conqueror and conquered. I include only a few Greek and Roman descriptions of non-Roman peoples, often called barbarians, who are also the nations to be defeated and assimilated.[60] Rather, literary representation of the nations, much like visual representation, provides a gendered lens through which to see Roman imperial power over the nations.

In the last part of this section, I discuss Josephus's famous speech of Agrippa in his *Jewish War* as an inscription concerning the nations in relationship to Roman rule. The speech, as James Scott has noted, can be greatly enhanced by a geographical and ethnographical understanding.[61] I include it here because, when seen alongside the other texts gathered, it is clear that the Jews are among the rest of the nations to be defeated and enslaved by the Romans as a matter of course.

Augustus as the Re-founder of Rome

Origin myths such as the *Aeneid* and Romulus/Remus stories predict, lead to, and in the case of the *Aeneid*, center upon the emperor Augustus. The "father of the fatherland" is mentioned several times as the one who will bring the Romans to the fulfillment of the "empire without end" prophecy, the man through whom Roman history reaches its zenith. He was prominently portrayed in the center of the Forum, where he was inscribed with the title *pater patriae*. At Aphrodisias, Augustus figures prominently among the imperial figures featured in the Sebasteion reliefs. In one such relief, he is portrayed as striding "over land and sea," that is, over the known world, a formula that also appears in the literature (see chapter 2). The Prima Porta Augustus statue also embodies such culmination by "him"self; the beautiful male body carries the divinely inspired good news that Rome has conquered the world on his cuirassed chest.

The predictions discussed in the previous section clarify Augustus's position as the re-founder of the Roman Empire, a position which he is thought to have endorsed when—just as one example—he famously remarked about his city/empire that he found it a city of brick and left it a city of marble (Suetonius, *Aug.* 28; Dio dramatically has this as the last thing he says before he dies; see 56.30.3). Certainly this is true concerning the city of Rome's topography—building projects soared during the age of Augustus.[62] But the "city of marble" could be applied to expansion projects outside of Rome across the empire. In fact, expansion, or perhaps penetration, is a major theme of Augustus's rule. The new regime installed by Augustus meant revisiting law, family values, entertainment, and much else in Roman society. It also meant penetration, acquisition, and assimilation of the nations in the name of making worldwide peace. Peace was enacted through pacification or victory in battle.

One such monument demonstrating the acquisition and pacification of the nations is the *Res Gestae Divi Augusti*.[63] It is one of three (Suetonius, *Aug.* 101) or four (Dio, 56.33.1) documents that Augustus had sealed the year before his death and deposited with the Vestal Virgins. The others included the directions for his funeral;[64] the *Breviarium totius imperii*, detailing the number and placement of troops under arms, state of the treasury, and accounts of public revenues; and, if Dio is correct, a document concerning advice on foreign and domestic policy given to the senate and, by implication, Augustus's heirs.

The *Res Gestae* was, according to Augustus's instructions, to be inscribed in bronze and erected in front of his Mausoleum at Rome. This is spatially significant, as the Mausoleum was situated on the Campus Martius (Mars Field) near the Ara Pacis, erected after the pacification of the west, and the *horologium*, which Augustus dedicated to the sun, from Egypt.[65] The Ara Pacis, another monument commemorating the Roman fertility and family values that come out of conquest and pacification, was situated on the equinoctial line that coincided with the birth of Augustus (21/23 September). This spatial combination served the purpose of "establishing a link between the *princeps*'s birth and world peace."[66] Placement on the Mars Field contributes to that space's programmatic scheme already celebrating the achievements of Augustus in the service of his new peaceful regime. The *Res Gestae* in the Mars Field also complements his Forum as a public monument detailing the state of the empire under Augustus, and is believed to have been not far from Agrippa's map of the world under Roman rule.[67]

Drawing on the logic of previous empire-builders, Augustus details what he has accomplished. In the *Res Gestae*, Augustus represents himself as having gone further and done more and, by implication, having fulfilled the prophecies concerning the Romans as lords of the world. In short, Augustus confirms his position as the Iulus who acts as a new Romulus, ushering in the empire without end Jupiter has given. Essential to limitless empire is the extension of peace to the nations who had never been encountered by anyone before him, as well as the submission of the entire known world to Roman power; this portion of the *Res Gestae* is discussed below.

The Nations in the Res Gestae

Augustus describes, in first person, the state of how he left his empire without end on the *Res Gestae*. His first act is to raise an army to avenge his dead father Caesar, and the inscription ends with his being bestowed with the title *pater patriae*. The entire "letter to the world" of Augustus is summarized by its superscription:

> (Latin): Below is a copy of the acts of the Divine Augustus by which he placed the whole world (*orbem terra[rum]*) under the empire of the Roman people (*imperio populi Rom.*), and of the amounts which he expended upon the state and the Roman people, as engraved upon two bronze columns which have been set up in Rome.
>
> (Greek): Below is a translation of the acts and gifts of Divine Sebastos, as he left inscribed on two bronze columns at Rome.[68]

While it is impossible to know the real intent behind the differences between these two superscriptions framing the *Res Gestae* (which Augustus did not write), it is possible to see both as a reflection of their potential audience's positioning vis-à-vis the inscription. The Latin, which was inscribed in the *pronaos*, makes clear what the Romans imagined about Augustus: he "placed the whole world under the empire of the Roman people." Such a sentiment would reflect the positioning of the Latin-speaking elite, namely governors and other officials, who would enter the temple. The Greek, inscribed on the outside of the temple, reflects the positioning of those subjected, who see the emperor as the supreme benefactor or divine gift-giver; such are terms for the emperor in the context of the imperial cult in the Greek east.[69] This placement, again, shows how space is used to manage social positioning and hierarchy: inside, the conquerors; outside, the conquered. Both superscriptions make it clear that the original is left at Rome, the capital of the world.

Even if the superscriptions differ in the way they do, the content of the inscription remains similar enough between the Latin and Greek. The *Res Gestae*'s content can be divided into three discernible topics, originally done by Mommsen and repeated by Nicolet: 1–14 concerns the political activity of Augustus's early years; 15–24 details his expenses and generosities to the Roman people; and 25–33 lists foreign activities, conquests, victories, or diplomatic achievements that "constitute the explanation and justification of the initial formula for the conquest of the *orbis terrarum*."[70] 34–35 provides a summary, affirming the inauguration of the new regime in 27 B.C.E.; the text culminates with the bestowal of *pater patriae* in 2 B.C.E., inscribed on Augustus's quadriga in his Forum.

The extensive mention of the fate of the nations in this inscription is of most concern. In *Res Gestae* 3, Augustus gives a short summary of his attitude toward the world:

> Wars, both civil and foreign, I undertook throughout the whole world (*toto in orbe terrarum, en holēi oikoumenēi*), on sea and land, and when victorious I spared all citizens who sued for pardon. The (foreign) nations (*exte[rnas] gentes*, in Greek just "the nations:" *Ta ethnē*) which could with security (*asphales*) be pardoned I preferred to *save* (*co]nservare, esōsa*) rather than *cut off* (*excidere, exekopsa*). [Emphasis added]

Augustus portrays himself here as a victorious yet merciful military leader. War is the constant throughout the entire world, but the consequences for the defeated are threefold. First, those who are defeated in civil wars and are citizens are granted a pardon if they demand ("sue for") it; they are absorbed back into the Roman race. Second, Augustus differentiates between two kinds of external (non-Roman) nations. In Latin, the noun *gentes* is qualified with the adjective *exte[rnas]*, outside, foreign, whereas in Greek there is no qualifier: *ta ethnē* denotes the nations other than Romans, different than the citizens. He is the "savior," pardoning the nations who would not pose a threat to the security of the Roman state. The other nations, by implication, get "cut off" in battle. They cannot be pardoned with security, thus leaving no option but destruction.

Distinction between the nations who can be saved and, by implication, assimilated, and those who cannot is helpful to remember as a key to reading the latter portion of the *Res Gestae*. In this section (25–33), Augustus recounts in first-person narrative his extension of the Roman Empire further across land and sea than anyone before him—Alexander, Pompey, or Caesar. The "more than anyone" level of achievement places Augustus in the role of having fulfilled the destiny of the Romans, those chosen to rule the world. More than fifty geographical terms are used to designate the pushing of boundaries, and the language of domination and peacemaking runs throughout. The fate of the nations includes a pattern of actively seeking friendship, sending envoys, showing allegiance, and being cut down by armies.

However, before the boundaries can be stretched, the existing ones must be made stronger. *Res Gestae* 25 has Augustus declare that he "freed the sea from pirates" and stamped out a slave revolt, a reference to his defeat of Sextus Pompey, son of Pompey the Great (who had previously claimed to have freed the sea of pirates, see below) and his army made of slaves.[71] Augustus quiets dissention in the Italian ranks and snuffs out the possibility of revolt from within. This action is followed by the claim to a unified Italy, as Augustus has all of Italy taking an oath of allegiance and, further, demanding that he serve as the (ultimately victorious) leader in the Battle of Actium. After Italy, the "provinces of the Spains, the Gauls (*Galliae*; *Galatia*), Africa, Sicily, and Sardinia took the same oath of allegiance to me."

Following the oath-taking of the provinces, Augustus opens *Res Gestae* 26 with a grand statement: "I extended the boundaries of all the provinces of the Roman people which were bordered by nations (*gentés, ethnē*) not yet subject to our empire." The theme now switches to the state of the nations, who are already there but not yet living their function of being subordinate to the Romans. He continues:

> The provinces of the Gauls, the Spains, and Germany, bounded by the ocean from Gades to the mouth of the Elbe, I reduced to a state of peace. The Alps, from the region which lies nearest to the Adriatic as far as the Tuscan Sea, I brought to a state of peace without waging on any nation (*genti, ethnei*) an unjust war. My fleet sailed from the mouth of the Rhine eastward as far as the nation of the Cimbri (Greek only: *ethnous Kimbrōn*) to which, up to that time, no Roman had ever gone into either by land or by sea, and the Cimbri and Charydes and Semnones and other nations (*popu[l]i, ethnē*) of the Germans of that same region through their envoys sought my friendship and that of the Roman people. On my order and under my auspices two armies were led, at almost the same time, into Ethiopia and into Arabia which is called the "Happy," and very large forces of the enemy of both nations (*gentis*, not present in Greek) were cut to pieces in battle and many towns were captured. Ethiopia was penetrated as far as the town of Nabata, which is next to Meroë. In Arabia, the army advanced into the territories of the Sabaei to the town of Mariba.

Augustus here mixes geographical reach with conquest over the nations not yet subject to Rome. He refers to the pacification of previous conquests-turned-provinces (Gauls, Spains, Germany). The boundaries of the provinces that were extended represent former enemy nations, who were all bordered by more ferocious barbarians.[72] War was waged on German nations, but never if they did not deserve it: Roman wars are just wars.[73] Eastward, "as far as the nation of the Cimbri," and southward, "into Ethiopia and into Arabia which is called the 'Happy,'" both places that had not yet been seen by the Romans.[74] Here we learn that the Germans to the northeast appear to receive better treatment due to their sending envoys and seeking friendship, unlike the Ethiopian and Arabian towns that were captured and "cut off" (*katekopsen*; note the same verb is used for these as for those who it is implied could not be saved), perhaps indicating a threat to security (see discussion of *Res Gestae* 3 above).

A similar combination of focused extension and conquest in the north occurs in *Res Gestae* 30:

> The nations (*gentes*, *ethnē*) of the Pannonians, to which no army of the Roman people had ever penetrated before my principate, having been subdued by Tiberius Nero who was then my stepson and my legate, I brought under the rule of the Roman people, and I pushed forward the frontier of Illyricum as far as the bank of the river Danube. An army of Dacians which crossed to the south of that river was, under my auspices, defeated and crushed, and afterwards my own army was led across the Danube and compelled the nations (*gentes*, *ethnē*) of the Dacians to submit to the rule of the Roman people.

The nations of the Pannonians and Dacians, both occupying territory north of Macedonia and east of Italy, represent "savage" enemies of Rome. Never before had the Romans gone into Pannonia or crossed the Danube to Dacia, yet the Dacians had, like the Gauls, invaded Roman territory on several occasions. They are the "Getae" of Greek literature, associated with Thracians and Scythians since Herodotus.[75] Pliny calls them among nations who are "generally Scythian" (*Nat.* 4.12.80),[76] and they are named in the *Aeneid* as one of the nations against whom the Romans make the sacred war ritual (7.601–17).[77] The Pannonians, consisting of various nations of Celtic and Illyrian heritage that are also represented, like the Dacians, at Aphrodisias,[78] are not geographically or ideologically far away from the Dacians. Like the Arabians and Ethiopians, the Dacians and Pannonians signify those nations that must be penetrated and conquered, that had not previously been conquered, and that Augustus personally handled during the state of world-war he (justly) waged against the nations in order to bring peace and stability.

Altogether, between *Res Gestae* 25 and 33 there are fifty-five geographical place names mentioned in relationship to Augustus's expansion and subjugation project.[79] Interestingly, victory over other Romans such as Antony and Sextus are only mentioned obliquely by place name (e.g., Egypt and provinces of the east). This further bolsters an ideological Romans/nations hierarchy and may be succinctly explained by a quip from Dio on the aftermath of Actium:

> [They] granted him the privilege of celebrating another triumph, this time over the Egyptians. For neither on the previous occasion nor at this time did they mention by name Antony and the other Romans who had been vanquished with him and thus imply that it was proper to celebrate their defeat. (51.19.5)[80]

It would be improper to celebrate victory over fellow Romans. Augustus maintains this public sentiment in the *Res Gestae* by presenting himself as the man who unified Rome and Italy, celebrating only the vanquishing of non-Romans. In addition to the examples of conquest and first contact over non-Romans described above, there are others penetrated and subjected, and colonies set up: "I settled colonies of soldiers in Africa, Sicily, Macedonia, both Spains, Achaea, Asia, Syria, Gallia Narbonensis (*Galatiai tēi pe||ri Narbōna*), Pisidia. Moreover, Italy has twenty-eight colonies founded under my auspices which have grown to be famous and populous during my lifetime" (*Res Gestae* 28). Those who sought friendship with the Romans through sending envoys and missions to Augustus are mentioned in 31–32.

The sending of embassies and dignitaries to the Romans indicates deference to Roman rule and the desire to be "saved" by the emperor—and perhaps cooperate in the Roman imperial project. Such demonstrations differentiate the nations from one another: again, those who must be conquered or cut off and those who might be saved have willing supplication in the balance. Leaders from nations as far away as India send multiple embassies seeking Roman friendship. This kind of national cooperation is reflected in visual representation as well: as C. R. Whittaker has explored, Roman imperial personifications of India exist, and she is never shown as conquered but as compliant with Rome and laden with attributes (animals, plants, ivory) denoting the fertility of her land.[81] Such is a similar case with the Parthian man on the Prima Porta Augustus: he is not defeated and personified as Gaul and Spain are (even if he is a feminized girly-man), but is shown approaching the Roman and handing the standards over.[82] Even the Scythians, possibly the oldest of the northern trouser-wearing barbarians, seek Roman friendship.[83] Finally, the Adiabeni and their suppliant king are mentioned for the first time in Roman literature here. Their inclusion as those who seek the friendship of the Romans is important for Jewish history: according to Josephus, Queen Helena and Izates, the royalty of the Adiabeni (near Armenia), converted to Judaism.[84] Eventually, they played a rather large role in the negotiation of Roman rule in Judea and the Jewish War of 66–70 C.E. The presence of the Adiabeni in the *Res Gestae* signifies Roman contact earlier than the conversion story of circa 30 C.E.

Especially poignant in this section is the Parthians' giving their children as pledges of friendship and assimilation, not because they had been defeated in war—they most certainly had not according to literary accounts—but because they *wanted* to. The Parthians must be represented as subdued for the Romans to create themselves as lords of the world. The handing over of children is a dynamic shown on Cup 1 of the Boscoreale treasure, where Gallic men hand over children and several coins.

While the far-away nations of the Parthians and Medes send delegations to Augustus for friendship, he also returns the favor by giving them the rule for which they so humbly ask:

> From me the peoples of the Parthians and of the Medes received the kings for whom they asked through ambassadors, the chief men of those peoples; the Parthians Vonones, son of King Phrates, grandson of King Orodes; the Medes Ariobarzanes, the son of King Artavasdes, grandson of King Ariobarzanes. (*Res Gestae* 33)

Kings Ariobarzanes and Artavasdes of the Medes are also the recipient of hard-won Armenia, whose subjugation is recalled along with the annexation of Egypt:

> Egypt I added to the empire of the Roman people. In the case of Greater Armenia, though I might have made it a province after the assassination of its King Artaxes, I preferred, following the precedent of our fathers, to hand that kingdom over to Tigranes, the son of King Artavasdes, and grandson of King Tigranes, through Tiberius Nero who was then my stepson. And later, when the same people revolted and rebelled, and was subdued by my son Gaius, I gave it over to King Ariobarzanes the son of Artabazus, King of the Medes, to rule, and after his death to his son Artavasdes. When he was murdered I sent into that kingdom Tigranes, who was sprung from the royal family of the Armenians. I recovered all the provinces extending eastward beyond the Adriatic Sea, and Cyrenae, which were then for the most part in possession of kings, and, at an earlier time, Sicily and Sardinia, which had been seized in the slave war. (*Res Gestae* 27)

This complicated handing-off of Armenia to various men of a royal succession, the acquisition of Egypt, and the recovery of the provinces indicates that which Augustus does not mention explicitly: the defeat of Antony and Cleopatra at Actium. According to the treaty of Brundisium in 40 B.C.E., the Roman world was divided into three parts: Lepidus received Africa to the south, Octavian received the west, and Antony was in charge of the east.[85] Following the departure of Antony from the picture, Augustus reunified the world by taking back the eastern provinces. In the service of presenting a unified Roman Empire dominating the nations, recovery of the east was not framed as the result of Antony's defeat.

Augustus, in the *Res Gestae*, presents himself unifying Rome, Italy, the provinces, and the world by putting all of the nations (*gentes, ta ethnē*) under the auspices of "the empire of the Roman people." He rules the nations not just by finding and conquering them, but also through showing mercy, should they recognize the universal sovereignty of the Roman Empire, and recovering that which was lost to other Romans like Antony. Exploration, penetration, recovery, and submission through diplomacy characterize *Res Gestae* 25–33. The end of section 32 indicates that world rule is delineated in detail only partially:

> And many other nations (*Plurimaeque aliae gentes, pleista te alla ethnē*) experienced the faith (*fidem, pisteōs*) of the Roman people (*populo Romano, dēmou Rhomaiōn*) during my principate (Greek: rule, *hēgemonos*) who never before had any interchange of embassies or of friendship with the Roman people. (*Res Gestae* 32)

The nations who experienced the faith of the Romans by submitting to them and seeking friendship are just too many to list. Beyond the already-extensive catalog presented in the inscription, there are many others who, during Augustus's time, met and interacted with the Romans. Their faith would have been cataloged in Rome, as treaties between Romans and others were kept in the temple of Fides, also believed to have been restored by Augustus, until at least the end of the first century C.E.[86]

The *Res Gestae* is a valuable first-person source from Augustus concerning Roman attitudes toward the nations. More than reflecting a sparse and unadulterated "truth" about his achievements, the text is an ideological justification of Rome's place as ruler of all the nations. Its plain language serves to make Roman expansion seem natural, like a matter of course in world history. Augustus posits himself as a fulfillment of Rome's destiny and the man who surpasses all others in terms of charting and conquering the world. A clear hierarchy between Romans and the rest of the nations emerges, especially in sections 25–33.

Through this reading of *Res Gestae* 25–33, I submit that Augustus also reveals a complexity in this Romans/nations hierarchy: dependent upon their level of willful submission to Roman rule (through sending envoys, for example), the nations are either spared and assimilated or excised. Thus, the nations who are vanquished and not saved bring it upon themselves by their hostility, justifying the war waged against them across the world. The *Res Gestae* is a prime resource for understanding the naturalization and justification of the fate of the nations in Roman imperial ideology.

The *Res Gestae* is and was not just a text in a book, however; it is an inscription—which means it is publicly visible and meant to be so. Below I consider the ideological implications of displaying inscriptions listing names of the nations conquered by Rome—not just at the capital, but in the conquered territories.

Res Gestae *as Monumental Inscription Displaying the Nations*

For many interpreters, it almost goes without saying that the *Res Gestae* is an inscription, the writing on the wall about the Roman Empire under Augustus. Usually, the fact that it is an inscription is quickly mentioned and then the work of unpacking the text is done. To some extent, this is what I have duplicated above. However, I also see this inscription as a monument, at least in part meant to show the relationship between Rome and the nations as central to Roman imperial world rule, and I see it as complementary to the visual representation discussed concerning the nations in chapter 2. In fact, the *Res Gestae* is another example of such representation of Rome's place over the *orbis terrarum*, including land and sea, and all of the nations. It is a visual narrative expressing the conquest of the world. The reason to read the text is to see the visual references alongside it and to imagine "how" the text means in its immediate spatial environment.

Specifically, the presence of the *Res Gestae,* as the writing on the wall of imperial cult complexes in major cities throughout the Roman province of Galatia, served to further enhance its status as a way to monumentalize the deeds of Augustus. It cemented the status of the cities who chose to mount it in their imperial cult complexes and "brought the beholder into contact with the larger reality of the empire of which he [sic] was a part."[87] Moreover, the content of the *Res Gestae* drew on other extant inscriptions, surpassing them all in world reach and rule.

The *Res Gestae* was intended to be seen in Rome. Augustus meant for the inscription to be installed there at a site with cosmic and dynastic connotations. The presence of the inscription of the emperor's deeds drew Romans and others into his accomplishments, seeing them near the dynastic procession and fertility themes adorning the Ara Pacis, as well as the personifications in Pompey's theater and the imperial Fora. But the inscription would have been seen differently in the east than in Rome due to the growth and presence of the imperial cult and the status of the east as a location of origin or relocation for many conquered nations. All copies are from the Roman province of Galatia and installed at temples there.[88] Thus the *Res Gestae* is an important, concrete monument for understanding Paul's Roman imperial ideological context.

Temples and complexes for the imperial cult were set up in eastern cities after Augustus gave permission for authorities throughout Asia and Bithynia to give him honors. This process is recalled in a passage from Dio:

> Caesar . . . gave permission for the dedication of sacred precincts in Ephesus and in Nicaea to Rome and to Caesar, his father, whom he named the hero Julius. These cities had at that time attained chief place in Asia and in Bithynia, respectively. He commanded that the Romans resident in these cities should pay honor to these two divinities; and he permitted the foreigners (*xenois*), whom he called "Greeks," to consecrate precincts to himself, the Asians to have theirs in Pergamum and the Bithynians theirs in Nicomedia.

> This practice, beginning under him, has been continued under other emperors, not only among the Greek nations (*en tois Hellēnikois ethnesin*) but also among all the others (*en tois allois*), in so far as they hear of the Romans. For in the capital itself and in Italy generally no emperor, however worthy of renown he has been, has dared to do this; still, even there various divine honors are bestowed after their death upon such emperors as have ruled uprightly, and, in fact, shrines are built to them. (51.20.6–8)

According to Dio, the instance of Augustus beginning to establish the imperial cult throughout Asia Minor, after his recovery of the east from Antony's defeat, begins with Asia and Bithynia, where the Romans are to pay honors to Roma and Caesar. The non-Roman foreigners (but native to their own cities!) are consolidated and renamed by Augustus into Greeks and permitted to consecrate precincts to him (and Roma). Dio reports that this implementation of imperial cult continued under the subsequent emperors among Greek nations and all others who had heard of (i.e., become subjected to) the Romans.

The foundation of provincial centers of emperor worship in Asia and Bithynia sets the tone for such provinces all over the empire.[89] Not so common in Rome ("no one dared,"),[90] the imperial cult in the east[91] was a tool of affirmation for the worldwide reach of Roman power. The presence of buildings, monuments, and altars for the imperial cult served to write Rome and Roman ideas into the fabric of an eastern city and its public life. Even if this was done in Greek style, or if the Roman structures are copies of Greek works, a Roman message still was sent. Such messages, incorporated into the plans and decoration of buildings, promoted specific ideas about social and cosmic order. Here myth and history were presented in tandem[92] to legitimize and, to a large extent, naturalize Roman world domination. In other words, if Roman rule is seen not just as a continuation or hijacking of Greek mythology, but as ordained from the very beginning of time, then the predestined aspect of Roman world domination cannot be questioned—it is presented as the logical culmination, fulfillment, and purpose of the "fundamental principles of the world."[93]

A good deal of material evidence for the imperial cult comes from Galatia,[94] indicating that honors to Augustus were established there soon after it was annexed.[95] There, as noted above, the *Res Gestae* inscription was installed on the outside (Greek) of the temple and in the *pronaos* (Latin). Romans and foreigners (called Greeks) in the city were both shaped, even unified, by the spatial arrangement of the inscription: even if the Greeks poured their resources into building and worship, they were still non-Romans and the subjects of Rome. The *Res Gestae* lays this out partially through its naming, five times, of Galatia as part of Augustus's extension project.[96] Though it is a longer conversation as to whether the Gauls in the north or Galatia in the east is meant here, I think it is at least possible that the eastern Galatians, descended from and related to the Gauls claimed as omnipresent enemies of the Romans,[97] would have been reminded of their place under Roman rule when confronted with the Greek term designating the Roman identification of their people.

The *Res Gestae* is further complemented and complicated by the list of Galatian priests who served the temple precinct.[98] This particular inscription shows the process of becoming loyal to the ruling power and the complexity of loyalty to Roman rule by conquered provincials. These inscriptions and other material evidence from the imperial cult in Asia Minor demonstrate that the imperial cult functioned as an ideological glue, holding together different cities that might otherwise have had little in common. Through implementation of the imperial cult, they became connected to each other: "Roman provincial officials and the local populations were bound together by their relations with the emperor."[99] While a hierarchy emerged among provincial elite who aspired to serve properly and "disappear" upwards into a Roman-sanctioned hierarchy, still visible were the non-elite members of the conquered, who lived in and negotiated their cities under Roman auspices. Still, the *Res Gestae* inscription operated as a visual and spatial narrative describing Roman sovereignty over the nations, encouraging a strategic form of literacy among provincial subjects: "know your place." Through this visual narrative, "these culturally heterogeneous and geographically distant audiences were deftly guided to become related through the common bond of an imperial vision personified by the quintessential emperor, Augustus, and his lofty ideals."[100] The inscription worked as a visual code naturalizing imperial dominion, literally written on the wall.

Res Gestae *among Inscriptions of the Nations*

Important for the study of Paul's travels and letters, the connection of the *Res Gestae* with the imperial cult strengthens an interpretation of the Aphrodisias Sebasteion as a visual elaboration upon achievements of the divinely ordained imperial family featuring Augustus "over land and sea," that is, the *orbis terrarum*. Other inscriptions remember the nations in relationship to Roman rule and also must have served to demonstrate and memorialize the massive extent of Roman rule. For example, Pliny the Elder describes and gives the inscription on a triumphal arch "in the Alps" (portions of which have been found in Nicaea, in Asia Minor), featuring a list of sixty conquered Alpine nations:

> To Emperor Caesar, divine son Augustus, supreme priest, in the fourteenth year of office as commander and seventeenth year of tribunal authority, erected by the senate and people of Rome (*SPQR*), to commemorate that under his leadership and auspices all the Alpine nations (*gentes Alpinae omnes*) pervading from the Adriatic Sea to the Mediterranean (*quae mari supero ad inferum pertinebant*) were reduced under the empire of the Roman people (*sub imperium P.R. sunt redactae*). Alpine nations defeated (*Gentes Alpinae devictae*): Triumpilini, Camunni, Venostes, Vennonetes, Isarchi, Breuni, Genaunes,

> Focunates, four nations (*gentes*) of the Vindelici, Cosuanetes, Rucinates, Licates, Catenates, Ambisontes, Rugusci, Suanetes, Calucones, Brixentes, Leponti, Uberi, Nantuates, Seduni, Varagri, Salassi, Acitavones, Medulli, Ucenni, Caturiges, Brigiani, Sobionti, Brodionti, Nemaloni, Edenates, Vesubiani, Veamini, Gallitae, Triullati, Ecdini, Vergunnii, Eguituri, Nematuri, Oratelli, Nerusi, Velauni, Suetri. (*Nat.* 3.20.136–37)

Pliny is sure to note that only the "fifteen states of the Cottani" who had *not* shown hostility to Roman military confrontation were not listed, implying that those who were had demonstrated a certain measure of resistance to Roman domination. Also not listed, according to Pliny, are those who "were placed by the law of Pompey under the tribute of the municipal towns" (*item adtributate municipiis lege Pompeia*; *Nat.* 3.10.138). Of those nations listed in the inscription, the Triumpilini also have been found as an inscribed base for a personification at the Aphrodisian Sebasteion's north portico.[101] They are described by Pliny before his recounting the inscription as a people who sold themselves and their land to the Romans, thus gaining the status of being among the "Euganean nations having the Latin rights" (*Nat.* 3.20.133, taking their name from the "good family" at 3.20.135). They are accompanied in this effort and status by the "Camunni and similar" nations. A number of nations listed above are also called "Rhaetian" by Pliny's estimation, and Rhaetians are among the bases found at Aphrodisias. This inscription on a triumphal arch, like the *Res Gestae* on a temple and the inscribed bases at Aphrodisias, served to map the terrain of Roman domination, inscribing it in popular consciousness. Similarly, the overlap between nations listed on different monuments points to the possibility of a centralized list approved at and disseminated from Rome in the service of portraying an ideology of world rule (such as the *Breviarium totius imperii* deposited by Augustus at his death; see above and Tacitus, *Ann.* 1.11.7).

Another example of a visual narrative detailing Roman domination over the nations inscribed on a public monument is reported by Strabo in his description of Lugdunum in Gaul, "the most populous of all the cities of Celtica except Narbo" (*Geogr.* 4.3.2).[102] This account references that the city had a temple to Augustus at its front, dedicated "by all the Gauls/Galatians in common (*hypo pantōn koinē tōn Galatōn*)." The temple complex included an important altar having "an inscription of the names of the nations, sixty in number, and images of each of these, and another great altar (*esti de bōmos axiologos epigraphēn exōn tōn ethnōn exēkonta ton arithmon kai eikones toutōn hekastou mia, kai allos megas*; 4.3.2)." Strabo then proceeds to mention the *ethnē* immediately subject to the city.

Augustus was not the first to make such inscriptions as those described above, nor was he the first to declare that the Roman Empire stretches over the *orbis terrarum*, to the ends of the earth, over land and sea, incorporating *omnes gentes/panta ta ethnē*.[103] The inhabitants of Asia might have found his claims familiar, as the *Res Gestae* draws on similar earlier inscriptions "commissioned by Oriental kings to celebrate their conquests and composed . . . in first person; the *cursus honorum* listing positions or honors, and the *elogia*, a tradition of Roman dynasties."[104] Though all such examples are expressive of power relationships, inscriptions listing the nations conquered by the Romans are closer to the former in content than the latter. One such inscription is recorded by Diodorus concerning Pompey's conquest of the east:

> Pompey the Great, son of Gnaeus, Imperator, having freed the seacoast of the inhabited world (*tēs oikoumenēs*) and all the islands this side of the Ocean from the war with the pirates—being likewise the man who delivered from siege the kingdom of Ariobarzanes, conquered Galatia and the lands and provinces lying beyond it, Asia, and Bithynia, who gave protection to Paphlagonia and Pontus, Armenia and Achaia, as well as Iberia, Colchis, Mesopotamia, Sophene, and Gordyene, brought into subjection Darius king of the Medes, Artoles king of the Iberians, Aristobulus king of the Jews, Aretas king of the Nabatean Arabs, Syria bordering on Cilicia, Judaea, Arabia, the province of Cyrene, the Achaeans, the Iozygi, the Soani, the Heniochi, and the all the nations (*panta ta ethnē*) along the seacoast between the Colchis and the Maeotic Sea, with their kings, nine in number, and all the nations that dwell between the Pontic and the Red Seas, extended from the frontiers of the empire to the limits of the earth (*tēs gēs*), and secured and increased the revenues of the Roman people—he, by confiscation of the statues and images set up to the gods, as well as other valuables taken from the enemy, has dedicated to the goddess twelve thousand and sixty pieces of gold and three hundred and seven talents of silver. (Diodorus, 40.4)

This inscription, in third-person, may have been erected at Rome in the temple of Venus,[105] linking the mother of the Romans with the conquest of the world. The sea is freed from pirates, all of the nations are subjected, many of whom with their kings, the borders extended. The world is mentioned twice, once as being freed all along the seacoast and once in the context of the empire's frontiers being extended to its ends. He took statues and images from their gods of origin, as well as other riches, and gave them to Venus.[106] Note the presence of the Jews and Judea, echoing Pompey's entry into the Jerusalem temple in 63 B.C.E., and the names of the eastern territories he conquered that also would become important to Augustus.

Pliny records a similar inscription set up by Pompey in the temple of Minerva that he "dedicated out of the proceeds of the spoils of war":

> Gnaeus Pompeius Magnus, Imperator, having completed a war of thirty years, routed, exiled, murdered, or accepted the surrender of 12,183,000 people, sunk or captured 846 ships, received 1538 towns and forts in faith, subjugated lands from the Maeotians to the Red Sea, rightly vows to Minerva. (*Nat.* 7.26.97)[107]

Pliny immediately follows this inscription with another, the announcement of Pompey's triumphal procession in 62 B.C.E.:

> After having rescued the sea coast from pirates and restored to the Roman people rule (*imperio*) over the sea, he celebrated a triumph over Asia, Pontus, Armenia, Paphlagonia, Cappadocia, Cicilia, Syria, the Scythians, Jews, and Albanians, Iberia, the island of Crete, the Basternae, and in addition to these, over King Mithridates and Tigranes. (*Nat.* 7.26.98)

Of all the great Roman men previous to Augustus, excluding the founders, Pompey covered the most territory and conquered the most cities and nations. Pliny further names the crowning achievement of his military career: he declared himself that he "found Asia the remotest of provinces and then made her the center of his fatherland" (*Nat.* 7.20.99; see also Cicero, *Prov. cons.* 31; Florus, 1.40.31).[108] Pompey's works were accompanied by public monuments, such as trophies in the Pyrenees and Alps, inscriptions such as the ones mentioned above, and of course his theater, the first stone theater in Rome, and believed to be the first to have included images of the nations.[109]

Julius Caesar also is remembered as a conqueror who showed the Romans as controlling the *oikoumenē/orbis terrarum*, making monuments to himself and Roman world domination.[110] Augustus inherited the world from masterful men like Pompey and Caesar, who also are part of his lineage as the sons of Mars and Venus. The *Res Gestae* and inscriptions and monuments like it create and manage a Roman imperial ideology of world rule over the nations. Seeing such inscriptions and massive lists of nations forced to submit, when paired with images of captives with and without trophies, indigenous weaponry, and personifications, served to demonstrate victory in battle and remind Romans and non-Romans alike of their ideal, natural place in the social order. Inscriptions concerning the nations, although commemorative, are part of the cultural grammar justifying Roman conquest over all the nations.

Judeans and Other Barbarians

In this section, I explicitly and briefly discuss ethnography, writing about the nations from the perspective of the victors. Ethnographic writing complements the inscriptions and visual representation I have discussed above and in the previous chapter. When I read the inscriptions above, I imagine gendered power relationships behind their representation in ethnographic writing. Most important for this project, ethnographic writing shows the gendered dimensions of literary representations of Roman conquest over all the nations. Such writing usually serves not to illuminate the voices of the nations themselves but reflects the voices, biases, and interests of dominant authors and social positioning. I do not take these accounts to be the "truth" about the nations; rather, I explore their texture for hints of Roman justification and naturalization of Roman rule over the nations.

Romans and Barbarians/Nations

Ethnographic descriptions of the nations are often couched in terms of foreigners being barbarian and other to Greeks and Romans, or outside of civilization.[111] To some extent, ethnography itself represents the practice of defining the world's contours, cultures, and limits from the perspective and on the terms of those who dominate it.[112] Describing the world's peoples and places, then, is an exercise in inscribing world-rule and power relationships. Detailed passages describing non-Roman nations, often called barbarians, occur in literature specifically devoted to describing the world, but also in historical accounts and stories about military encounters. Literary representations of how barbarians look, particularly their clothing, weapons, and hair, are often reflected with great consistency in visual representations of barbarians and personifications of conquered barbarian nations. Many have posited that the Romans worked on their representations of others on account of actually encountering them, in battle for instance.[113] Usually, the further from the center (Rome) those are who dwell at the margins (nations), the more savage and strange the clothing, hair, and customs. At the edges of the world live the strangest people and barely-people, attested in writings from Herodotus to Strabo, from Caesar's *Gallic Wars* to Book 7 of Pliny's *Natural History*.

Those in the center, of course, are the Romans, and they are the most fit to rule through conquest on account of their nature and native geographical location. Pliny summarizes the differences, what he calls in his table of contents "differences of the nations according to the law/rationale of the world" (*differentia gentium ad rationem mundi*). He blames difference not on human invention or military conquest but the arrangement of the earth in relation to the sun:

> For it is beyond question that the Ethiopians are burned by the heat of the heavenly body near them, and are born with a scorched appearance, with curly beard and hair, and that in the opposite region of the world the nations (*gentes*) have white frosty skins, with yellow hair that hangs straight; while the latter are fierce owing to the rigidity of their climate but the former wise because of the mobility of theirs; and their legs themselves prove that with the former the juice is called away into the upper portions of the body by the nature of the heat, while with the latter it is driven down to the lower parts by falling moisture; in the latter country dangerous wild beasts are found, in the former a great variety of animals and especially of birds; but in both regions men's stature is high, owing in the former to the pressure of fires and in the latter to the nourishing effect of the damp; whereas in the middle of the earth (*medio . . . terrae*), owing to a healthy blending of both elements, there are tracts that are fertile for all sorts of produce, and men

> are of medium bodily stature, with marked blending even in the matter of complexion; customs soft (*ritus molles*), senses clear, intellects fertile and able to grasp the whole of nature; and they also have empire (*imperia*), which the outermost nations (*extrimis gentibus*) have never possessed, any more than they have ever been subject to the central ones, being quite detached and solitary on account of the savagery of the nature that broods over these regions. (*Nat.* 2.80.190)

The middle of the earth, of course, is Rome. Here Pliny delineates the natural superiority of the Romans. The nations to the north (Celts/Gauls, Germans, Britons, etc.) are too white, and the ones to the south (named here Ethiopians) are too black. Others are too big, and the middle-of-the-earth people are just right. The middle region, in between the hot and the cold, is naturally the location of the best land, animals, and people. The people in this place have empire, which the nations of the northern and southern regions do not possess, but do experience since they have been subject to the mid-climate people. Pliny, in a way, sets the boundaries of Roman imperial self-understanding in this passage: Rome is located at the center of the world, in the best possible place, and by nature is inhabited by the best and most temperate people. Everything outside of the center is other, wrong, unbalanced in some way, due to its very positioning on the earth. Those in the center, who know government, might bring temperance and order to the outskirts, but this is the only way the outsiders will know of civilization, since they naturally do not have it.[114]

Pliny's project is to describe the entire known world from the perspective of its center.[115] He interrupts his own description of Italy's nations (included among them: the Gauls and other barbarians) to sing Rome's praises:

> I am aware that I may with justice be considered ungrateful and lazy if I describe in this casual and cursory manner a land which is at once the nursling and mother of all other lands (*terra omnium terrarum alumna eadem et parens*), chosen by the providence of the gods to make heaven itself more glorious, to unite scattered empires (*sparsa congregaret imperia*), to make customs soft (*ritusque molliret*), to draw together in converse by community of language the jarring and uncouth tongues of many peoples, to give humans civilization, and in a word to become throughout the whole world the one fatherland of all the nations (*breviterque una cunctarum gentium in toto orbe patria fieret*). (*Nat.* 3.5.39–40)

Pliny's comments indicate a presupposition that his world is divided into Romans and other nations. His project makes explicit what writing about the nations expresses: a manipulation of socio-cultural practices and prejudices into scientific observations, thereby naturalizing Roman domination. Someone has to rule the world, and the nations to the north and south are naturally not predisposed to possess empire. Thus, their subordination to the Romans is justified. Additionally, Rome's positioning in Italy is not only natural but completely justified, since it is "chosen by the gods" to bestow civilization, unite scattered empires, and be the mother of all while simultaneously the fatherland.

Celts/Gauls/Galatians as Exemplary Non-Roman Nations

The Celts/Gauls/Galatians serve as exemplary non-Roman nations for this project, both because there are extended descriptions of them from a dominant Greek and Roman point of view and also because I assume they are the addressees of Paul's letter. The Gauls, Celts, and Galatians (the terminology is similar in Greek: *Keltoi/Galatai*) are, in many respects, the quintessential barbarian. They spread far and wide over the ancient Mediterranean, having contact with many other nations the Romans identified, described, conquered, memorialized, and assimilated. They have been preserved in text and image as stereotypical representatives of those who must be conquered, initially on the bottom side of a Romans/nations, civilized/uncivilized, male/female hierarchy. Finally, in literary representation, they often are mentioned as having appearance and practices in common with other barbarians, or are used as an exemplary point of comparison.

Diodorus gives an extended and detailed description of the Gauls (Book 5), showing all the ways in which they as a nation differ from civilized (i.e., correct in appearance, stature, gender, performance) people. He locates their origin from a woman who was so vain that she could not take any lover for herself, so she waited for Herakles to visit and conceived with him—so the Galatians were born. As for how they look and live, they inhabit a land with many different nations and speak their own language. Additionally, they are tall of stature and have very blond hair that they wash with lye and wear in what is described as a wild and unruly manner, "like Satyrs and Pans, since the treatment of their hair makes it so heavy and coarse that it differs in no respect from the mane of horses" (Diodorus, 5.28.1). Animal-like, their bodies are soft yet fierce, and they wear fanciful, very colorful clothing of their own design:

> . . . shirts which have been dyed and embroidered in various colors, and breeches, which they call in their tongue "bracae," and they wear striped heavy coats, fastened by a buckle on the shoulder, heavy for winter wear and light for summer, in which are set checks, close together and of various hues. . . . (Diodorus, 5.30.1–2)[116]

Clearly foreign and not civilized in their hair and appearance, the Gauls are easy to identify as outside of the normative cultural codes for men, therefore being labeled barbarian due to their animallike appearance. Both men and women are adorned with gold jewelry (gold being abundant in "Celtica"). They also have deep and harsh voices,[117] they like to speak in riddles and hyperbole, yet they are thought not to be so smart. The most savage of them, the ones who, according to Diodorus, made contact with the Scythians in the north, eat people, like the Britons (5.32.2–3). They cannot stand the heat, so they must stay where it is cool,[118] and they keep bees. They also are not exactly the picture of moderation in food and drink, according to Diodorus's description: they do not drink wine modestly, they eat excessively, they fall into madness when they are drunk from beer at their own meals—to which they invite total strangers.[119]

Gender transgression, particularly male effeminacy and female masculinity, is a common characterization for ancient barbarians/nations in ethnographic literary representation, and the Galatians are no exception.[120] Diodorus poses the Galatians and other barbarian nations as gender outlaws or transgressors: rather than maintain a proper family structure, as one would expect Greeks and Romans to do, they intermarry and take more than one sexual partner:

> . . . they have very little to do with them (their women), but rage with lust, in outlandish fashion, for the embraces of men. It is their practice to sleep on the ground on the skins of wild beasts and to roll together with sexual partners (*tōn merōn parakoitois sunkyliesthai*). And the most astonishing thing of all is that they have no concern for propriety, but prostitute out their bodies easily, nor do they consider this disgraceful, but rather when any of them is thus approached and refuses the favor offered, they consider it a dishonorable act. (Diodorus, 5.32.7)

Galatian men lust after other men.[121] They take to "rolling" with multiple partners, not their wives, and the women do this as well.[122] This wife-swapping is something common to different non-Roman nations: Strabo reports, for example, that the Irish, more savage than the Celts/Gauls or Britons, openly have intercourse with "not only other women, but also with mothers and sisters" (*Geogr.* 4.5.4); this is mentioned in the same sentence as the pervasive cannibalism that they have in common with Scythians, Celts, Iberians, and "several others" (*Geogr.* 4.5.4).

Gender trouble is manifest among the Galatians in body-type and the performance of their sex-based duties. Such problematic gender performance is represented as consistent among barbarian nations in ethnographic literature. Galatian women are like the men in terms of size and are a match with their courage (Diodorus, 5.31.2), suggesting that they are not submissive in a vertical, social arrangement with their men—a feature that irritates the Romans as a mark of "uncivilization." Strabo reports that their custom relating to men and women is "opposite to us," as the tasks have been exchanged—and this gender role-reversal is something they have in common with other barbarians (*koinon kai pros allous suchnous tōn barbarōn esti, Geogr.* 4.4.3). Other barbarians include the Cantabrians in Spain, among whom "it is the custom . . . for the men to give dowries to their wives, for the daughters to be heirs, and for the brothers to be married off by their sisters. For they have some kind of gynocracy, but this is not at all a mark of civilization" (Strabo,

Geogr. 3.4.18).[123] Gender role-reversal also plagues the legendary Amazons, who represented a threat to civilization and, in some ways, exist only to be defeated by a civilized masculine-defined social order.[124]

The Celts/Gauls/Galatians, much like other barbarians, cannot wage war in the right (i.e., Roman) way. They do not line up as the Romans would like, they take weapons and knock soldiers off of their horses, they ride horses two at a time, they scream and shout while they are fighting, and they have those horrendous *carnyx* horns.[125] At the same time, they are portrayed as skilled and ruthless warriors (especially the Celtiberians, who are related to them and far more savage: see Diodorus, 5.33 and Strabo, *Geogr.* 4.4.2). When they are victorious in battle, they do not take the land or imprison slaves, and they "just are in it for the money." For example, the Gauls could have taken over Rome for themselves, but decided to leave. The speech of Brennus in *Camillus* before the Gauls reach Rome has Plutarch inserting a telling analysis of Roman treatment of those they conquer in a conference with the Romans over the fate of the Clusians:

> You march against these peoples, and if they will not share their goods with you, you enslave them, despoil them, and raze their cities to the ground; not that in so doing you are in any way wise or cruel or unjust, but you are obeying the most ancient of all laws which gives to the stronger the goods of his weaker neighbors, the world over, beginning with God himself and ending with the beasts who perish. For these too are so endowed by nature that the stronger seeks to have more than the weaker. Cease, therefore, to pity the Clusians when we besiege them, that you may not teach the Gauls to be kind and full of pity toward those who are wronged by the Romans. (Plutarch, *Camillus* 27.3–4)

Repeated encounters and threats from the Gauls appear to have been fairly embarrassing for the Romans, and this kind of humiliation is apparent through the useful portrayal of the Gauls as paradoxical barbarians: simultaneously effeminate non-men and super-manly opponents of the highest worth (see the "Dying Gaul" sculpture, for example). Such a paradox makes it all the more important for the Romans to defeat and incorporate them into their rule: doing so both properly reins in effeminacy and bolsters the competence and strength of the victors.

Stereotypes of Gauls are productively utilized in Roman assertions of superiority. In Cicero's *Pro Fonteio*, the Gauls are presented in a stereotypical way—despite their assimilation and cooperation with the Romans occupying their land, evident throughout this speech—to persuade the court of the Romans' innocence and benevolence in the attempt to contain these wily and threatening barbarians. In an attempt to discredit the testimony of the Gauls and win the case for provincial employee Fonteius, Cicero employs the same old sentiments and Roman historical anxiety concerning the Gauls:

> [D]o you think that nations (*nationes*) like that are influenced, when they give evidence, by the sanctity of an oath or by the fear of the immortal gods, differing so widely from all the other nations (*gentium*) as they do in habit and character? Others wage war in defense of their religion, they do against the religion of all, others in waging war entreat the favor and pardon of the immortal gods, they wage war against the immortal gods themselves. These are the nations (*nationes*), who in old days set forth upon a far journey from their homes and came to the oracle of the Pythian Apollo at Delphi, the resort of the whole world, to vex and despoil. It was these same nations (*gentibus*) of upright and punctilious oath-regarders who beset the Capitol and the temple of that Jupiter with whose name our ancestors chose to seal their plighted troth. Finally, can anything appear holy or sacrosanct to men who, if ever they are so worked upon by some fear as to deem it necessary to placate the gods, defile the altars and temples of those gods with human victims, so that they cannot even practice religion without first violating it with crime? (Cicero, *Pro Fonteio* 30–31)

Cicero privileges the historical sacking by the Gauls, whom he singles out as different from all the other nations, and makes that event into a religious offense of the highest degree against Rome. Further, he asks if "the most honorable native of Gaul is to be set on the same level as the meanest citizen of Rome?" (Cicero, *Pro Fonteio* 27). Setting natives against citizens, Gauls against Romans, Cicero affirms that there is a hierarchical difference between Romans and barbarians/nations. This divide is conceived as stereotypically hostile in the following statement:

> Can you hesitate to believe, judges, that it is a blood-feud which is cherished and waged by all those nations (*gentes omnes*) against the name of the Roman people (*populi Romani*)? Do you think that they stand here, in *sagi* and *bracae*, their mood is the meek submissive mood of the victims of outrage who betake themselves, as humble lieges, and appeal for aid to a jury? (Cicero, *Pro Fonteio* 35)

Cicero uses national stereotypes to justify the domination of the Roman people over all the nations who threaten them. The superiority of Fonteius—and by extension that of the Romans, as a whole upright and religious people—rests on the collective degradation of the Gauls:

> [L]et the world see that you place more credibility in the evidence of our countrymen than in that of foreigners, that you have greater regard for the welfare of our citizens than for the licentiousness of our enemies, that you set more store by the entreaties of her who presides over your sacrifices than by the effrontery of those who have waged war against the sacrifices and the shrines all over the world. (Cicero, *Pro Fonteio* 49)

Cicero shows some of the dialectics involved in the hierarchy between Romans and barbarians: countrymen versus foreigners, welfare against licentiousness, citizens against enemies, religion against those who attack it. In short, the sentiment expressed here is that the Gauls are anti-civilization, or everything that is right with civilization, that is, the Romans and their gods and power.

The Gauls collectively as barbarian nations serve a particular ideological function for the Romans, that of the outsider. This function legitimates the power of Roman military might and expansion, the taking of slaves from the conquered, and taking the land and people in order to civilize them. While the Gauls might be the quintessential barbarians according to dominant accounts of their appearance and ways from the second and first centuries B.C.E., they also make cameo appearances throughout ethnographic and historical literature of the first century C.E. as having intermingled with some other conquered or not-yet-reached nation, thus rendering them more or less like Celts or like Gauls. Even when Gauls themselves have disappeared somewhat by being assimilated into the Roman Empire or becoming Romanized,[126] they still also function as a familiar non-Roman quantity, a comparison point for other barbarian, non-Roman nations. Descriptions of Britain and Ireland, for example, use Celts/Gauls as a reference for the comparative savagery of the more-northern Britons, Irish, and what we know as Scottish peoples (Strabo, *Geogr.* 4.5.1ff).[127] The same is true of the Iberians, specifically the Celtiberians (who intermarried with the Celts) and the Cantabrians, who are said to have "gynocracy" (see above) and wash their bodies and teeth in urine "like the Keltoi," which indicates that they "have no regard for rational living."[128] Gynocracy also extends north to nations of the Germans, according to Tacitus—a characteristic that makes them "lower than slaves."[129] The Romans, while maintaining distinctions between the Galatians and between Gauls/Galatians and other nations to some extent in literary and visual representation, also distribute similar stereotyping using gender constructs throughout the dominated world while maintaining, through their natural and divinely ordained just-rightness, their position as rightful rulers.

Writers explicitly concerned with geography and ethnography such as Pliny and Strabo mention Gauls among just about all of the nations found represented in the Aphrodisias Sebasteion and in the *Res Gestae*, with clear descriptions of them as sufficiently outlandish, often in gendered terms, and in need of sustained conquest by the Romans. Aside from the more famous enemies (Jews, Egyptians) and locations of revolt (Sicily),[130] the less well-known nations are described in terms that designate their otherness, similar to those used for Gauls, and whole swaths of nations in the north are even called Galatians (Strabo, *Geogr.* 4.4). The Dardani are "savage" (Pliny, *Nat.* 4.1.3). The Alpine Bessi are "called brigands even by the brigands," murdering all men and women their seers said were pregnant with men when they raided a city (Strabo, *Geogr.* 3.369, 3.383). The Spanish Callaeci are "godless" and sleep on the ground "like the Keltoi," are interbred Gauls and Iberians, tattoo their bodies, and have women who switch roles with men (Strabo,

Geogr. 2.65, 2.67, 2.77, 2.103). The Iapodes, who are called "Keltoi," are known for being brutal pirates (Strabo, *Geogr.* 2.287). Additionally, the non-personifications in the Sebasteion's south portico are wearing the *sagi* and *bracae* common to northern barbarians, marking them as recognizably Gaulish.

Representation of the nations, such as Gauls, as promiscuous and yearning for boys, gender-role switching, sleeping with many people at once, trouser-(not toga) wearing, and irreligious or offensive to Roman religion, also places them outside of Roman gender constructs. Ideologically, they function as feminine and chaotic, or lacking the self-control central to ancient masculinity. This means, of course, that they are not fit to control anyone else, and they must take a feminine role where they relinquish control to those (men) more powerful by nature.

Roman Military Violence as Sexual Conquest over the Nations

Roman justification of male/female relations such as the impenetrability of the male and receptivity of the female extends far beyond the individual body and its activity to Roman corporate, national ideology. The feminine is to be conquered by force or to be complicit in the impenetrability of the male. The early walls of Rome that Remus leaped over and then was killed for penetrating serve as a poignant metaphor in this regard. Those who try to permeate manly Rome's boundaries must be destroyed. The walls of Rome, however, also extend to the empire's edge, where the military defeated nations in the service of preserving Roman impenetrability and spreading manly civilization.

The display of the Roman phallus plays a significant role in the guarantee of male impenetrability and virility. It is telling in this context that Fascinus, the spirit of the phallus, was "the protector of the boundary and of the general who fought beyond it;" the phallus also was placed in strategic public locations to ward off evil.[131] Roman boys and triumphing generals wore the phallus as amulet to protect them from danger and to signify their bodies as impenetrable, manly, and in control. The conquest or subjugation of whole nations is represented as legitimate and necessary to keeping Roman social and cosmic order by noting their gender and/or sexual configurations as transgressive or deviant and, in the case of the colonial encounter, essential to civilize, in order to bring and keep peace.[132]

The writing about the nations that I explore above has as a main theme the non-Roman barbarians as feminine and the Romans as masculine. This makes a powerful metaphor for territorial expansion: conquest of new lands and conquest of women are equated. Sexual violence and military violence are intertwined. That Rome is endowed with *virtus*, and that the nations over which the Romans by right and divine decree exercise *imperium*, is a gendered dynamic.[133] Those with unlimited *virtus* control themselves in such a way that they are fit to rule the world. *Imperium* is exercised through feminization and subsequent defeat of the nations.

There are not many extant literary representations of wartime rape of the nations during the Roman principate, perhaps because it was "taken for granted as a consequence of defeat,"[134] and perhaps because we do not have the majority of the voices of those conquered.[135] However, Tacitus puts a famous description of Roman conquest as rape into the mouth of Calgacus, the British leader of what appears to be the last people free of Rome's grasp:[136]

> Rapists of the world (*raptores orbis*), now that earth fails their all-devastating hands, they probe even the sea; if their enemy has wealth, they have greed, if he is poor, they are ambitious; east nor west has satiated them; alone of all they covet with the same passion want as much as wealth. Robbery, butchery, rape (*rapere*) they falsely name *imperium*, they make deprivation, they call it peace. Children and kin are by nature each man's dearest possessions; they are swept away from us by conscription to be slaves in other lands: our wives and sisters, even when they escape a soldier's lust, are defiled by them pretending to be guests and friends. Our goods and chattels go for tribute; our lands and harvests in requisitions of grain; life and limb themselves are worn out in making roads through marsh and forest to the accompaniment of gibes and blows. Slaves born into slavery are sold once and for all and are fed by their masters free of charge; but Britannia pays a daily price for her own enslavement, and feeds the enslavers; and as in the slave-gang the newcomer is a mockery even to his fellow-slaves, so in this world-wide, age-old slave-gang, we, the new hands, worth least, are marked out to be made away with. (Tacitus, *Agricola* 30.4–31.2)

Usually, only the part of this speech that explicitly mentions rape of the British women is referenced, and the "they make deprivation, they call it peace" statement is one of the most often-quoted sentences of Roman literature. But Tacitus here provides an analysis of Roman conquest as sexual violence and slavery from the perspective of those enslaved. Instead of lords of the world, Calgacus calls the Romans "rapists of the world"; if we remember that the *orbis terrarum/oikoumenē* was personified by a woman's body in Roman visual representation, the sexual connotations become obvious. Further, Calgacus links the slavery of his nation (children taken away to be slaves elsewhere) with that of others under Roman rule and speaks of slavery on a worldwide level. Britannia (Tacitus uses the feminine) is enslaved, and she pays a price to the Romans for her own enslavement, even feeding them. Calgacus positions Britannia on the newest, and therefore lowest, position on the "world-wide slave-gang," that is, the nations ruled through slavery to the Romans. The entire nation is feminized and enslaved, marking her as in need of control.

Control of gender and sexuality by those who enjoy positions of social and political power is crucial to the maintenance of social order, upright morality (or morality at all), and respectability.[137] Such politics draw boundaries around insiders and outsiders. The Romans, as insiders, are corporately represented as a masculine people. The conquered, as outsiders, are corporately represented as a feminine nation. The process of conquest—sexual violence, real or metaphorical—is powerfully expressed by the relief of Claudius over Britannia at Aphrodisias and is stated in Calgacus's speech concerning the Romans as world-rapists. But these dynamics, I would argue, are consistent and behind Roman imperial representation of a conquered nation, visual or literary. These representations do not have to be as explicit as Claudius over Britannia to be gendered. Such gendered ideology and its connection to sexual violence and slavery was a given in the context of Roman expansion and rule over all the nations.

Jews among the Conquered Nations

In Tacitus's speech of Calgacus, Roman conquest and rule over all the nations is equated with worldwide slavery, with (the woman) Britannia occupying a low position on the slave-gang. Tacitus also has Calgacus positing elsewhere that, within Rome's own army, there will be northern barbarian nations who will become allies to help his people (Tacitus, *Agricola* 32.1, 3–4). He worries that the Britons anticipate that the Gauls and Germans, who previously were defeated and incorporated into Roman rule and serve in the same army that defeats others, might desert their military duty and join with the Britons in their fight against impending Roman domination. In one other place, Tacitus alludes to the idea that the nations should not show love for one another, lest it mean trouble for the Romans:

> Long may it last, I pray, and endure among the nations (*gentibus*), this—if not love for us—at least hatred for each other; since now that the fates of empire drive it on, Fortune can guarantee us nothing better than discord among our enemies. (Tacitus, *Germania* 33.2)

Here Rome was spared going to battle with several savage German nations because they found and destroyed each other. Sixty thousand men were killed, and Tacitus reports that this was "an even greater triumph" for the Romans, since the fall of so many was "merely a delight to our eyes" (Tacitus, *Germania* 33.2).

The characterization of Roman rule as unfriendly servitude and the isolation of the nations from working with one another in the service of resistance to the Romans is also a theme in Josephus's speech of Agrippa to the Jews.[138] This speech is a list of the nations under Roman rule, an "inscription" of Roman world domination. The Jews are configured as one among many of the conquered nations, and they are the last to try to resist, so it is useless. The speech already was noted for its geographical sweep[139] and in it, Agrippa clearly expresses the inevitable, God-ordained dominance of Rome. The hopelessness of Jewish resistance comes from the Jews being weak and not having the assistance of the other defeated nations, rather than from having a poor reason to fight against the slavery of Rome.[140] Importantly for the study of the New Testament, Josephus positions Roman world-rule as "slavery," and in Agrippa's list of the nations repeatedly refers to tribute and pacification by Rome as enslavement.

Before the catalog of all the nations under Roman rule, Agrippa points out that the time to resist in the name of freedom has come and gone: "for slavery is a painful experience and a struggle to avoid it once and for all is just; but the man who having once accepted the yoke then tries to cast it off is a contumacious slave, not a lover of freedom" (Josephus, *B. J.* 2.356).[141] The time to think about freedom and keeping the Romans out was when Pompey invaded Jerusalem in 63 B.C.E.[142] At that time, he says, the ancestors of the Jews were fighting a small Roman army. This time, however, the Jews have fewer resources, and they want to "defy the whole of Roman hegemony" (*pros holēn anthistasthe tēn Rōmaiōn hēgemonian*, Josephus, *B. J.* 2.357).

Agrippa shows the other nations in the "whole of Roman hegemony" by mapping them out for the Jews. Many of the same nations appearing in the lists and inscriptions commemorating Roman power discussed above appear here, except they are explicitly named as being enslaved. Mentioned foremost as an example of the formidability of the Romans are the Greeks. The Athenians, who once fought so diligently for the freedom of Greece, "now are slaving to Romans" (*nyn douleuousin Rōmaiois*; 2.358). The Lacedaemonians, that is, the Spartans, "love the same masters" (*agapōsin tous autous despotas*; 2.360). The Macedonians, who with Alexander "scattered the seeds" (*paraspeirousin*) of the rule of the world (*tēn oikoumenēs hēgemonian*), bow (*proskynousin*) to the ones to whom Fortune has given favor (2.360). Agrippa implores the Jews to see that when they say it is hard to be enslaved by Rome, it is more difficult for the Greeks, the noblest and smartest of all, who are under six Roman rods (2.365).

In addition to these three formidable Greek nations now under the Roman thumb, Agrippa states that "myriad other nations" (*alla te ethnē myria*) who have greater reasons to fight for freedom than the Jews have yielded, prompting him to ask "and will you alone disdain to slave to those to whom all things have been subjected?" (*monoi d' hymeis adoxeite douleuein hois hypotetaktai ta panta*; 2.361). The Jews are a weak nation without arms or help; the Romans, by contrast,

> ... [are] not content with having for their frontiers on the east the Euphrates, on the north the Ister, on the south Libya explored into the desert regions, on the west Gades, they sought another world beyond the ocean and have carried their arms as far as the Britons, previously unknown to history. I ask you, then, are you wealthier than the Gauls, stronger than the Germans, more intelligent than the Greeks, more numerous than all according to the world (*pleious tōn kata tēn Hellēnōn este pantōn*)? (2.364)

The catalog of nations here turns from the civilized nations of Greece to the barbarians. The Romans have defeated the whole world with arms and have sought more due to dissatisfaction with their own boundaries. Many of the nations mentioned are already inscribed elsewhere as being under Roman rule: Asia, the nations of which "formerly knew no master, not even one of their own household, are now in submission to 3,000 soldiers, while 40 battle-ships bring peace to that once unnavigated and savage sea" (2.367).[143]

Famous northern barbarians also are named, in succession, as examples for the Jews, of Rome's extensive and unmatched reach. Thracians, who are stronger and live on more difficult terrain to reach and subdue, obey the Romans (2.368); neighboring Illyrians and Dacians; Dalmatians, who "often have reared their heads for freedom, whose constant defeats have only led them to muster their forces for a fresh revolt, now live in peace" (2.369–70); Galatians, who have the most reason to revolt, submit to the orders of 1,200 soldiers, even though they have almost as many cities to outdo the Romans (2.371–72);[144] and Iberians, including the Lusitanians and Cantabrians and their "fever for war," fought for freedom and lost and were reduced to slavery (2.375–76).[145] Even though ferocious, the Romans have installed Germans as captives everywhere, so that even the Jews have seen them, and the Germans are reduced to slavery (2.376–78); Britons, who have in the sea a greater wall than Jerusalem, were still approached and enslaved by the Romans (2.378).

Agrippa then moves southward in his catalog of all the nations. Even the Parthians, "ruling so many nations," sent hostages to the Romans, "and it is upon Italy to see, in the false pretext of peace, the nobility from the east enslaved" (*kai estin epi tēs Italias idein en eirēnēs prophase douleuousan tēn apo tēs anatolēs eugeneian*; 2.379). Southern nations such as Carthage, Arabia, Cyrene, and Numidia are all among those who pay homage to Roman arms (2.380–82). Even the so-called third part of the world, the southern regions mentioned by Pliny (above) as too hot to have empire, such as the Ethiopians, feed Rome for months and pay their tribute without any trouble, "far from seeing, as you do, an outrage in the orders which they receive" (2.382–83).[146] Egypt, right next door, does not mind submitting to Roman domination so much, even if Alexandria itself is reason enough to resist (2.385–86).[147]

In this speech imploring the Jews not to go to war with Rome, Josephus gives Agrippa impressive geographical and ethnographical knowledge. This knowledge is bolstered and communicated by using an array of the better-known barbarian stereotypes discussed above: the Gauls are rich, the Greeks smart, the Ethiopians unwitting, Asia untamed before the Romans, the Germans and Spaniards savage and brute. Here it is impossible for the Jews to win any war, as the nations who have been defeated before them—more savage, more fortified, more wealthy—all have lost to the Romans and are now enslaved and reduced to peace through conquest and continued military presence.[148] The nations are portrayed here as all different from one another in temperament and location according to the well-known ethnographic designations, but they all have enslavement to Roman rule in common. In fact, this is a reason the inhabited world will not help the Jews: for "all are Romans upon the world" (*hoi men gar epi tēs oikoumenēs pantes eisin Rōmaioi*; 2.388).[149] Not the inhabited world, not the Adiabene, not even God will help the Jews, for all are on the side of Rome.[150] Agrippa warns that the Romans will make the Jews into a "model for the other nations" (*eis hyodeigma tōn allōn ethnōn*) by burning the whole city and annihilating the Jewish race, which would have an impact on Jews all over the world.[151]

Josephus's maneuver in Agrippa's speech is to simultaneously inscribe Rome as the most powerful and extensive rule the world has ever known and characterize such rule—which the Romans call civilization itself—as enslavement. To do this, he uses the names of the nations well known from inscriptions, other visual representation, such as a portico of nations or perhaps Agrippa's map, and ethnographic writings. Known stereotypes are employed in order to have Agrippa persuade the Jews—who are small and weak and not as savage or rich as other nations—to not go to war with the Romans, who are strong and never satisfied with the extent of their empire. All the nations might differ from one another, and yet what they have in common is their enslavement, as well as the fact that they will not help the Jews.

Moreover, in this speech, it is clear that the Jews are not, from a Roman perspective, ideologically opposed to the nations. According to Agrippa, they are a nation, one of many, even if they will serve as an example to the others should they decide to go to war. This also means that they, like other nations, have been collectively placed on the bottom half of a Romans/nations hierarchy along with Gauls, Greeks, Egyptians, Germans, Spaniards, Britons, and so on.

Summary

The Romans were destined and determined to rule the whole world, which was composed of all the nations. The literary representation I examine in this section focuses on conceiving Roman domination of the nations as natural and universal.[152] Consistency in the display of the nations publicly and strategically in inscriptions, such as the *Res Gestae* as part of imperial cult complexes, served to solidify the social order and hierarchy. Writing about the nations, much like visual representation, affirms that gender constructs serve to differentiate nations from Romans, barbarians from civilized, and femininity from masculinity. The nations, imagined and written as collectively female, naturally must be found, conquered/penetrated, and pacified by their collectively male conquerors. Male/female hierarchy, assumed to be natural, justifies the defeat of all the nations. These nations included the Jews, as evidenced by Josephus's speech of Agrippa. Rather than being opposed to the nations, according to Roman imperial ideology, the Jews fit among the rest.

The Ritualization and Eternalization of Roman Conquest

One more small exploration will complete this collection of literary representation concerning the fate of the nations in Roman imperial ideology. The nations were defeated in Roman state mythology and origin stories. They were written about and listed throughout Greek and Roman literature. They were carved in stone and hung up around various parts of the Roman Empire. They also were paraded regularly as images, placards, and live captives in Rome as part of triumphal processions.[153] Like ethnographic writing about the nations, texts concerning triumphal processions are scattered throughout Greek and Roman literature of the late republic and early empire, including an extended description in Josephus.

My concern with triumphal processions is precisely with the element of display.[154] Particularly important is the display of images of the nations and carefully chosen captives from those nations. Within the context of the display of the gods (native and Roman) and the spoils of war, as well as the framing of the triumphator as god/king, the triumph takes on a religious character. But I am not so concerned with the various religious aspects of the triumph here, nor am I particularly interested in the origins of this Roman institution (even if it is telling that the Romans chose to write the triumph into their history as far back as Romulus himself, and two of the predictions in the *Aeneid* that I discuss above include processions).

I am interested in the ability of the triumphal procession to function as a ritualization and eternalization of Roman imperial ideology of conquest over all the nations. The triumph is an elaborate display at Rome designed—carefully designed!—to commemorate victory over the nations in battle. As a mode of representation, it is part of the self-conscious political performance on the part of the emperor.[155] It allows the spectators at the city of Rome to participate safely—on a highly constructed, managed, and censored level—in Roman world conquest. The triumph is a ritual activity that enables the viewers to engage first-hand the fate of the nations: to see what it was like for the army to do battle in far-flung lands, to ogle at the natives in their indigenous dress and note cultural differences, and to see the animals, gems, works of art, and other spoils brought back from afar. Its explicit linkage, through display, of the triumphator with the Roman gods eternalizes Roman rule over the nations, bringing it full circle back to all of the predictions about divine genealogies and empire without end.

Description of the Roman Triumph

Before I discuss how the Romans/nations hierarchy is portrayed in the triumph, a general description of the procession's elements, based on what we know from sources, is in order.[156] Although the triumph may have originated as a festival in Etruscan times with rulers dressed as deities for annual sacrifices, by the late republican period, the king-god had been replaced by the victorious military general (Diodorus, 14.117.6, Plutarch, *Camillus* 7.1). The general acted as Fortune's messenger or apostle, bringing the good news of victory back to the people of Rome. The transition to the principate brought changes in the triumph as well: by the time of Paul's activity, and as early as the second decade of the first century B.C.E., the victor enjoyed exclusive rights to be triumphator. During the first century C.E., the triumph became once again the domain of god-men, as emperors played the role of gods during the processions—thus combining the gospel of conquest with the deification of the savior during this public display.

The triumph was not to be celebrated following civil wars or rebellions. To qualify for a triumph, the Romans must have been victorious in foreign battle. Even when the foreign battle involved defeating Romans, as it was between Octavian and Antony, it was considered improper to drag fellow Romans through the streets, so foreign captives were readily produced. In this way, it appears that the Romans/nations hierarchy is built into the very architecture of the triumph. During the processions, which are believed to have entered Rome through the Porta Triumphalis and marched on to the temple of Jupiter Capitolinus, the emperor would be dressed very much like the Father of the Gods himself: he wore a purple toga and crown, painted his face red, and carried a scepter with an eagle on it. He rode a chariot, and a slave was to hold a laurel crown over his head without it touching; Tertullian reports that the job of such a servant also was to whisper "Remember, you are a man" in the ear of the Jupiter-triumphator (*Apol.* 33). This chariot was surrounded by choice soldiers returning from battle.

Though the emperor appeared as god, his car was not first in the triumphal procession. That spot was reserved for the bound kings and nobles of the conquered, who almost always were put to death following the triumph (Plutarch, *Aem.* 33.3–34.2; Josephus, *B. J.* 6.433–34).[157] Wagons displaying precious metals and other valuable spoils, such as art and statues from the conquered, followed, then (usually bound) captives. Sometimes everyday objects carried in from the conquered lands would do. In Livy's account of Manlius Vulso's triumph over the Asiatic Galatians, for example, "foreign luxuries" were introduced to the Romans for the first time: bronze couches, exotic tapestries, and pedestal tables (Livy, 39.6–7).[158] Musicians and dancers provided added entertainment on the route. Images, placards, and float-like constructions, including portraits of famous Romans, lists and images of the defeated cities and nations, paintings of gods and battle-scenes, replicas of rivers and mountains crossed, and animals came next. The legions and, finally, the triumphal chariot brought up the rear.

Triumph as a Display of the Nations

The triumph was, at its core, a public celebration of Roman defeat over foreigners. The nations were displayed in the flesh, using human representatives of captured peoples, as well as in images and inscriptions developed for such occasions. Historical accounts of Roman triumphs narrate the triumphal processions as featuring a pageant of images of nations and/or sufficiently stereotypical specimens of the conquered, in traditional dress parading through Rome's streets. In one farcical example that reveals the performative dimensions of the triumph, Gaius gathers his Germans together for a procession:

> [I]n addition to a few captives and deserters from the barbarians he chose the tallest of the Gauls, and as he expressed it, those who were "worthy of a triumph" (*axiothriambeuton*), as well as some of the chiefs. These he reserved for his parade, compelling them not only to dye their hair red and let it grow long, but also to learn the language of the Germans and assume barbarian names. (Suetonius, *Gaius* 47)[159]

Gaius does not have any real Germans to display, so he manipulates his Gauls.[160] More than yet another indication of how terrible or licentious this particular emperor was, the detail of what it means to be German is made visible. If what Suetonius reports is true, Gaius is relying on the people's ability to recognize proper Germans or tell the difference between barbarians. To create Germans for the triumph, the emperor relies on the stock stereotypes available to him and known to the Roman public. Attention to ethnic differences in the clothing and attributes shows that real-life national representatives also differed in dress and appearance to signify racial diversity and the vastness of the inhabited Roman world.

It was apparently not just images of the ethnographically-accurate conquered nations *du jour* that were represented in the triumph. Collections of many nations served to signify the extent and universality of Roman domination. Dio's account of Augustus's funeral (itself styled as a triumph, according to his wishes) states that the procession included images of ancestors (except divine Caesar) and accomplished Romans, then Pompey and "all the nations that he had acquired, each represented by a likeness which bore some local attribute" (Dio, 56.34.3). According to Tacitus, "the names of the nations conquered by him were to be carried in front," in the position of the captives (*Annals* 1.8.4) during the funeral procession. According to Dio, this included more than forty nations.[161] Pertinax's funeral (in 193 C.E.), perhaps in imitation, included twenty bronze plaques featuring defeated nations in national dress; these were followed by distinguished Romans (Dio, 74.4.5).

The most complete report of a triumphal procession is that over the Jews following the destruction of Jerusalem.[162] Josephus's account of the Flavian triumph—arguably a very rare description of the parade from the perspective of a would-be "loser"—describes how the spectacle included selected Jewish prisoners such as Simon, dressed and tied up, beaten and executed even before the procession reached the Capitoline (in "fatherly custom," *palaion patrion*; Josephus, *B. J.* 7.153). Other prisoners were traditionally robed and made to stand in suggestive postures while perched precariously on top of float-like constructions that included tapestries detailing how Roman soldiers defeated them.[163] In that same procession the Torah was carried as an image of the God of Israel along with the menorah, the table for the showbread, and other holy objects. Notably, Josephus writes that all the jewels, foreign silver and ivory, expensive cloth, and so on are nearly impossible to describe

(Josephus, *B. J.* 7.132). This triumph is vividly commemorated on the still-standing Arch of Titus in Rome, where treasures of the razed Jerusalem temple are riding high on marching shoulders, the quadriga chariot rides in, and Titus is atop an eagle to heaven inside the arch.

It could very well be that images of the nations were female, like the personifications of Roman imperial visual representation, again using gender constructs to designate power relationships. Jocelyn Toynbee remarks that the personifications in stone might be "regarded as studies of . . . unfortunate captives as they walked in chains, were dragged in wagons in the train of their conqueror, or were herded in sullen groups through the streets of Rome."[164] Ovid's *Ars Amatoria* imagines the triumph as a great place to solicit women for sex, and along the way he manages to describe a figure "Persia, born of Danae" walking along in line (1.217–28). And in Silius Italicus's imaginary procession following the Punic Wars, Carthage is styled as a woman kneeling and raising her arms to the sky along with icons of Spanish cities (*Punica* 17.635–42). Whereas the nations might have been female, the manliness of the triumphator was emphasized through his display of the phallus under his chariot,[165] ostensibly to avert danger but also to assert the phallic power bound up with worldwide Roman *imperium*. The combination of personifications and enhanced phallus suggests a sexual relationship between the Roman emperor and the nations.

The triumphal procession provided an opportunity to display the nations in a manner consistent with their representation in sculpture and other media: captured, defeated, and deferential to Roman world rule. Through bringing the world to Rome, the people could become involved in the ongoing dramatic ritual of Roman world expansion. Through the equation of the triumphator with Jupiter, the cosmic and eternal qualities of Roman worldrule are emphasized. Through recognizable stereotypes of the conquered, including gendered stereotypes, hierarchical differences between Romans and nations are reinforced. Like the other materials discussed in both this and the previous chapter, the triumph is a means to show Rome's domination over all the nations.

Conclusion

Roman imperial ideology expresses the order of the (conquered) world and is critical to the enforcement of imperial social order and the making of a preordained master race whose father (of the fatherland, naturally) rules over land and sea, day and night. I maintain that gender imagery is a primary mode of delineating hierarchical distinctions between Jews and Greeks, slaves and free, and male and female. The production of Roman difference from and superiority over the others involves representing barbarians and nations in gendered terms.

The examples I have chosen are particularly relevant here because they use gender constructs to differentiate Romans from non-Romans, signifying a convergence of race, gender, and class. This convergence complicates the politics of Roman conquest significantly because when fully assimilated or Romanized, the nations may have looked no different than Romans. However, the dynamic of changing appearance, much like Aeneas's eventual shedding of his "Trojan clothes" to become a man in the *Aeneid*, points to the importance of appearance to identity and status in a Romans/nations hierarchy of which gender is an integral part. Further, in several accounts the process of conquering nations involves an explicit equation of military violence with rape/sexual violence. Through this literary representation it is possible to see that the logic of the Romans/nations relationship equated barbarism with sexual licentiousness, expressed in terms of gender transgression and specifically femininity, whereas Roman virtue and fitness to rule over land and sea is the ideological domain of masculinity.

The coherence and implications of the victorious-Romans-over-defeated-nations message should not be underestimated. Representation of this world amounts to a mapping of the empire's boundaries through attention to gender and ethnic interconnectedness. The whole world is composed of individual, racially distinct parts, as evidenced by attention to clothing and attribute diversity. Through representing the world in this manner, Roman imperial ideology creates and maintains the notion that the whole world is within reach and is attainable. The nations, in spite of whatever perceived or real differences they exhibit, together are united in their status and relationship to Roman rule.

Paul's use of gender and sexual categories and allusions must be better contextualized in order to deepen a transgressive understanding of his rhetoric. An examination of the specificity of Roman gender/sexual and ethnic categories and how they were linked directly to imperial power, militarism, and nation-building is relevant to show how this works. Such examination should lead to a much different analysis of Paul's self-presentation and rhetoric as a member of a defeated nation. Such examination will assist in a gender-critical re-imagination of a defeated Paul, then as apostle to the defeated nations, formulating a deeper understanding of some of Paul's very difficult language concerning gender, ethnicity, class status, and family in Galatians. This integrative exegetical task is the focus of chapter 4.

CHAPTER FOUR

Re-Imagining Paul as Apostle to the Conquered

I have argued in the previous chapters that the visual and literary language of Roman imperial ideology and power is necessarily gendered. Paul also uses gendered language to navigate, critique, and re-imagine the very same patriarchal structure that so many have used him to affirm and propagate. I contend that Paul, like many of the New Testament writers, provided intervention into Roman imperial ideology. In other words, insofar as Paul articulates a political anti-Roman stance in his letters, he does so using gender constructs and imagery. Insofar as the New Testament itself represents a rare textual glimpse of Roman imperial society from "below" and suggests struggle and resistance, gender is at work. I find gendered imagery that challenges "natural" gender order as the Romans represented it throughout Paul's rhetoric.

A gender-critical re-imagination of Paul, as apostle to the defeated nations, largely involves redescribing and recontextualizing the Gentiles as the nations defeated by Roman imperial power and positioned as those destined to serve Rome's empire-without-end. Paul, a Jewish man, should also be redescribed as a complex figure who may be a Roman citizen from a Hellenized, highly respected intellectual community in Asia Minor, as well as a member of a conquered nation that the Romans saw as especially menacing to their world-domination project.[1] To that end, the nations are those who are to be defeated by Rome *and* those reincorporated into Israel under the one God. The aim of this section is to continue my exegetical emphasis on gender-critical re-imagination by attending to Paul's work within the context of Roman imperial ideology and gender constructs. To do this, I focus on Paul's own self-presentation and performance as a transformed apostle to the defeated nations. Since the bulk of Paul's autobiography and some lucid gender-based suggestions about community are both in Galatians, I concentrate on re-reading specific elements of that letter, while relating to the letter as a whole as a window to addressing some wider issues raised by the realignment of the sources I have proposed throughout this project.

— "Conversion," "Call," and "Consciousness" (Gal 1:13–17) —

Gender-critical lenses have not been trained to look at Paul's mission to the Gentiles as having implications for gender and power, particularly Roman imperial power.[2] Gentile inclusion "in Christ," as recounted in Paul's letters and Acts, is admittedly central to Pauline theology. But Paul's mission to the Gentiles begins not with the trips across the Mediterranean, or with the so-called Jerusalem conference, or even with the scales falling from his eyes.[3] The mission to the Gentiles starts with Paul's own transformation, what in the history of interpretation has been called his conversion and call, and in his desire to represent himself as someone who has changed. Paul's mission begins with his own transformation in relationship to others, particularly others he had been persecuting. Because the mission to the Gentiles—the defeated nations—begins with Paul's transformation and reorientation, I consider this pattern in some detail.

As part of my gender-critical re-imagination of Paul as apostle to the defeated nations, I submit another interpretation of Paul's transformation, building on the hermeneutical tradition of his call as the Jewish apostle to the Gentiles, as exemplified most succinctly by Krister Stendahl and increasingly affirmed by scholars within the so-called new perspective in Pauline studies (see below). The new perspective also has informed more recent work on Paul as a Jewish person operating in his Roman imperial context. However, a further distinction I propose is that Paul's transformation and subsequent life-in-relation is connected with the ideological Romans/nations hierarchy, expressed through gender constructs, that I have explored in the previous chapters. I do not think that Paul ever leaves the tradition of his fathers, but his body and orientation to the world around him undergo a substantial, time-consuming shift from persecutor to persecuted, or more specifically from Roman-aligned conqueror to conquered nation—and from impenetrably-male-identified to penetrably-female-identified. As such, interpretation of Paul's relationships with others, and specifically his work among the nations, should necessarily change as well. Paul works within his context from a marginalized position, using imagination to respond to his world.

Traditional Perspective: Paul Converts from Judaism to Christianity[4]

As is well known, even infamous, to people who study Paul's life, thought, and theology, Paul has traditionally been interpreted as a Jew who experienced an entirely inward-focused and religious conversion to Christianity.[5] Although we may have difficulty imagining an original moment for this naturalized, scholarly position, several influential studies have emphasized Paul's experience within a subdiscipline, studying the process and effects of religious conversion reaching as far back as Augustine's fourth-century reflections on his own experience as recounted in his *Confessions*[6] and, even further, to Alexander the Great.[7]

The pattern of Paul's conversion as psychological and religious also is represented as dramatic and sudden in text, art, and tradition.[8] It has informed what it means to repent and be born again and converted in our contemporary cultural context, particularly among evangelical Protestant Christians in the United States. Paul's conversion also is tied to what is commonly referred to, even in scholarly literature seeking to overcome the language of religious conversion, as his "missionary journeys,"[9] which in turn has influenced the history of Christian missionary activity to the "heathens"—notably, the preferred translation of *ethnē* in the King James Version of the Bible[10]—across the world. In this schema, Paul, blinded and then healed by the light of Christ, tried to convince other Jews to convert to his new religion, was unsuccessful, and turned his attention to persuading non-Jews who were more accepting. The conversion was then complete: lawful Judaism was discarded for law-free Christianity, and Paul preached the same to anyone who would listen. The communities to whom he wrote his letters, then, were composed of converts seeking advice about Christian dogmatics and ethics for their new lives.

Using a gender-critical re-imagination, I argue that Paul's self-presentation of the character of his life before and after, especially in Galatians, has underexplored gendered dimensions that provide a key to reading his overall project regarding the nations defeated by Roman rule. Paul additionally does not cease talking about how his life has changed with the classic conversion pericopes that seem to describe a sudden change of religion; in Galatians, Paul's transformation occurs as the letter progresses and is much less abrupt than usually represented in biblical interpretation and culture.

New Perspective: Paul Is Called, Not Converted

The traditional perspective on Paul's conversion is both enduring and correctly identified as both representative of a later, individualized development in Western consciousness and psychology, as well as anti-Jewish in motivation and implication.[11] The so-called new perspective in Pauline studies has considered a shift in focus from conversion in light of a reassessment of Paul in light of first-century intra-Jewish, and not modern Protestant-Catholic or Christian-Jewish, conflicts.[12] The reframing of conversion as prophetic call is best exemplified by Krister Stendahl's landmark book of collected essays *Paul Among Jews and Gentiles*. According to Stendahl, a main criticism of traditional Christian theological perspectives concerning Paul's life-change is that such work has paid less attention to the texts themselves and more attention to Luther's interpretation and the psychological tradition, which he terms the "introspective conscience of the west."[13]

For Stendahl, in the new perspective's[14] outlook, Paul is called, as were prophets (most closely, Isaiah, Jeremiah, and Ezekiel) before him. The content of Paul's call is to bring the good news of a crucified Jewish messiah to differing communities where he is certainly "among Jews and Gentiles." He is chosen by the God of Israel to go among the Gentiles, in particular, and declare the restoration of Israel (Jer 1:5; Isa 42:1). Paul is reconfigured as someone who stays Jewish and expands his Judaism to include Gentiles/non-Jews in a messianic religious assemblage. This Paul brings the monotheism of Israel ("God is one") to the polytheistic, pagan Gentiles, who are then "grafted" onto the Jewish tree under the one God (cf. Rom 9–11).

However, New Testament interpreters who affirm Paul's life-long Jewishness[15] tend to still think of his self-presentation and rhetoric as exclusively religious and theological. Scholars differ as to how, after his call, Paul configures the requirements of Torah (circumcision, food laws) for the formerly morally dubious Gentiles who seek, after their own conversion,[16] participation in the religious demands of service to the God of Israel. The main question here is whether or not Torah observance matters equally to both Jews and Gentiles, relying on the theological law-faith dichotomies central to Pauline studies.[17] Paradigmatic to this approach is a focus on the details of Jewish ritual observance in Palestine and the Diaspora as far as we can tell from the first-century C.E. and Paul's use of his textual tradition to make his arguments to non-Jews. The question of ritual observance is also inextricably bound, in the new perspective, generally and explicitly to the identity of Paul's so-called opponents in Galatians.[18]

Jewish observance of Torah, and circumcision in particular for Galatians, is more complicated than simply a matter of legal interpretation within an exclusively religious framework. To be sure, it could be said that circumcision is the core issue of Galatians. However, circumcision is not simply a cultic issue special for (male) Jews, but is a social—and political—issue in the wider material world.[19] Although it might be the case that "from the Jewish side, circumcision was not a useful marker of Jewishness,"[20] it could be said that in Paul's context, circumcision functions as a marker of national identity, intelligible and assigned a category within a Roman-defined social hierarchy that includes many peoples, circumcised and not. In some sense, observing the precepts of the Torah by practicing circumcision renders Jews visible as a countable ethnic group to those who can see,[21] particularly Roman authorities. But Paul, inasmuch as he uses scripture, is in tune with a tradition of prophetic criticism[22] and not simply discarding the idea of legalistic observance of circumcision; it is observance *to what end* that matters. I will return to the implications of this issue for Paul in his Roman imperial context below.

Aside from the obvious lack of concern for issues of gender and imperial power among proponents of the so-called new perspective, the Gentiles as a category still remain undifferentiated. The approaches inspired by the new perspective still take for granted a two-dimensional definition of the Gentiles as non-Jews, the objects of Judaizing from Paul's opponents. Such a view of the Gentiles pre-empts a full examination of the implications of Roman imperial ideology for the interpretation of Paul's mission.

Empire-Critical Perspective: Paul Is Called, but to Politics

Recent empire-critical work in Pauline studies has built upon the new perspective and positioned Paul as profoundly opposed to Roman imperial ideology and religion from his Jewish standpoint.[23] In this mode of interpretation, Paul turns away from his previous life in Judaism and becomes a different kind of zealot, a politically oriented Jewish person encouraging religio-political resistance to the Roman Empire through declaring a crucified Christ as savior from the evil age. This opposition mainly manifests itself, according to Richard Horsley and similar proponents, against the Roman imperial cult, the primary religio-political system operative in Paul's context. Here the emperor was worshiped as god and called lord, benefactor, and savior.[24] Positioning the God of Israel as the *only* and most powerful god, the best benefactor and law-giver, who guaranteed certain destruction of Roman-configured peace and security, constitutes the political view of Paul. Such a view positions salvation as not concerning individuals from the law or Judaism, but the whole of humanity from Caesar's world. Jesus, ironically enough, becomes the lord of all flesh, and his resurrection from the very real capital punishment he endured from the Romans signifies not a literal bodily reconstitution but the transgression of death-dealing.[25] Paul, then, is nothing without his observations on the crucified Christ in relation to his Roman imperial context. The aims of this work in empire-critical studies include the recognition that religion and politics are not so separate in the world of the earliest Christians, nor are the two isolable in the contemporary world.[26] Paul is called by the God of Israel to a different politics from "Caesar is lord of all."

However, as I have discussed above and elsewhere, there are sustained methodological inadequacies to recent work on Paul in his Roman imperial context. The first concerns the intersections of gender, sexuality, race, and power. This shift to empire-critical studies and politics in recent Pauline studies regrettably has been met with little investigation of controversies concerning race, gender, and sexuality—even as the refusal to separate religion and theology from politics in the ancient and modern contexts could be seen, through feminist eyes, as a result of liberationist hermeneutical challenges over the past almost-half century in theological and religious studies.[27] The shift to empire-critical perspectives has not yet fully incorporated major insights from the analysis of how, specifically, gender operates in Paul's Roman imperial context. Interpreters have yet to move beyond naming gender as a moral issue concerning the status of women in Pauline assemblies vis-à-vis the Roman Empire's social structures and constrictions, or otherwise relegating gender and sexuality to private issues that have nothing to do with public or civic hierarchy. Ignorance of the gendered texture of Roman imperial ideology prevents New Testament scholars and other interpreters from fully grasping the alternativeness of Paul's call and subsequent work among the Gentiles.

An obvious second methodological inadequacy in empire-critical approaches to the New Testament relevant for this project concerns descriptions of Paul's Gentiles. Too often an empire-critical focus on Paul positions him as a Jewish cultural critic and/or political opponent to the Roman imperial cult or social order, yet still maintains the theological category of Gentiles. Even in work that takes ethnicity seriously, Gentiles remain ambiguously non-Jewish.[28] Put simply, even though we have started to ask difficult and overdue questions about the complexity of New Testament terms of authority, such as *lord* and *savior*, the Gentiles have not enjoyed the same attention. Gentiles as a category constitute a concern to much empire-critical work insofar as they represent (sexual) immorality,[29] those who might be willing to participate with the Jews in the context of the collection for the saints,[30] and idolatry. If, according to empire-critical perspectives, major Pauline categories such as *sin*, *faith*, *lord*, and *world* should be re-imagined as having something to do with Roman imperial ideology, so too should (Jews and) Gentiles. Yet what the Gentiles look like, literally and ideologically, is underexplored in New Testament interpretation that reconsiders the Roman Empire as the religio-political context for Paul's life and mission, as well as the overall emergence of earliest Christianities.

To begin to redress this lacuna, I have privileged Roman imperial visual and literary representation about the Gentiles, that is, the nations, in order to provide a richer interpretive context for Paul's use of the very same terminology. In my recontextualization, the Jews are not ideologically opposed to the nations—they *are* a nation, with specific attributes, one of many that must be defeated by Rome. Defeating the nations, personified as female bodies in visual representation and conceptualized as not-really-male (i.e., effeminate) in Roman ethnographic literary representation, is the Roman mandate as sons of Mars and impenetrably virtuous men. So it may be the case that nations are people who are outside of Jews—however, they are also sculpted and named by, and outside of, Romans. I discuss below what this dynamic has to do with what, precisely, is the substance and outlook of Paul's call. A shift to the Romans/nations hierarchy as the more meaningful one in Paul's context provides a way to see his call as a gendered consciousness-raising experience. Paul uses this experience as an integral part of his self-presentation and apostolic performance in Galatians.

Gender-Critical Re-Imagination: Paul Is Called to Consciousness

Privileging an examination of the fate of the nations in Roman imperial ideology according to visual and literary representation contributes to a more nuanced understanding of the term Gentiles or nations in Paul's Roman imperial context and in his own rhetoric. To be sure, Paul's use of this term to stand for those who are not Jewish is still relevant, but this meaning is not the whole picture. What the visual and literary representation I consider in chapters 2 and 3 clarifies about the Gentiles, from a Roman imperial ideological perspective, is that the power relations between Romans and nations is such that all other nations should all show deference to Roman *imperium*, including the Jews. To the Romans, Jews are a nation just like the rest, even if we have tended to see them as special in their rebelliousness and textual traditions (including the tradition of the texts that ultimately came to be the New Testament) that we have inherited.[31] Jews and Gentiles opposed to each other, and not helping one another, ultimately serves a Roman interest: divide and conquer.[32] Paul's project involving the inclusion of Gentiles must be interrogated in light of worldwide resistance to Roman rule.

Whether or not Paul saw the *specific* Roman imperial visual representation explored above—and we do not know for sure all the things he did see, read, touch, or hear—he must have been exposed to and fluent in the thoroughgoing language of images communicating Roman domination in his context. Visual representation of Roman victory through conquest was consistent enough in the Julio-Claudian period—during Paul's lifetime—that he would have encountered its various expressions. He would have seen it in various cities of Asia Minor (including his birthplace, Tarsus), in Corinth, in Philippi, and in Rome. According to Acts, he explicitly commented on such visual ideology in Athens, calling the images idols.[33] Even in light of variances in the historical and epistolary traditions represented in the New Testament, it is not too much of a stretch to posit that Paul and his addressees not only would have seen portraits of emperors and monuments commemorating historical victories over enemies, including commemorative arches, monumental reliefs, theater decorations, and imperial cult complexes.

I also submit that Paul would have been able to read such visual narratives. He may have seen and read a *Res Gestae*, or similar inscription, on an imperial temple in Asia Minor. While he never saw *Judaea Capta* coins and attendant Flavian visual imagery depicting Jerusalem's destruction, Paul might have seen and held similar Roman coins with other defeated peoples and cities already in circulation at his time, as "coins could remain in use for over a century."[34] He would have seen female personifications of conquered foreign nations and conquering Roman imperial males. And evidence indicates that, in all likelihood, the Jews were represented alongside other captive and defeated nations, named as such and shown as ethnically specific women's bodies, such as in the Sebasteion at Aphrodisias—a "free" city, "chosen" by Augustus[35] on the Roman road, itself perhaps adorned with images, between Ephesus and Laodicea and Colossae. Paul could have taken that route further along an adjoining road to reach some Galatians in Ancyra.[36]

Paul would not only have been exposed to the visual representation communicating Roman victory and incorporation of all the nations, however. Such visual representation complemented and crystallized a Roman imperial ideology of world conquest over all the nations. Visual representation appears to effortlessly make natural and easily acceptable what the Romans worked tirelessly to bring into being, promote, and protect: themselves, as master "nation of the toga" and rightful rulers of the known world. Much of literary representation of the late republic and early principate also served to historicize, justify, naturalize, and eternalize such rule. Display of the nations—including the Jews!—live and in various media as subordinated to Romans served to portray a fulfillment of Roman prophecy as given in the *Aeneid* and the Romulus and Remus narratives.

To enter into a gender-critical re-imagination of what Paul *was* versus what he *becomes*, I attempt a structural analysis of the Romans/nations hierarchy in light of which I re-read Paul's first-person account of his consciousness-raising process in Galatians. Roman imperial visual and literary representation can be imagined as a pattern expressing Roman order, which is based on strong hierarchical oppositions between insiders and outsiders, or selves and others. Brigitte Kahl has proposed the following using the semiotic diagram as a methodological tool for such imagination. Though she uses it in reference to the Great Altar of Pergamon as a world-expressive monument relevant to Paul's time, the concepts easily apply to the material I have been examining as well, and I modify this structure below.

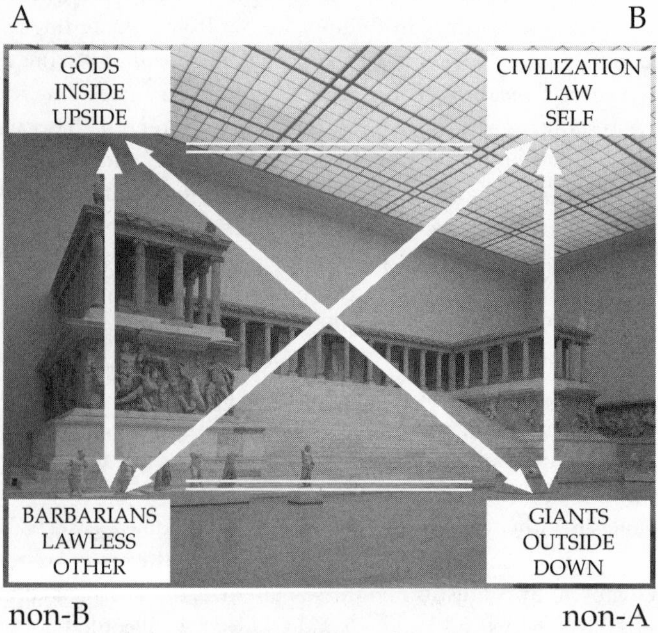

Figure 15. Spatial Semiotics (of the Great Altar of Pergamon)

In this schema, "we can depict a structure shaped by strongly bi-polar oppositions between A and non-A, B and non-B, as well as between A and non-B, and B and non-A."[37] The structure, as portrayed in figure 15 above, is described as follows: "The inside and upside (A) in this arrangement represents the positive values of city, civilization, law, order, proper religion (B), whereas the counter-positions of lawlessness, barbarism, chaos, blasphemy, and otherness (non-B) are linked to the opposite location of outside and underside (non-A)."[38]

According to the logic of the Roman visual and literary representation of the nations I have discussed in chapters 2 and 3, I modify this semiotic square as follows to reflect a Roman imperial ideology of world order and rule over all the nations:

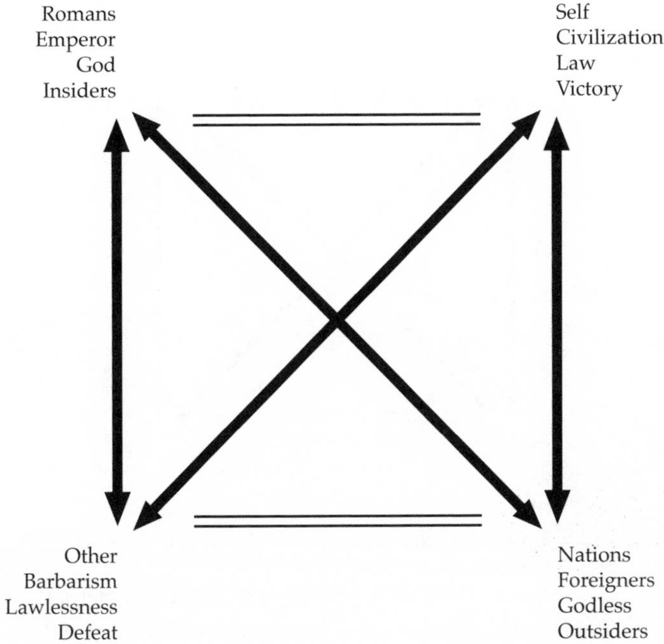

Figure 16. Roman Imperial World Order: Over All the Nations

Here the relationships are similar to those shown in figure 15, and I have filled out the square with several details that are ideologically relevant. The Romans, as the Emperor and *populus,* are situated on the upside (A) with God and insiders; these correspond to the positive values of self, civilization, law, and victory (B). They are opposed to and vertically situated above the godless, *gentes/ethnē/* nations, outsiders/foreigners (non-A), who represent the negative qualities of others, barbarism, lawless(ness), and defeat. Such oppositional relationships are clear in the *Res Gestae* inscription, for example, and in the spatial arrangement of conquered nations in relation to conquering Romans. Within this structure it becomes apparent how social divisions between Romans and others work in tension with one another to reinforce a vertical hierarchy. The Romans celebrate themselves through celebrating victory over their enemies, which they call the process of making peace.[39] Such victory and peace are closely linked to law and civilization. Those nations at peace, that is, who have been defeated, are associated with the potential for unrest and chaos by virtue of their being called barbarians and being depicted as women's bodies.

I also add a component to this semiotic structure that reflects the gendered and sexual texture of visual and literary representation concerning the fate of the nations according to the Roman sources (described as outside of Roman masculinity) and art (consolidated into racially specific female personifications and displayed in series):

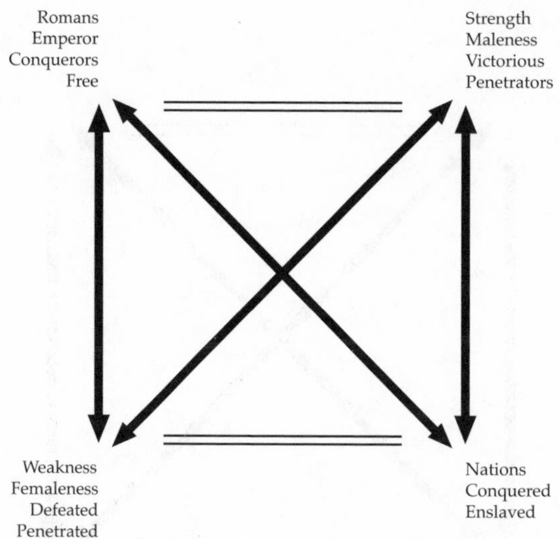

Figure 17. Roman Rule Over All the Nations as Patriarchal Power Relationships

The Romans, represented with and by the emperor, are conquerors who are free (A); they are designated by strength, maleness, and status as victorious and capable of penetration (B) on the upper side of this vertical hierarchical equation. Such maleness, achieved through victory and strength, is defined by and defines the weakness, femaleness, and penetration symbolizing defeat (non-B). Those defeated are the nations, who are conquered and enslaved (non-A). This construct also can be mapped easily using the spatial arrangement of the relief of Claudius over Britannia from the Sebasteion at Aphrodisias (see chapter 1) to reinforce the power relationships between conqueror and conquered expressed by that relief:

Figure 18. Mapping Roman Patriarchal Relationships with Visual Representation

So far I have used semiotic square diagrams to succinctly describe how Roman rule and order over all the nations worked in imperial ideology. Whatever actual historical circumstances, the Romans consistently positioned themselves in a vertical hierarchical relationship to all the other nations. No matter how ethnically diverse the world that produced the texts representing early Christianities in the first four centuries C.E., the Romans still occupied the position of being in charge, or more to the point, on top. Outside of archaeological investigation, another way that we know that the ancient Mediterranean world was so diverse is, as I have noted in the previous chapter, that the Romans wrote about the nations and justified their rule over them by describing them as barbarian outsiders. Aside from being displayed as female bodies in visual representation and events like triumphal processions, the nations are described as simultaneously less manly and more fierce/savage in relation to the Romans, which places them in an inferior position of needing to submit to civilization and order. The civilizing process that culminates in the changing of clothes to the toga is regrettably violent: the Romans bring peace through conquest, capture, and persecution.[40]

Paul also occupies the position of persecutor, according to his own account in Galatians and the historical re-telling of Acts. He, too, was forcing the "assemblies of God," presumably including fellow Jews and members of other nations, to submit to him through violence. He tells the Galatians something he supposes they already know:

> You have heard of my manner of living then in Jewishness/Judaeanism, that I was excessively persecuting the assembly of God, even annihilating (*eporthoun*) it (*autēn*, "her"). I was ahead in Jewishness/Judaeanism, above many contemporaries in my race (*genei*), as I was more abundantly being a zealot for the traditions of my fathers (Gal 1:13–14).[41]

Paul admits to a life defined by upward mobility (moving ahead of and above his contemporaries), accompanied by violence (persecuting the assembly of God) and exclusion of the others. Commentators have tended to focus on the identity of the assembly and whether or not it is a Christian church community Paul is attacking.[42] I do not presume a religious orientation called Christianity for the assembly Paul was persecuting. More interesting for my gender-critical re-imagination is Paul's self-presentation as someone who was not only persecuting (*diōkō*), but annihilating (*eporthoun*).

Much less common than *diōkō*,[43] *portheō* appears only three times in the canonical New Testament, all in relationship to Paul's activity toward the assembly (Gal 1:13 and 1:23; Acts 9:21).[44] This particular term is also not used frequently in extant literature outside of the New Testament, where it consistently denotes total destruction of a collective entity, usually a city or the countryside, in military conflict; it is also used as a participle in that regard (e.g., "ravager").[45] The only usage of *portheō* in the LXX is twice in 4 Maccabees to designate what the tyrant Antiochus does to the Jews. I include it here to give an example of the type of violence associated with the term:

> . . . when he ravaged (*eporthēsen*) them he issued a decree to the effect that all who were seen to conform to the law of the father must die. And when by his decrees he failed completely to destroy our nation's respect for the law, and observed that all his threats and penalties were entirely discounted, even to the extent that women . . . were hurled headlong from the walls with their infants because they had their children circumcised; when, I say, his decrees were despised by the people (*tou laou*), he himself sought to force each one of the nation (*hena hekaston tou ethnous*) under torture to eat unclean food and to abjure Judaism (*ton Ioudaismon*). (4:23–26; see also 11:4)

Power relationships are clearly implied by this term. Philo uses *portheō* seven times in all of his texts to signify a similar level of violence at the hands of a political authority over the Jews. Several times he means the Romans.[46] A particularly graphic example concerns Flaccus, who, while acting as "accuser, enemy, witness, judge, and executioner," added to his public declaration of all Jews, as "aliens and foreigners" and his destruction of their synagogues and constitution, the decree that anyone who wished could "destroy" the Jews as prisoners of war (*Flacc.* 54). Josephus uses this particular term a total of forty-five times, twenty-eight of which are concentrated in his *Jewish War* and describe either how the Romans dealt with Jerusalem[47] or how insurgents destroyed the countryside.

The semantic field of *portheō* signifies more than religious persecution; it is a war term that includes sexual violence as a consequence of battle, usually taken for granted.[48] In this sense, the personification of lands as women's bodies expresses a quality of total annihilation. It is not so much the point that Paul might have raped a woman, but that he describes himself as previously being in a position of perpetrating extreme violence, as being in the position of a war-maker.

Paul hints that he previously thought violence toward others was natural to the "traditions of his fathers," or the "way it is supposed to be," for which he describes himself as being more zealous than most. This pattern is what we might call Paul's confidence in the flesh, according to Philippians 3:4–6, where he claims his right lineage and social position as stemming from an impeccable genealogical and racial construct: "circumcised on the eighth day, out of the race of Israel, the tribe of Benjamin, a Hebrew out of Hebrews, a Pharisee according to the law" (*genous Israēl, phylēs Beniamin, Hebraios ex Hebraiōn, kata nomon Pharisaios*). This presentation is also gendered: Paul is a man above all, blameless (and without blemish?) and wanting to destroy others for the sake of self-preservation. Paul presents himself as having ample historical justification for his violent behavior toward others.[49] If we are to believe the account of Acts, we learn there the character of Paul's persecution: he was threatening to murder the students of the Lord and requested letters from the high priest so that he could ferret out people of "the way," bind them, and lead them to Jerusalem.[50] The assembly of God probably includes Jews and Gentiles, and according to Acts, does include both men and women (9:2; presumably implied by "all" in 9:14; cf. the list of women among the apostles in Rom 16).

A map of Paul's previous attitude toward others as he presents it in Galatians can also be drawn using the same hermeneutical diagram as above. Kahl calls this the "Pre-Damascus Paul."[51]

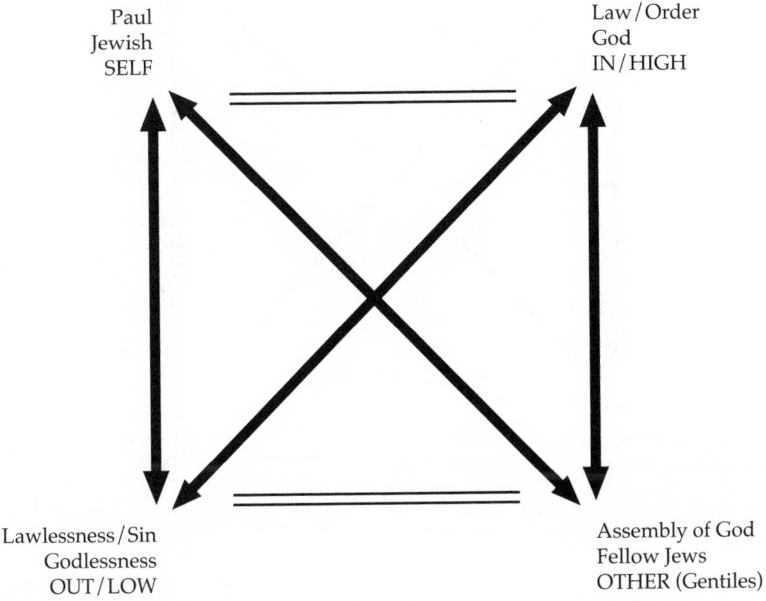

Figure 19. Pre-Damascus Paul

Kahl describes Paul as presenting himself as militant in his approach to others (what he calls assembly of God), who must be pushed out and pushed down violently in the name of self-preservation. In the symbolic language of Kahl's main reference point, the Great Altar of Pergamon, this means that Paul works himself upward toward the gods by defeating the Giants, who may be "creeping into the body of Israel"[52] and corrupting what he thought of as the order of the world. This Jewish order as Paul presents it converges with what Kahl labels Jewish and Roman Law.[53]

I agree that there could be a confluence in how Paul and the Romans construct behavior toward and hierarchy over others. I again add a gender-conscious level to such a characterization of Paul. The gods on the Great Altar behave in a dominating, (literally) penetrative way toward the Giants, who are depicted as hybrid and unruly monsters. Such monstrosity and chaotic inclination also are what the Greeks and later Romans would have associated with so-called barbarian peoples slated for conquest, and as I have discussed above, are expressed in terms of gender transgression and femininity. The gods, as victorious conquerors of the Giants and protectors of civilization, are aligned with the Roman emperor and army, and are therefore linked with gender conformity and particularly, with impenetrable maleness (see figure 17). That Paul behaves in a masculinist way according to his

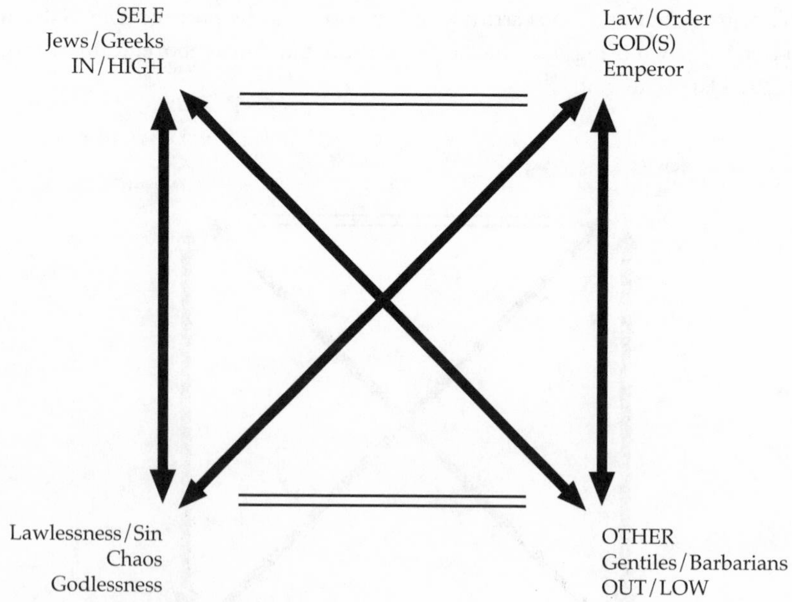

Figure 20. Jewish and Roman Law

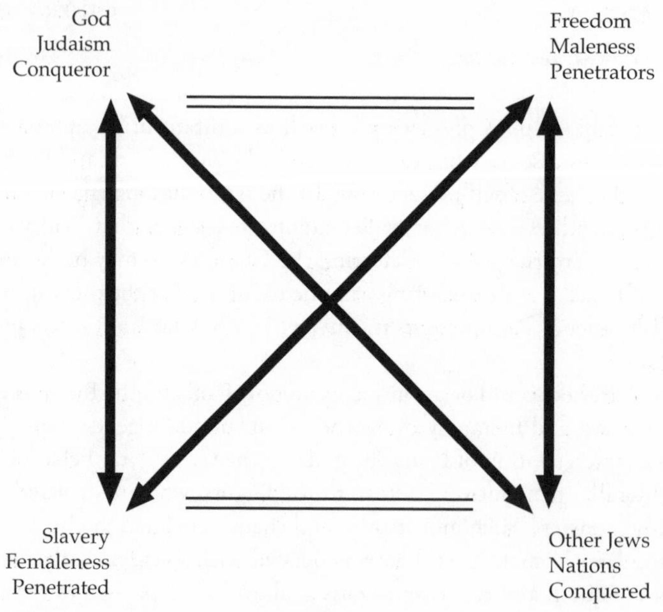

Figure 21. Paul's (Former) Identification with Roman Patriarchal Order

own admission signifies an identification with the patriarchal construct I have been describing.

Here Paul's attitude toward himself and others is shown in high relief. The semiotic oppositions demonstrate that Paul, by using violence toward others in the name of self-aggrandizement and protection, reproduces the same ideological configuration as the Romans. Paul equates God's approval of Judaism with the ability to conquer (A), which is a demonstration of freedom, maleness, and penetration (B) of the assembly of God composed of other Jews and nations (non-A). The penetrated and conquered, again, are associated with femaleness and slavery (non-B). The assembly of God could be represented by a woman's body reminiscent of gendered ethnic personifications and the literary representation designating the nations as enslaved.

Paul represents himself as behaving in a manner vaguely reminiscent of a manly Roman soldier,[54] even like the emperor as a representative of divinely ordained conquest and rule over all the nations. The obvious linkage of Paul's appearance to the mechanisms of Roman imperial ideology and power, and relevant implications for Paul's shift in consciousness and activity to a lower(ed), injured, and crippled man, have rarely been explored by scholars. The present project seeks to begin to make such connections and ask different questions about what Paul's soldier-dress signifies—as well as how his change of clothing affects his life-in-relation. Such is the task below.

Paul presents himself as a man who formerly was advancing beyond his own people and defeating others; I have linked this to a Roman imperial gender construct of impenetrable masculinity. Paul then indeed becomes a different person after what he terms a revelation from God in Galatians. The life Paul lives before this experience and the life he lives after diverge radically, but not because he left Judaism and converted to what moderns have come to name and live as Christianity. As recent scholarship from the new and empire-critical perspectives have proposed, Paul becomes a different kind of Jewish person through his experience. But difference in theological and/or religious orientation is hardly the entire picture: he also presents himself as a different *man*, and even a *woman* of sorts. As such, he models a different kind of consciousness toward and relationship to others.

Paul's self-presentation of his former life shows what kind of man he was and is, and how he has changed. Wandering around the eastern portion of the Roman Empire is only part of this change. In the context of the gendered and sexual facets of Roman imperial ideology Paul was, in his former life, reproducing the very same power structure that the Roman metanarrative portrays as natural. He was persecuting and ravaging those who differed from him. He was at the top, having advanced beyond others of his race. Paul was behaving as a proper Roman man according to imperial ideology: dominating others, policing boundaries, and employing his right of *imperium*. If Acts 9:1–2 is reliable for Paul's biography, he was on his way to tell synagogues to collect prisoners, bind them in chains, and lead them through the capital as the Romans might do with barbarian captives following victory in battle.

In Paul's recollection, his bodily alteration begins with his reflection on his life before and after God intervened. Paul was changed by what he saw (which, according to Acts, rendered him temporarily unable to see). In Galatians 1, his revelation includes a retelling of his birth story:

> . . . when God, the one who set me apart while in my mother's womb and called me through his grace, was pleased to reveal his son in me so that I might proclaim him among the nations (*en tois ethnesin*)."[55] (Gal 1:15–16)[56]

Paul, who mentioned the fathers as those for whose traditions he was previously zealous, is now somewhat fatherless. Paul presents himself as a mother's son called by God in a manner consistent with First Testament prophets. Jeremiah, for example, is known by God before being formed in the womb and is appointed a prophet "to the nations" (Jer 1:5). Isaiah is also chosen from the womb (Isa 49:1). God reveals to Paul that what he is "born to do" is proclaim Christ among the nations. To do this, he must stop persecuting people. His turn from violence is rumored among the assemblies of Judea, who did not see him but heard that Paul was "proclaiming the faith he was once ravaging" (Gal 1:23).

The difference in Paul's activity after his revelation is not only that he believes in Christ, but that his image of self and behavior towards others moves from sole dominator to among the dominated, and from impenetrable masculinity to penetrable femininity. One key to picking up this pattern, I submit, is that the direct result of the (prophetic) revelation he receives is that he is to go among the nations, not just the ones he has persecuted personally but those who were part of Israel from the beginning (i.e., in the table of nations in Gen 10 and reconciled to Israel in the prophets) and have been conquered and assimilated into Roman rule.

A relevant question, perhaps, is what the point of Paul going among the nations is if not to convert them to Christianity. I suggest that Paul's consciousness is raised in two identifiable ways in Galatians, pointing again to the multiple Jewish-Roman contexts of his rhetoric. First, the prophetic echo of Jeremiah and Isaiah in Paul's self-description is not accidental. Jeremiah is called to be a "prophet to the nations" (1:5). Isaiah has God designating Israel as the servant who will teach the true way, that is, the justice of God, to the nations (Isa 42:1), to be a "light" to them (Isa 49:6). In First Testament prophetic literature, particularly Isaiah and Jeremiah, it is common to acknowledge that Israel and the rest of the nations should not be opposed to one another, but actually that Israel should understand their God's justice as the "light to the nations": "Listen to me, my people / hear me, my nation / The law will go out from me / my justice will become a light to the nations / My righteousness draws near speedily / my salvation is on the way / and my arm will bring justice to the nations / The islands will look to me / and wait in hope for my arm" (Isa 51:4–5).[57] Such reconciliation between Israel and the nations is linked to the common genealogical heritage of all the nations from God in Genesis 10 and the blessing of Abraham as the "father of many nations" in Genesis 12.

The nations, together, all over the world, are descended from the same origin. They are related and connected to one another, and they ultimately will be reconciled with Israel as their light in the making of justice and right-relation. Paul's consciousness is partially centered, I submit, around a realization that also is fully according to the tradition of his fathers: the project of Israel is not to persecute the nations, but to reincorporate them and make justice with them, to turn them from idolatry and toward a relationship with the one imageless God.[58]

The Jewish construct of the nations, particularly in Genesis and prophetic literature, presents them as different but interconnected through their creator. As we have seen, the nations serve another purpose in Paul's Roman imperial context. They are not just persecuted by Paul—the nations are also those who are related to the Romans through conquest. In Roman imperial ideology, the nations are not remembered as descended from the same place as their conquerors. They occupy space at the frontiers that must be expanded as well as at the bottom of a gendered hierarchy that is presented as predestined, justified, naturalized, and eternal. Paul's previous view of the nations is a distorted version of Israel's connection to them and is more in line with the Roman view than the potential of the Jewish view.

What Paul is forced to come to heightened consciousness about is that to the Romans, the nations include the Jews—and they all are persecuted and ravaged, and re-created, by a larger force. God reveals to Paul that he has Christ "in him," that he has the dynamics of defeat by the Romans within him. In this sense I am proposing a departure from the traditional scholarly view about what it means that Christ is revealed in Paul.[59] In Galatians, when Paul qualifies his words about Christ, he does so mainly in connection to violence, particularly crucifixion, and includes himself and the Galatians in that configuration. Paul says he is dead to the world and crucified with Christ, who inhabits Paul's body (2:19); the Galatians saw Christ "openly portrayed" as crucified "before [their] very eyes" (3:1); Christ became a "curse" for "us" by hanging on a tree (3:13); Paul likens his weak body to Christ's when he first visits the Galatians (4:12); the cross of the Lord Christ Jesus is the only thing Paul wants to boast about (6:14); and Paul has the marks of Christ in his body (6:17). Crucifixion did not just happen, nor was it meant to happen only to Jesus; it was a means of Roman capital punishment, a means of keeping criminals in check, promoting fear, and representing victory. And, it was meant to be seen.[60] Crucifixion, as violent punishment of state enemies, is also a core image of divinely ordained Roman domination over all the nations. Christ in Paul signifies awareness of that theo-political imagery, its pervasiveness, and his role in affirming the world order it naturalizes.

Persecution is not something Paul should do to others, since he himself is persecuted by the very dynamics he duplicates. Violence is not outside of Paul, but something he in fact has in common with the nations under Roman rule and in Roman imperial consciousness as those to whom all nations should bow. Paul's call to a consciousness shift about his place in Roman order can be mapped below.

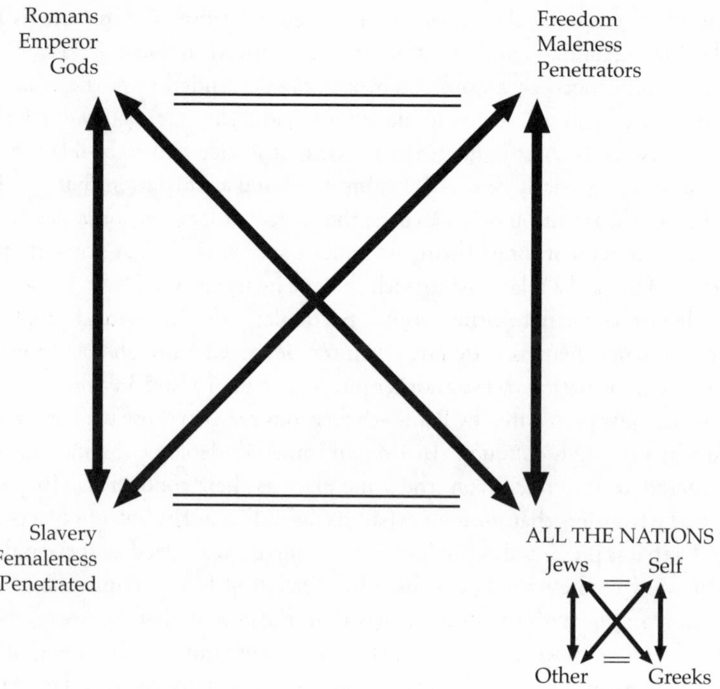

Figure 22. Paul's Shift in World Consciousness

Paul's place as a member of a nation destined to be conquered and assimilated by the Romans, along with all the other nations, is graphically transparent. Paul perceived himself as on top and above the others, but according to the wider dynamics of Roman imperial ideology he is actually on the bottom and below. I have also included the gendered component to these relationships as I have discussed and shown above. The top position is not occupied by Paul after all, but the Romans, represented by the emperor/god(s) (A), who are associated with freedom, maleness, and conquerors (B). They are above all of the nations, Jews, Greeks, and others (non-A), who must show deference by occupying the position indicated by slavery, femaleness, and conquered people and land (non-B).

Paul's antagonism toward and oppression of others becomes that which disables him from seeing the wider dynamics of oppression and slavery represented by what Tacitus's Calgacus calls the "world-wide, age-old slave-gang" (*Agricola*, 31.2) owned by the Romans. The scenario on the bottom is almost like a square-on-top-of-a-square, with the dynamics of oppression by the world-wide dominant masters being duplicated between dominated and enslaved minority peoples. It is the dynamics on the bottom, among the defeated nations, and in line with what the dominant portray as natural, that Paul seeks to overcome in the name of solidarity—among the subjugated—that will eventually subvert domination over all the nations as practiced by the Romans.

Paul's shift in consciousness results in a different configuration of knowledge about the world and results in a renunciation of his previous affirmation of the power relations made natural and inevitable by Roman imperial ideology. Paul appears more conscious of the particularity of his Jewishness, as well as his commonalties with members of other nations throughout the Roman Empire. In other words, Paul comes to consciousness as a marginalized person. This consciousness affects how he sees Jewishness operating in the Roman context (e.g., the Temple as aligned with Roman power through, for example, the tax structure and performance of sacrifices to the emperor) as well how he sees himself as a Jewish man. Paul's conversion, as consciousness, does not stop with his realization that he is on the bottom. In what follows below, I examine how Paul revises his self-presentation in the rest of Galatians, culminating with his transgendered appearance as a mother, as well as how he approaches the question of what it means to be among the nations.

The Politics of the New Creation

A gender-critical re-imagination of Paul as apostle to the defeated nations begins with examining his self-presentation, starting with his so-called conversion or call story, as a performance demonstrating his previous alignment with Roman imperial ideological masculinity in the name of Judaism. Paul's realization leads him to put down his weapons and literally change his path—and his gender configuration. In this section, I further trace this transformation from dominator to dominated and male to female. I sketch a link of this transformation to his life-in-relation among the (other) defeated nations as suggested in Galatians and other such self-descriptions in his letters. Galatians in particular contains some of the most famous passages concerning gender formation and expression in all of the New Testament and early Christian literature. However, as far as I know, such passages have not been fully examined in light of their Roman imperial context.[61] I seek to begin to ask different questions along gendered lines.

Paul Adopts the Subordinate Position among the Other Defeated Nations

Paul's change does not end with God's revelation, and his different consciousness is not merely theoretical or theological. It has worldly political implications for community formation in his Roman imperial context. In Galatians, Paul presents his body as the vehicle for his articulation of new relationships between Jews and other defeated nations: "considering his physique to be a major form of communication, alongside the words of his letter, Paul points literally to his own body. He can do this because his body tells the story of the forward march of the gospel, as do his words."[62] For interpreters such as J. Louis Martyn, the wounds and somatic brokenness Paul reports in his letters, particularly Galatians, are evidence of his participation in God's war—they are marks of valor or marks of persecution from fellow Jews and Gentiles about Paul's conversion to Christianity.[63] The implications are that Paul's body remains strong throughout his travels and missions all over the Roman Empire. Paul may have changed with his experience of Christ, but a manly warrior he remains through and through.

In a gender-critical re-imagination, we should not take Paul's masculinity for granted: upon closer inspection in light of the realignment of sources I am proposing in this project, Paul is not a manly man at all in legend or letter.[64] After his realization that he is not on the top or A (masculine) position in his larger Roman world but on the bottom" with those in the non-A (feminized) group he was persecuting according to his own rhetoric in Galatians, he immediately goes out to Arabia, the "end of the earth."[65] Paul was there for three years, after which point he goes to Jerusalem to meet Cephas/Peter and stay with him for fifteen days. During this time there are rumors of his change: the assemblies of Judea do not see him face-to-face, but they had heard that "the one once persecuting us is now proclaiming the faith which he was once ravaging" (*ho diōkōn hēmas pote nun euangelizetai tēn pistin hēn pote eporthei*, Gal 1:23).[66]

During all this time out of touch, Paul becomes vulnerable in a manner that he would not have been as a manly soldier and persecutor, imitating Roman hierarchical patterns. He has "died to the law" and "been crucified" with Christ (Gal 2:19) so that he might live to God, and it is a life of penetrated, defeated masculinity. In 2 Corinthians 11, for example, he tells of the "strength out of weakness" of which he can boast:

> . . . among more abundant labors, among more frequent imprisonments, among far more beatings, among death often. Five times under Jews/Judeans I received forty minus one (lashes), I was beaten with rods three times; once I was stoned. Three times I was shipwrecked, for a night and day I was in the deep. On frequent journeys, in danger from rivers, danger from robbers, danger out of (my) race (*ek genous*), danger out of nations (*ek ethnōn*), danger in a city, danger in a desert, danger in a sea, danger among false brothers. By labor and toil, among sleeplessness often, among hunger and thirst, among fastings often, among cold and nakedness. . . . (2 Cor 11:23–27)

As Jennifer Glancy has recently discussed, excessive beatings and danger from everywhere in the world, among people of Paul's own race and other nations, on land and sea, do not necessarily indicate elite male status or success in military confrontation. Such bodily dangers and trauma, particularly whipping, flogging, and beating, are common to persons of slave status.[67] Visually, Roman men would never be portrayed as having lost the war, so to speak. Paul models a *defeated*, and not heroic, male body. His defeated body is identified with slavery and with Christ, who is in him and crucified alongside him.[68] In the semiotic terms presented above, Paul goes down to the bottom position within a vertical hierarchical arrangement.

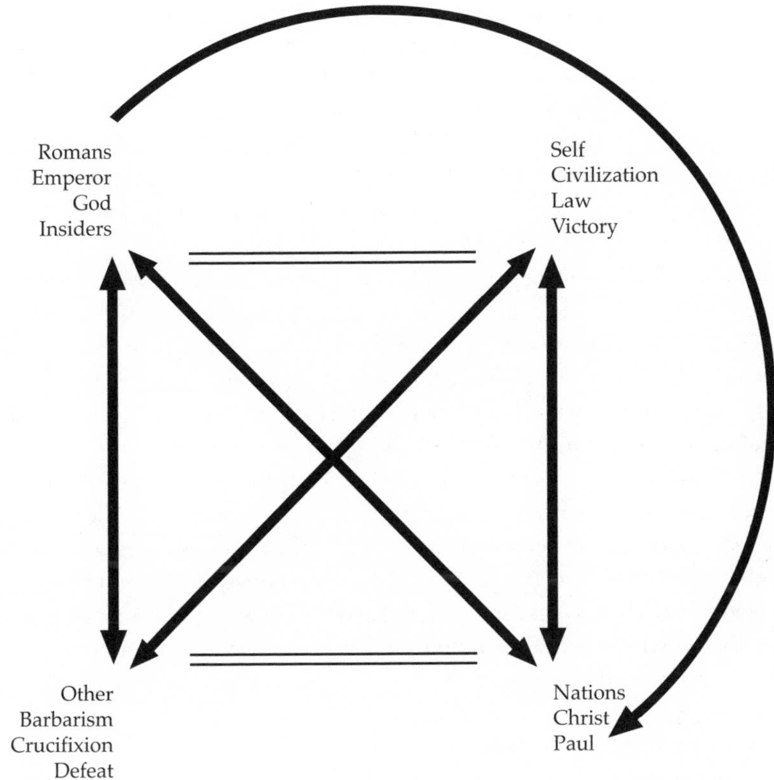

Figure 23. Paul Identifies with the Crucified Christ/Defeated Nations (Gal 2:19)

Paul identifies himself as dead, defeated, and weak on the underside of a world-wide power structure. Instead of ravaging and persecuting, Paul performs as a man for and with, and not against and above, others, including the nations. Instead of Claudius (A), now he sits with Britannia (non-A); instead of Augustus, now a defeated nation on his cuirass. There is nothing extraordinarily warrior-like or heroic about Paul's defeated, penetrated male body: it is a body reminiscent of numerous casualties of Roman encounters with barbarian nations. It bears the "marks of Christ" (Gal 6:17), again, the marks of capital punishment. It is a body depicted as bound and chained in visual representation; it is a body led in triumph to express (Roman) peace through victory.[69] Instead of endeavoring to stand in a line of *summi viri*, Paul's consciousness concerning his marginalization enables him to go down and stand in a line with all the defeated nations. Standing in line with the defeated nations means that he has "become like them" (Gal 4:13).

Paul presents himself as a man without others to dominate, both in terms of assemblies he was formerly persecuting and in terms of his relationships with other bodies. He is not necessarily a manly soldier in the most impenetrable way throughout his letters. He is also a man who is not married, nor is he an ardent supporter of traditional marriage arrangements.[70] Paul does not act as the traditional household-head, or *paterfamilias*, who has dominion over wives, children, and slaves; not once does he narrate himself as being like a traditional father who enjoys dominion over others.[71] It could be that when Paul reports of his previous life in zealousness for the traditions of his fathers in Gal 1:14, he imagines himself as acting in a fatherly role; his placement in the A position in the semiotic diagrams I present here certainly would resonate with father behavior, such as that of the "father of the fatherland," who conquers the female lands.

However, after Paul's revelation from God in Galatians, he does not again persecute others; spatially, he goes down ("I did not go up . . .") and away. When he finally does go up[72] to Jerusalem with Barnabas, he tells the Galatians that he brought Titus, a Greek who apparently was not circumcised and not "compelled" to be (Gal 2:3).[73] Titus is a bodily symbol of Paul's consciousness concerning the Gentiles; it is telling that Paul has not hurt him as he had previously done to others. Paul brought Titus up to Jerusalem in order to show, perhaps, what he has learned about how he is connected to others. This knowledge and consciousness, called freedom, place them in danger of being enslaved by the "false brothers," who were secretly brought in to spy on them (Gal 2:4). Paul does not damage Titus's uncircumcised, non-Jewish body, but brings him along to Jerusalem. Jew and Greek stand together before the apostles, where Paul announces his good news of freedom from worldwide slavery for the defeated nations.

The Defeated Paul among the Nations: "Become Like Me" (Gal 4:12)

Paul's non-dominant male body is beaten and broken; he is no longer the beater and breaker, and this material and ideological position puts him in a state of having a lot in common with the defeated nations who are conquered and enslaved by Rome. The nations also occupy the bottom position in the hierarchy I propose. It is in the state of being weak, in fact, that Paul says he first met the Galatians: "you know that through weakness of the flesh I first brought you good news, and you did not despise or loathe your trial in my flesh, but you received me as a messenger of God, as Christ Jesus" (Gal 4:13–14).[74] The Galatians, rather than treat Paul as an enemy to destroy (as they might be expected to do!),[75] cared for his weakness in the flesh when he first arrived—even as he was ethnically different than they, and perhaps they had heard of his previous warrior behavior as had the assemblies in Judea.

Though Paul claims that goodwill has vanished and the Galatians now treat him as an enemy (Gal. 4:16), it is his report of this initial encounter and his declaration that he has "become as you are" that reveals a commonality in suffering between defeated peoples on the bottom, in the non-A position. That Paul has "become as you (the Galatians) are" signifies both his bodily state (suffering at the hands of those more powerful than he, as captives and slaves would) and consciousness (the recognition that all nations live under the same threat of violence at the hands of the Romans). Such a statement also signifies that he understands the Galatians as those who are beaten and suffering as he, and not just politely engaged in dogmatic theological debates about law and faith in a power-vacuum.

Paul has not just become as the Galatians are, however; he tells them to become as he is (*ginesthe hōs egō, hoti kagō hōs hymeis,* Gal 4:12). This phrase could be understood as Paul asking the Galatians to become like, or imitate him, possibly in relation to his conversion experience. Such becoming like one another is not necessarily a measure of assimilation or "call to sameness,"[76] but an acknowledgement that Paul has had a similar experience to the Galatians under Roman rule. To be sure, Paul elsewhere calls for "imitation" (1 Thess 1:6–7, 2:14; Phil 3:17; 1 Cor 4:16, 11:1), and such imitation is not without resultant power relationships and possible hierarchies of its own.[77] But, when examining Paul's own rhetoric in its Roman imperial context and shelving the over-theologized implications of Paul's conversion experience, we must ask what precisely is being imitated, and what is at stake in such imitation. For example, what, precisely, does it mean to become like Paul's body, which is unheroically broken and unmanly? Paul has gone down, and occupies a position on the bottom of the Romans/nations hierarchy holding up the world order. His weakness of the flesh is a documentation of persecution by mechanisms of strength, who have more corporeal and structural power than Paul. Imitating weakness and a dominated, penetrated Jewish male body in the context of Roman imperial ideology does not automatically register a vertical hierarchy and upward assimilation; in fact, such imitation requires downward mobility, away from the conquerors toward the conquered.

In a gender-critical re-imagination concerning Galatians, Paul's movement downward and outward, toward the crucified Christ and among the conquered nations, should no longer be seen as an effort to superimpose a unitary Christian faith onto an obsolete Jewish law. It is also not the story of upward mobility characterized by becoming real men in Christ. Becoming like Paul means giving up the dynamics of domination symbolized by impenetrable imperial masculinity, unveiling a larger umbrella of patriarchal power relationships. Disidentification with such hierarchy includes (re)turning to identification with the other, feminized, nations destined to be conquered by the Romans. If we attend to the ideology communicated by the visual and literary representation I have discussed above, it becomes clear that Paul is not the same man as what is represented as ideal or heroic, for which the victorious emperor serves as the example *par excellence*. Paul's masculinity changes from dominant to non-dominant and undergoes further shift toward femininity in Galatians.

The Defeated Paul as a Suffering Mother (Gal 4:19)

Paul transforms his non-dominant, non-A masculinity, exemplified by a loss of status, death, and weakness of the flesh, into the suffering of a woman in labor soon after he recalls the suffering that characterized how he first visited the Galatians: "my children, for whom again I suffer birth pains until Christ is formed in you . . . " (*tekna mou, hous palin ōdinō mechris hou morphōthē Christos en hymin*, Gal 4:19). I aim here not to make all of the connections between instances of maternal imagery in the New Testament or the Bible as a whole, but to begin to re-connect Paul's appearance as a woman and (single!) mother with the transformed consciousness and downward mobility among the defeated nations in the context of Roman imperial ideology. The weakness and brokenness characterizing the Paul of just a few verses earlier in Galatians is here manipulated into an act of creation. But this creation does not appear to happen the proper or natural way, that is, with a man. It is a creation out of nothing, from the bottom, by a seemingly defeated woman. I suggest that Paul's birth pains are a symbol of the labor for a new creation of different relationships between Jews and other defeated nations on the bottom together, echoing his scriptural context and challenging his exilic situation under Roman rule.

Paul, sent among the defeated nations, is in a painful way also becoming their mother. When commentators attend to this verse at all, they usually emphasize its difficulty and metaphorical nature. Then they point out the places where Paul refers to himself as a father or otherwise a man and, therefore, the defender of gender hierarchy (more specifically, patriarchy).[78] My re-imagination of Paul's self-presentation questions the seemingly unproblematic naturalness of Paul's manhood *and* womanhood. To fully draw out the obvious modern (hetero)sexism and fear of gender transgression, specifically female-identified males, driving the history of interpretation of Paul's maternal imagery is another, related, project.[79] It is sufficient to say, at the moment, that Paul as a mother crying out in labor with her Christ-shaped children is a provocative (trans)gendered image that should be just "sat with" in its complexity.

In other words, the metaphor of birth and birth pains does not allow us to ignore taking Paul's reconfigured self-image seriously. Paul's description of "her"self as a mother in labor pains is unique to Galatians among the letters, but only in terms of its describing the moment of birth. Elsewhere Paul fashions "her"self a mother when s/he narrates "her"self as "a nurse cherishes her own children" (*alla egenēthēmen nēpioi en mesō hymōn, hōs ean trophos thalpē ta eautēs tekna*; 1 Thess 2:7) and describes the Corinthian "brothers" as "infants" (*nēpiois*) to whom Paul gives "milk, not solid food" (1 Cor 3:1–2). S/he has given birth to Onesimus, whom s/he calls "my child" (. . . *tou emou teknou, hon egennēsa en tois desmois, Onēsimon*, Phlm 10), using the same language of generation as the genealogical lists in the LXX and Matthew, to be sure, but also as s/he does for Hagar and the free woman just a few short sentences later in Gal 4:21—5:1 (see below for discussion).[80] The memory of Paul as a mother who (breast)feeds children also exists beyond the canonical letters; it is milk, and not blood, that pours out of Paul's body and onto a Roman soldier's breastplate immediately following the beheading according to the *Acts of Paul*.[81]

Anxiety about masculinity in light of maternal imagery has no doubt prevented us from fully seeing that Paul's narrative act of personifying "her"self as a mother in birth pains (*ōdinō*) in Galatians 4:19 also has critical resonance with the Israelite prophetic tradition of movement toward the reconciliation of Israel and the nations, just as his call does. This movement is signified by the reinstitution of Jerusalem as the chosen city of the God of Israel, where all the nations shall serve together. Zion is, of course, also personified as a woman,[82] and she is transformed from being ravaged and in mourning[83] to writhing and in birth pain.[84] In the prophetic material such pains are eventually transformed into characterizations of a new Jerusalem, as a mother who does not suffer birth pains (see below in relationship to the free woman in Gal 4:21–31).[85] Sometimes the city is personified, and sometimes the people, but in each case the birth pangs signal the pain of making a different situation for God's people and the turning away from idolatry. In Isaiah,[86] for example, the gates of Zion open for the righteous nation calling on the name of the LORD, who will call all other nations to join "her" in doing so, and the people describe their state of being as "like a woman with child approaching childbirth, writhing and screaming in her pangs, so are we become because of you, O LORD . . ." (Isa 26:17). In Jeremiah, Zion gone astray from God is portrayed as a heavily adorned woman in labor: "I hear a voice as of one in labor pains; Anguish as of a woman bearing her first child; The voice of fair Zion; Panting, stretching out her hands: 'Alas for me! I faint before the killers!'" (Jer 4:31).

The intense labor of personified lands and peoples is set in the context of exile that the prophets address.[87] Zion is devastated and in pain due to her ravaging and exile at the dominating hands of an empire, and the birth pangs denote the struggle of a dominated people. Birth pains also designate several other cities/nations struggling and moving toward recognition of the God of Israel as theirs. In Jeremiah's protracted judgment on all the nations where many of them are personified as women, Edom's warriors are depicted as being like "a woman suffering birth pains" (Jer 49:22), and Damascus has grown "weak" and "turned around to flee . . . Pain and anguish have taken hold of her; Like a woman in childbirth" (Jer 49:24). Micah's characterization of Zion directly associates her birth pains with exile: "Why do you utter such cries? / Is there no king in you / Have your advisors perished / That you have been seized by writhing like a woman suffering birth pains? / Writhe and scream, fair Zion / Like a woman in labor! / For now you must leave the city / And dwell in the country / And you will reach Babylon" (Mic 4:10).[88]

In each case briefly presented here, Israel and other nations are personified as women suffering in the pain of birth during a time of exile (for Israel) leading to restoration (including the nations). The potential implied in rendering the struggle of collective peoples as birth, however, is that the children will serve the one God—and not "not-gods." Most especially in Isaiah, the suffering of Zion—characterized by her birth pains—will be transformed into that which redeems the nations, bringing the blessing of restoration and *shalom* to all peoples (Isa 53:5).[89]

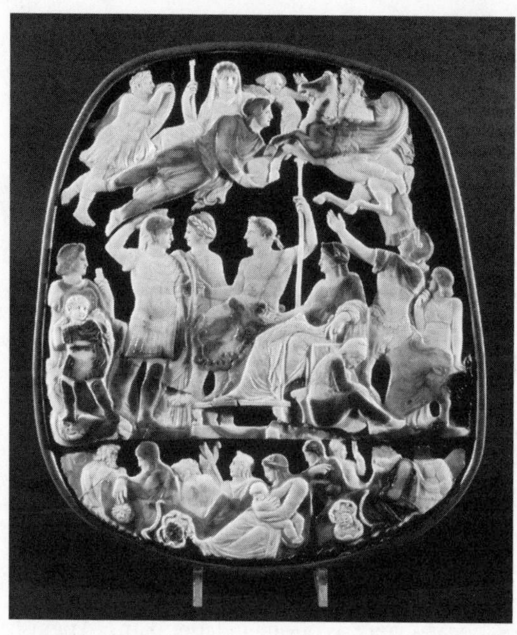

Figure 24. The "Grande Camée de France," the largest known gem, cut in Rome around 20 C.E. *In the center, Livia sits beside her son Tiberius and other family members; the now divine Augustus watches from above. In the lowest register sit barbarian families. Cabinet des Medailles, Bibliothèque Nationale, Paris. Photo © Erich Lessing / Art Resource, N.Y.*

The universality of the one God, the creator of all, is expressed through all the nations gathering to serve in peace, putting down swords: "Nation shall not take up / Sword against nation / They shall never again know war" (Mic 4:3).[90] All will serve the God of Israel, and Jerusalem will be restored as a place of freedom from the slavery and exile, characterized by submission to imperial power, for all the nations.[91] Paul uses gendered imagery to signify a major current in his tradition: exodus, exile, restoration.[92] Whether this pattern is called apocalypticism or prophecy, it symbolizes a new relationship and world-order born of non-violent reconciliation among enemies[93] that lies in dramatic contrast to what Paul himself calls "the present evil age" (*tou aiōnos tou enestōtos ponērou*, Gal 1:14).

When we cease worrying about the implications for Paul's manhood of the metaphorical gender transformation in Gal 4:19, we become able to see that Paul too uses birth pangs to signify the formation of new relationships among her children in a new creation within her "present evil age"—the Roman imperial context—likened to exile and defined by domination over all the nations. At this moment, she too moves from a penetrated and ravaged non-A position to the potentially transformative exodus position of bringing forth a new creation where all the nations will enjoy the *shalom*—the worldwide peace—the one God of Israel provides. In this peace, nations no longer are at war with one another, but are united at Jerusalem in restoration.

The image of Paul as a generating mother is a comment on and contrast to the dominant fertility paradigm of the Roman Empire as shown in visual and literary representation concerned with the fate of the nations. While Roman emperors guarantee racial fertility and reproduction through conquering and plundering the nations in the name of their version of peace, Paul's fertility with the Galatians is born of the physical pain and struggle of care and support among the conquered. Paul's model of manipulated fertility is a counter-impression of that portrayed on the Grand Camée de France, for example (figure 24). On this imperial gem, representatives of barbarian nations sit in the slavery of the bottom register with their children; they sit underneath the imperial family, where their reproduction is captured. Paul's birth pains, echoing the prophetic tradition of Zion and the nations in a struggle to turn toward the God of Israel who will restore them, herald the end of suffering and new relationships between the nations under God's—and not Caesar's—universal sovereignty.[94]

In Galatians 4:19 Paul—the defeated woman, the laboring mother—is concerned for her children inside whom Christ is taking shape. Christ has also taken shape inside Paul according to his own birth story in Gal 1:15–16 and now, from a defeated position, Paul births a new batch of children who should display the same dynamics of Christ, thus "becoming like me" even more. Some have suggested that this particular dynamic or metaphor is difficult to picture.[95] I suggest that Paul's birth pains give us a clue about the prophetic path toward a restructured Jerusalem and reconciliation for all of the nations through abandonment of the beings "who by nature are not gods" (Gal 4:9), that is, the emperor and other human representatives of imperial domination acting as gods, toward whom the Galatians acted as slaves. It is the birth pangs, born of consciousness concerning the dynamics of empire and defeat—Christ in me (Paul) and in you (Galatians)—that provides the way for Paul's children of all nations to recognize their connectedness with one another and act accordingly.

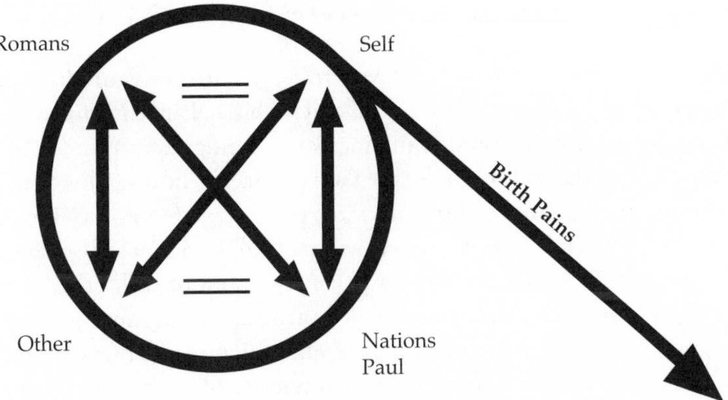

Figure 25. Birth Pains of New Creation among the Defeated Nations (Gal 4:19)

Paul, already in the non-A position within the Romans/nations hierarchy, becomes a mother-conduit for a different relationship among the defeated nations to whom he has gone as a result of her own altered consciousness and (re)birth. The birth pains mark the transition to an alternate structure characterized by inter-national solidarity among the defeated—literally, solidarity between the defeated nations.[96] As such, on the above diagram, the birth pains label the line from the non-A position going out from the vertical hierarchy of the semiotic diagram into a different, horizontal pattern of relationships among Jews and Gentiles. Through this semiotic diagram I have also hinted at the position of Paul's children that I discuss in the next section.

Many studies have focused on imagining Paul as a stern father or have simply taken his domineering manhood for granted;[97] very few have thought seriously about what the implications of Paul's self-presentation—alternately as ruthless soldier, broken man, *and* mother—are for how s/he behaves toward others and what kind of relationships s/he imagines are possible between Jews and Gentiles on the bottom of the Romans/nations hierarchy. In a gender-critical re-imagination, Paul's self-presentation is marked by its gender instability. Such instability is not necessarily uncommon to gender constructs upon closer inspection. But striking here is the transformation—from conquering male, to conquered male identified with other defeated peoples, to laboring mother—and how that results in both a loss of status and the creation of something new from below. This transformation appears most *unnatural* in the context of Roman imperial ideology, which promotes upward gender mobility and curtails the fertility of those who are conquered and assimilated. Paul's motherhood in Gal 4:19 serves as the creative impetus for alternative relationships among the defeated nations—Jewish and others.

Bear One Another's Burdens: A Movement of Inter-national Solidarity

Going out of the vertical, hierarchical pattern represented by Paul's Roman imperial context requires more than labor pains and (re)birth. Paul encourages the Galatians to model unnatural, non-dominating power configurations in the service of reunification of all the nations under the God of Israel. S/he does this by modeling deconstructed masculinity and transformed, procreative femininity him/herself. But those in the assemblies of Galatia to whom Paul writes must also endeavor to fully live into their new Christ-shape and consciousness of each other's suffering. After they, like Paul, have been transformed themselves, they must also act differently with one another. In Galatians, part of what this means is that circumcision is no longer the crucial marker of hierarchy or difference. However, this is not because the details of the Israelite law have been overcome in favor of Christian faith.

Paul makes clear at the end of Galatians that the circumcision debate is a red herring of sorts, a futile controversy among her progeny since "neither circumcision nor foreskin is anything, but a new creation (is everything)" (*oute gar peritomē ti estin oute akrobustia alla kainē ktisis*, Gal 6:15). This is not necessarily because Jewishness needs to be overcome. Circumcision could be seen as a marker of Jewish difference, but difference from whom must be asked—circumcision may differentiate Jews from nations, but it also differentiates Jews and Romans. Even if circumcision is not exclusive to Jews, one of the stereotypes used by the Romans to label Jews is circumcision.[98] Circumcision is a stereotypical marker of difference insofar as it locates non-Roman ethnic affiliation—just as pale skin, limed hair, *sagus*, and *bracae* are for Gauls; dark skin is for Ethiopians; bored ears, turbans, and big moustaches are for Arabs; and strange headgear is for Spaniards.[99] The linkage of these attributes with their proper non-Roman designation is important to naturalize patterns of domination. Paul, as boundary-transgressor at the margins, is aiming for a disruption of this natural order by insisting that such stereotypes be overcome. In the counter-hegemonic new creation, the signals for what counts as Jewish (circumcision) and not-Jewish (foreskin) are scrambled to dominant eyes and sensibility. Assimilation into one stereotype will not accomplish the goal of solidarity among the defeated.

The longing and pain for new creation and freedom are appropriate characterizations for Paul's Galatian situation in the face of the exilic conditions represented by the Roman Empire. In a context of marginalization, in-fighting among dominated groups (the nations) can seem small in the face of the larger problems, such as whether to adhere to the Roman imperial order that Paul calls slavery. In what follows, I give a sketch of what this new creation entails on the ground, among the defeated nations, according to Paul's impassioned pleas to her children.

The Politics of the New Creation

The new creation, once born, is marked by solidarity and mutual relationship among defeated nations. Let me return for a moment to Paul as mother of all the defeated nations to address this issue in proper perspective. In Gal 4:19, Paul is giving birth to children who also appear to be pregnant, but with a not-fully-formed Christ. As if this were not confusing enough gender-wise, the children (*tekna*) all are born at once. There is no first son here. No rightful heir is painfully coming out of Paul as he should according to law, Jewish or Roman. Those circumcised and those with foreskins are being (re)born at the same time. The form of Christ is in Paul and the impetus for his going among the nations, who also are incubating the same shape. Furthermore, the Christ-shape is not readily identifiable in a place within the vertical social hierarchy as one (A) or other (non-A).

Paul has come to the consciousness that his nation is as endangered as others throughout the Roman Empire—that is, it will inevitably be conquered and made to serve the empire as slaves. He puts down his weapons of domination, asks others to do the same, gives birth to children of this non-violent shape of the defeated, and tries to share a table in peaceful solidarity at Antioch in Galatians 2.[100] The table shared by Jews and other nations is presumably a part of Paul's "gospel for the nations," for which he receives the "right hands of fellowship" from Cephas, James, and John. In such meal settings, Paul consistently requests that the strong care for the weak (Rom 14 and 15), that the rich wait for the poor to start eating (1 Cor 11). Paul recalls that uncircumcised and circumcised share meals together, that the "truth of the gospel" (Gal 2:14) requires the different groups of the defeated to connect with one another in the same space without duplicating vertical hierarchical domination. This is the task of the new creation ushered in by mother Paul.

Such solidarity among the defeated would be a substantial challenge to Roman world rule. Kahl has called this movement the "one-an(d)-other" pattern in Paul, characterized by what she calls the "Jerusalem Agreement"[101] occurring before the Antioch meal in Galatians.[102]

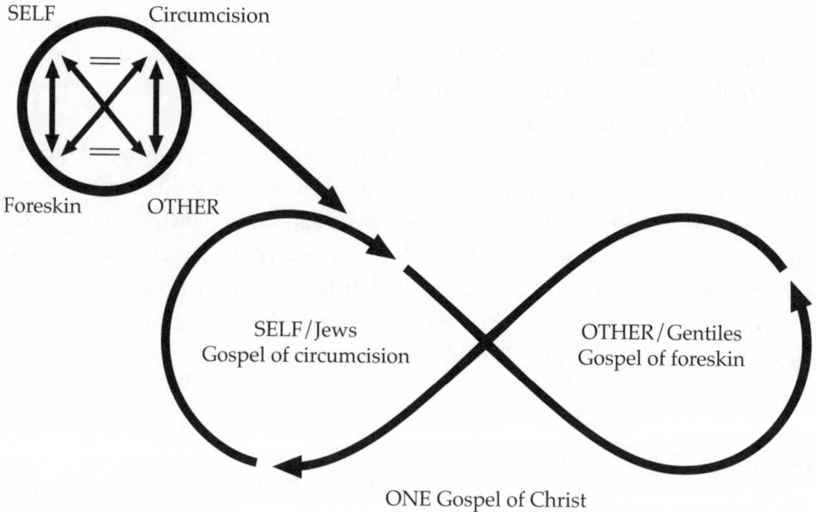

Figure 26. Jerusalem "Agreement"

This agreement is what finally is able to overcome the battle order represented by conquest and capture. Jews and Gentiles are connected to each other in a non-hierarchical way, which does not fit into the world order represented by the semiotic square diagram. I add the new creation element represented by Paul's labor pains here, maintaining that this movement happens as a result of overcoming a battle order promoted by Paul that is actually occurring on the bottom of a larger battle order represented by the Roman Empire. And, the dynamics of new creation and birth pains continue to signify the struggle involved in reconciliation between defeated nations (figure 27).

It is telling that, though Paul calls Jews and other nations her children, they are also one in Christ. Here, again, "one" does not have to mean "same"; from the view on the bottom—Paul's marginalized view, and the view among the nations—it can mean solidarity. The rendering of vertical hierarchy obsolete does not require assimilation into sameness and denial of difference; such assimilation, it would seem to me, characterizes identification with the top rather than

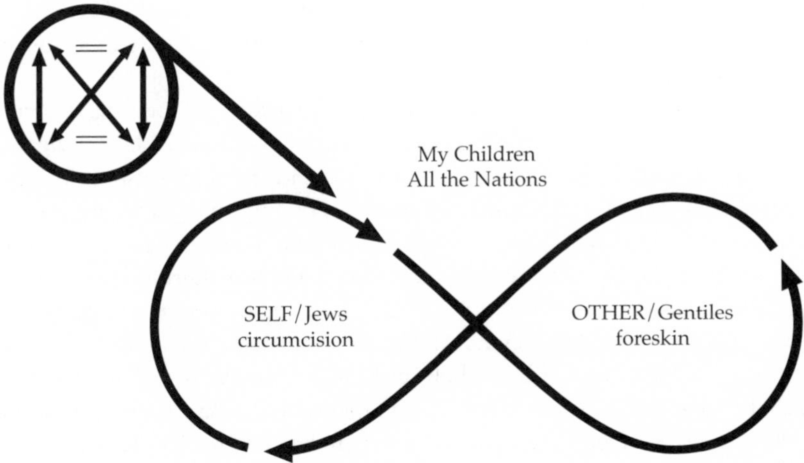

Figure 27. New Creation: One-an(d)-other, All the Nations

labor among those on the bottom. In fact, in Galatians Paul goes to great lengths to say that those who are not circumcised should not, under any circumstances, do so—if the Galatians become circumcised, "Christ will be of no profit" to them (Gal 5:2). Yet they are still to participate in the new creation designated by "oneness in Christ" while maintaining physical differences. It is their heritage as sons of Abraham, through whom all the nations, regardless of differences or location, are blessed (Gal 3:8, see below).

The Uniform of International Solidarity (Gal 3:26–29)

Physical differences—marked on and by the body—are lurking under the "clothing of Christ" that all of the (Galatian) children are to put on in 3:26–28,[103] culminating in the famous statement "there is not Jew or Greek, there is not slave or free, there is not male and female, for you all are one in Christ Jesus" (*ouk eni Ioudaios oude Hellēn, ouk eni doulos oude eleutheros, ouk eni arsen kai thēlu; pantes gar hymeis heis este en Christō Iēsou*, Gal 3:28). This phrase has tended to be interpreted as "no longer . . . ," emphasizing the temporal difference-erasing quality of Christian initiation, as if to implicitly say, "Galatians, previously you were observing the (Jewish) law, and now you are baptized into (Christian) faith, like me, where none of that matters any longer."[104] Much recent interpretation, particularly of the feminist variety, has focused on the question of equality, sameness, and differences between men and women in the Pauline, and therefore Christian, assemblies.[105] In both cases, the bodies of participants undergo shifts from presumably among one of the categories to One in Christ.

When we take a developed sense of Christianity over and against Judaism out of Paul's logic, however, such interpretations largely fall apart. Though this particular statement has a long and varied history of interpretation in its own right, there has not been much of a concentrated effort to see this phrase, like much of Galatians, as an expression of minority consciousness, or even resistance, in light of Roman imperial ideology.[106]

Gender-critically—remembering the dynamics of defeat and suffering structuring Paul's letter—there are some observations to make about hierarchy linking this statement to Roman imperial, and Paul's own transformed, consciousness. The categories of identity and status mentioned here are not only opposed to one another in the vertical hierarchy represented by the semiotic diagrams discussed above. They also designate visible markers of the bodies under Roman rule. Jews, Greeks, slaves, free, male, female—all are submitted to Rome by destiny and force, and all are part of one world under Caesar. A similar phrase in deutero-Pauline Colossians gives categories more explicitly symbolic of Roman enemies, as well as important to Paul in Galatians: "Greek and Jew, circumcision and foreskin, barbarian, Scythian, slave and free" (Col 3:11). What if we were to begin to see Gal 3:28 as part of Paul's broader argument for a transformed consciousness and solidarity among the defeated?[107] In a Roman imperial ideology concerning the fate of all the nations, conquest and enslavement of all those presumed naturally inferior to the Romans includes, and even creates and manages to some extent, the categories Paul mentions here. Jew and Greek, slave and free, male and female—all are one under the banner of the emperor, through his violent peacemaking process.

Paul, as an apostle who goes down among the defeated nations, has had to come to terms with the ideological configuration designating all as other and inferior to Roman rule. In the prophetic new creation Paul is struggling so hard in labor to usher into being, all of the nations must turn away from idolatry—civic worship of the one master of the world—and turn as children toward the God of Israel, the creator of the world, who will reconcile them with one another and end war forever. If this is the case, then Micah's call for all nations to put down their weapons and stop fighting one another has special application in relation to Gal 3:28. In the new mode of relationships among the defeated, the bodies on the bottom of a Romans/nations hierarchy should cease their perpetuation of divisions between one another and understand that there are larger dynamics of violence and persecution structuring their world. They might realize that there are no divisions between them, as persecuted minority groups, that matter. The little details of conflict (e.g., over circumcision, table manners, and so on) should not constitute the basis for continued strife among the defeated; the conflict should be relocated between the conquered (all the nations) and their conquerors (Rome) and eventually transformed by reincorporating into Jerusalem. The difference here is spatial, not temporal. Paul brings the possibility of reconciliation *toward* the nations at the ends of the earth, rather than imploring them to return to the geographic locality of a new Jerusalem *from* those same ends. He goes *out* to the frontiers to bring the news of an alternative central capital to the one they currently serve.

To overcome the dynamics of worldwide suffering, death, and victimization, the defeated should enter into a new creation of a mutual sharing relationship, crystallized by the meal, but extending into daily life under Roman rule. Additionally, the "no Jew and Greek . . ." phrase does not end with no male and female. All are one in Christ, the same crucified Christ in Paul and her children. In Gal 3:29 all are designated the "seed" (*sperma*) of Abraham and heirs (*klēronomoi*) according to the promise. All of the nations are related to one another as children and heirs of the new creation. Therefore, I locate Gal 3:28 as a call to solidarity among the defeated, as further evidence of the "one-an(d)-other" paradigm Paul promotes. I map it onto the new creation below.

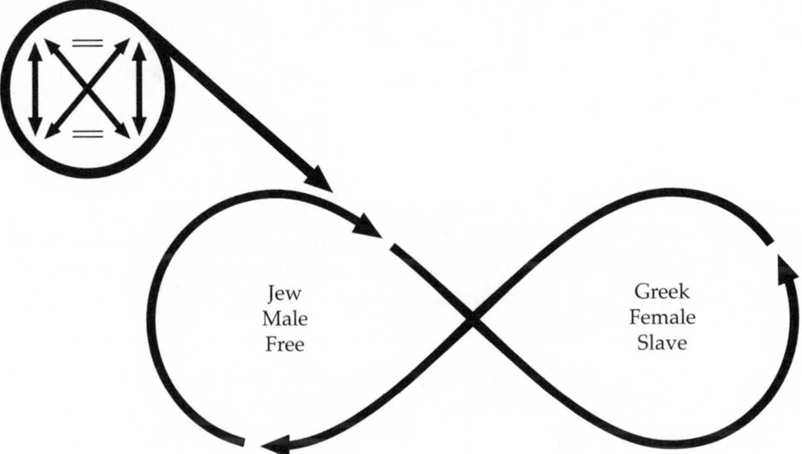

Figure 28. Galatians 3:28 in Paul's New Creation

The new creation is born among the defeated, at the bottom, yet is right in the middle of a world interested in maintaining a divide-and-conquer approach to humanity. These social divisions are not just imitated in the moment of battle, but in everyday life. This solidarity among the defeated is called one in Christ, and is Christ-shaped. It is a unity under the banner of Roman capital punishment among those who are suffering largely because of violence that is all too familiar in their environment. The Galatians themselves, who Paul hopes have not "suffered in vain" (*tosauta epathete eikē*, Gal 3:4) have seen Christ crucified "before their very eyes" according to Gal 3:1.

If we take seriously the extensive visual representation commemorating conquest and the actual practice of execution throughout the Roman Empire, we do not have to imagine that the Galatians were there at Golgotha for Christ's actual crucifixion, or that they had some sort of theological vision of the savior. Rather, Paul is imploring the Galatians to remember that they, too, are weak, just as so many others are who are under the emperor's wing.[108] But gaining strength does not require cosmetic upward mobility through assimilation (i.e., circumcision) into another weak group perceived to be less weak, for example, because of exemption from certain civic taxes and honors. It requires staying on the bottom and opposing vertical hierarchy from that location by making an alternate structure.

The uniform of this alternate structure is the clothing of Christ that the Galatians are to put on through baptism (Gal 3:27). Such clothing confirms membership as children in the new creation. It renders vertical ethnic, gender, and social status hierarchies, communicated by the outward appearance of bodies, obsolete, or at least invisible to the eyes.[109] The care the Romans take to represent real men as stable, virile, and free, and the nations as penetrated women enslaved to their conquerors, is challenged by this statement. Oneness in Christ and the one God of Israel is a unification of defeated nations from below in defiance of Roman imperial ideology consolidating the whole world, composed of all the nations, as one under Roman law and hierarchy. Paul presents this oneness as gender transgression and solidarity that destabilizes racial, gender, and cosmic order.

Performing International Solidarity (Gal 5:9—6:2)

The contrast between a paradigm of Roman domination and that of inter-national solidarity is expressed in Galatians 5 in the contrast between "works of the flesh" (including "divisions and sects"; see Gal 5:20) and "fruits of the spirit." Paul directs the Galatian children to "serve one another as slaves" (Gal 5:13) and "love your neighbor as yourself," a quotation from Lev 19:18 that Paul calls a summary of every law (*pas nomos*, Gal 5:14), and not to provoke or envy one another (Gal 5:25). If the children, representatives of the nations, "bite and devour" one another, they might consume each other (Gal 5:15). Those who behave in divisive, dominating ways "will not inherit the *basileian theou*" (Gal 5:21). The reign of God is indeed a challenging inheritance: it is a new creation against and beyond Caesar's natural cosmic structure. The new creation arises through Paul's birth and the Galatian children's after the world (*kosmos*) is crucified to Paul and s/he to it (Gal 6:14). The new creation is also likened to "faith working through love" (Gal 5:6).[110] The love works if it is that love for the other that enables the Galatians to sit with one another and "bear the burdens" across boundaries and differences from each other.

As a final reminder that Paul is penetrable and therefore what the Romans would have considered unmasculine, s/he states that s/he "bears the marks of Christ" on his/her body (Gal 6:17). This reading of Paul, as being on the bottom the whole way through Galatians, signifies a dwelling among the defeated. The new creation (life) out of old world (death), privileging those who are supposed to be dead and stay dead, is a Jewish criticism of Roman cosmic order and peace. What is promoted as natural in Roman imperial ideology is challenged by the unnaturalness of Paul's good news to the nations. Again, these virtues should be seen as desirable for an assembly among the defeated.

The image of oneness and unification of Jews and other nations under the banner of Israel's God requires solidarity and cooperation, not the division or assimilation characterized by allegiance to Caesar's world order. This image is gendered: instead of living up to male/female imperial expectations of unequivocal domination and subordination, Paul models uncharacteristic vulnerability. S/he advocates living into an-other world, the new creation, through inter-national community resistance and nonconformity to the Roman imperial structure, the metanarrative ordering the world and helping to keep peace at the time. This resistance is born of the consciousness required in Christ to break the cycle of violence, to turn one's back on persecuting and annihilating other peoples and places. By turning around and away from violence toward the outside and lowly, Paul models a masculinity and femininity that defies the Roman obligation to conquer and promotes allegiance among the defeated: Jews and other nations, captive women's bodies, bound (male and) female barbarians, those rendered inevitably powerless by Roman might.

Summary

Paul critiques and reconfigures his/her world on gendered terms. Such gendered terms include a redefinition, or re-imagination, of how Jews and Gentiles are related to one another from the beginning of the story of Israel and should continue to act as siblings toward one another. Such familiarity is a prophetic criticism of, again, a Roman imperial ideological configuration of genealogy and family relative to the nations where they are destined to be defeated. Paul articulates an alternative "fate of the nations" with the God of Israel rather than that which they are to experience with Rome. In the following section, I describe the fate of the nations according to Pauline imagination through a discussion of Paul's familial imagery and use of personifications in the "Sarah-Hagar Allegory" of Gal 4:21—5:1.

The Fate of the Nations in Pauline Imagination (Gal 4:21—5:1)

In this final section, I complete my exegetical overview of a gender-critical re-imagination of Paul as apostle to the defeated nations through a re-reading of what I consider to be his lynchpin argument, the Sarah-Hagar Allegory in Gal 4:21—5:1. The transformed Paul, in this letter, invokes a different theo-political destiny for all the nations than enduring conquest and submission to imperial designs. He implores the Galatians to turn away from complicity in systematic oppression—away from Egypt, from Babylon, and from Rome—and the making of another way through transformation of relational circumstances in the new creation. Paul provides justification of these alternative power relations through invoking family constructs all the way back to Israel's founding narrative, Genesis, and continues an emphasis on the interrelationship, prophetic integration, and restoration of Israel and other nations.

It is in the scriptural context of prophetic restoration against the ideological backdrop of the Roman Empire that I propose an alternative gender-critical re-imagination of this allegory through the transformed Paul I have presented throughout this chapter. Rather than an aberration or theological turning-around of Paul's rhetoric, this passage is fully part of his/her articulation of the fate of the nations as divergent from and resistant to the fate represented in image and text by Roman imperial ideology. This allegory represents a counter-hegemonic discourse indicative of Paul's strategy of imagination.

Paul insists that all the nations are descended from Abraham and belong to the God of Israel before the covenant is sealed with circumcision. Such interrelationship, which Paul draws upon to argue for reconciliatory relationships in the new creation s/he is laboring over, is brought to the fore through and not negated by the Sarah-Hagar allegory. Paul also uses a Genesis story, with echoes of the prophets who do the same, to say something about the Galatians' current situation. But, as allegory, it is also not precisely the Genesis story to which Paul alludes. Rather than the two women being opposed to one another (which is a reading of how the Genesis story proceeds), Paul positions the mothers as two options ("covenants") for the city of Jerusalem personified: isolation/slavery/exile or interrelation/freedom/restoration. Third, I understand the Galatians' current situation to be faced with integration into Roman imperial order through conquest. In that light, Paul's insistence on the restoration/freedom option embodied by "Jerusalem above" brought about by all the nations turning toward the God of Israel (the one God) and away from the Roman emperor and family (the not-gods), serves in this allegory as a further call toward inter-national solidarity from below, among the defeated.

Abraham as the Father of the Nations

Galatians 4:21—5:1 is positioned as the so-called capstone to Paul's argument in Galatians 3 and 4. Whereas traditional, idealist interpretation would rather focus on these two chapters as heavily dogmatic elaboration of Paul's Christian supersession and the battle of law against faith, in a gender-critical re-imagination I see the language Paul uses as delineating the genealogical priority and interrelationship of all the nations from Abraham onward, drawing on the world genealogy or table of nations given in Genesis 10. Mother Paul voices her allegorical call to freedom after what is thought to be one of the clearest pronouncements that she is angry with the Galatians. Perhaps still metaphorically in labor, Paul states that s/he wants to be present with you (Galatian children being born) and "change my voice because I am at a loss about you" (Gal 4:20).[111] Then Paul switches from her own desires to what s/he says are those of the children: "Tell me, the ones who want to be under the law, do you not hear the law? For it has been written, Abraham had two sons . . ." (*legete moi, hoi hypo nomon thelontes einai, ton nomon ouk akouete?*

. . . *Abraam dyo hyious eschen*, Gal 4:21–22). Those who want to be under the law should understand something about Abraham: his genealogical status as father of many nations. The Galatians should listen, because Paul makes some points that refer to earlier parts of the letter's discourse.

Earlier in Galatians 3 and 4, Paul invokes the Genesis tradition of all the nations being generated from the God of Israel and Abraham. Abraham's first appearance in these two chapters is as the one who believed God. Abraham is Paul's own answer to the series of questions, from 3:1–3:5,[112] of how exactly the Galatians received the spirit—through works of law or hearing faith. Since they saw Christ "openly portrayed as crucified," how could they have any doubt about how to receive the spirit and faith? Abraham trusted God, according to Paul, and was made righteous out of his situation. The faith that Abraham has in God comes out of the promises God made in Genesis, including the blessing of many nations and that his offspring will inherit the land (Gen 12:1–2; 17:4–6). Abraham, when told that many nations will issue forth from him, does what he is told: he drops what he is doing and leaves on a journey toward the land. As has been recently discussed by David Petersen, he also models non-violent behavior and conflict resolution toward others;[113] issues of disagreement are settled by Abraham's turning around and going the other way rather than making war, as in the story of the near-confrontation with Lot in Genesis 16. It is after this peaceful resolution with Lot that God tells Abraham that he and his offspring (who will be countless, like the "dust of the earth," Gen 16:16) will have all of the land, stretching out forever.

Paul argues that Abraham, the nations, and faith are closely connected through fatherhood and sonship: the ones "out of faith" are sons of Abraham (Gal 3:7). The nations, among whom Paul is dwelling, are connected to God through Abraham—through the writing that "out of faith" God would justify the nations (Gal 3:8). In fact, through Abraham, God promised to bless *panta ta ethnē*/all the nations (Gal 3:8). These nations include the circumcised and uncircumcised (Rom 4:1–12); Abraham is the father of all the nations, because he followed God before his own circumcision. It is Christ, the defeated one "hung on a tree," that becomes the curse activating the blessing of (all the) nations in Abraham (Gal 3:14). Christ is also the "seed," with Abraham, to whom was given the promise (Gal 3:16). The promise is not only that through Abraham all nations will be blessed, but that the "seed" he receives will be from his and Sarah's own, basically dead, bodies.[114] Life and land, for all of the nations, out of what appears impossible is the result of the promise in Genesis that Paul is invoking in Galatians.

Defeated Paul is sent to declare that all the nations are sons of God (and Abraham) through faith in Christ. But the Galatians are not only sons: Paul also calls them heirs of the promise, which connects them to Jerusalem above (see below). In Gal 4:1–7 Paul delineates how exactly slaves become sons, become heirs. There is a contrast between slavery, characterized by service to "elemental principles of the world" (*stoicheia tou kosmou*, Gal 4:3; see also 4:9) and "those who by nature are not gods" (*tois physei mē ousin theois*, Gal 4:8), and sonship, characterized by "knowing God" (Gal 4:9). Knowing God in this sense entails the turn from not-gods, as part of the prophetic call to engender consciousness among the nations as belonging to Israel and having a different destiny than being the victims of empire without end. In this sense, the transformation from slavery to inheritance can be thought of as the same movement into the new creation paradigm using the same semiotic structure as previously. The elemental principles represent Roman world order over all the nations, which the Galatians serve as slaves and is represented by not-gods. To become sons and heirs, the Galatians should enter into the consciousness and life-practice of the new creation among the nations.

In Galatians 3 and 4 Paul expresses the new creation using genealogical constructs, naming Abraham as the father of all the nations and then moving into birth pains, "her"self as the fashioner of different relationships among the defeated so as to engender inheritance. I will discuss the new Jerusalem that guarantees freedom from slavery for the heirs—the humanity who has a different shape—below.

Paul as a Mother among the Defeated Nations

In terms of gender and genealogy, Abraham is not the sole parent, nor Paul the only mother, of the Christ-formed children in Galatians. Through the only explicitly named allegory in all of his extant rhetoric, Paul manipulates the Hagar-Sarah mother entanglement from Genesis to further his unnatural genealogical justification of alternative power alignments[115] among the defeated. It is here, in Galatians 4:21—5:1, where Paul is most transparently attentive to a Jewish genealogical and prophetic framework as well as Roman political propaganda and imperial ideology, particularly personifications of lands and cities as female bodies. Paul identifies Hagar and the free woman (Sarah) as personifications of enslaved and free lands, respectively. Hagar is "Mount Sinai in Arabia," corresponding to "Jerusalem now," and is "in slavery with her children" (Gal 4:25). The other woman is "Jerusalem above," who is free and is "our mother" (Gal 4:26). Although Paul affirms that the Galatians are children of the free woman (Gal 4:31), it is clear that they know what it means to be children in slavery with their mother because he admonishes them not to "again be held by a yoke" (Gal 5:1).

After Paul quotes the text that gives Abraham as a father of two sons, he immediately says "which things are allegorized" (*hatina estin allēgoroumena*, Gal 4:24). Paul links his explanation of the "things allegorized" to an image using the women as examples. The women (*hautai*: note the feminine plural) represent

> . . . two covenants: one away from Mount Sinai, giving birth into slavery, who is Hagar. Hagar now is Mount Sinai in Arabia, and stands in line with

> Jerusalem now, for she slaves with her children. But Jerusalem above is free, and she is our mother. (Gal 4:24–26)[116]

The two women are two covenants and two cities, and appear to be opposed to one another. It is often supposed that Paul uses this allegory as a tour de force,[117] an explanation of the "contrast between the 'slavery' of the Israelites, who have the present Jerusalem as their 'mother,' and the 'freedom' of the Christians, whose mother is the Jerusalem above."[118] The women are further contrasted by linkage to law and promise.

Paul's use of *allēgoreō* indeed triggers all sorts of associations with textual references, metaphorical biblical exegesis, and veiled interests in predicting the end of Judaism and the beginning of Christianity.[119] Invoking allegory—the practice of using one thing to say something else and knowing, or hoping, the audience understands the double meaning intended[120]—also leaves room to make deep Christian-Jewish conflict out of this text. The use of women's bodies is a means to express corporate identity, particularly the identity of religions: Hagar-slavery-Judaism, Sarah-freedom-Christianity.[121] Hagar and Sarah as Paul present them have traditionally been read as allegorizing a battle-order of their own through their supposed opposition, despite Paul's own insistence that law is not opposed to the promises of God (Gal 3:21; see also Rom 3:29–31[122]). The battle order proposed by much of the history of interpretation corresponds to precisely the same world order Paul is also transgressing. Rather than show the women as columns next to each other, I map them out according to the dominant history of interpretation as follows:

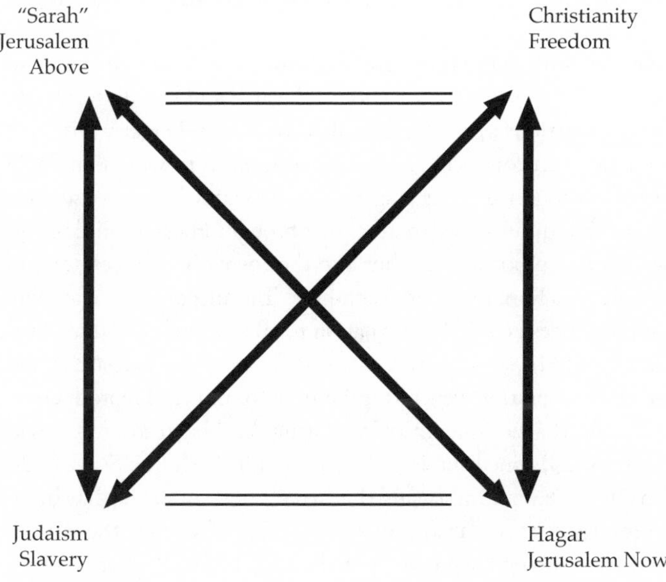

Figure 29. Battle Order According to the "Sarah-Hagar Allegory"

The spatial arrangement of this semiotic diagram shows the dominance of Jerusalem Above/Sarah (A) over Jerusalem Now/Hagar (non-A), who occupies the slave position associated with Jewish law, the synagogue, and flesh (non-B). Victorious Sarah occupies the position of promise/Christian spirit associated with the church (B).

The history of interpretation of this passage is unfortunate. However, the bound and cast-out Synagoga is not too far from another image of Paul's Hagar. It is unavoidably the case that Hagar in Galatians, as "Jerusalem now," is in slavery with her children. But we must ask who is doing the enslaving and what, precisely, should be cast out in the name of freedom. It is not necessarily the Jewish law (Torah) enslaving Hagar, nor need it be the case that the Pauline Sarah-church should defeat the Hagar-synagogue for all time. Church and synagogue are not valuable place-names for Paul's argument at all. And, again, there are larger power dynamics at work than these two women fighting each other.

I submit, alternatively, that Paul re-imagines a story from his Jewish prophetic tradition within and referring to his Roman imperial context to produce a political allegory for marginalized Jews and Gentiles alike in Galatia. When Paul says "these things are allegorized," he does not give a proof for Christian dogmatics against Jewishness but something closer to a Jewish critique of Roman imperial ideology that he has been articulating throughout Galatians using gendered imagery. The transformation of Paul and the restoration of all the nations from below is also continued in this allegory by naming "Jerusalem above"—that is, the transformed Jerusalem, the "light to the nations"—as our mother. This mother is, with Paul, the matriarch of the transformed, the city space where inter-national solidarity is practiced.

The examples of Roman visual representation I discuss in chapter 2 show some striking similarities between the allegorical Hagar[123] and the allegorical personifications of defeated nations as the Romans depicted them. Hagar is a dejected foreign woman who has been conquered and made to submit; to whom, in Paul's context, should now be obvious. Paul calls Hagar a slave woman who bears a son born according to flesh. Flesh indicates the dynamics that brought Hagar a child in Genesis: desperate coercion and probably rape, but also the coercion, conquest, and rape facing the nations in Paul's Roman imperial conquest. The allegorical Hagar who generates a son according to flesh could be any nation for Rome: Judea, Gallia, Armenia, Britannia, Germania, Hispania, Africa. She is defined by the patriarchal dynamics of submission and co-optation, generating children for imperial reproduction.

Paul gives a more specific identity by relating this Hagar to a place twice, Mount Sinai (Gal 4:24, 25); once she is "away from" (*apo*) Mount Sinai (4:24).[124] This Mount Sinai is in slavery, indicating that what Sinai stands for has been captured and enslaved. The phrase "away from Mount Sinai" echoes the situation of the nations and Israel being alienated from the God of Israel, that is, being engaged in separation and idolatry, before exile and restoration. Paul becomes even more specific by saying that Hagar "stands in line with Jerusalem now."[125] She is an allegorical personification of Jerusalem taken captive, and her enslaved children with her. Such a characterization also recalls the mourning Zion of First Isaiah; ideologically, "Jerusalem now" serves another master besides God. Paul's Hagar is parallel to Britannia in Tacitus's speech of Calgacus to the Britons on the verge of going to war with the Romans: "Britannia pays a daily price for her own enslavement, and feeds the enslavers, and . . . we, the new hands, worth least, are marked out to be made away with" (*Agricola* 31.2). In the same speech, we learn that women and children are carried off into slavery (see chapter 3).

Hagar, in other words, represents a Jerusalem where the (Israelite) people are enslaved, feeding others, paying a price to the masters for her enslavement. In Josephus's speech of Agrippa (see chapter 3) to dissuade the Jews from going to battle with Rome, several nations are also designated as being enslaved to Rome. The Hagar enslaved to Rome with her children is a woman that we can imagine representing her people and "standing in line with" a series of defeated nations, such as those in the Aphrodisias Sebasteion. As the city of Jerusalem, she is not figuratively enslaved to Torah, but rather she stands for imperial co-optation and resultant distortion of that same Torah. The Galatians should hear that law: it cries out as a bound captive. As such, Hagar in Galatians represents Jewish adherence to Roman world order, "away from Mount Sinai," away from the law of Moses. Images of the golden calf (Exod 32:1–8) and desire to turn back to the slavery of Egypt immediately arise. Hagar, then, sits in the slave position in the semiotic representations of world-order I have been using throughout this chapter.

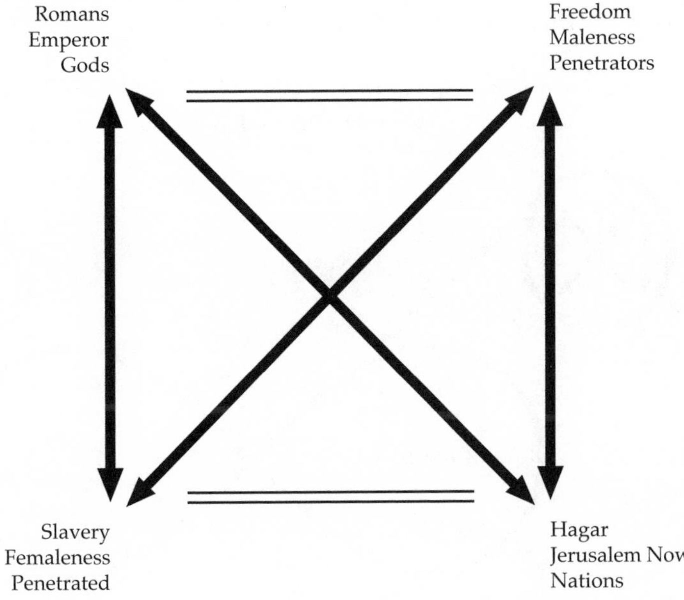

Figure 30. Hagar/"Jerusalem Now" Enslaved to Roman World Order

In this diagram (figure 30) I have placed Paul's Hagar in the non-A position, as in figure 29. However, the top A position has changed from Sarah to the enslavers, the Romans. Jerusalem now stands in line with the rest of the defeated nations. I see Paul's line of thought as a continuation of the consciousness-raising process exhibited throughout Galatians: Jews, Gauls, all the nations are enslaved. Paul has realized that Jerusalem now, of whom he was a product of sorts, is not in a strong or singular position.

Paul's contrast of the slave and free woman is not limited to denigrating one and celebrating the other, nor are the women necessarily engaged in a fight against each other as in Genesis.[126] While Hagar represents the dynamics of worldwide slavery, the free woman stands for the God-sponsored resistance and exit-pattern Paul has insisted upon, and even is giving birth to, in Galatians. She belongs not on top of Hagar, but as the mother of all the nations participating in the one-an(d)-other pattern designating the new creation.

Figure 31 maps both options for Jerusalem according to Paul's allegory. "Our mother" is that of the transformed, reconfigured Jews and nations in the new creation. The birth pains endured by Paul provide the way out of the vertical hierarchical structure and into relations of solidarity. The new creation represents the reconciliation of all the nations into Jerusalem above through their service to the God of Israel—that is, to the one God and *proper* life-giving relationship through following the Law of Sinai. In this re-imagination, law is not overcome, but freed from captivity. Here I call "away from Sinai" the dynamics leading back to the non-A Hagar position in the larger world order. Kahl has called the going back from the new creation (in my schema this is back into the womb!) Paul's Anathema (Gal 1:8–9).[127]

The allegorical free woman in Galatians is not a captive and therefore does not figure in a procession of conquered nations. Her son is born according to promise,

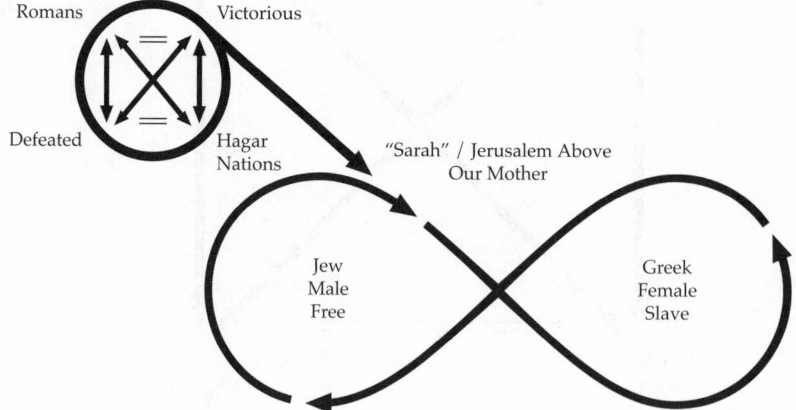

Figure 31. Sarah/Jerusalem Above as (Co-)Mother of All the Nations in the New Creation

that is, the Genesis promise from God that Sarah will bear an heir who will ultimately develop into many nations. But, according to Genesis 15:13, the offspring will be in slavery to a foreign power before attaining that freedom. "Jerusalem above" is designated by such freedom, again echoing the Exodus pattern of liberation.

But Genesis and Exodus are not all: through Paul's quotation of Isa 54:1, it becomes even clearer that "Sarah" is transformed into "Jerusalem above"—from the Zion in mourning to the Zion and the nations in the birth pains of new creation out of exile to the restored Jerusalem that is the "light to the nations":

> Rejoice, O barren one, the one not giving birth,
> Break forth and shout, the one not suffering birth pains,
> Since many are the children of the desert rather than the one having a man.[128]

This Jerusalem does not have a man but is barren, indicating that she has not been submitted to the same patriarchal procreative dynamics as Hagar. Yet her children will be many. This is a city, in contrast to Hagar's Jerusalem, who is activated by Abraham's seed gathered from the ends of the earth (Isa 41:8). As a reconstituted Jerusalem made for "the new heaven and earth," her people:

> shall build houses and live in them
> And plant vineyards and eat their fruits.
> They shall not build houses for others to live in
> Or plant for others to eat.
> For the days of my people (*tou laou mou*) shall be
> As long as the days of a tree.
> My chosen ones (*hoi eklektoi*) shall outlive
> The work of their hands.
> They shall not work for no reason
> They shall not bear children into a curse (*eis kataran*)
> Since (the) seed is blessed by God
> And their offspring will stay with them. (Isa 65:21–23 LXX)[129]

The freedom of "Jerusalem above" from the procreative coercion of imperial capture marks her as our mother. Of course our mother appears to be Sarah from Genesis—but I think there is a good reason Paul does not name her in his allegory. She is the Sarah who, like Paul, has been transformed from someone who persecutes to someone who is an organizer of an alternative structure with God's help—one where the people will not build for and feed those who dominate them, but build and grow and eat for themselves. As such this city is no longer the same Sarah as presented in Genesis.

Roman destiny dictates that the master race is entitled to ferret out and acquire all of the nations, and (re)name them in the spirit of making peace through conquest.

The free woman's lack of name signifies that she is an unrecognizable place, owned by no one. Empire cannot claim this land, this nation: "Jerusalem above" is out of the army's grasp, outside of territorial boundaries. She is beyond the inhabited world, beyond the margins. She is not captured and therefore unnamed. She does not produce children for the perpetuation of the master race, and neither should her Galatian children. The free woman is the co-mother, with Paul, of the new creation, in which the circumcised Jews and nations with foreskins are arranged in such a way that they no longer have any reason to imitate a divide-and-conquer approach to humanity. In relation to Roman imperial visual ideology, this Jerusalem is invisible and undetectable.

Two Covenants: with Caesar and with God

In Paul's imagination the free woman is the reconstituted Jerusalem who is the light to the nations, where all peoples should gather in peace, reconciliation, and self-determination according to First Testament prophetic rhetoric. The people of this city are called out of exile, and the peoples from the ends of the earth—all the nations, all those defeated—are called to enter her gates. That the two cities are women should not distract us from attention to Paul's manipulation of gendered power relationships. The cities represent two political choices: continuation under Roman rule (Hagar, slavery, natural reproduction of domination) or service to the one God and collective self-determination (Sarah, freedom, unnatural motherhood breaking the cycle of domination). Paul, similar to both the Israelite prophetic tradition and Roman imperial ideology, uses women here as signifiers of group identity, indicating that s/he is conversant in imperial propaganda. However, Paul manipulates these tropes—the women stand for something else, as their designation as "allegorized" signals—into two possibilities for the very same city of Jerusalem. I still would call these two covenants: a covenant with Caesar (slavery/Hagar) and a covenant with God (freedom/Sarah).

Given that the Roman imperial personification of conquered lands as women also functions as allegory for patterns of world domination and slavery for those defeated and their children, it follows that what is at stake in Paul's story is not necessarily a degradation of the actual Hagar or abandonment of Judaism. Rather, the two mothers of the Galatians—Paul and Sarah—represent the fertility and abundance flowing from the freedom of oneness in Christ and not curtailed reproduction and false unification under Caesar's self-serving interests.

Hagar's children in Paul's allegory are born into slavery, and they in turn persecute the children of the free woman. The "casting out" refers not to Hagar and Ishmael themselves, but to the conditions that create and maintain ethnically specific division and conquest. Paul uses allegory to identify the dynamics of resisting the worldwide slavery of imperial domination. In 5:1 s/he makes clear that the Galatians have a choice: "for freedom Christ has set us free; stand firm, therefore, and do not again be held to a yoke of slavery." In other words, the Galatians can choose their covenant: with Caesar, continuing slavery, or with the God who liberates. Paul may have made it difficult with allegory, yet the message remains: the Galatians might have been akin to Hagar's children, born into slavery, but they do not need to submit again to this yoke. They can be of transformed consciousness, becoming like each other, bearing each other's burdens. They can be Sarah's offspring. They can belong to Jerusalem above. They can be children out of empire's violent reach. The fate of all the nations, according to Pauline imagination, is to reconnect under the banner of Israel's God and put an end, finally, to their suffering at the hands of their dominators.

Conclusion

From a Roman imperial ideological perspective, Paul was a member of a conquered nation. He would have seen (and experienced) the totality and forced coherence of Roman imperial ideology and its relentless imaging. When he implores the "senseless" Galatians to see differently in order to escape their state of being bewitched, or fallen under the evil eye, he entreats them to remember "it was before your very eyes" that the Christ was "openly portrayed" as crucified (Gal 3:1–2). Paul's Galatians (north *or* south, all were defeated in the Roman province) did not see Jesus' crucifixion, but they did not have to. There were plenty of examples before *everyone's* eyes (in real life, in stone, on coins) of capture, torture, bondage and execution of the others in the name of affirming Rome's universal sovereignty through domination.

A gender-critical re-imagination of Paul as apostle to the defeated nations in Roman imperial and Jewish contexts raises the need for correctives regarding both the new perspective situating Paul as a Jew among Gentiles, as well as work that takes seriously a reconsideration of the Roman Empire as the politico-religious context of early Christian literature and social formations. The new perspective has rightly pointed out the thorough Jewishness of Paul and the New Testament writers, and empire-critical work has situated that Jewishness as being shaped by and responding to Roman claims of universal domination over all the nations. I submit that traditional cultic and theological separations are inadequate for understanding Paul's mission to the Gentiles and alleged rejection of the Jews.

However correct recent work is for re-orienting scholars and other interpreters of early Christianity, lenses are not trained to look at the pictures or fully see how imperial power and Jewishness are linked to gendered constructions of power relationships. Further attention to how power operates on gendered and sexualized terms will only benefit a redescription of early Christianity, particularly as represented in the New Testament, as a series of negotiations of and resistance to the imperial project that indelibly shaped the world in which these texts were produced. In my view, a recontextualization and re-imagination of the Gentiles as the feminized nations defeated by masculine Roman rule is only one step in this process.

CHAPTER FIVE

Dislocating Paul's Universalism

Do not submit again to a yoke of slavery! (Gal 5:1). I begin this concluding chapter with a restatement of one of Paul's core admonishments in his letter to the Galatians. This statement guides the observations and reflections I offer below.

Representing Imperial Civilization as a "Yoke of Slavery"

Two often-quoted Roman voices provide an opportunity for reflection on civilization, enslavement, empire, and Paul.

> In order that a people dispersed and uncivilized, and proportionately ready for war, might be tamed by comfort to quiet and leisure, he would exhort persons, help communities, to build temples, fora, and houses; he praised the quick, rebuked the lazy, and the competition for his compliments took the place of coercion. Moreover, he began to train the sons of the chieftains in the liberal arts, and to give a preference to the native talents of the Briton as against the trained abilities of the Gaul. As a result, those who rejected the Latin tongue began to aspire to eloquence; further, the wearing of our clothing became an honor, and the toga came into fashion, and little by little they went astray into alluring vices: to the portico, the bath, the elegant dinner-party. The simple-minded called civilization (*humanitas*), these parts of their slavery (*servitutis*). (Tacitus, *Agr.* 21.2)

> I am well aware that I might with justice be considered ungrateful and lazy if I describe in this casual and cursory manner a land (Italy) which is at once the nursling and mother of all other lands, chosen by the providence of the gods to make heaven itself more glorious, to unite scattered empires, to effeminize their customs (*ritusque molliret*), to bring together the harsh and coarse tongues of so many peoples into contact by community of language, to give men civilization (*humanitatem*), and in a word, to become throughout the world the single fatherland of all the nations (*breviterque una cunctarum gentium in toto orbe patria fieret*). (Pliny, *Nat.* 3.39)

The first excerpt describes a process at the edge of Roman territory. Tacitus relates what his father-in-law Agricola accomplished during his mission to the Britons, the peoples on the northern frontier "who had not yet been effeminized (*emollierit*) by long years of peace" like the Gauls (Tacitus, *Agr.* 11.4). Agricola's strategy for giving peace to the Britons includes their being lulled by products of Roman city-planning and culture. In order that the Britons should be "tamed" by the "quiet and leisure" represented by Roman peace, they get a "proper" education, learn Latin, and drop their native dress for the toga. Roman social institutions, planted in Britain by Agricola's initiative, further soften or effeminize the previously warlike barbarians. Life appears grand for the Britons, as they receive the material rewards of Roman occupation. Then Tacitus offers an observation: their becoming like the Romans was aligned with "alluring vice." What they thought was upward mobility was a sign of their status as a dominated nation. What the Britons called civilization was actually slavery.

The second statement quoted above is at the beginning of Pliny the Elder's description of Italy in his encyclopedic *Natural History*. It is, basically, an encapsulation of what the Romans were chosen by their gods to do. They are to populate heaven with glorious men, bring "scattered empires" together and "effeminize" their customs, to bring peoples of widely variant (barbarian) languages to one place, to give civilization to men. Italy—Rome—is to become a unifying force, a "single fatherland" of "all the nations" throughout the whole world. The mother and fatherland of all the nations has a mandate to give the gift of civilization to the conquered through effeminizing tactics. Elsewhere Pliny describes the visual and spatial environment of Rome as follows: "this is indeed the moment for us to pass on to the wonders of our own city, to review the resources derived from the experiences of 800 years, and to show that here too by our architecture we have vanquished the whole world" (*Nat.* 36.101).

The fatherland imposed civilization through a variety of means, and they were noticeable in the very fabric of public spaces and visual culture. By architecture, Pliny states and Tacitus observes, the world is vanquished. It is erased and then reproduced on terms that naturalize the imperial center and remind those at the margins to whom they should be deferent and to whom they should assimilate. But it is not just the buildings as such that showed the superiority of the Roman Empire. Roman imperial productions of space and visual representation also served to eternalize the memory of conquest. Programmatic spatial reconstruction in the borderlands included explicit depictions of vanquished effeminized peoples who were often a part of the building process themselves; in other words, they participated in the depictions of their own status as conquered by being in the same space with portrayals of themselves, alongside others, as defeated and assimilated. Such is peace, which is more than the absence of war: it is the totality of Roman civilization itself. Likewise, slavery is more than an economic institution to be taken for granted in the ancient world (since there were so many slaves, and slavery is what kept the empire running and the elite fed); it is a term that describes the very relationship between whole nations and the Romans in the name of civilization.

I have been describing throughout this book how the Romans represented themselves as the hyper-manly chosen race, destined to enact a specific fate for all the nations: conquest, capture, and domination. Such relations were consistently represented—that is, they configured the reality of the world—in an obviously gendered way: masculinized Romans violated effeminized nations. Given what Pliny and Tacitus relate above, it seems as though a primary contradiction in Roman imperial ideology is that the adoption of Roman customs and settling into newly built Roman buildings is also called softness or effeminization. In this sense the nations are not effeminized before Roman peacemaking penetrates their world, even if in the "writing about the nations" I explore in chapter 3, the outsiders' native effeminacy is what designates them as needing to be harnessed by civilization.

But here the Romans also display effeminizing dynamics not by forcing nations to the ground in conquest, but by having them imitate their own decadent, effeminate ways. Is the Roman encounter with barbarian others to be characterized as a clash of feminizations? To the contrary: the feminization of the nations through assimilation into Roman decadence represents the continuation of conquest. Peace, or pacification, is accomplished and maintained through the two mechanisms of imperial power: the military and the city. The military feminizes the nations, rendering them defenseless and victimized; the city makes them passive objects or receptacles of Roman civilization. In each case, the shape of what is to be called humanity is a Roman shape. It is the Roman worldwide mission to the nations to bring them into the one fatherland. To do so requires a de-humanization and re-humanization process on Roman terms. The bodies of the nations, then, are in captivity to civilization.

Therefore, when Paul calls the Galatians out of slavery he is referring to precisely these dynamics. He identifies "two covenants" in Gal 4:21–31: one that is a city enslaved, and one that is a free city, out of reach. This criticism of Paul's goes further, beyond simple resistance to the rituals of the imperial cult as practiced in the free eastern cities of Asia Minor. It attacks what the Roman imperial cult represents: civilization through enslavement to empire. The totality of empire as imposed on the nations is the yoke out from under which Paul pulls the Galatians toward freedom. The New Testament concept of idolatry, then, should be expanded to denote a political criticism of self-referential world order created and maintained by those who dominate. To be sure, idolatry is rightly located as a designation for worship of images. However, as I hope this project has made clear, images as such are never neutral. Idolatry, in Paul's context, includes the worship of penetrative patriarchal power constructs, naturalizing Roman conquest over all the nations.

(Dis)Locating Universalism

In this book I have argued that the universality of Roman rule over all the nations is a thoroughgoing notion in Roman imperial ideology, consistent in image and text. In visual representation, the personification of conquered nations as women's bodies and Roman conquerors as men's bodies communicates hierarchical power relations between Romans and nations. Textually, lists of nations added to Rome's empire through military conquest are spread throughout extant literature and public inscriptions of the early imperial age. The whole world itself is composed of Romans and *omnes gentes*, or *panta ta ethnē*. The nations, as tribes and peoples conquered and acquired by the Romans, have in common that they comprise the inhabited world.

I have discussed aetiological material in some detail because such material is what drives a preordained Roman imperial ideology of world conquest. Origin stories serve to mythologize and historicize the present, to give the way things are a predestined quality. For the Romans, universal sovereignty and peace through patriarchal conquest and assimilation were the prime directives according to the will of the gods. Through the presentation of literary accounts detailing the conception, life, and rule of Romulus (and Remus) as well as three main predictions from Virgil's *Aeneid*, I have argued that Roman rule over all the nations is given a predestined and inevitable character and is channeled through a line of select men. According to the logic of these particular texts, Roman rule is to be acknowledged as the preordained outcome of imperial succession, a prophecy given by the gods that has naturally come to pass in precisely the way it should.

I have also endeavored to examine this material as representative of the world to which Paul belongs and to which he responds. It is true that Paul uses the language of universalism, and this truth is unfortunately what has led to interpretations of Paul as a patriarch himself who conquers otherness in the name of oneness. But we must ask how Roman universalism and Pauline universalism compare to one another: is it hermeneutically responsible to say that the metanarratives of Rome and Israel are the same, or merely mirror images of one another? An implication of this book's re-imagination of Paul is that he can no longer be called an enemy of Judaism, but must be seen as an enemy of Roman imperial order. He is an enemy not of the local synagogue, but of the worldwide drive toward civilization/slavery. His integration program, or alternative destiny, for the nations is relief under the umbrella of the father of the promised land, not of the father of the fatherland. And the terms of integration, according to Paul's Galatian formulation, are not conquest and slavery but interconnectivity and freedom.

The concept and image of the Gentiles is, in my view, the connective tissue between this clash of Roman and Jewish metanarratives. The nations are described as other to both Israel and the Roman Empire. If the Gentiles are those not previously included in salvation history according to Christian dogmatics, attention to Roman imperial ideology reveals that there, too, the nations must be saved in the name of peace; they are those who must be reincorporated into the salvation history represented by Roman imperialism.

As a consequence of the intersectional schema I have attempted to articulate throughout this book, Paul's representation of Judaism more clearly emerges as a counter-narrative to the Roman imperial project of world conquest, which can be called universalism from the top or *universalism through patriarchal domination*.

In Roman imperial ideology, all of the nations—lands and peoples, far and wide—are predestined to show deference to Roman rule consolidated in the figure of the emperor as father. I contend that Paul, on the other hand, promotes a universalism from the bottom, a *universalism through solidarity among the defeated*, in which all of the nations are predestined to turn away from allegiance to their oppressors (Rome, not the Jews) and toward the invisible one God of Israel. Paul is, then, not just the apostle to the Gentiles; he is the apostle to the defeated nations.

Paul's universalism is much discussed elsewhere and is variably celebrated as revolutionary and lamented as oppressively hierarchical. It is, in my view, attention to empire and gender constructs together that makes the difference in decisions on whether to lament or celebrate, and for what reasons. The characterization of Paul's project as *universalism through solidarity among the defeated* gains a certain density and transformative potential through a reconsideration of the Roman Empire as the New Testament's primary socio-political, historical context. In Galatia, Paul implies, this is not accomplished by cosmetic (hierarchical) assimilation into another conquered nation (*Judea*) instead of Rome. It is accomplished by the de-civilizing task of taking off the toga and putting on the crucified Christ. It is accomplished through all the nations working together, not fighting or insisting that they go first, but through seeing themselves in the others.

In the alternative vision that a gender-critical re-imagination fosters, continued theological reflection on justification by faith should be re-imagined as *reconciliatory justice-making through solidarity*. Justification is not something that is handed down from the sky for free, but is done among the people of God through material service to one another. In an imperial context that promotes universalism through conquest and domination of others (nations/female) and worship of the impenetrable self (Romans/male) by imposing the self onto the others, a universalism through solidarity among all those affected is what transforms people, places, and the world. Paul's universalism is a significant departure—a dislocation—from Roman universalism.

Toward Visually Literate New Testament Studies

In the previous chapters I have proposed a methodological shift toward a gender-critical re-imagination of Paul as apostle to the defeated nations. A gender-critical re-imagination is necessarily interdisciplinary; I have identified theoretical perspectives and conversation partners informing my work, as well as provided a sketch of selected analytical tools. The point of methodology is not to insist on its correctness, value-neutrality, or universal applicability, but to participate in the necessary situatedness of all intellectual perspectives through self-disclosure and self-conscious scholarship. My work seeks to contribute to larger conversations within the fragmented field of New Testament studies concerning gender and sexuality, imperial designs, the use of art and archaeology, and the facility of New Testament interpretation for liberation.

One of the guiding principles of this project is that a realignment of the primary sources available to New Testament scholars makes a difference for an alternative reading of Paul. To that end, I have emphasized a reading of primary materials over secondary literature. This is a deliberate choice. To deepen and radicalize an understanding of Paul in his Roman imperial context, I have chosen to engage the primary materials rather than rely heavily on what previous interpretations have concluded. Interpreters have not endeavored to fully put Paul or the rest of the New Testament in the same space with Roman imperial ideology, except to notice their remarkable congruency. Even more, visual representation has been all but dismissed as peripheral to grasping meaning of core concepts as they appear in Paul's letters. I have attempted redress in these areas; I submit the results for review, conversation, and development.

With respect to method, I contend that seeing differently, or rather learning how to interpret what we see, is a severely underexplored area in academic New Testament studies. This is unfortunate, as seeing has historically been a primary way that people work with scripture. Historically, it has been the interplay of text and culture—including oral and visual culture—that has made stories intelligible beyond their original contexts. The production of spatial arrangement and visual representation in different reading contexts—houses, public squares, churches and basilicas, monasteries, sacred and secular—matter. The presence of Paul's body in these places matters to how people experience text, and in some sense representations of the body in such spaces, as well as the spaces themselves, *are* texts. Re-imagination, then, on some level, has always been tied to space, place, and visual representation. This reality speaks even further to the need to (re)connect visual representation and spatial relationships to the study of the New Testament, or to engender what I call *visually literate* readings of the New Testament.

But it is not just that visual representations of scripture like biblical art have been ignored by traditional contemporary scholarship as viable interpretive practices. Images and spatial arrangement, including what scholars categorize as art and archaeological remains, have also been downplayed as an integral part of the Roman imperial context in which the New Testament was produced. The Roman Empire, as a material context where many people were illiterate and many local dialects were spoken, was rich with imperial visual imagery geared toward a multicultural populace, who could probably "read" it. Often, the ideological message of an image provided the primary medium through which to express power relationships and reinforce hierarchical social order. Conquered ancient barbarian peoples, for example, might get the point of a triumphal arch, altar, or coin bearing their likeness being crushed by those of Roman soldiers, real or mythological, regardless of whether they read Latin or Greek. If they saw such images everywhere, they would probably have accepted such crushing as necessarily real; indeed, the evidence suggests that many did, and it could be said that this is what kept the empire running for so long.

We New Testament scholars are currently ill-equipped to deal with such dynamics. For too long research in New Testament studies has promoted a scholarly iconoclasm, focused solely on elite literary models of representation for parallels and context. The possibility that New Testament texts, with rich visual imagery of their own, might also be responding to their visual context shaped by Roman imperial ideology should be considered in a thoroughgoing manner. I have proposed "reading" visual representation in this book as central to doing Pauline studies, and yet such a process requires much refinement and investigation in relation to myriad other textual representations of early Christianity—within the canon and beyond. To present more striking pictures of the New Testament in its Roman imperial context and pictures of, and for, modes of contemporary resistance, we must entertain a broader sense of what it means to read, and partake in teaching and learning how to read images and performances alongside requisite languages and other tools of the trade.

The Roman Empire's legacy as a largely benevolent, order-producing political machine, a "global civilizing agent," is built into and naturalized by its architecture and art. Attention to visual representation as a powerful mode of communication provides a conduit for understanding parallels between the Roman Empire and the inheritance of empire today. Images—primarily branding, advertising, design, and also art—undeniably constitute a primary mode of communication in the contemporary United States. Scholarly iconophobia and iconoclasm should not be overcome regarding ancient material alone, but in the contemporary, constructive context as well.

As part of a gender-critical re-imagination, interpreters must also learn more about how to produce our own contemporary transgressive images reflective of progressive engagement with the New Testament and early Christian literature. Such production is related to understanding how texts are experienced in community, that is, through performance and ritual in said spaces, as well as how spaces and images and texts are chosen to occupy the same semantic system in different contexts. Beyond such recognition, however, is the assertion of art and performance as critical modes of interpretive agency that threaten to disrupt dominant ideology and re-activate imagination among the marginalized. Creative possibilities in the employment of pictures, graphic design, and artistic expression should be taken seriously as modes of contemporary commentary on, and resistance to, empire in the service of building a more just human community.

Visualizing Significant Others

Basically, I have proposed a "Roman reading" of Paul's Gentiles. But I have also done a "Pauline reading" of Roman imperial ideology. Taking these two perspectives together—Roman ideology and Pauline imagination—reveals counter-impressions as to how to understand and navigate differences in hierarchy and power relationships. This is an ancient and modern problem of "two covenants" that has had immense consequences. Seeing the other by contrast to the self is the lens of difference, in Paul's context and ours. Constructions of minority groups in public consciousness are often dependent on their relation to the dominant group. Women are constructed in hierarchical relationship to men; to find a "room of one's own" has been a project of feminism for quite some time. Non-white racial groups are defined in relationship to whiteness. LGBT people are defined in relationship to compulsory heterosexuality. Two-thirds world people are defined in relationship to the "first" world. In every case, a hierarchical differentiation grants "people" status to the dominant group and denies it to the subordinate groups.

The task of liberationist hermeneutics—feminist, queer, black, postcolonial—is to return personhood and agency to those who have had it taken from them, remembering that those labeled "non-people" are at the center of the Bible. This is what has happened to the nations. Not only is it the case that we think we know what we are talking about when we use the term Gentiles, but we have also colonized and domesticated the Gentiles with myriad other terms that keep them anonymous, as the others.

The examination of the fate of the *ethnē*/nations personified by women's bodies in Roman visual representation, and attention to patterns of literary representation concerning attitudes toward the nations can contribute to a more nuanced understanding of the term Gentiles in Paul's rhetoric. In this sense, the New Testament's Gentiles become more than a scriptural echo or allusion. This term is political and not solely what we moderns might call theological. It can signify both non-Jewish ethnicity and the non-Roman nations conquered by, and incorporated into, Roman universal rule. The term *ethnos*, *ethnē*, rather than simply a theological stand-in for non-Jewish Christian in Paul's letters, is therefore multivalent. To be sure, Paul's use of this term to designate "those who are not Jewish" is still relevant, but this meaning is not the whole story. What visual and literary representation makes clear about the Gentiles, from a Roman perspective, is that the power relations between Romans and nations is such that other nations (the Jews included) were expected to show deference to Roman *imperium*.

For those of us interested in reading Paul as a Jewish critic of the Roman Empire—crystallized as a narrative of inevitable patriarchy—and in analyzing early Christianity as a complex of social formations variably using "rhetorics of resistance" to comment on imperial designs, an approach that takes the power of images seriously provides rich material for consideration, as well as complication of some familiar interpretive problems such as representations of women and the various others in early Christian literature. Attention to gender constructs further illuminates and localizes the power issues at stake and enables us to "see" imperial power operating on racialized, gendered, and sexualized terms. A gender-critical re-imagination enables us to visualize the nations as significant others, in fact the most significant others in the New Testament's constructions of community relationships.

A gender-conscious reading of Roman imperial ideology and culture is not necessarily new in and of itself. It is re-imagining Paul in light of such a reading that constitutes a shift from received scholarship concerning his mission to the nations and a proposal for relationship between Jews and Gentiles. My proposal that the Pauline mission to the nations is a movement toward, and among, peoples destined to be defeated by Roman *imperium*, including the Jews, proposes overcoming a hierarchical dichotomy between Jews and Gentiles in Pauline rhetoric. Supporting this shift, and most striking as surviving *ethnē* bases from the Sebasteion in Aphrodisias show, is that among the vast array of nations conquered by the Romans and rendered as female bodies are those of the Jews. Thus, in the logic of Roman imperial ideology (at least as visually implemented in, for example, one of the most famous ancient cities of Asia Minor), the Jews were among "all the nations" to be defeated and ruled.

"All the nations," according to Roman imperial ideology, are the marginalized others. They are those whose humanity has been denied; whose only hope for life is to be resurrected from the dead into imperial civilization. By contrast, Paul does not uphold or imitate the model naturalized by Roman imperial ideology. He goes and meets others where they live, in the public spaces (re)constructed as civilized across the Roman Empire. By doing so, he is on a counter-mission. He does not advocate the continued dehumanization and impoverishment of the others, the Gentiles. He is relentless about making sure the nations, including the Jews, treat each other not as other, but as brother; not as object, but as subject. If they become the same as each other, they run the risk of reproducing the dehumanizing hierarchical pattern of slavery represented by Roman imperialism. Paul calls on his own formidable minority tradition of liberation, which includes a different model of relationships and relatedness among the others, in order to proclaim the "release of the captives." In contrast to the imaginary of a whole world composed of captive peoples effeminized into passivity and complacency, Paul's "gospel among the nations" is a world-wide cultivation of loyalty among those who are not-human according to imperial standards. It is the reactivation of the "gospel for the marginalized" that is the distillation of biblical consciousness.

Paul's "new creation" model of solidarity among Jews and other nations, as a gender-critical re-imagination of its own, would have been radical in its Roman context, as the surviving visual representations from the early imperial period demonstrate. Such an imagination, as a visibly resistant performance on a grand scale among minority peoples, is creatively subversive and politically dangerous to divisive imperial rule. Against this background Paul's mission to the Gentiles can be understood to represent a program for, with, and among defeated and disenfranchised nations that each experienced a degree of assimilation to (and humiliation by) Roman territorial domination calling itself civilization. This civilization, both Tacitus and (I submit) Paul warn, is in fact slavery. Paul's mission to the nations is a transformative humanizing project that seeks to render the rejected stones—the female personifications pinned underneath the heft of male penetrative conquest—into the cornerstones.

Resistance and resentment among the conquered was, of course, not unknown in Paul's time. The Romans had persistent anxieties about the stability of their frontiers, as increased military presence makes clear. Quite possibly, they also knew that solidarity among the defeated could mark the end of the world as they knew it. Remember Emperor Nero's dream that the images of the nations from Pompey's theater rose up together, surrounded him and kept him from moving. This very dream, that the nations could work together to stop the emperor, was tied to Nero's final fall. The nations—the defeated and marginalized across the inhabited world—worked together to weigh him down. They did not fight one another, they did not exclude one another based on perceived differences. In this light, Paul's plea for disloyalty to imperial intercolumniations and solidarity among the nations, marked by a refusal to "stay in place," appears as a nightmare for those vested with, and invested in, imperial power.

Abbreviations

Acts	Acts
Aem.	*Aemilius Paulus*
Aen.	*Aeneid*
Agr.	*Agricola*
Ann.	*Annales*
A.J.	*Antiquitates judaicae*
Apol.	*Apologeticus*
BAGD	Bauer, W., W. E. Arndt, F. W. Gingrich, and F. W. Danker (*Greek-English Lexicon of the New Testament and Other Early Christian Literature*)
BDAG	*A Greek-English Lexicon of the New Testament and Other Early Christian Literarue, 3rd edition*
Bapt.	*De baptismo*
Bell. civ.	*Bella civilia*
B.J.	*Bellum judaicum*
BJRL	*Bulletin of the John Rylands Library*
BMCRE	*British Museum Coinage of the Roman Empire*
1–2 Cor	1–2 Corinthians
De Arch.	*De architectura*
Desc.	*Description of Greece*
Dom.	*Domitianus*
DPL	*Dictionary of Paul and His Letters*
Ep.	*Epistulae*
Epod.	*Epodi*
Exod	Exodus
Ezek	Ezekiel
Flacc.	*In Flaccum*
Gal	Galatians
Geogr.	*Geographica*
Georg.	*Georgics*
Gos. Thom.	*Gospel of Thomas*
Hatch and Redpath	A Concordance to the Septuagint
Hist.	*Historiae*
Hist. rom.	*Historia romana*

ILS	*Inscriptiones Latinae Selectae*
Isa	Isaiah
JBL	*Journal of Biblical Literature*
John	John
JRA	*Journal of Roman Archaeology*
JRASup	*Journal of Roman Archaeology* Supplement Series
JRASSup	*Journal of the Royal Asiatic Society* Supplement Series
JRelS	*Journal of Religious Studies*
JRS	*Journal of Roman Studies*
JRSSup	*Journal of Roman Studies* Supplement Series
JSNT	*Journal for the Study of the New Testament*
JSNTSup	*Journal for the Study of the New Testament* Supplement Series
JSOT	*Journal for the Study of the Old Testament*
JSOTSup	*Journal for the Study of the Old Testament* Supplement Series
Lev	Leviticus
Liddell and Scott	*A Greek-English Lexicon, 9th edition*
LIMC	*Lexicon Iconographicum Mythologiae Classicae*
LXX	Septuagint
Mark	Mark
Matt	Matthew
Metaphys.	Metaphysica
Mos. 1, 2	De vita Mosis I, II
Nat.	Naturalis historia
NovTestSup	*Novum Testamentum* Supplement
NTS	*New Testament Studies*
Num	Numbers
Pan.	Panegyricus
Phil	Philippians
Pol.	Politica
Prov. cons.	De provinciis consularibus
Rom	Romans
Rust.	*De re rustica*
Sat.	*Satirae*
Spec.	*De specialibus legibus*
TAPA	*Transactions of the American Philological Association*
TDNT	*Theological Dictionary of the New Testament*
Theog.	*Theogonia*
1–2 Thessalonians	1–2 Thess
USQR	*Union Seminary Quarterly Review*
Vit.	*de Vitis Philosophorum Graece* [*Lives and Opinions of Eminent Philosophers*]
WUNT	Wissenschaftliche Untersuchungen zum Neuen Testament
ZPE	*Zeitschrift für Papyrologie und Epigraphik*

Notes

1. The Nations in Nero's Nightmare

1. A literary account of the legend of Paul's execution can be found in the second-century *Acts of Paul*. His execution also figures prominently as an illustration of his life story in illuminated manuscripts, and is in several examples displayed next to Peter's upside-down crucifixion; see Luba Eleen, *The Illustration of the Pauline Epistles in French and English Bibles of the Twelfth and Thirteenth Centuries* (Oxford: Clarendon, 1982), 103–4. Paul also "leaves the world" in 1 Clement 5:6 after being imprisoned seven times, being in exile, and being stoned.

2. This statement constitutes only a part of a sentence in Suetonius: *afflicti suppliciis Christiani, genus hominum superstitionis novae ac maleficae*. The Christians are punished, the chariot drivers sanctioned, and pantomimic actors and their followers banished. Suetonius's statement differs slightly from that of Tacitus, who notes that Nero purposefully blamed the followers of Christus for the great fire at Rome, and they were convicted, not so much for the fire itself, but for their hatred of humanity.

3. I discuss this relief in detail, as well as the *simulacra gentium* in Pompey's theater, in chapters 2 and 3.

4. I discuss the line of defeated nations, including *ETHNOUS IOUDAIŌN,* displayed in the Sebasteion's north portico in chapter 2.

5. One of the most vigorous debates in Pauline studies of the last three decades, and especially in the most recent one, is whether Paul is a theological or political figure. The emergence of the "new perspective" and the "empire-critical" approaches have, as one of their explicit aims, to emphasize historicity and politics over theology.

6. Warren Carter asks a similar question regarding Matthew 28:19–20 in light of Roman imperial structures ("Therefore go and make students of all the nations . . . " *poreuthentes oun mathēteusate panta ta ethnē*); see "Matthew and the Gentiles: Individual Conversion and/or Systemic Transformation," *JSNT* 26 (2004), 259–82.

7. Here I consider volumes such as *BDAG* and *TDNT* to represent the "major reference works" of philological relevance in the field of New Testament studies.

8. E.g., the first definition under "*ethnos, ous, to*" in *BDAG*, 276. The entry for *ethnos* in Liddell-Scott uses primarily the group-identity definition, adds its linkage with Roman *provinciae,* and also mentions "Gentile Christians" as a separate definition (480). For a full exploration of the racial group-identity implications of this term in Greek antiquity, see Johnathan M. Hall, *Ethnic Identity in Greek Antiquity* (New York: Cambridge University Press, 1997) and Hall, *Hellenicity: Between Ethnicity and Culture* (Chicago: University of Chicago Press, 2002). I discuss a wider semantic field for this term relating to New Testament studies below.

9. The second definition under "*ethnos, ous, to*" in *BDAG* notes that the term conveys a general sense of foreign (276). No explicit New Testament references are considered to fall under this designation.

10. E.g., the "2a" and third definition under "*ethnos, ous, to*" in *BDAG*, 276–77. Here *ta ethnē* are those "who do not belong to groups professing faith in the God of Israel" and "Christian congregations composed of more than one nationality and not limited to the people of Israel." Paul's

references in Galatians (2:12) and Romans (3:29; 9:24; 15:10; 16:4) are categorized under these two definitions according to this lexicon, thus already placing these two communities firmly in the realm of Christian groups and signifiers in distinction from Jews.

11. Georg Bertram and Karl Ludwig Schmidt, "*ethnos, ethnikos*," *TDNT* 2/11 (ed. Gerhard Kittel; trans. Geoffrey W. Bromiley; Grand Rapids: Eerdmans, 1978), 364–372, esp. 367. To be sure, this article does not take into account the new perspective on Paul. Nevertheless, it summarizes a vast amount of scholarship on the issue. I have found that many scholars do not stray too far from these characterizations, using Gentiles for heathens as well as a stand-in for or precursor to Christians.

12. Bertram and Schmidt, "*ethnos, ethnikos*," 371. Schmidt posits that there is "some trace of Hellenistic influence" on the New Testament's use of this term, acknowledging that "prior to the Romans the Greeks described foreigners as *ethnē* in distinction from the Hellēnes." But, in the Bible, this discussion still maintains that foreigners are outsiders insofar as they are alienated from the Jewish religion. For a recent discussion of how Gentiles are related to universal salvation history, see Terence L. Donaldson, *Paul and the Gentiles: Remapping the Apostle's Convictional World* (Minneapolis: Fortress Press, 1998).

13. *Laos* usually translates *'am* in the LXX and translates *goy/im* only thirteen times—in Joshua (3:17, 4:1), Psalms (66 [67]:2), Zachariah (14:14), Isaiah (9:3, 26:2, 55:5, 58:2, 60:5), Jeremiah (9:9 [8], 40 [33]:9), Ezekiel (20:41, 28:25). There is a complex of twelve other Hebrew words that translate as *laos*. For the data, see Edwin Hatch and Henry A. Redpath, *A Concordance to the Septuagint and the Other Greek Versions of the Old Testament,* 2/2 (Graz, Austria: Akademische Druck-U. Verlagsanstalt, 1954), 853–62.

14. Bertram and Schmidt, "*ethnos, ethnikos*," 369.

15. And, to a lesser extent, *laos* and *dēmos*. However, as Bertram and Schmidt see it, the nonpolitical and, therefore, theological nature of *ethnos* is confirmed by the rarity of *dēmos*, which is seen as an exclusively political term for people, in the Bible. Furthermore, they assert that *laos* designates people almost solely in the sense of "people of God" in distinction from the *ethnē*, who are not such people. This is the case in the Bible even if Hellenistic Jewish writers like Philo and Josephus use the term to relate to the Jews, i.e., *to Ioudaiōn ethnos* (especially Philo, *Spec.* 2.163; see also the New Testament phrase *ethnos tōn Ioudaiōn* in Acts 10:22). Interestingly, this is the case for scholars even if it does not precisely work in the closed semantic system of oppositions, where Jew-Gentile and Greek-Barbarian are hierarchically opposed to one another. As will become clear, reinsertion of Paul's language into its Roman context provides some clarity on the power relationships behind the use of these terms.

16. G. Windisch, "*Hellēn*," *TDNT* 2/11, 504–16, esp. 507.

17. Ibid., 513.

18. See e.g., Edith Hall, *Inventing the Barbarian: Greek Self-Definition through Tragedy* (New York: Oxford University Press, 1989).

19. I am not arguing for a dismissal of the traditions of Judaism in any construction of the Gentiles. I am saying that scholars have leaned too heavily on seeing the Gentiles through a construction of ancient Jewishness. Maintaining that Jewishness is only about religion to the exclusion of politics as a methodological maneuver legitimating the fortification of idealist readings of text and tradition. Such a construction relies on a fixed category called Judaism that is conceived of as a somewhat dominant theological group; Paul's writings express, then, a Jewish self where the Gentiles are the other. The difference with the Jew-Gentile divide in the New Testament is that, when the Roman Empire is brought to bear on the material, Jews are not in a dominant position—theologically or otherwise. Yet the Gentiles are still constructed through Jewish eyes as if they were, and as if Judaism constituted a closed system unto itself. The shift I propose is seeing these constructions of difference as occurring on the bottom, *among minority groups* in relation to the Romans in charge, and not between Jews who are positioned to be in charge and Gentiles who are not. Therefore, the Gentiles are others to the Jews and to the Romans, to whom the Jews are *also* others. Nevertheless, the hierarchical opposition I outline above is pervasive in Pauline scholarship, where the Jew-Gentile dichotomy is

a basic presupposition. The literature is too extensive to recount here, but the above constitutes a consistent summary. After Krister Stendahl's watershed criticisms collected in *Paul Among Jews and Gentiles and Other Essays* (Philadelphia: Fortress Press, 1976), major studies concerned with Paul and his Jewishness have focused on the details of ancient Judaism and how the Gentiles might have been included. But still, the Gentiles remain theological and without substantive investigation or definition except through the lens of Jewishness and opposition. Even one of the more recent thorough investigations, that of Mark Nanos, describes the Gentiles as "marginals," who are being taught by Jewish "influencers" and want to gain "ingroup" status. The consideration of who the Gentiles are is dependent upon the answer to the question of who the influencers, that is, Paul's Jewish opponents, are. This is the case before and beyond Nanos however, as scholars generally tend to see the Gentiles as linked to the opponents even if Paul never connects them to the Gentiles in his apocalypse to go to them. See a summary in Nanos, "The Inter- and Intra-Jewish Political Context of Paul's Letter to the Galatians," in *Paul and Politics: Ekklesia, Israel, Imperium, Interpretation*, ed. Richard A. Horsley (Philadelphia: Trinity Press International, 2000), 72–102.

20. I am fully aware that the historical-critical approach, in some interpretative circles, is treated with much suspicion, and in many cases rightly so. I maintain that alternate readings of history "from below" are possible in a less-naïve manner, using some of the same tools to turn history upside-down and liberating that which has been repressed by dominant positivist historiography, for the purpose of freeing the imagination and production of a different future. I understand, however, that the development of biblical interpretation as such is indelibly associated with Western imperialism and capitalism, as is the development of many academic disciplines. For a collection of appraisals of the historical-critical approach to biblical texts from a variety of feminist and postcolonial perspectives, see *Her Master's Tools? Feminist and Postcolonial Engagements of Historical-Critical Discourse,* ed. Caroline Vander Stichele and Todd Penner, Global Perspectives in Biblical Scholarship 9 (Atlanta: Society of Biblical Literature, 2005). In their introduction, Vander Stichele and Penner discuss three options for engagement of historical-critical discourse: uncritical use of the tools, their outright rejection, or a "third way": "one can engage the dominant discourses and create counterdiscourses and communities, reconfiguring and reconstituting traditional tools, methods, and aims in alternative directions and contexts. In the latter case, voices within and without of the guild find each other, and those at the center and the margins can establish (some) common cause. Herein also lies the possibility and prospect for the creation of shifting identities and the development of subversive discourses amidst the employment of alternative ones" (28). This third way is where I would locate non-idealist critical perspectives: in this process, historical-critical discourse regains its critical edge; interpreters and others who struggle for justice (e.g., the poor and marginalized) work together; and the development of subversive identities and liberationist discourses can be forged out of such contact. See also Susanne Scholz, "'Tandoori Reindeer' and the Limits of Historical Criticism" (47–70); Scholz traces the radicalism of historical-critical biblical interpretation, from the case of Charles Augustus Briggs whose "heresy" led to the official break of Union Theological Seminary in the City of New York from the Presbyterian Church in the late-nineteenth century to the current case of Gerd Lüdemann in Germany (who has been removed from his academic post for his historical approach to Jesus). However, the *uncritical* use of historical-critical approaches toward difficult texts, such as rape stories in the First Testament, can lead to "feminist complicity in androcentric readings" (56).

21. Brigitte Kahl, "Toward a Materialist-Feminist Reading," in *Searching the Scriptures: A Feminist Introduction* (ed. Elisabeth Schüssler Fiorenza with Shelly Matthews; New York: Crossroad, 1993), 225–40; 226. In this article Kahl situates "materialist" exegetical approaches in the specific context of the social movements of post-1968 Europe. Largely indebted to the historical-materialist analysis of Karl Marx, delineation of materialist approaches to the Bible and theology were interspersed among three interrelated schools. The *lecture matérialiste*, represented by Fernando Belo, Michel Clévenot, and Georges Casalis in France (though Belo was a Portuguese ex-priest in exile there) and Kuno Füssel in Germany, employed a blending of Marxist structuralism and linguistic/semiotic analysis to decode biblical texts. I return to semiotic analysis as a tool for analyzing New

Testament texts later. See Belo, *Lecture matérialiste de l'évangile de Marc: récit—pratique—idéologie* (Paris: Cerf, 1976); Clévenot, *Materialist Approaches to the Bible,* trans. William J. Nottingham (Maryknoll, N.Y.: Orbis Books, 1985); *Introduction à la lecture matérialiste de la Bible*, ed. Georges Casalis (Geneva: WSCF, 1978); and Füssel, *Sprache, Religion, Ideologie: von einer sprachanalytischen zu einer materialistischen Theologie* (Frankfurt am Main: Peter Lang, 1982). In Germany, proponents of materialist approaches to the Bible that form a "socio-historical school," represented by Frank Crüsemann, Luise and Willy Schottroff, and Ekkehard Stegemann, introduce specific and detailed questions about the social contexts of the Bible and patterns of exploitation/domination. See Crüsemann, *The Torah: Theology and Social History of Old Testament Law,* trans. Allan W. Mahnke (Minneapolis: Fortress Press, 1996); Luise Schottroff, *Let the Oppressed Go Free: Feminist Perspectives on the New Testament* (trans. Annemarie S. Kidder; Louisville, Ky.: Westminster/John Knox Press, 1993); Schottroff, *Lydia's Impatient Sisters: A Feminist Social History of Early Christianity,* trans. Martin and Barbara Rumscheidt (Louisville, Ky.: Westminster/John Knox Press, 1995); Luise and Willy Schottroff, *Die Macht der Auferstehung: sozialgeschichtliche Bibelauslegungen* (Munich: Chr. Kaiser, 1988); and Ekkehard Stegemann, *The Jesus Movement: A Social History of Its First Century,* trans. O. C. Dean (Minneapolis: Fortress Press, 1999). In the "Amsterdam School" of the Netherlands, proponents advocate for the Old-New Testament unity of the Bible. This hermeneutical strategy sees the Bible as a narrative whole, marked by structurally thoroughgoing intertextuality. Biblical texts, then, refer to each other through the remembrance of the Exodus story, the core of the liberation message for the poor. Proponents were (and still are) especially influenced by the theology of Martin Buber and Franz Rosenzweig, as well as the effects of the Holocaust in the Netherlands; their synchronic approach is explicitly concerned with Dutch constructive theology and ethics. See Frans Breukelman, *Bijbelse Theologie,* 10 vols. (Kampen: Kok, 1980–); *De Bijbel maakt school: een Amsterdamse weg in de exegese* (ed. Karel Deurloo and Rochus Zuurmond; Baarn: Ten Have, 1984); *Inleiding tot het studie van het Nieuwe Testament*, ed. A.F.J. Klijn (Kampen: Kok, 1982); and a Dutch scholar working in Germany, Ton Veerkamp, *Autonomie und Egalität: Ökonomie, Politik und Ideologie in der Schrift* (Berlin: Alektor Verlag, 1993). Much of the literature has not been translated into English, thus impeding full appreciation outside of Dutch-speaking circles. But see *Voices from Amsterdam: A Modern Tradition of Reading Biblical Narrative*, ed. Martin Kessler (Semeia Studies; Atlanta: Scholars Press, 1994). For an application of the principles of the "Amsterdam School" in a theological setting, see Johanna Wijk-Bos, *Making Wise the Simple: The Torah in Christian Faith and Practice* (Grand Rapids: Eerdmans, 2005).

For explicitly political readings that draw on historical-materialist traditions in the English-speaking context, see especially Norman Gottwald, *The Tribes of Yahweh: A Sociology of the Religion of Liberated Israel, 1250–1050 BCE* (Maryknoll, N.Y.: Orbis Books, 1979); Ched Myers, *Binding the Strong Man: A Political Reading of Mark's Story of Jesus* (Maryknoll, N.Y.: Orbis Books, 1989); Christopher Rowland and Mark Corner, *Liberating Exegesis: The Challenge of Liberation Theology to Biblical Studies* (Biblical Foundations in Theology; London: SPCK, 1991); *The Bible and Liberation: Political and Social Hermeneutics,* rev. ed., ed. Norman Gottwald and Richard A. Horsley (Maryknoll, N.Y.: Orbis Books, 1993). More recently, Roland Boer has been involved in forging alternative hermeneutical directions at the intersection of materialist concerns, cultural studies, and First Testament studies; see, e.g., Boer, "Marx, Method, and Gottwald," in *Tracking the Tribes of Yahweh: On the Trail of a Classic*, ed. Roland Boer, JSOTSup 351 (Sheffield: Sheffield Academic Press, 2002), 98–156; and Boer, *Marxist Criticism of the Bible* (London: T&T Clark, 2003).

22. This phrase is owed to the title of the book by Casalis that heavily informed the *lecture matérialiste*: *Les idées justes ne tombent pas du ciel: Éléments de "théologie inductive"* (Paris: Les Éditions du Cerf, 1977).

23. I remain convinced that the Bible is, at its core, about protest against and liberation from political oppression and suffering. The real subject of the Bible is the marginalized; the Bible is a counter-history. That does not mean that there is not contradiction, or that liberation shines through from every word, or that the texts are not androcentric or produced by certain elites who could read

and write. The overall story, that God acts in history for and with the poor, is enduring. My own early impulses for this kind of reading stem from interaction with post-Holocaust Jewish practices of biblical interpretation and theology that see the Bible as primarily a "people's book" and the process of reading and interpretation as a conversation. In such conversations, massive suffering is not forgotten, and healing is sought. See Ilana Pardes, *Countertraditions in the Bible: A Feminist Approach* (Cambridge, Mass.: Harvard University Press, 1992); David Blumenthal, *Facing the Abusing God: A Theology of Protest* (Louisville, Ky.: Westminster/John Knox Press, 1993).

24. Recognition of the thoroughgoing biblical subjectivity of the poor, which is not just limited to isolated pericopes that mention poor people or poverty, is central to the non-idealist task. Such recognition does not come from a theoretically abstract position, but is expressive of experiences reading the Bible with and among base communities of non-academics and non-clergypeople. It is important to note that the Bible is often not the only or most important text in these encounters. See Kuno Füssel, "The Materialist Reading of the Bible: Report on an Alternative Approach to Biblical Texts," in *The Bible and Liberation*, 116–27.

25. Vincent L. Wimbush uses this phrase to describe the dynamics represented by the New Testament and by interpreters who resist the temptation to continue along an idealist path. In his early work on Paul, he gives an appropriate rationale for situating Paul as a respondent to his world in a resistant way: "given the present-day anxiety and confusion among both the religiously committed and uncommitted about the appropriate ways to engage the world as it manifests itself in the form of awesome political, military, and economic structures and powers, and given the tendency of many to fall back upon tradition and old landmarks, including authoritative texts, for clarity and simple answers, not a little is at stake in an attempt to understand more clearly what counsel Paul has given" (Wimbush, *Paul the Worldly Ascetic: Response to the World and Self-Understanding According to 1 Corinthians 7* [Augusta: Mercer University Press, 1987], 10). In this work, Wimbush ultimately concludes that Paul's advice is rather lukewarm and represents a compromise. However, if the world of the early Christians was the Roman Empire, as the evidence suggests, then Paul's engagement of the world must necessarily be the engagement of the Roman Empire's "awesome political, military, and economic structures." Although the advice to the Corinthians might look like a compromise even in light of imperial dynamics, I would contend that the compromise is perhaps due to the fact that the community is in danger of further persecution at the hands of political authorities. Wimbush's later work develops a designation of the New Testament as a "rhetoric of resistance" to signify the productive capacity of world-criticism, or the "otherworldliness," its writers reflect. See Wimbush, "'Not of this World': Early Christianity as Rhetorical and Social Formation," in *Reimagining Christian Origins: A Colloquium in Honor of Burton L. Mack,* ed. Elizabeth Castelli and Hal Taussig (Philadelphia: Trinity Press International, 1996), 23–36; and *Rhetorics of Resistance: A Colloquy on Early Christianity as Rhetorical Formation*, ed. Vincent L. Wimbush (Semeia 79; Atlanta: Scholars Press, 1999). What Wimbush takes as a given here is that the task is not to prove "whether" early Christianities constituted resistance to the Roman Empire, but "how, why, and with what consequences" ("Introduction: Interpreting Resistance, Resisting Interpretations," in *Rhetorics of Resistance*, 6).

26. Those who "excavated" the Roman imperial world and connected it to the New Testament at the beginning of the twentieth century include most especially Adolph Deissmann, *Light from the Ancient East or The New Testament Illustrated by Recently Discovered Texts of the Graeco Roman World,* rev. ed., trans. Lionel R. M. Strachan (New York: Kessinger, 2003); Sir William M. Ramsay, *St. Paul the Traveller and Roman Citizen,* 3rd ed. (New York: Baker, 1949); Ramsay, *Historical Commentary on Galatians,* rev. ed., ed. Mark Wilson (Grand Rapids: Kregel, 1997).

27. It should be noted that "empire-critical" is what I am calling this relatively recent body of scholarly literature and not necessarily how the participants in this work would identify themselves. I speak as a relatively new active participant in this working group of scholars now calling itself the "People's History" group, stemming from the Society of Biblical Literature's "Paul and Politics" section led by Richard Horsley. Coming from only a few perspectives, many of the contributors to "empire-critical" studies are traditionally trained New Testament scholars, who have rediscovered

the Roman Empire as part of historical-critical methodology. Interestingly, among empire-critical circles, these more traditional New Testament scholars conduct work alongside scholars whose interest in the Roman Empire as the New Testament's socio-political context arises from liberationist/justice-oriented agendas, as the variety of essays in the few collected volumes attests. However, it has been my experience that several scholars doing this work seek to promote the Roman Empire as the historical context to the New Testament as a remedy to overtheologized approaches without sustained re-evaluation of Paul's theology in light of historical resituation. In my view, a major public battle over who reads and makes meaning of the Bible is lost when we abandon the interpretive task that includes attending to the contours of how Christian theology can both be held accountable and reconfigured. Earlier work (e.g., *Images of Empire*, ed. Loveday Alexander [JSOTSup 122; Sheffield: Sheffield Academic Press, 1991]; Horsley [ed.], *Paul and Empire*) seeks to connect empire-critical readings of biblical texts with broader currents in ancient studies—in ancient history, classics, and archaeology, stressing the connections between religion and politics in the ancient world. Still this work is undertheorized and underappreciates the potentially transformative contributions of historically dominated peoples to New Testament scholarship, particularly around controversies involving race, gender, and sexuality.

28. Edward Said, *Culture and Imperialism* (New York: Knopf, 1993), 68.

29. I discuss this contribution in chapter 4.

30. However, it should be clear that Christianity, as such, is non-existent at Paul's time. See, e.g., Richard A. Horsley and Neil Asher Silberman, *The Message and the Kingdom: How Jesus and Paul Ignited a Revolution and Transformed the Ancient World* (Minneapolis: Fortress Press, 1997).

31. Musa W. Dube, *Postcolonial Feminist Interpretation of the Bible* (St. Louis: Chalice, 2000), 15.

32. Ibid., 16.

33. Homi Bhabha articulates that "postmodernity, postcolonialism, and postfeminism are terms that insistently gesture to the beyond . . . they transform the present." See *The Location of Culture* (New York: Routledge, 1994), 4. Postcolonial interpretation and argumentation is not about dwelling on what has happened in the past, but is present and forward-looking about seeking transformation for liberation.

34. I am aware that the term *postcolonial* is contestable, and the literature is massive and complex. Nevertheless, postcolonial studies are a way to negotiate the study of empires and cultures throughout time in a non-innocent, non-compliant, and non-ideal way. For an idea of how variant its appropriation is manifest in biblical studies, see *The Postcolonial Biblical Reader*, ed. Rasiah S. Sugitharajah (London: Blackwell, 2005).

35. Such subjectivity is indebted to Gayarti Spivak's essay "Can the Subaltern Speak?" in *Marxism and the Interpretation of Culture,* ed. Cary Nelson and Lawrence Grossberg (Urbana: University of Illinois Press, 1988).

36. Dube, *Postcolonial Feminist Interpretation,* 15–16. See also Fernando F. Segovia, "Biblical Criticism and Postcolonial Studies: Toward a Postcolonial Optic," in *The Postcolonial Bible*, ed. Rasiah S. Sugitharajah (Sheffield: Sheffield Academic Press, 1998), 49–66.

37. See, e.g., the contributions to *The Postcolonial Bible*. For an earlier exploration focusing specifically on the problems and prospects for historical-critical methodology in light of divergent social locations within the globalization of biblical studies, see *Reading from This Place,* ed. Fernando F. Segovia and Mary Ann Tolbert, 2 vols. (Minneapolis: Fortress Press, 1995).

38. Rasiah S. Sugitharajah, "Biblical Studies after the Empire: From a Colonial to a Postcolonial Mode of Interpretation," in *The Postcolonial Bible*, 12–23; 16.

39. Sugitharajah, "Biblical Studies after the Empire," 16–18; Dube, *Postcolonial Feminist Interpretation*, 12–14. See also The Bible and Culture Collective, *The Postmodern Bible* (New Haven: Yale University Press, 1995).

40. Dube, *Postcolonial Feminist Interpretation,* 23.

41. Füssel, "The Materialist Reading of the Bible," 122.

42. For example, Roland Boer diagnoses postcolonial biblical criticism as a homeopathic solution to a real dilemma that might be better served by a renewed allegiance with materialist (Marxist, non-idealist) approaches. Of course this assertion is not unproblematic, nor is historical materialism a perfect alternative. Boer is clear that the popularity of postcolonial biblical criticism in the United States is due to a main allegiance with cultural studies arising from uncritical postmodernism and, perhaps, not always actual analysis of political and economic structures and struggles for justice in the face of globalization of capitalist modes and relations of production. See Boer, "Remembering Babylon: Postcolonialism and Australian Biblical Studies," in *The Postcolonial Bible*, 24–48.

43. This conflict can be illustrated by two mirror-image readings of Mark by Richard Horsley and Tat-siong Benny Liew. Horsley contends that Mark is a template for anti-colonial resistance, whereas Liew maintains that the text of Mark imitates and reifies colonial structures. It could be argued that neither view is nuanced enough or incorporates sufficient attention to the *dialectics* of resistance and accommodation among marginalized, colonized peoples. See Horsley, "Submerged Biblical Histories and Imperial Biblical Studies," in *The Postcolonial Bible*, 152–73; Liew, "Tyranny, Boundary, and Might: Colonial Mimicry in Mark's Gospel," *JSNT* 73 (1999): 7–31. For a summary and critique of the debate plus bibliography, see Stephen D. Moore, "Postcolonialism," *in Handbook of Postmodern Biblical Interpretation,* ed. A. K. M. Adam (St. Louis: Chalice Press, 2000), 182–88.

44. Dube's work in feminist postcolonial approaches seeks to provide redress here but still is largely concerned with how women have been left out of postcolonial biblical interpretation and not with the gendered aspects of the colonial enterprise as such. But see also *Postcolonialism, Feminism and Religious Discourse* (eds. Laura Donaldson and Kwok Pui Lan; New York: Routledge, 2001).

45. The Gospels and, to a lesser extent, Revelation are prime targets for postcolonial analysis. The authors in the *Paul and Empire* volume would not necessarily claim postcolonial orientation, and hardly any of the essays cite postcolonial theories. A notable exception is Sze-Kar Wan, "The Collection for the Saints as an Anti-Colonial Act," in *Paul and Politics*, 191–215. Much empire-critical work on Paul has focused on the Corinthian correspondence; that discourse seems easier to decipher in terms of relations with imperial power than Galatians or even, ironically, Romans. This could be because of an aversion to the perceived dogmatics in Galatians and Romans. I know of no explicitly postcolonial treatments that mention Galatians with any frequency—besides Wan. Even though empire-critical and postcolonial streams of scholarship argue for no cleavage between politics and religion, the shift to empire studies in this formulation over the past twenty years still pays insufficient attention to race, gender, sexuality, and power. Again, even though there is a consciousness of Jews under Roman rule and attention to the structure of the Roman Empire, including the emergence of Christianity as an anti-structure, who the Gentiles could be in Paul's anti-Roman formulation is an outstanding question.

46. Paul Zanker, "The Power of Images," in *Paul and Empire*, 72–87. This essay is basically a summary of the portion of Zanker's *The Power of Images in the Age of Augustus* that deals with the Roman imperial cult, thus limiting the discussion of images among New Testament scholars to a category determined by religion (idolatry) rather than seeing visual representation as a central element in the expression of imperial social hierarchies and order. The decision to limit discussion of images to a particular context that scholars of the New Testament would recognize as religion actually re-inscribes the religion-politics divide.

47. Strikingly, Sugitharajah's essay "Biblical Studies after the Empire" does begin with two images of colonialism, where the Bible is being handed to exotic others—"Hindoos" and an African man—by white European colonizers. The connection of these images to those operative in the context of the New Testament concerning gendered and ethnic differences in hierarchy, and the implications for shifts in meaning-making, are missing from this argument.

48. Vincent L. Wimbush, "In Search of a Usable Past: Reorienting Biblical Studies," in *Toward a New Heaven and a New Earth: Essays in Honor of Elisabeth Schüssler Fiorenza*, ed. Fernando F. Segovia (Maryknoll, N.Y.: Orbis Books, 2003), 179–98. I share Wimbush's basic premise that such re-orientation involves what he calls "radical excavation." This means the unearthing of not only

submerged biblical histories or new insights about the world of the New Testament but also the world created by its strategic employment throughout time, particularly among historically dominated communities who have come to call the texts scriptures, for one reason (i.e., slavery, colonization) or another. I find Wimbush's rather consistent use of archaeological metaphors for biblical studies to be a sign that central to his agenda is precisely the task of learning how to see the world differently through examining its objects and affects. This outlook is rather congruent with what I call re-imagination. I additionally contend that vigorous attention to visual representation, and by extension performance, are necessary to more adequately see the world. I thank Hal Taussig for helping me "come out of the closet" about my own background, training, and interests in performance, as well as modeling how to incorporate critical attention to performance in biblical interpretation.

49. I cannot provide a full history of feminist New Testament interpretation here. Further, such interpretation has not often met empire-critical work. Much of the vast body of literature pertaining to feminist New Testament studies is related to a gender-critical re-imagination of Paul as apostle to the defeated nations inasmuch as feminist approaches employ gender as a primary category of analysis. In some ways, the term *feminist* itself has become as contentious as *postcolonial.* Regardless of the varieties of definition, I continue to claim the emancipatory goals of feminist organizing and theoretical insights. For a distillation of feminist methodologies in New Testament studies, see Luise Schottroff, Silvia Schroer, and Marie-Theres Wacker, *Feminist Interpretation: The Bible in Women's Perspective,* trans. Martin and Barbara Rumscheidt (Minneapolis: Fortress Press, 1998). Much of Elisabeth Schüssler Fiorenza's work has been devoted to articulating a feminist-emancipatory method of New Testament interpretation; see Schüssler Fiorenza, *Bread Not Stone: The Challenge of Feminist Biblical Interpretation* (Boston: Beacon, 1984); *But She Said: Feminist Practices of Biblical Interpretation* (Boston: Beacon, 1992); *Sharing Her Word: Feminist Biblical Interpretation in Context* (Boston: Beacon, 1998); *Rhetoric and Ethic: The Politics of Biblical Studies* (Minneapolis: Fortress Press, 1999); *Wisdom Ways: Introducing Feminist Biblical Interpretation* (Maryknoll, N.Y.: Orbis Books, 2001). Another hallmark of feminist biblical interpretation and, indeed, of feminist studies and organizing generally, is the demystification of epistemology as an individualized endeavor and a hallmark of patriarchy. To that end, cooperation is a feminist value. In the field of biblical studies, collaborative feminist interpretive/commentary projects include *The Women's Bible Commentary,* ed. Sharon Ringe and Carol Newsom (Louisville, Ky.: Westminster/John Knox Press, 1992); *Searching the Scriptures,* ed. Elisabeth Schüssler Fiorenza with the assistance of Shelly Matthews, 2 vols. (New York: Crossroad/Herder, 1993); *Kompendium Feministische Bibelauslegung,* ed. Luise Schottroff and Marie-Theres Wacker (Gütersloh: Gütersloher, 1998); the *Feminist Companion to the Bible* volumes, edited in two series: Series 1, ed. Athalya Brenner (Sheffield: Sheffield Academic Press, 1993–97); Series 2, ed. Athalya Brenner and Carole Fontaine (Sheffield: Sheffield Academic Press, 1997–); and the *Feminist Companion to the New Testament and Early Christian Writings Series,* ed. Amy-Jill Levine (Cleveland: Pilgrim Press, 2002–).

50. For a provocative summary of how feminist and gender-interested New Testament interpretation has dealt with the ever-complicated issue of social location, see Mary Ann Tolbert, "The Politics and Poetics of Location," in *Reading from This Place,* vol. 1, 305–18.

51. I mean here specifically feminist interpretation explicitly conversant with historical materialism; I also am aware that feminism and Marxism have historically had an "unhappy marriage" even if I see these two orientations as inseparable from one another. See Kahl, "Toward a Materialist-Feminist Reading." For materialist-feminist theoretical contributions linking gender formation to economic structures that are applicable to biblical studies see Michèle Barrett, *Women's Oppression Today: The Marxist/Feminist Encounter,* rev. ed. (London: Verso, 1988); Barrett, "Words and Things: Materialism and Method in Contemporary Analysis," in *Destabilizing Theory: Contemporary Feminist Debates* (eds. Michèle Barrett and Anne Phillips; Stanford: Stanford University Press, 1992); Rosemary Hennessy, *Materialist Feminism and the Politics of Discourse* (New York: Routledge, 1990), and *Materialist Feminism: A Reader in Class, Difference, and Women's Lives* (eds. Rosemary Hennessy and Chrys Ingraham; New York: Routledge, 1997).

52. For "discipleship of equals" as a hermeneutical key to the New Testament's liberating message, see Elisabeth Schüssler Fiorenza, *In Memory of Her: A Feminist-Theological Reconstruction of Christian Origins* (Tenth Anniversary Edition; New York: Crossroad, 1993). A focus on the radical inclusivity of Jesus and the patriarchalism of Paul over and against the sexism and even more oppressive patriarchy of Judaism rightly has been criticized as anti-Jewish; see Judith Plaskow, "Anti-Judaism in Feminist Christian Interpretation," in *Searching the Scriptures, Volume 1*, 117–29; Katharina von Kellenbach, *Anti-Judaism in Feminist Religious Writings* (Atlanta: Scholars Press, 1994).

53. This question is intimately related to the "is the New Testament pro- or anti-gay" line that keeps the Bible, again, in chains regarding gender and sexuality. I maintain that as long as interpreters of all stripes keep entertaining the "pro-con" approach as implicitly central to biblical interpretation, we will not be able to understand or complicate the issues, nor will we be able to overcome the patriarchal dynamics still associated with simplistic and overdetermined readings.

54. I discuss Galatians 3:28 in chapter 4.

55. Such passages are mostly in Paul's letters (1 Corinthians 11 and 14 being the prime examples), thus bringing Paul the designation as, in Ernst Troeltsch's historic formulation, a promoter of "love-patriarchalism" as opposed to the "love-communism" of Jesus. For an alternative view that significantly advances the discussion of such troubling Pauline texts through thorough attention to gender theory, ancient constructions of gender, and space studies, see Jorunn Økland, *Women in Their Place: Paul and the Corinthian Discourse of Gender and Sanctuary Space* (JSNTSup 269; London: T&T Clark, 2004).

56. This study probably will not settle this very real debate. I do not propose either returning to old ways or abandoning the interpretive enterprise. Critical re-imagination of Paul as a non-dominant, fallible, male figure who should no longer be used as a tool to perpetuate the subordination of women, but as an agent of transformation, requires fashioning different historical tools and theoretical allegiances. I try to accomplish that here by making a firmer, gendered, link between Paul's Gentiles and the nations in Roman imperial ideology.

57. The danger in this approach is the conflation of patriarchy with Judaism and liberation with Christianity. I contend that the Roman Empire is the real patriarchy to which the Jewish writers of the New Testament respond.

58. The "essentialism-social construction" debates extend beyond biblical studies to feminist and queer theoretical discourses and have parallels and links to postmodernist investigation where Lyotard and Foucault serve as main reference points. A full bibliographical delineation of these debates, the bulk of which have been developed since the late 1980s, is beyond the scope of this project. In my view, a lesson of these debates is implicated in the realization that gender and sexuality operate in more complex, historically situated, and power-laden ways than based only on the givenness of biology. Moreover, gender and sexuality are never isolable as social issues or expressions of hierarchy. The crux of the essentialist-social construction debates can be followed in, for example, Elizabeth Spelman, *In/essential Woman: Problems of Exclusion in Feminist Thought* (Boston: Beacon, 1988); *Feminism/Postmodernism*, Linda Nicholson, ed. (New York: Routledge, 1990); *Forms of Desire: Sexual Orientation and the Social Constructionist Controversy*, Ed Stein, ed. (New York: Routledge, 1991); Judith Butler, *Bodies that Matter: On the Discursive Limits of "Sex"* (New York: Routledge, 1993); Seyla Benhabib, Judith Butler, Drucilla Cornell, and Nancy Fraser, *Feminist Contentions* (New York: Routledge, 1995); *Feminism Meets Queer Theory,* ed. Elizabeth Weed and Naomi Schor, Books from *Differences: A Journal of Feminist Cultural Studies* (Bloomington: Indiana University Press, 1997). In fact, the idea that biology is immutable is itself a construction and appeal to power; see, e.g., the discussion of differing accounts of anatomy throughout history in Thomas Laqueur, *Making Sex: Body and Gender from the Greeks to Freud* (Cambridge: Harvard University Press, 1990); the debates over appeals to science as necessarily biased in *The Science Question in Feminism*, ed. Sandra Harding (Ithaca: Cornell University Press, 1991); and the cultural construction of the body in Anne Fausto-Sterling, *Sexing the Body: Gender Politics and the Construction of Sexuality* (New York: Basic Books, 2000).

59. Debates about homosexuality in public contexts in the United States, no matter where situated, somehow find their way back to a discussion of whether the Bible permits homosexuality. A few book-length examples stand out among the written material: Robert L. Brawley, ed., *Biblical Ethics and Homosexuality: Listening to Scripture* (Louisville, Ky.: Westminster/John Knox, 1996); Robert A.J. Gagnon, *The Bible and Homosexual Practice: Texts and Hermeneutics* (Nashville: Abingdon Press, 2001); Robin Scroggs, *The New Testament and Homosexuality: Contextual Background for a Contemporary Debate* (Philadelphia: Fortress Press, 1983). The very title of Jeffrey Siker's edited volume *Homosexuality in the Church: Both Sides of the Debate* (Louisville, Ky.: Westminster/John Knox Press, 1994) describes the point exactly: the terms of this debate are determined by the idea that there can be only two sides, pro- or anti-gay. Both sides must address a single set of questions posed by those in charge: is homosexuality okay? Can adherents to religious traditions that doctrinally are against homosexuality be gay themselves? If so, how are they to be included into the religious structure? What must they (gays) do to be acceptable to us (straights)? In all of the previously mentioned texts, the perennial anti-gay stance of the Bible is assumed as a given, and the dilemma of what to do in a contemporary context with an ancient but living anti-gay set of scriptures is under consideration. On the other hand, Bernadette Brooten, in *Love Between Women: Early Christian Responses to Female Homoeroticism* (Chicago: University of Chicago Press, 1996), takes a plainly pro-gay position in her examination of Rom 1:18–32, perhaps more popularly known as Paul's anti-gay manifesto. No one has assembled more primary and secondary material on female same-sex relationships in the first four centuries C.E. from as wide a variety of sources. By concluding that Paul is culture-bound in his condemnation of an ancient form of homosexuality in Romans, however, she does not fully interrupt the persistent story about this text. Instead, Brooten recommends that Christians might discontinue its use as "authoritative" since, even in its own historical context, it *is* so anti-homosexual. I am not sure that this position has helped or hindered the contemporary debate, but I do think that the two-sided problem persists—and even rigorous historical analysis cannot unhinge the historical association of key biblical texts with recommendations concerning homosexual activity.

60. From my own participation in various public speaking experiences on precisely these passages, I attest that engagement of the debates on this level is fruitless. Any nuance or suggestion for transformative practice is funneled back into the "so, are you saying the Bible is pro-gay?" line of conversation. It is clear to me that dwelling on the few biblical phrases that may—but probably do not—have to do with homosexuality as we currently understand it obscures both consideration of sexual orientation alongside other expressions of power relationships (military, racial, geographic) and attention to the gendered and sexual texture of (biblical) texts as a whole beyond the select passages. Agreeing to engage in debate on these passages amounts to an agreement that they do, in fact, concern homosexuality as such—a social identity consolidated out of sexual acts between two persons of the same sex—and are not about larger political dynamics via sexual imagery.

61. The heterosexual imaginary is basically the dominant political structure promoted as predestined, ahistorical, unchangeable, and eternal that has heterosexual male-female relationships and male power at its core. I discuss the imaginary later. See Chrys Ingraham, *The Heterosexual Imaginary* (New York: Routledge, 1994).

62. The modern study of the history of sexuality, including sexual orientation, within the humanities as has been thoroughly discussed in works too numerous to list here, is largely indebted to Michel Foucault's *La Valonté de savoir* (1976), also known as Volume 1 of his *History of Sexuality.* The text that is considered to have broken open the field of queer studies in the last part of the twentieth century is Eve Kosofsky Sedgwick, *Epistemology of the Closet* (Berkeley: University of California Press, 1990). See also Judith Butler, *Gender Trouble: Feminism and the Subversion of Identity* (New York: Routledge, 1990); David M. Halperin, *One-hundred Years of Homosexuality and Other Essays on Greek Love* (New York: Routledge, 1990) and *Saint=Foucault: Toward a Gay Hagiography* (New York: Oxford University Press, 1995); Annamarie Jagose, *Queer Theory: An Introduction* (New York: New York University Press, 1996); and Nikki Sullivan, *A Critical Introduction to Queer Theory* (New York: New York University Press, 2003).

63. Some queer interpreters attribute the rise of a modern identity category called lesbian, gay, bisexual, or transgendered to diagnosis by medical science and the disciplines of psychology, as well as the rise of capitalism. Two classic essays on the matter: John D'Emilio, "Capitalism and Gay Identity," *Powers of Desire: The Politics of Sexuality,* ed. Ann Snitow, Christine Stansell, and Sharon Thompson (New York: Monthly Review Press, 1983), 100–16; and Gayle Rubin, "Thinking Sex: Notes Toward a Radical Theory of Sexuality," *Pleasure and Danger: Exploring Female Sexuality,* ed. Carole S. Vance (New York: Pandora, 1984), 267–319. For a materialist-feminist critique of abstract queer theory that posits revolutionary love and solidarity as a transformative power from below, see Rosemary Hennessy, *Profit and Pleasure: Sexual Identities under Late Capitalism* (New York: Routledge, 2001). For additional perspectives integrating materialist approaches with queer theory see *Fear of a Queer Planet: Queer Politics and Social Theory,* ed. Michael Warner (Minneapolis: University of Minnesota Press, 1993) and *Sexual Politics, Queer Identities,* ed. Mark Blasius (Princeton: Princeton University Press, 2001). In her recent work, Judith Butler has reconsidered her previous approach to gender performance and has taken especial note of the intersection of gender and sexuality with globalized economic domination and social norms; see *Undoing Gender* (New York: Routledge, 2004).

64. See David M. Halperin, "Queer Studies Now and Then," a lecture presented to the Center for the Study of Sexuality and Society, New York University, on February 11, 2003. Excerpted as "Renewing the Radical Potential of Queer Theory," *Center for Study of Sexuality and Society Newsletter,* vol. 3:1 (Spring 2004), 3. See also Halperin, *How to Do the History of Homosexuality* (Chicago: University of Chicago Press, 2002).

65. An earlier effort by Robert Goss (*Jesus Acted Up: A Gay and Lesbian Manifesto* [San Francisco: HarperSanFrancisco, 1993]) includes a nascent "queer hermeneutics of solidarity" aimed to overcome the fundamentalist use of "texts of terror" in conversations about homosexuality. Goss's queer hermeneutics of solidarity seeks to connect LGBT existence with the Exodus event, reclaiming the gospel for the marginalized as congruent with a queer politics that seeks to eliminate oppression and make justice (87–111).

66. Halvor Moxnes, *Putting Jesus in His Place: A Radical Vision of Household and Kingdom* (Louisville, Ky.: Westminster/John Knox Press, 2003). It cannot be emphasized enough how important it is that Jesus' personal sexual orientation has nothing to do with his manifestation as a queer character.

67. It should be noted that not all LGBT or queer biblical interpreters would claim liberation—of the Bible, of the marginalized—as their project. My observation is that such claims are dependent upon political positioning (traditional, liberal, or radical) and level of engagement with more abstract models of queer theory. Many LGBT or queer readings stop at the level of recognition by the dominant society; for a liberationist reading, this is inadequately liberal. For a sketch of the difference that includes attention to the moral directives arising out of queer biblical interpretation, see Daniel T. Spencer, "A Gay Male Ethicist's Response to Queer Readings of the Bible," in *Queer Commentary on the Hebrew Bible,* ed. Ken Stone (Sheffield: Sheffield Academic Press, 2001), 193–209. To my knowledge, no such collection about queer commentary on the New Testament yet exists. See, however, the variety of readings from queer, though mostly interested in LGBT recognition, perspectives spanning both Testaments in *Take Back the Word: A Queer Reading of the Bible,* ed. Robert Goss and Mona West (Cleveland: Pilgrim, 2000). See also Deryn Guest, *When Deborah Met Jael: Lesbian Biblical Hermeneutics* (London: SCM, 2005). Guest, an interpreter of the First Testament, also proposes a hermeneutical movement beyond the usual texts used to talk about homosexuality that involves: *resistance* to heteronormativity; *rupture* out of ordinary sex-gender binary constructions; *reclamation,* or reappropriation of the Bible by sexual minorities; and *re-engagement* in struggles for justice with the Bible as conversation companion.

68. This is especially the case with homosexuality, the terminology for which was not even coined or introduced into translations of the biblical text until the nineteenth century. For a tracing of the unclear meanings and significations of Greek terms now translated as homosexual in New Testament texts, see Dale B. Martin, "*Arsenokoitēs* and *Malakos*: Meanings and Consequences," in

Biblical Ethics and Homosexuality, 117–36. Before homosexuality, sodomy was an equally hollow yet harmful term; see Mark D. Jordan, *The Invention of Sodomy in Christian Theology* (Chicago: University of Chicago Press, 1997).

69. Louis Althusser, *Lenin and Philosophy and Other Essays,* trans. Ben Brewster (New York: Monthly Review Press, 1971), 52. Althusser draws on Lacan's conceptualization of the imaginary, or the unmediated contact an infant has with its mother where the world is experienced not as full of contradiction and danger, but as being just fine.

70. An obvious manifestation of the imaginary in the contemporary context can be found in what Chrys Ingraham has called the "heterosexual imaginary." The heterosexual imaginary is defined as "that way of thinking that conceals the operation of heterosexuality in structuring gender (across race, class, and sexuality) and closes off any critical analysis of heterosexuality as an organizing institution. It is a belief system that relies on romantic and sacred notions of heterosexuality in order to create and maintain the illusion of well-being. At the same time, this romantic view prevents us from seeing how institutionalized heterosexuality actually works to organize gender while preserving racial, class, and sexual hierarchies as well . . . through the use of the heterosexual imaginary, we hold up the institution of heterosexuality as timeless, devoid of historical variation, and as 'just the way it is' while creating social practices that reinforce the illusion that as long as 'this is the way it is' all will be right in the world"; Ingraham, *White Weddings: Romancing Heterosexuality in Popular Culture* (New York: Routledge, 1999), 16. Queerness presupposes the imaginary as "compulsory"; see Adrienne Rich, "Compulsory Heterosexuality and Lesbian Existence," in *Pleasure and Danger*. For an evaluation of the contours of ideological critique in biblical studies, see *The Postmodern Bible*.

71. This is part of the fall-out according to contemporary debates over the role of identity politics in justice-making: is it preferable for marginalized groups to be recognized as legitimate within a dominant structure without actually changing that structure, or should the structure be changed? Nancy Fraser calls this the struggle between "recognition" and "redistribution"; with recognition, diverse marginalized groups are accepted into the dominant socio-economic structure that gives the false security of acceptance through celebration of diversity, whereas in a mode of redistribution, the socio-economic structure itself is changed. See Fraser, *Justice Interruptus: Critical Reflections on the "Postsocialist" Condition* (New York: Routledge, 1997).

72. For a delineation of the concept of imagination as a tool of the marginalized and application to traditional historiography, see Hjamil Martínez-Vásquez, "Breaking the Established Scaffold: Imagination as a Resource in the Development of Biblical Interpretation," in *Her Master's Tools?* 71–91. Martínez-Vásquez draws on the contributions of historical-materialist, feminist, postcolonial, and *mestiza* (mixed-race/mixed-language/borderlands consciousness, best exemplified by the work of Gloria Anzaldua) lenses to articulate imagination as a critical practice engaged by those at the margins, often multiply. Imagination is not entirely foreign to biblical studies, as it has been identified as a main motif in prophetic and apocalyptic writings; see Walter Brueggemann, *The Prophetic Imagination* (rev. ed.; Minneapolis: Fortress Press, 2001).

73. Martínez-Vasquez, "Breaking the Established Scaffold," 89.

74. Each of these disciplines has its own internal methodological problems and prospects and its own culture of border-policing. The study of the Roman Empire in light of decolonization and globalization is especially fraught with political meaning and consequences. The study of visual and material culture is still subordinated to the "real" study of philology and texts. And still, from the side of the disciplines of religion, there is a divide between what counts as religious and what does not, as well as whether it is appropriate even to have an interested perspective in order to study religion. Nevertheless, a broadening of the primary sources considered important by New Testament scholars necessarily includes gaining some familiarity with whatever tools will assist in deepening an understanding of the rich context that produced these texts.

75. Tonio Hölscher, *The Language of Images in Roman Art,* trans. Anthony Snodgrass and Annemarie Kunzl Snodgrass (New York: Cambridge University Press, 2004), 2.

76. Ibid., 126.

77. Ferdinand de Saussure, *Course in General Linguistics,* rev. ed., trans. Wade Baskin (New York: Philosophical Library, 1974), 80. The title says it plainly: though Saussure is the "father" of structural semiotics, his construction of a theory of signs being defined as a union of signifier and signified that do not have meaning outside of a system was intended to be applicable to words. Later developments in semiotics include attention to images, as such, and modes of communication more broadly. Saussure insisted that the development of language and systems of signification was directly dependent upon there being a community of speakers and listeners; thus, language is socially embedded.

78. The double-faced nature of signs—that they are made up of opposites—is based on the oldest of such constructions, the Pythagorean "table of opposites" quoted by Aristotle; see below.

79. V. N. Voloshinov, *Marxism and the Theory of Language,* trans. Ladislav Matejka and I. R. Titunik (New York: Seminar Press, 1973), 10.

80. According to Roland Barthes, images provide a special way to understand ideology and culture, playing a role termed mythological. Images are coded just as words, and images play a large role in the everyday dissemination of ideology. See especially Barthes, "Rhetoric of the Image," in *Image, Music, Text,* trans. Stephen Heath (London: Fontana, 1977); Barthes, *Mythologies* (Paris: Editions du Seuil, 1957).

81. Greimas developed a version of structural semiotics that he called "generative semiotics," focusing less on the formal analysis of signs themselves and more on systems of signification. For Greimas, the "semiotic square" is the basic structure of signification that conveys the oppositional logic of semantic and symbolic content. More than one semiotic square for the same narrative or semantic system is possible; each conveys a different level of a text's "diegesis," or created world. A reader's engagement with the analysis of texts necessarily entails entering into a text's diegesis. See Greimas, *On Meaning: Selected Writings in Semiotic Theory,* trans. Paul Perron and Frank Collins (Minneapolis: University of Minnesota Press, 1976). Greimas's semiotic square has been quite influential in narratology. Frederic Jameson also has appropriated the Greimasean semiotic square as a tool to analyze the structures and contradictions of dominant ideology. For Jameson, the semiotic square is a "cognitive map" of ideological critique; it exposes the contradictory structure of ideology, so it may be recognized and transformed. See, for example, *Postmodernism, or the Cultural Logic of Late Capitalism* (Durham: Duke University Press, 1991). For an application of Greimas's structural semiotics to biblical studies, see Daniel Patte, *The Religious Dimensions of Biblical Texts* (Atlanta: Scholars Press, 1990). For further exegetical explorations using Patte's structuralist and ethically interested model(s), see *Reading Communities, Reading Scripture: Essays in Honor of Daniel Patte,* ed. Gary Phillips and Nicole Wilkinson Duran (Harrisburg, Penn.: Trinity Press International, 2003).

82. In Aristotle's Pythagorean table, oppositions are placed in relation to each other in vertical columns. The Aristotelian table of oppositions includes: finite/infinite, odd/even, one/many, right/left, rest/motion, straight/crooked, light/darkness, good/evil, square/oblong, and male/female. Each is that which it is not: finite is not infinite and vice versa. Such oppositions also represent hierarchical power relationships. Aristotle linked male to active and female to passive; male to self-control and female to no-control. Grammatically, maleness is active in self-control and the control of others; it is the subject. Femaleness is that which is out of control and must be acted upon; it is the object. Further, Aristotle's observation of the four elements—air, fire, water, earth, developed out of his basic oppositions hot/cold and wet/dry—also transfers easily to gender constructs. Air and fire, as active elements, are linked to maleness and subjectivity; water and earth, as passive or still elements, are representative of femaleness and objectivity. Land/woman is that which is acted upon. Aristotle's table of oppositions has had enormous influence on and consequences for the history of philosophy and science, including constructions of gender and sexuality. For a thorough review of such constructs' manipulation over time, see Sister Prudence Allen, R.S.M., *The Concept of Woman: The Aristotelian Revolution, 750 BC–AD 1250* (Grand Rapids: Eerdmans, 1985). Allen discusses the Roman adoption of Aristotelian concepts in the context of Stoicism, and though she does mention female personifications for abstract concepts like *pietas* and *philosophia*, she does not consider the link between Roman imperial consciousness, gender differentiation, and the subordination of lands. For a thorough review

of Aristotle's oppositions and their use for ancient constructions of gender as part of Paul's context, and in light of feminist critiques, see Økland, *Women in Their Place*. For an application of Aristotle's table of oppositions as context for gender constructs in Roman imperial art, especially the personification of conquered lands as women's bodies, see René Rodgers, "Female Representation in Roman Art: Feminizing the Provincial Other," in *Roman Imperialism and Provincial Art,* ed. Sarah Scott and Jane Webster (New York: Cambridge University Press, 2004), 69–93.

83. E.g., as Greimas and others have done. Kahl develops this particular shift in a number of published essays, most explicitly and in relation to spatial and visual representation in "Reading Galatians and Empire at the Great Altar of Pergamon," *USQR* 59:3–4 (2005): 27–41.

84. I discuss in chapter 4 how Paul operates with these and related oppositions to imaginatively subvert and transform them toward a position of solidarity at the margins.

85. The term *ethnē* in nominative/accusative (52), genitive (46), and dative (32) cases appears a total of 130 times in the New Testament (Vulgate: *gentes*). Of those times, there is a certain concentration in Romans and Galatians; see below. By contrast, Paul does not use the singular *ethnē* at all (though it appears eighteen times in the New Testament: in the Gospels, Acts, 1 Peter, and Revelation), and when he does use the singular *ethnei* (which appears seven times and only in Mark and Acts), it is in the context of quoting the LXX (see the following footnote). Even if he did frequently use the term in the singular, though, it still should be understood collectively and not necessarily in the sense of an identity one possesses. The related term *ethnikos* is rarer still in the New Testament; it appears once in the singular (Matt 18:17) and three times in the plural (Matt 5:47 and 6:7; 3 John 1:7). It is translated in the Vulgate as *ethnicus* (Matthew) and *gens* (3 John). Finally, Paul is the only New Testament author who uses *ethnikōs*, the adverbial, nation-like, in Galatians 2:14; the Vulgate uses *gentiliter*.

86. This quotation should be understood in its immediate literary context (Rom 9–11) about the integration of Jews and Gentiles under the God of Israel; a geographical interest and the contrast between Jews and other nations is present in 10:18–21, where Ps 19:4, Deut 32:21, and Isaiah 65:1–2 are quoted right after one another. "Their voice [the ones "calling on the name of the Lord, Jew or Greek," see Rom 10:12] went out into all the earth (*eis pasan tēn gēn*), and their words to the ends of the world (*eis ta perata tēs oikoumenēs*). But I say, did Israel not know? First Moses says, 'I will provoke you (Israel) to zealousness by a not-nation (*ouk ethnei*); I will make you angry by a senseless nation (*ep' ethnei asunetō*).' But Isaiah is very bold and says, 'I was found by the ones not seeking me, I showed myself to the ones not asking for me.' But to Israel he says, 'the whole day I stretched out my hands toward a disobedient and oppositional people (*laon*).'" Here I assume that it is the nations who are "not seeking" God and find God anyway, in contrast to the people of Israel who are caught in idolatry.

87. See Gal 1:16; 2:8 and 9 (discussed below). At Rom 1:13, Paul is hoping that he can reap some harvest among the saints at Rome, as he has "among the rest of the nations" (*en tois lopois ethnesin*), for he is indebted to "both Greeks and barbarians, both wise and foolish (ones)" (*Hellēsin te kai barbarois, sophois te kai anoētois*, Rom 1:14). The opposition "both Greeks and barbarians" indicates not only a historical hierarchy between those two categories of peoples, but also they are two categories of peoples under Roman rule over all the nations. At Rom 11:13 when Paul switches from speaking directly to Jews to directly to the nations, he says he speaks to them "inasmuch as, therefore, *I am* the apostle of the nations" (*eph' hoson men oun eimi egō ethnōn apostolos*).

88. The term *ethnos, ethnē* does not appear in Philippians or Philemon. It is rare in 1 and 2 Corinthians (1 Cor: three times; 2 Cor: once, in 11:26, "danger from nations;" see chapter 4 for discussion), and Paul is not clear that he is the "apostle to the nations" in those letters. It appears twice in 1 Thessalonians (2:16 and 4:5).

89. Paul mentions *Ioudaios* and *ethnē* together in the context of having the same God: see Romans 3:29 ("Is God the God of the Judaeans only? . . . "). Romans 9:24, demonstrating who God has called, states "he called us, not only out of Jews but also out of nations (*ou monon ex Ioudaiōn alla kai ex ethnōn*)." Here he uses Hosea to show a quality of transforming un-chosenness into chosenness: "as

also in Hosea he says, 'I will call the not-people of me "my people" (*laon* both times), and the not-loved "loved" and it will be in the place where it was said to them "You are not a people (*laos*) of me," there they will be called "sons of a living God"'" (Rom 9:25–26). When Paul opposes Peter in Galatians, he reports that he said to him, "If you, being *Ioudaios*, live *ethnikōs* and not *Ioudaikōs*, how can you compel *ta ethnē* to *Ioudaizein*? We are by nature *Ioudaioi* and not sinners of nations (*ex ethnōn hamartōloi*)" (Gal 2:14–15). In 2:15 especially, the contrast seems to be between *Ioudaios* and *hamartōloi*, who come out of *ethnē*. When Paul discusses his own position and heritage, he uses *genos*, another collective term (*en tō genei mou*, Gal 1:14; and *ek genous Israēl*, Phil 3:5). The use of *genos* to denote a Jewish collectivity is consistent in Paul. Unlike Philo and Josephus, he does not use the phrase *ethnos tōn Ioudaiōn*.

90. One place this contrast is developed is in Gal 2:7–9. "Jews/Judaeans" does not appear, but *peritomē* appears three times in relation to Peter's apostleship. In Galatians 2:7, Paul is entrusted with the gospel *tēs akrobustias* as Peter is *tēs peritomēs*. But in 2:8 and 2:9, Paul switches to being entrusted with the gospel for *ta ethnē*, whereas Peter still receives the *peritomē* (for the same linguistic contrast, see also Rom 15:8–9). *Ioudaioi* does not appear in Galatians until 2:13, when *hoi loipoi Ioudaioi* join *tous ek peritomēs* and Peter in refraining from eating *meta tōn ethnōn*. While Jews are circumcised, it is not clear that "the rest" initially agree with the "those of the circumcision" that they should not share with the nations. What is clear is that "circumcision" consistently with Peter and Paul is concerned with the foreskin, also called nations.

91. *Akrobustia* appears mainly in Paul's authentic letters: Romans (2:25–27; 3:30; 4:9, 10 [twice], 11 [twice], 12), Galatians (2:7; 5:6; 6:15), 1 Corinthians (7:18). It also appears in Ephesians (2:11) and Colossians (2:13; 3:11), as well as Acts (11:3). In Romans and Galatians the term is directly related to law observance and justification of the nations. For a brief encapsulation of the relations between circumcision and foreskin in Galatians, see Brigitte Kahl, "Gender Trouble in Galatia? Paul and the Rethinking of Difference," in *Is There a Future for Feminist Theology?* ed. Deborah F. Sawyer and Diane M. Collier (Sheffield: Sheffield Academic Press, 1999), 57–73; Nanos, *Irony of Galatians*, 88–91.

92. One body, many members: Rom 12:4 (note: it is the refusal to conform to "this age" that helps the Romans understand that they are connected to one another); 1 Cor 12:12–26; "all are one in Christ Jesus" at Gal 3:28.

93. Paul uses *ethnē* nine times in Romans 9–11; importantly, in 11:26 he makes the case that Israel will not be completely "saved" until "the fullness of the nations" (*to plērōma tōn ethnōn*) arrives, followed by a quotation from Isaiah. This demonstrates that the prophetic tradition of reconciliation is linked to Paul's view of the nations. For discussion, see James M. Scott, "'And Then All Israel Will Be Saved' (Rom 11:26)," in *Restoration: Old Testament, Jewish, and Christian Perspectives*, ed. James M. Scott (Leiden: Brill, 2001), 489–528.

94. Paul uses *ethnē* ten times in Romans 15, again with a reconciliation theme (15:9 [twice], 10, 11, 12 [twice], 16 [twice]) and twice in reference to the collection (15:18 and 27).

95. What we know of this table from Paul is in terms of how he says fellowship among Jews and nations went wrong with Peter, Barnabas, and the rest of the Jews, leaving the table for fear of the "circumcision faction" (Gal 2:11–13).

96. See James M. Scott, *Paul and the Nations: The Old Testament and Jewish Background of Paul's Mission to the Nations with Special Reference to the Destination of Galatians* (WUNT 84; Tübingen: Mohr Siebeck, 1995). Scott maintains that Paul's use of *ethnos* signifies mostly the nations apart from Israel (122–34), and does not fully explore the familial implications of common descent in relation to a Roman imperial ideology of conquest over all the nations. Scott has provided a definitive catalog of the use of *ethnos*, *ethnē* in the LXX and Hellenistic Jewish literature and posits that Paul learned Jewish geographical constructs exemplified by the "Table of Nations" tradition.

97. Ibid., 135–180.

98. E.g., the Jewish geographical conception is a counter-tradition. Geography was no less sacred to the Romans, particularly in the late republic and early principate. I discuss this issue in chapter 3.

For how the Romans saw geography, history, and mythological destiny as inseparable, see Rhiannon Evans, *Forma Orbis*, and Claude Nicolet, *Space, Geography, and Politics in the Early Roman Empire* (Jerome Lectures 19; Ann Arbor: University of Michigan Press, 1991).

99. On the interpretation, or "appropriations," of Abrahamic traditions in the first century C.E., see Halvor Moxnes, *Theology in Context: Studies in Paul's Understanding of God in Romans* (NovTestSup 53; Leiden: Brill, 1980), 117–206. See also Caroline Johnson Hodge, *"If Sons, Then Heirs": A Study of Kinship and Ethnicity in Galatians and Romans* (Ph.D. diss., Brown University, 2002).

100. For a discussion of lists of nations, including inscriptions like the *Res Gestae*, as integral to Roman political propaganda expressing the universal dominion of the Roman Empire under the emperor/*princeps*—and how analysis of such materials can shift and how scholars view the purpose and agenda of Luke-Acts, see Gary Gilbert, "The List of Nations in Acts 2: Roman Propaganda and the Lukan Response," *JBL* 121/3 (2002): 497–529. I use much of the same Roman material as Gilbert and largely agree with his assertion that "Luke-Acts presents Jesus and the church as existing in competition with Rome and its leaders over the claim of universal authority" (525). However, similarities and differences in gendered (and genealogical) expressions of "universal authority" from Roman and New Testament perspectives remain relatively unexplored in this article, which indicates inattention to the "deep structure" of power relations suggested by Roman and New Testament claims of world dominion and sovereignty.

101. It is also not the case in the pre-Alexander Greek context, where *ethnos* also has a primarily political range of meanings. Before Alexander, *ethnē* were peoples who were either different from the polis (since the polis had autonomy) or had a large population (Arist., *Pol.* 1326b). For elaboration on the contours of *ethnos, ethnē* in the literature of this period, see Hall, *Ethnic Identity in Greek Antiquity*, 34–67. Between Alexander and Augustus, the concept of *ethnos* shifts to designate outsider groups, such as the Jews, who had acquired a particular kind of right to exist following a military encounter. In the Hellenistic period, according to Hall, a sense of ethnicity between Greeks and barbarians is created through their interaction in the colonial encounter (*Hellenicity*, 172–228; see also Carla M. Atonaccio, "Ethnicity and Colonization," in *Ancient Perceptions of Greek Ethnicity*, ed. Irad Malkin, Center for Hellenic Studies, Harvard University [Cambridge, Mass.: Harvard University Press, 2001], 113–57). This means that to be represented as an *ethnos* a group must be conquered, consolidated, and reincorporated into the dominant political structure; the designation is imposed from the perspective of the conquerors. Hall also usefully notes the direct correlation between ethnicity and genealogy; that is to say, in his formulation one of the primary factors in delineating an "ethnonation" in the Classical period is a shared fictive or mythological genealogy (*Ethnic Identity in Greek Antiquity*, 40–51. He also makes this observation about the Hellenistic period; see *Hellenicity*, 220–26). For an analysis of the transformation of the collective sense of distinct Greek nationhood from Herodotus to Pausanias, see David Konstan, "*To Hellēnikon ethnos*: Ethnicity and the Construction of Ancient Greek Identity," in *Ancient Perceptions of Greek Ethnicity*, 29–50. The Romans certainly predicated their mythological genealogies on (gendered) conquest and assimilation of outsiders; see chapter 3. The Romans, however, differ from the Greeks in that their *aitia* include outsiders from the beginning (much like the Jews); there is no pure Roman nation. On the question of Roman mixed-ethnic identity, see Emma Dench, *Romulus's Asylum: Roman Identities from Alexander to Hadrian* (New York: Oxford University Press, 2005). On the designation of others as nations as arising out of ancient perceptions of cultural differences, as well as through conquest and imperialism, see Benjamin Isaac, *The Invention of Racism in Classical Antiquity* (Princeton: Princeton University Press, 2004). For an examination of ethnicity in early Christian literature, see Gay Byron, *Symbolic Blackness and Ethnic Difference in Early Christian Literature* (New York: Routledge, 2002); and Denise Kimber Buell, *Why This New Race? Ethnic Reasoning in Early Christianity* (New York: Columbia University Press, 2005).

102. The distinctiveness of Roman imperial constructions of gender and sexuality have begun to be explored only recently by classicists and ancient historians. Amy Richlin and Marilyn Skinner have made this point well: the preoccupation with Greek formulations of sexuality and gender—as

formulated, for example, by Michel Foucault—has obscured Roman specificity and the "non-coincidental" parallels between Roman conceptions of imperial/patriarchal power and later colonial and imperial contexts. See Richlin, "Foucault's *History of Sexuality:* A Useful Theory for Women?" in *Rethinking Sexuality: Foucault and Classical Antiquity,* ed. David H. J. Larmour, Paul Allen Miller, and Charles Platter (Princeton: Princeton University Press, 1998), 138–70; Skinner, "Zeus and Leda: The Sexuality Wars in Contemporary Classical Scholarship," *Thamyris* 3:1 (1996): 103–23; and *Roman Sexualities,* ed. Marilyn B. Skinner and Judith P. Hallett (Princeton: Princeton University Press, 1998). For a full-length treatment that discusses the transformations of gender and sexuality between Greece and Rome, see Marilyn B. Skinner, *Sexuality in Greek and Roman Culture* (London: Blackwell, 2005). The same preoccupation with Greco-Roman constructions of gender and sexuality, most often pederasty, pervades New Testament scholarship concerned with sexuality; this formulation serves to further devalue or hide the Roman Empire as the socio-political context of New Testament texts. I submit that a similar preoccupation with individual sexual practices has obscured treatment of the gendered and sexual connotations of ideology.

103. For a concise treatment, see Jonathan Walters, "Invading the Roman Body: Manliness and Impenetrability in Roman Thought," in *Roman Sexualities,* 29–46; for a lengthier and more detailed investigation, see Craig Williams, *Roman Homosexuality: Ideologies of Masculinity in Classical Antiquity* (New York: Oxford University Press, 1999).

104. C. R. Whittaker, "Sex on the Frontiers," in *Rome and Its Frontiers: The Dynamics of Empire* (London: Routledge, 2004), 129.

2. The Fate of the Nations in Roman Imperial Representation

1. A notable exception is Halvor Moxnes, "'He saw that the city was full of idols' (Acts 17:16): Visualizing the World of the First Christians," in *Mighty Minorities: Minorities in Early Christianity—Positions and Strategies. Essays in Honour of Jacob Jervell on his 70th Birthday, 21 May 1995,* ed. David Hellholm, Halvor Moxnes, and Turid Karlsen Seim (Boston: Scandinavian University Press, 1995), 107–32. Moxnes asks whether it could *not* be the case that the early Christians were not influenced by their visual environment and calls for the development of "methods to study the interrelations between urban structures, architecture and art and the social and ideological world of the community" (109). Such methods find a fruitful beginning in *Picturing the New Testament: Studies in Ancient Visual Images,* ed. Annette Weissenrieder, Friederike Wendt, and Petra von Gemünden, WUNT 2 (Tübingen: Mohr Siebeck, 2005), which features a number of essays by biblical scholars interested in approaches to and conversations between image and text. For a thorough consideration of John's Apocalypse in light of archaeological finds connected to the Roman imperial cult in Asia Minor, including the Sebasteion at Aphrodisias, see Steven Friesen, *Imperial Cults and the Apocalypse of John: Reading Revelation in the Ruins* (New York: Oxford University Press, 2001). However, the intersections of social issues, image, and space vis-à-vis the New Testament, and particularly Paul's letters, are yet to be given more flesh.

2. Natalie Boymel Kampen, "Epilogue: Gender and Desire," in *Naked Truths: Women, Sexuality and Gender in Classical Art and Archaeology,* ed. Claire L. Lyons and Ann O. Koloski-Ostrow (London: Routledge, 1998), 267–77 (267).

3. Roman imperial visual representation, in my estimation, is more like contemporary advertising; it is designed to communicate a narrative to an audience. Whereas those who control the production of what becomes dominant visual representation might be elites, the viewing public always includes non-elites. For the Romans, this meant that the same conquered people they displayed would also see such monuments. For a framework that provides some important grounding as to how wider publics might have viewed and "read" Roman visual representation in a variety of media, see John R. Clarke, *Art in the Lives of Ordinary Romans: Visual Representation and Non-elite Viewers in Italy, 100 BCE–AD 315* (Berkeley: University of California Press, 2003). In addition to numerous

insights concerning how the masses interacted with their visual environment, Clarke argues that some kind of textual "literacy" must have been required to read some of the "minor" wall paintings in Pompeii that incorporated visual imagery and words together (160–80).

4. C. R. Whittaker, "Imperialism and Culture: The Roman Initiative," in *Dialogues in Roman Imperialism: Power, Discourse, and Discrepant Experience in the Roman Empire*, ed. D. J. Mattingly (JRASSup 23; Oxford: Oxbow, 1997), 143–64, esp. 144.

5. The term is Henri Lefebvre's. See *The Production of Space,* trans. Donald Nicholson-Smith (London: Blackwell, 1991). Lefebvre's influential theorization of space as "social" and as a site of production means that it is created and shaped by the social activities in which it is invested. "Ancient space" is increasingly a site of scholarly production in biblical studies, in certain circles indebted to the work of Lefebvre and geographer David Harvey. See Moxnes, *Putting Jesus in His Place*; and Roland Boer, "Sanctuary and Womb: Henri Lefebvre and the Production of Ancient Space," in *Redirected Travel: Alternative Journeys and Places in Biblical Studies,* ed. Roland Boer and Edgar Conrad, JSOTSup 382 (New York: T&T Clark, 2003), 162–84.

6. Richard Hingley, *Globalizing Roman Culture: Unity, Diversity, and Empire* (New York: Routledge, 2005), 72.

7. Larissa Bonfante, "Introduction," in *The World of Roman Costume,* ed. Larissa Bonfante and Julia L. Sebesta (Madison: University of Wisconsin Press, 2001), 5.

8. On [il]literacy rates in the Roman Empire, see William V. Harris, *Ancient Literacy* (Cambridge: Harvard University Press, 1989), 147–284. Harris defines literacy as being able to read and write words. Visual literacy is not addressed; such is the provenance of art historians. Yet Roman imperial communication happened, I submit, largely through the control of public space and its imagery; such design was geared toward a mass of people who could probably understand its core messages. In other words, it is not just the proliferation of Roman-style city-planning and architecture all around the empire that mattered, but a whole range of communicative aspects involved in the manipulation of space by those who have political power. Images formed a more consistently intelligible language across an empire that contained vast amounts of local dialects and different spoken languages. See also *Literacy and Power in the Ancient World,* ed. Alan Bowman and Greg Woolf (New York: Cambridge University Press, 1994).

9. Hölscher, *The Language of Images in Roman Art,* is expressly concerned with delineating this grammar.

10. Paul Zanker, *The Power of Images in the Age of Augustus,* trans. A. Shapiro (Ann Arbor: University of Michigan Press, 1991).

11. Peter J. Holliday, *The Origins of Roman Historical Commemoration in the Visual Arts* (New York: Cambridge University Press, 2002), 112. Hölscher notes that allegorical abstraction enabled the Romans to communicate ideas like virtues (*fides, pietas, concordia, victoria*) and conquest in a consistent manner (*Language of Images*, 120).

12. Natalie Boymel Kampen, "Gender Theory and Roman Art," in *I, Claudia: Women in Ancient Rome,* ed. Diana E. E. Kleiner and Sandra B. Matheson (New Haven: Yale University Art Gallery and Austin: University of Texas Press, 1996), 14–25; 14.

13. Additionally, personified virtues were taken out of the realm of philosophy and came to be "owned" by the emperor and his friends; see Hölscher, *Language of Images,* 91. In this sense, abstraction (personifications) and actuality (ruler) came to be displayed in the same space, anchoring "reality."

14. R. R. R. Smith, "*Simulacra Gentium*: The *Ethne* from the Sebasteion at Aphrodisias," *JRS* 78 (1988): 50–77; 70.

15. See Smith, "*Simulacra Gentium,*" who draws on Toynbee's short summary of pre-Hadrianic personifications, as well as F. W. Hamdorf, *Griechische Kultpersonifikationen der vorhellenistischen Zeit* (Mainz: von Zabern, 1964).

16. On rivers as male bodies, see Janusz A. Ostrowski, *Personifications of Rivers in Greek and Roman Art* (Studia z Archeologii Sródziemnomorskiej, vol. 12; Kraków, 1991). This is the only

full-length art-historical treatment that traces a tradition of personifications for water using maleness. Ostrowski notes that in Roman imperial art, personifications of rivers served a propaganda function, as they were associated with military events such as the crossing of a river by the Roman army into enemy territory. He also draws out examples from the ancient literature that depict the river personifications as being part of the same processions as *simulacra oppidorum* or *gentium*, images of the towns or nations (47, n. 99), thus linking the rivers with that which the Romans acquired and assimilated through victory. After all, the trampling over rivers indicated an intention to go to battle in many respects.

17. Scholars disagree on whether Hellenistic geographical personifications were used to denote defeat. R. R. R. Smith argues that such figures were not used in Hellenistic victory art, implying that they were not depicted as captives ("*Simulacra Gentium*," 70). Ann Kuttner labels Hellenistic personifications as "falling into two basic categories—the celebratory or friendly and the domineering or hostile" (*Dynasty and Empire in the Age of Augustus: The Case of the Boscoreale Cups* [Berkeley: University of California Press, 1995], 74) noting that cities and lands were shown as submissive toward a captor or friendly toward one another or a liberator. Notable examples of this latter, friendly type include the Tyche of Antioch, and those friendly toward a liberator include a Ptolemaic procession of 276 BCE that celebrated Alexander's liberation of the Greek city-states of Asia Minor (*Dynasty and Empire*, 75). A well-known example of a late-Hellenistic assemblage of cities survives from Lagina. There the cities of the League of Asia had themselves represented on a frieze of the Temple of Hekate together with Roma, and the image was linked to relations of patronal power in the sense that this was a site where a Cult of Roma developed in return for Roman gifts and support. This representation and the space seems to have had importance for relations with Rome; this sanctuary instituted a Cult of Roma, including games, in return for Sulla's benefactions. Kuttner argues that Romans would have traveled to and seen this spot and that they probably picked up on this kind of politico-religious organization of cities as shown by the Altar of Rome and Augustus at Lugdunum and the Augustan arch at Susa in the Cottian Alps (*Dynasty and Empire*, 75).

18. Kuttner, *Dynasty and Empire*, 76.

19. Ibid., 76 (=*ILS* 103); there are *comparanda* in coins showing Pompey the Great flanked by (female) personifications of Tarraco and Baetica.

20. Hölscher calls this an element of the semantic system in the Roman context (*Language of Images*, 38–45). The other elemental pattern is the state ceremonial, e.g., the procession on the Ara Pacis.

21. The mythological battle as allegory for historical conquest is crystallized most impressively by the monumental Gigantomachy on the Great Altar of Pergamon. Here the Olympian gods, led by Zeus and his motherless daughter Athena, battle the monstrous Giants in a frieze that wrapped all the way around the outside of the inflated altar. It is impossible to extract this representation of "good vanquishing evil" from an assertion of Attalid dynastic power after Alexander's conquest of Asia and the establishment of Pergamon as a seat of Greek cultural opulence and political power, which then collaborated with and conceded to Roman imperial power. And, as Mary Beard and John Henderson state rather plainly, "in the strain to build an unbeatable sum of cosmic, heroic, and human valor, the Great Altar can stand for any and every state's aspirations for glory, self-glorification, vainglory—as much the triumph *of* barbarism as triumph *over* barbarism" (*Classical Art: From Greece to Rome* [Oxford History of Art; New York: Oxford University Press, 2001], 158). The Gigantomachy is a common depiction in ancient visual representation of the Hellenistic period, as are its "siblings," the Amazonomachy and Centauromachy. In these cases, mythological battle is enacted between those who have power (Olympians, Greeks, Heroes) and those who threaten it (Giants, Amazons, Centaurs). These image programs communicate historical conquest on cosmic, divinely ordained terms. This mode of expression was taken up by the Romans to express their emergent consciousness as the race destined to rule the whole world. A mythological battle on the scale of the Great Altar of Pergamon (and the Pergamene school as a whole) appears to have had concrete influence on Roman literature and art, particularly in the translation of the Olympians' battle against the Giants into a

Roman statement on "Gods-with-us" regarding its own expansion; see Ann Kuttner, "Republican Rome Looks at Pergamon," *Harvard Studies in Classical Philology* 97 (1995), which draws on Philip Hardie, *Virgil's Aeneid: Cosmos and Imperium* (New York: Oxford University Press, 1986). As Hardie notes, the battle-order represented by the Great Altar is perhaps most graphically alluded to in literary representation on Aeneas's prophetic shield in *Aeneid* 8 (see chapter 3).

22. Hellenistic dying figures include mythological types Like Amazons, Giants, and Centaurs, as well as their translation into historical outsiders and enemies of the Greeks, Attalids, and Romans like Gauls, Thracians, and Persians. Such figures were part of larger friezes depicting battle-scenes with their conquerors, and sometimes they also appear as singular figures, without depiction of the conquerors. Some of the most famous pieces of this type, such as the "Dying Gaul" and the "Suicidal Gauls," are believed to have been part of an Attalid victory monument and/or the spatial program of the Great Altar. Pausanias reports that various emblematic battles were commemorated by Attalos at the Athens Acropolis, using small figures: "by the south wall, Attalos dedicated the legendary battle of the Giants, the battle of the Athenians against the Amazons, the battle against the Persians at Marathon, the destruction of the Gauls in Mysia—each figure being about two cubits (three feet)" (*Desc.* 1.25.2). Big Gauls were also displayed at Rome, as reports indicate (e.g., Suetonius, *Nero* 41.2, a description of the "overthrow of a Gaulish soldier by a Roman horseman who was dragging him along by the hair") and several small-scale Roman copies of unknown purpose survive. Gauls seem to be especially popular as enemies; for discussion and plates, see Piotr Bienkowski, *Die Darstellungen der Gallier in der Hellenistischen Kunst* (Vienna, 1908); and John R. Marzsal, "Ubiquitous Barbarians: Representations of Gauls at Pergamon and Elsewhere," in *From Pergamon to Sperlonga: Sculpture and Context,* ed. Brunilde S. Ridgway and Nancy T. deGrummond (Berkeley: University of California Press, 2001). Iain Ferris also claims them as the barbarians *par excellence* in ancient visual representation (*Enemies of Rome: Barbarians through Roman Eyes* [London: Sutton, 2000], 6–13). The mythological figures exist in order to be defeated; they represent the outsider who must be destroyed to create order.

23. It is ideologically provocative that several dying types survive without a portrayal of those who killed them. Clearly, historically the victor in the proposed victory monument of which the dying and dead Gauls were supposedly a part was the Attalid dynasty as representative of Greek civilization. However, if there is no image of a clearly identified vanquisher, it could be anyone in the position of terminating the represented Gauls. The absence of the victor provides an opportunity for the viewer to reflect on who, precisely, are winners and losers—and with whom the viewer identifies. Such absence in an ancient viewing context would have provided a special opportunity for the Romans, who counted the Gauls among their most pernicious and persistent enemies.

24. Hölscher, *Language of Images*, 39.

25. See Isaac, *Invention of Racism in Classical Antiquity*, 55–124.

26. While the Greek system may not have allowed room for barbarian mobility due to its concretization of the inscrutable differences and hierarchy between Greeks and non-Greeks, the Romans were different. As Ferris notes: "the Roman imperial system allowed for the possibility of transformation, a metamorphosis. Barbarian peoples, those outside the empire, could be transformed into citizens and subjects of the empire by conquest and incorporation. Whether this incorporation gave them equality is open to question, but certainly in state art they then became invisible, unless being celebrated at death for their service to the Roman state or by self-advertisement as new citizens following manumission from slavery" (*Enemies of Rome*, 4). Important to the Roman imperial system as transformative is this expression of what steps must be taken by barbarians to experience a metamorphosis into citizenship. Outsiders must be conquered first and then incorporated. All those barbarians who were incorporated, therefore, must have been defeated in order to enjoy Roman status and mobility. Conquest represents the first step in the civilization process, the result of which is described by Ferris as becoming invisible under the imperial umbrella, at least in Roman state art. The peace and world rule of the Romans is accomplished through victory over foreigners and consequently offering an assimilatory alteration of their shape. This dynamic is crucial to keep in mind

when examining Roman imperial portrayals of ethnic and provincial personifications. Even tribes and territories that are pictured as friendly or less hostile or assimilated by Greek draping or a standing position should be seen as having been captured and redefined on Roman terms.

27. E.g., Greeks recorded their travels and encounters with barbarians as predicated on a sort of natural, inborn inequality—and the Romans before the empire did the same but also presupposed superiority over other Italians. The rhetoric of civilized–barbaric served the Romans, who sought dominance over Italy, as well. In addition and unlike the Greeks, the Romans also promoted incorporation-through-battle of non-Roman Italians into their brand of civilization, signifying a unity among Italians that was extended to non-Italian peoples later in the creation of empire. An important dynamic distinguishing this period from the later imperial one is that of who is doing the conquering, and therefore who can celebrate the victory. In the pre-Augustan period, emphasis was placed on victorious generals as war heroes, and each general was able to celebrate his own victory and triumph. The shift to imperial configurations entailed a shift in consolidation of power from heroes to emperor-as-solitary-hero.

28. Kuttner, *Dynasty and Empire*, 78–80; Erich Gruen, *Culture and National Identity in Republican Rome* (Ithaca: Cornell University Press, 1992).

29. I discuss several such inscriptions in chapter 3.

30. I discuss the *carnyx* as attribute below.

31. See chapter 3 for a consideration of the Roman triumph as a means to display images of the nations.

32. Roman depiction of defeated barbarians is an area of scholarly research on its own, and one that is unfortunately beyond the scope of this study. Ferris has compiled a diachronic examination of images of barbarians in Roman representation in *Enemies of Rome* that also includes an extensive bibliography.

33. For a discussion of the mourning pose in Roman women's body language, see Anthony Corbeill, *Nature Embodied: Gesture in Ancient Rome* (Princeton: Princeton University Press, 2004), 67–106.

34. For more examples of the "chained to a tree" barbarian type, see Ferris, *Enemies of Rome,* and Holliday, *Origins of Historical Commemoration*. Several panels from the Aphrodisias Sebasteion also feature the emperor standing near a trophy with a bound captive nearby; I discuss some of these below.

35. For the most part, the literature focuses on sorting out what exactly in the Roman period counts as a provincial personification and what is simply another representation of a conquered barbarian. Less attention is given to expressions of gender and power relations of such images. See the classic treatments by Percy Gardner, "Countries and Cities in Ancient Art," *Journal of Hellenic Studies* 9 (1888): 47–81; Piotr Bienkowski, *De simulacris barbararum gentium apud Romanos. Corporis barbarorum prodomus* (Cracow: Imprimerie de l'Université des Jagellons, 1900); Michele Jatta, *Le rappresentanze figurate delle provincie romane* (Rome: E. Loescher & Co., 1908); Jocelyn M.C. Toynbee, *The Hadrianic School: A Chapter in the History of Greek Art* (Cambridge: Cambridge University Press, 1934); Janusz Ostrowski, *Les personnifications des provinces dans l'art romain* (Travaux du Centre d'Archéologie Méditerranéenne de l'Academie Polonaise des Sciences 27; Warsaw: Comer, 1990); and Liane Houghtalin, *The Personifications of the Roman Provinces* (Ph.D. diss., Bryn Mawr College, 1993). Houghtalin in particular provides a comprehensive catalog of provincial personifications from the Late Republic to the third-century C.E. according to a narrower definition than previous works: ". . . a figure in literature or art which embodies in human form a land outside Italy possessed and administered by Rome" (6). In art-historical scholarship, a personification is ethnic if it represents a conquered people or territory that does not constitute a province under Roman auspices, and it is provincial if it does designate such a territorial delimitation. In my reading of the Roman imperial practice of representing nations in series such as at the Aphrodisias Sebasteion, the official status of a conquered tribe or land does not seem to make a great deal of difference in terms of appearance (woman's body, dress and attribute, standing pose), spatial arrangement (all in a line together,

deferent to the emperor), or designation of the personification as ἔθνος (*ethnos*). The exception from the Sebasteion's north portico centers on the lack of an *ethnos* inscription for the three islands of Crete, Cyprus, and Sicily. Another distinction is possibly around native or classicizing dress, yet I do not think enough survives to make such decisions without reservation. So for the purposes of this project, I interchangeably call the personifications ethnic and ethnic/provincial.

36. For discussion, see Kuttner, *Dynasty and Empire*, 77.

37. Carlos F. Noreña, "The Communication of the Emperor's Virtues," *JRS* 91 (2001): 146–68 (154 n. 44).

38. Numismatists and historians debate how the images on coins were chosen; whether they were the choice of the emperor, senate, or only of those who actually minted them; the implications of that process; and what coins can actually reveal about Roman imperial ideology. As a scholar of the New Testament, I see coins, and especially the images on them, as an important and often overlooked component of the material record during the time of the textual production of the New Testament. I agree with art historians who posit that Roman imperial portraits, regardless of the medium, tended to have been state-approved. I also see coins as an everyday conduit for official dissemination of imperial ideology through iconography. For a succinct summary of the major conflicts surrounding the political significance and intentions of ancient Roman coins and their usefulness for the study of early Christian texts, see Richard Oster, "Numismatic Windows into the Social World of Early Christianity: A Methodological Inquiry," *JBL* 101 (1982): 195–223. For a constructive use of Roman coins in the interpretation of New Testament literature, see Larry J. Kreitzer, *Striking New Images: Roman Imperial Coinage and the New Testament World* (JSNTSup 134; Sheffield: Sheffield Academic Press, 1996).

39. Despite Maecenas's urging Augustus to prohibit conquered Roman territories to "have currency or weights or measures of their own; instead let them use ours," there still was a vast amount of indigenous coinage throughout the Roman Empire. Many local officials helped their regions show deference to Rome by minting their own coins in honor of, for example, the imperial cult, featuring iconography similar to that used at the empire's capital. For Maecenas's plea to Augustus, see Dio, *History of Rome* 52.30, cited in Kenneth W. Hall, *Coinage in the Roman Economy, 300 BC to AD 700* (Baltimore: Johns Hopkins University Press, 1996), 97.

40. P. J. Casey, *Understanding Ancient Coins: An Introduction for Archaeologists and Historians* (Norman: University of Oklahoma Press, 1986), 37.

41. Also issued was a closely related *Judaea Devicta* ("defeated") coin with similar iconography, often appearing with single, male, bound captives. These coins are frequently pictured in major reference works as New Testament or biblical coins. Sometimes they are the only Roman coins discussed. For an example, see John W. Betlyon, "Coinage," *ABD* 1:1076–89. In contrast, Kreitzer (*Striking New Images*) extends Oster's discussion of coins as a window onto early Christianity, systematically arguing that attention to the range of Roman coins minted during the period of early Christian textual production will enhance our understanding of that world.

42. All of the image entries and discussions concerning Judea in the *Lexicon Iconographicum Mythologiae Classicae* focus on coins from this series. See Herbert A. Cahn, "Iudaea," *LIMC* 5: 531–33 (plates), 811–13 (discussion).

43. The presence of the palm tree could be a definitive signifier of the location of the suppressed revolt (i.e., that it was situated in Judea). This, along with the fact that Titus and Vespasian did not take the title "Judaicus" after their joint triumph, could be an indicator that they did not want to associate the destruction of Jerusalem with the Diaspora (i.e., all Jewish people). See E. Mary Smallwood, *The Jews under Roman Rule: From Pompey to Diocletian* (SJLA 20; Leiden: Brill, 1976), 229.

44. Smallwood designates her as a Jewess who represents "a personification of the province" (ibid., 229–30).

45. Luise Schottroff, *Lydia's Impatient Sisters*, 190–91.

46. Ibid., 187–90. This dual significance also speaks to the polyvalency of the symbolism involved in using a woman's body to represent a whole people. I discuss the mother of Zion in chapter 4.

47. See Kreitzer, *Striking New Images*, 137; and Harold Mattingly and Edward Sydenham, *The Roman Imperial Coinage: Vespasian to Hadrian* (vol. 2 of *The Roman Imperial Coinage*; London: Spink, 1967), 427.

48. See Isaac, *Invention of Racism in Classical Antiquity*, 251.

49. This statue was found in 1863 in the so-called Villa of Livia at Prima Porta near Rome and is now housed at the Vatican museum. This representation of Augustus is one of the most familiar and widely discussed examples of imperial portraits of the Augustan age and perhaps of Roman imperial art as a whole. An extensive bibliography on the statue itself and its place in the Augustan program is included in Heinz Kähler, *Die Augustusstatue von Primaporta,* Monumenta Artis Romanae 1 (Cologne: DuMont Schauberg, 1959), 29–30; more recent work on this statue is included in Niels Hannestad, *Roman Art and Imperial Policy* (Aarhus: Aarhus University Press, 1988), 50–56; C. Brian Rose, *Dynastic Commemoration and Imperial Portraiture in the Julio-Claudian Period* (New York: Cambridge University Press, 1997), 11–21; and Zanker, *Power of Images*, 188–92. On Roman imperial cuirassed statues as a whole, see the classic work of Cornelius C. Vermeule, "Hellenistic and Roman Cuirassed Statues," *Berytus* 13 (1959): 1–82, continued in *Berytus* 15 (1964): 95–110; 17 (1966): 49–59; 23 (1974): 5–26; 26 (1978): 85–123; as well as Klaus Stemmer, *Untersuchungen zur Typologie, Chronologie, und Ikonographie der Panzerstatuen,* Archäologische Forschungen 4 (Berlin: Mann, 1978). Vermeule's *Hellenistic and Roman Cuirassed Statues* (Boston: Department of Classical Art, Museum of Fine Arts, 1980) contains relevant images and serves as a concordance for the *Berytus* articles and Stemmer's work.

50. Though the Romans made fairly extensive use of the cuirassed statue as a means to communicate imperial ideology, they were not the first to erect statues of victorious men wearing military armor. Many of the elements on the Roman portrait statues are similar to those employed on examples from the Classical and Hellenistic periods.

51. There are more than 600 known cuirassed statues from the Roman imperial period. Of these, about 150 depict conquered peoples and nations. Richard A. Gergel provides a valuable discussion (and notes) in "Costume as Geographic Indicator: Barbarians and Prisoners on Cuirassed Statue Breastplates," in *The World of Roman Costume*, 191–208. The proliferation of cuirassed statues featuring (and indeed celebrating) conquered peoples underscores the point that such representation is key to portraying military victory as a core concept underlying the Roman imperial ideology of peace that is premised on subduing and assimilating non-Roman peoples.

52. Cornelius C. Vermeule posits that erecting a statue through which to honor the emperor in Greece or Asia Minor would be the easiest (and perhaps cheapest) way of making gratitude to Rome known. The other options would be to manipulate already-existing Hellenistic-era monuments and/or make Roman-style ones such as arches, historical reliefs, and so on; see his *Roman Imperial Art in Greece and Asia Minor* (Cambridge: Harvard University Press, 1968), 41–46. Rose notes the likelihood of a patronage relationship leading to the erection of portrait statues and other dynastic monuments in the provinces, where the provincial city gives statues as gifts in anticipation of favors from the imperial family (*Dynastic Commemoration*, 8).

53. Zanker discusses how the portraits in various parts of the Roman Empire, east and west, corresponded to identifiable types believed to have been standardized at Rome (*Power of Images*, 300–16). For an extensive discussion of the evidence for the imperial cult in Asia Minor, see Simon R. F. Price's seminal work *Rituals and Power: The Roman Imperial Cult in Asia Minor* (New York: Cambridge University Press, 1984). For a discussion of the ways the city of Rome itself responded to imperial cult, see Ittai Gradel, *Emperor Worship and Roman Religion* (New York: Oxford University Press, 2002).

54. This point is discussed extensively in Zanker, *Power of Images*, 188–238. It is not so much the point that people throughout the Roman Empire would view the exact same statue portrait of the emperor in the identical place, but that the themes represented on the statues, as well as the faces of the emperors themselves, would be familiar. It is well known that following the Egyptian example, the Romans made statues with changeable heads—so a portrait would be updated with a new head

whenever, and for whatever reason, it was needed. It is therefore imaginable that, at the very least, the emperor's head would be recognizable in a larger geographical area.

55. Zanker argues for bare feet as an allusion to divine status (drawing on a classical Greek Polyclitan imagery), underscoring Augustus's own divinity (*Power of Images*, 189). Karl Galinsky takes a more utilitarian approach to Augustus's feet, postulating that the lack of shoes is a symptom that the statue is a copy, whose boots have been removed after his death to highlight more fully his divinity (*Augustan Culture: An Interpretive Introduction* [Princeton: Princeton University Press, 1998], 161). See later examples of the same phenomenon throughout Vermeule, *Roman Imperial Cuirassed Statues*. Cf. the divine Claudius relief represented at Aphrodisias, discussed below.

56. Suetonius, *Aug.* 79–81. The Romans tied the success of an emperor to how good-looking he was, highlighting a preoccupation with the dependency of virtuosity on appearance. Such good looks were also a cause for desire and identification on the part of conquered and subject peoples as well. Pliny's account of Trajan arriving in Rome, with none of the assembled being able to avert their eyes from his beautiful likeness (including women rejoicing over having children to live and serve under his command), is an example of this kind of identification (*Pan.* 22.3). It probably is not a coincidence that Trajan, responsible for subduing the Dacians and "securing borders," is looked up to, even desired by, his subjects, who, Pliny ensures to point out, are ready to serve with pleasure. See also the contrast, peppered throughout historical literature and visual representation, between the idealized beauty of the Romans as indicative of possessing the civility and fitness to rule the world and the strange and not-so-pretty features and wardrobes of barbarians of various types (some of which I discuss in chapter 3).

57. Gergel, "Costume as Geographic Indicator," 194.

58. This feature is viewed most productively as Roman imperial theology, contrasted with the anti-imperial theology of Judaism. See Crossan and Reed, *In Search of Paul*, 13–68; Warren Carter, *Matthew and Empire: Initial Explorations* (Harrisburg: Trinity Press International, 2003), 9–32.

59. There is much discussion about how this figure could have any number of identities, including an association with Mars. Gergel has seen it as a representation of the Roman army (*exercitus*); see "Costume as Geographic Indicator," 195.

60. Galinsky, *Augustan Culture*, 155, referring to calls for Julius Caesar's revenge.

61. The identity of this figure is also the subject of much discussion. Is it King Phraates IV, who returned the standards to the Romans, or perhaps Mithridates I, founder of the Parthian nation? The personifications elsewhere on the cuirass seem incongruent with a definitive personal portrait for these two central figures. Therefore, the identification of this figure as a stereotypical representative, even personification, of the Parthian people and not a particular Parthian individual seems sound. Likewise, the Roman figure is not a specific man, but perhaps a personification of the victorious Roman army. Whatever the case, the power relationships between the figures are clear: active/winner, passive/loser. For a discussion of these figures as personifications, see Gergel, "Costume as Geographic Indicator," 195; Hannestad, *Roman Art and Imperial Policy*, 53; and more thoroughly, John Pollini, *Studies in Augustan "Historical" Reliefs* (Ph.D. diss., University of California, Berkeley, 1978), 8–74.

62. In visual representation, eastern barbarians like Dacians, Armenians, and Parthians usually wear similar loose-fitting trousers while northern barbarians like Gauls and Germans wear tight-fitting pants. For examples of coinage featuring eastern barbarians, see Gergel, "Costume as Geographic Indicator," 195 and 208 n. 12.

63. This element is also reflected in quips like "On humbled knees Phraates accepted the law and rule of Caesar" (Horace, *Ep.* 1.12.27–28, cited in Galinsky, *Augustan Culture*, 156).

64. Zanker notes that the image of the kneeling Parthian was originally created by the Senate, and, apparently, Roman elites also displayed such images on their rings (*Power of Images*, 187–91).

65. See Craig A. Williams, *Roman Homosexuality: Ideologies of Masculinity in Classical Antiquity* (New York: Oxford University Press, 1999), 132–35.

66. On the spatial representation of these gods on the cuirass as being indicative of the Roman imperial pantheon, see Frances Van Keuren, "Cosmic Symbolism of the Pantheon on the Cuirass of the Prima Porta Augustus," in *The Age of Augustus,* ed. Rolf Winckes (Louvaine-La-Neuve: Center for Old World Archaeology, Brown University, 1985), 177–88.

67. Although Pax and Cybele are certainly possible identifications for this figure, Tellus/Earth seems apt because of her attributes (cornucopia, two infants), her dress (fully clothed and draped) and her reclining pose. Tellus also is appropriate when her relation opposite Caelus and the rest of the gods above (in the heavens) is taken into consideration. The two central figures appear to be standing above or on her. This interpretation is further bolstered by the appearance of a similar woman sitting and holding two infants on the Ara Pacis. Her positioning at the bottom of this composition also recalls the mythological defeat of Gaia, mother of the Giants, famously commemorated visually on the Attalid Altar of Zeus at Pergamon (now in Berlin), as well as a panel from the Sebasteion at Aphrodisias (see below). The imperial new life of abundance comes out of the defeat of the borderlands, as well as the surrender of the earth herself. I thank Brigitte Kahl for this helpful observation linking Roman imperial art to this earlier Attalid monument still in use at Paul's time. For an in-depth discussion of the Great Altar as an exemplary monument in light of which Paul's rhetoric to the Galatians can be understood, see Kahl, "Reading Galatians and Empire at the Great Altar of Pergamon," *USQR* 59:3–4 (2005): 21–43.

68. See the discussion of these two figures in Ferris, *Enemies of Rome,* 35–36.

69. Celts and Gauls are often described in Greek and Roman sources as wearing *bracae*, shirts, and *sagi* (cloaks), fastened to their shoulders with a clasp. All clothing items are brightly colored and patterned and form a significantly outlandish appearance when seen with their stiff limed hair, tattoos, and plethora of shining torque cuffs. They also often are depicted as fighting while nude. See, for example, Diodorus, *Library* 5 and 30; and Strabo, *Geogr.* 4.4.3. I discuss Roman stereotypes of the Gauls based on appearance and behavior in chapter 3.

70. The *carnyx* was a tall horn used by Celtic peoples across Europe, from Britain and Gaul (France) to the German Alpine region and Dacia (Romania). Several well-known examples of the head portion survive, the most notable one being the Deskford Carnyx of northern Scotland. Accounts of its use include the Gauls' sack of Delphi in 279 B.C.E., the Battle of Telamon in Etruria in 225 B.C.E., and Caesar's various battles with Gallic tribes. According to Diodorus, the Celts would use such barbaric trumpets to startle their enemies, making a harsh and confusing noise (*Library* 30). Polybius (*Hist.* 29.5–9) describes there being so many of these loud horns in battle that the piercing sound was not as if it were from humans but from the whole countryside itself. An international instrument, the *carnyx* must have been common enough to capture the Roman imagination, thereby becoming a stereotypical attribute designating Celtic and Gaulish peoples in visual representation. A keystone at the Palazzo dei Conservatori in Rome, for example, features a crouching woman next to one, identifying her as a representative or personification of a Celtic or Gaulish nation. A silver denarius coin issued circa 48 B.C.E., whose obverse side features a stereotypical head (complete with the famed limed hair) of a personified figure identified as Gallia (a representation of the Gauls) or simply a female Gaul, also has a *carnyx* behind it. See D. R. Sears, *History and Coinage of the Roman Imperators, 49–27 BCE* (London: Spink, 1998), Coin #19.

71. Gergel notes that consistency in the potential national representatives of this personification points to identification with Alpine or Gaulish tribes (Pannonia, Dalmatia, Gallia herself); see "Costume as Geographic Indicator," 196 and 208 n.16.

72. The *Res Gestae* mentions Hispania/Spain as experiencing the hand of Roman rule a number of times, including the following references: that it takes the "same oath of allegiance" as Italy and demanded Augustus to lead them after Actium (25); the "Spains" were "reduced to peace" with Galatia/Gallia and Germany (26); Augustus claims to have settled military colonies in Africa, Sicily, Macedonia, "both Spains," Achaia, Asia, Gallia/Galatia Narbonensis, and Pisidia (28); and the Roman standards were recovered from Spain, Gallia/Galatia, Dalmatia, and the Parthians (29). I discuss this inscription as a text and visual monument in chapter 3.

73. There is a military trophy on Augustus's back without an attendant body near it. Some have theorized that this trophy, due to its inclusion of northern barbarian armor, weapons, and helmet, represents Dalmatia in the Alpine region. This identification would be consistent with the *Res Gestae*'s placement of Gallia, Hispania, and Dalmatia as regions conquered within close range of each other. See Gergel, "Costume as Geographic Indicator," 196; and Hannestad, *Roman Art and Imperial Policy*, 56.

74. Her appearance could additionally refer to the long and contested relationship the various Spanish tribes had with Rome before Augustus finally defeated them in 25 B.C.E. (marking a premature closing of the Temple of Janus's doors to signify peace, since the Cantabrians revolted again in 22 B.C.E.) and divided the land. Some defeated Spanish tribes, such as the Numantines in 133 B.C.E. and the Cantabrians, preferred to commit suicide and destroy their own towns rather than submit to the Romans, thus depriving the latter of prisoners and slaves from among their ranks. Such behavior is a show of their love of valor and freedom according to Dio (44.5) and Appian (*Hist. rom.* 6, the "Spanish Wars" account).

75. Ancient Aphrodisias of Caria (near modern Geyre) is still undergoing excavations that were started by New York University (NYU) in 1961 under the leadership of Kenan T. Erim (d. 1990) and have continued under R. R .R. Smith and Christopher Ratté. For up-to-date reports on ongoing archaeological work, including a fairly comprehensive bibliography from 1961 to the present, see the website of the Aphrodisias project at: http://www.nyu.edu/projects/aphrodisias. For extensive bibliographical information and discussion of excavations until the mid-1980s, see Kenan T. Erim, *Aphrodisias: City of Venus Aphrodite* (New York: Facts on File, 1986); and Juliette de la Genière and Kenan T. Erim, eds., *Aphrodisias de Carie, Colloque de l'Université de Lille III* (Paris: Éditions Recherche sur les civilisations, 1987). Subsequent reports on excavations have been made and discussed in Kenan T. Erim and Charlotte Roueché, eds., *Aphrodisias Papers 1: Recent Work on Architecture and Sculpture*, JRAM 1 (Ann Arbor: Department of Classical Studies, University of Michigan, 1990); Kenan T. Erim and R. R. R. Smith, eds., *Aphrodisias Papers 2: Theatre, a Sculptor's Workshop, Philosophers, and Coin-types*, JRAM 2 (Ann Arbor: Department of Classical Studies, University of Michigan, 1991); and Charlotte Roueché and R. R. R. Smith, eds., *Aphrodisias Papers 3: Setting and Quarry, Mythological and Other Sculptural Decoration, Architectural Development, Portico of Tiberius and Tetrapylon*, JRAM 20 (Ann Arbor: Department of Classical Studies, University of Michigan, 1996). For designation of the complex as an imperial cult sanctuary and consideration of the imperial cult's proliferation in Aphrodisias, see Joyce M. Reynolds, "New Evidence for the Imperial Cult in Julio-Claudian Aphrodisias," *ZPE* 43 (1981): 317–27; Reynolds, *Aphrodisias and Rome: Documents from the Excavation of the Theatre at Aphrodisias*, JRS Monograph 1 (London: Society for the Promotion of Roman Studies, 1982); Reynolds, "Further Information on Imperial Cult at Aphrodisias," *Studii Clasice* 24 (1986): 109–17; and Reynolds, "Ruler-Cult at Aphrodisias in the Late Republic and under the Julio-Claudian Emperors," in *Subject and Ruler: The Cult of the Ruling Power in Classical Antiquity*, ed. A. Small, JRAM 17 (Ann Arbor: Department of Classical Studies, University of Michigan Press, 1996), 41–50. For images of the Sebasteion reliefs, I rely here on the high-quality presentation in R. R. R. Smith, "Imperial Reliefs from the Sebasteion at Aphrodisias," *JRS* 77 (1987): 88–138; and Smith, "*Simulacra Gentium*: The *Ethne* from the Sebasteion at Aphrodisias," *JRS* 78 (1988): 50–77, as well as the images available from the NYU excavations.

76. Smith, "Imperial Reliefs," 90. Inscriptions show that the complex was most likely started under Tiberius and finished under Nero. An earthquake damaged it during its construction, and restorations were made. Some time after Nero's *damnatio memoriae* in 68 C.E., reliefs bearing his likeness were removed from display and used as floor panels within the Sebasteion complex and as stone for a theater renovation elsewhere in the city, thus explaining why they were found away from the Sebasteion's location and in such remarkably good condition.

77. Venus's identification as such is preserved from an inscription on a statue base of the *propylon*; see Erim, *Aphrodisias*, 123.

78. Ibid., 107.

79. Ibid., 122.

80. Kuttner has suggested that the Sebasteion's sculptural and architectural program may have had the Fora of Caesar and Augustus as its template (*Dynasty and Empire*, 82).

81. Smith ("Imperial Reliefs") was one of the first to publish reliefs together as a group and discuss them as imperial images, thereby offering an interpretation of the iconography of the Roman imperial cult on Greek terms. See Plates 3 and 4 for examples.

82. For a proposed sequence of the myth panels, see R. R. R. Smith, "Myth and Allegory in the Sebasteion," in Erim and Roueché, *Aphrodisias Papers 1*, 89–100.

83. This scene recalls representations of the mythological opponents Achilles and Penthesilea. According to the *Iliad*, Achilles killed Penthesilea, the Amazon queen who came to the aid of the Trojans during that war; he only realized how beautiful she was after he killed her. The death scene is a popular representation in art showing Greeks battling Amazons. Virgil has Aeneas looking at one such frieze depicting the Trojan War in a Carthaginian temple and commenting on Penthesilea's valor (*Aen.* 1.490). In Aphrodisias, another relief of Achilles and Penthesilea is part of the mythological series in the Sebasteion, and a sculpture group believed to be the two foes has been found in Hadrian's baths there (see Erim, *Aphrodisias*, 115; and Smith, "Myth and Allegory," 95–97). An Amazonomachy (which depicts the legendary battle between the Amazonians and the Athenians) was also found in Aphrodisias at the Agora Gate. See Pascale Linant de Bellefonds, "The Mythological Reliefs from the Agora Gate," in Roueché and Smith, *Aphrodisias Papers 3*, 174–86.

84. Notably, of the published reliefs, all of the anonymous, non-personified captured figures save one (who is buried up to his waist) are wearing the tight breeches characteristic of northern, Gallic and/or German barbarians. For the published reliefs featuring captives, see Smith, "Imperial Reliefs," Plates 4, 10, 12, 18. See also figures 3 and 4 in this chapter.

85. They are identified as such by an inscription underneath their image: *TIBERIOS KLAUDIOS KAISAR*) and *BRETANNIA* on either side of a satyr's head. See Kenan T. Erim, "A New Relief Showing Claudius and Britannia from Aphrodisias," *Britannia* 13 (1982): 277–81; and Smith, "Imperial Reliefs," 115.

86. For the significance of the bared breast in ancient visual representation, see Beth Cohen, "Divesting the Female Breast of Clothes in Classical Sculpture," in Lyons and Koloski-Ostrow, *Naked Truths*, 66–98.

87. Ferris, *Enemies of Rome*, 58.

88. Ferris notes that the sexual intimations of the Claudius and Britannia relief have made interpreters uncomfortable; see ibid., 56–58. Rodgers argues that Britannia's dishevelment indicates "the highest degree of Otherness" ("Feminizing the Provincial Other," 85). However unsettling, the linkage of sexual conquest with conquering land is a recurring theme in the history of imperial politics, colonialism, and nation-building. Sexual conquest is a palpable tool of state control and a metaphor for expansionism where those doing the penetrating are male, and the land is constructed as female, with native inhabitants being [ef]feminized by overly masculine conquerors. See Richard Trexler, *Sex and Conquest: Gendered Violence, Political Order, and the European Conquest of the Americas* (Ithaca: Cornell University Press, 1995); and David Tombs, "Crucifixion, State Terror, and Sexual Abuse," *USQR* 53 (1999): 89–110. It should be noted that the God of Israel does not rape the nations; a theme to which I return in chapter 4.

89. Kampen, "Gender Theory and Roman Art," 20; and Ferris, *Enemies of Rome*, 38.

90. The women were only sold into slavery if barbarian men rebelled any further or disregarded Roman friendship (Suetonius, *Aug.* 21). Additionally, Augustus took children as hostages and in some cases, raised and educated them with his own (i.e., Roman) children (*Aug.* 48; cf. *Res Gestae* 32, where he mentions that client-kings sent children as pledges because they wanted to; see chapter 3 for discussion).

91. Even though they were incorporated, the women were still in slavery with their children. Augustus's social reforms made it more difficult for Roman citizenship to be attained by foreigners (Suetonius, *Aug.* 48).

92. This is also the case with the Nero and Armenia scene. Britannia and Armenia represent personified conquered nations and geographical outlines of the Roman Empire: Britannia to the far north and Armenia to the eastern extremity. These two relief panels have the following in common: geographical boundaries, conquest and Amazon imagery, and scantily clad emperors. They also are the only two of the found and published imperial reliefs where an emperor is shown in action, that is, in the course of victory actually touching conquered people. In other reliefs, emperors are shown next to trophies and captives and are also in many cases nude (or almost nude), cloaked, and holding weapons. They are standing and receiving crowns or presented in a *concordia* pose with a draped Roman female figure or with a male personification of the Roman *populus*. Also, see a panel depicting a fully dressed and cuirassed Nero receiving a crown from a woman, probably his mother Agrippina, who is dressed in the manner of Tyche (Fortuna) and pictured bearing a cornucopia (Smith, "Imperial Reliefs," Plate 24).

93. Smith, "*Simulacra Gentium*," 50.

94. Some of the names are fragmentary. Smith, following Reynolds ("New Evidence for the Imperial Cult"), has argued for the following identifications: Egyptians, Andizeti, Arabs (fragmentary), Bessi, Bosporans, Dacians, Dardani, Iapodes, Judeans, Callaeci, Piroustae, Rhaeti, and Triumpilini.

95. Smith, "*Simulacra Gentium*," 58–59. The nations mentioned in the Sebasteion additionally differ in administrative status. Cyprus, Egypt, Judea, Sicily, and Rhaetia were all separate administrative provinces. Crete was part of a province with Cyrene. Arabia and Dacia were not technically part of the Roman Empire until Trajan, and the Bosporans never fully were. The other *ethnē* (Andizeti, Bessi, Callaeci, Dardani, Iarodes, Piroustae, Triumpilini), all in the west or in a area north of Asia Minor, were peoples within provinces of the Roman Empire. The Bessi were part of the Thracian client kingdom that became a province only in 46 C.E. The previously mentioned nations are described in historical and geographical literature (e.g., throughout Diodorus, Strabo, and Pliny the Elder) as sufficiently foreign or barbarian to warrant the civilizing force of Roman rule, and many were perceived to be fierce brigands, robbers, and similarly resistant to being ruled.

96. Unfortunately, personifications of both Judea and Ethiopia to match the bases have not been found. See Smith, "*Simulacra Gentium*," 55, Plate 7.

97. Both Reynolds and Smith argue that this portico served as a visual representation of the inhabited conquered world, encompassing mainly the conquests of Augustus. In this sense, the series serves as a visual *Res Gestae* of sorts. The islands of Crete, Cyrene, and Sicily have the honor of being returned to Augustus from Cleopatra and Antony after the Battle of Actium. See Reynolds, "New Evidence for the Imperial Cult," and Smith, "*Simulacra Gentium*."

98. On Day and Ocean, see Smith, "*Simulacra Gentium,*" 53, Plate 7; and on Augustus, see Smith, "Imperial Reliefs," 104–6, Plate 6.

99. This panel is identified as such by an inscribed base. In another panel Roma also is shown crowning a personification of Aphrodisias, including her in the victory pattern with the emperors (see Erim, *Aphrodisias*, 117).

100. See Susan Fischler, "Imperial Cult: Engendering the Cosmos," in *When Men Were Men: Masculinity in Classical Antiquity,* ed. Lin Foxhall and John Salmon; London: Routledge, 1999), 165–83.

101. The only full-length discussion of the silver cups of the Boscoreale treasure is Kuttner, *Dynasty and Empire*. A brief recent exploration that draws heavily on Kuttner's work is in Crossan and Reed, *In Search of Paul*, 284–88. Kuttner's work makes the cups relevant because, as she argues, they are items of the "minor arts," whose decoration is almost certainly based on a now-lost public monumental relief program. Therefore, the study of the cups is not about the cups at all, but

about another instance of a relief program involving a depiction of peace brought through defeat of the nations.

102. The men are not bound and not disheveled; this could indicate that they were not conquered recently, i.e., that they show some measure of Romanization. See Kuttner, *Dynasty and Empire*, 100.

103. Ann Kuttner makes this point in *Dynasty and Empire*; also see Ferris, *Enemies of Rome*, 1–25.

104. These more domesticated personifications (i.e., represented as friendly to Rome) are consistent with Hadrian's later iconographical program in the Hadrianeum that depicts the world's provinces and territories as free-standing reliefs living in harmony with their rulers. Sixteen provincial reliefs and six trophies survive in at least four museum collections throughout Europe. For images and discussion of the Hadrianeum reliefs, see *Provinciae fideles: Il fregio del Tempio di Adriano in Campo Marzio,* ed. Marina Sapelli and Amanda Claridge (Milan: Electa, 1999); for the province series in coins and reliefs, as well as for a thorough examination of pre-Hadrianic personifications that still serves as a standard reference, see Toynbee, *The Hadrianic School.*

105. See Jane M. Cody, "Conquerors and Conquered on Flavian Coins," in *Flavian Rome: Culture, Image, Text,* ed. A. J. Boyle and W. J. Dominik (Leiden: Brill, 2003), 103–24.

106. Cody, "Conquerors and Conquered," 109.

107. See further A. N. Sherwin-White, *The Roman Citizenship,* 2d ed. (Oxford: Clarendon, 1973), 437–44.

108. Ramsay MacMullen notes that the Roman Empire—of the third and fourth centuries, but alluding to Paul's first-century context as well—was in fact composed of hundreds of tribes that constituted outsiders prone to various degrees of alienation. See *Enemies of the Roman Order: Treason, Unrest, and Alienation in the Empire* (New York: Oxford University Press, 1966), 192–241.

109. R. R. R. Smith has suggested that the sculptural program in the Sebasteion's north portico belongs to the victory art pattern involving groups of conquered peoples that was definitively Roman in production; a consensus is emerging to this effect.

110. For the texts, see Pliny, *Nat.* 36.41; Suetonius, *Nero* 46.2. At *Nat.* 7.3.34–35, Pliny mentions that Pompey also exhibited "images of celebrated marvels" as ornaments in the theater, such as monstrous births (considered prodigies and portents, as well as a form of entertainment, to the Romans) and women who generated an exceptional number of children set alongside images of the nations.

111. Cited in Smith, "*Simulacra Gentium*," 71. Such a portico has not been found. However, Kuttner argues that such a portico could easily have been part of the program at the Forum of Augustus (*Dynasty and Empire*, 81–82). I think this is entirely plausible and agree that the Sebasteion at Aphrodisias provides compelling conjecture that the portico came from Rome and was not designed by the Aphrodisians themselves. The later, greater Forum of Trajan is thought also to have included images of Dacian captives holding up the roof alongside their weapons, which could also imply development of the program at the earlier Fora in continuation of the pattern of sculpting and displaying the conquered. See James Packer, *The Forum of Trajan in Rome: A Study of the Monuments,* 3 vols. (Berkeley: University of California Press, 1997). The Hadrianeum is another example; these later developments are outside the present scope of this project and will need further investigation upon its elaboration.

112. In Virgil's description, the nations were parading as part of the triple triumph for Augustus. Framing the procession were three hundred shrines, games and shouting, as well as slaughtered steers on altars in all of the temples, further indicating the celebration of conquest. Interestingly, the Carians, representing Caria where Aphrodisias is located, are mentioned explicitly along with the Africans, Leleges, Morini (called "the furthest of mankind"), and Dahae. I discuss this passage in chapter 3.

113. This is most likely a description of the Forum of Augustus and is of uncertain accuracy; it could represent either portions of the actual Forum as it was built or the plans for it (that were

already under way before the Battle of Actium). The description is a relatively close parallel to Ovid's representation of the Forum at *Fasti* 5.550 ff.

114. For a reconstructed plan and extensive discussion of the Forum of Augustus, see Paul Zanker, *Forum Augustum* (Tübingen: Wastmuth, 1968).

115. The *caryatides* (columns shaped like women's bodies) in the Forum may be modeled after those at the Parthenon in Athens, but they are not simply a design element (i.e., evidence of Romans copying Greeks) or gender-neutral. Vitruvius, writing in the early imperial period, provides a probably contrived explanation for the *caryatides* in the context of discussing how architects should be historically informed, knowing that when they employ elements from previous structures, they should be aware of the message they send. The women represented as Cariatids were the Carians conquered by Greece after a failed conspiracy with the Persians. They were led in a triumph and placed in slavery as an eternal warning; architects then designed figures of women who were to carry burdens (i.e., hold up the roof) for inclusion in public buildings "so the penalty of the sin (*peccatum*) of the Cariatid women would be known to posterity and historically recorded" (*On Architecture* 1.1.5). Whatever the history, their appearance as women's bodies should not be ignored. Noteworthy is Vitruvius's inclusion of the story in a treatise discussing appropriate architecture for the Roman Empire, where it seems to make the point that the image of women's bodies in Roman public buildings could send a handy and familiar message of defeat already communicated by the Greeks. For an extensive discussion of the Roman reception of this female-as-column form as presented at the Erechtheion in Athens, see Alexandra Lesk, "A Diachronic Examination of the Erechtheion and Its Reception" (Ph.D. diss., University of Cincinnati, 2004).

116. Ferris, *Enemies of Rome*, provides the most recent and thorough discussion and bibliography of barbarians in Roman imperial art, considering personifications alongside other, "nameless" visual portrayals of conquered people.

117. Rhiannon Evans suggests that, due to their close spatial proximity, it would not be difficult to read these two geographically inclined items together. See her "Containment and Corruption: The Discourse of Flavian Empire," in Boyle and Dominik, *Flavian Rome*, 255–76; cf. R. Moynihan, "Geographical Mythology and Roman Imperial Ideology," in Winckes, *Age of Augustus*, 149–62.

118. For particularly vivid descriptions of how foreign gods traveled to Rome, see Ovid's *Fasti*. For a discussion of Roman cultural appropriation as a part of imperialism, as well as how non-Romans reacted to the plundering of their homelands and to the display of their sacred images at Rome, see Catherine Edwards, "Incorporating the Alien: The Art of Conquest," in *Rome the Cosmopolis*, ed. Catherine Edwards and Greg Woolf (New York: Cambridge University Press, 2003), 44–70.

119. On the Greek and Latin inscription, see the still-reliable study *Monumentum Ancyranum*, ed. E. G. Hardy (Oxford: Clarendon, 1923); on the inscription's location at the temple of Augustus and Roma in Ancyra, see Daniel Krencker and Martin Schede, *Der Tempel in Ankara* (Berlin: de Gruyter, 1936).

120. According to Josephus, Herod built two theaters: one was an amphitheater "in the plain" where games in honor of Caesar were celebrated every five years "opposite to Jewish custom." For an account of the theater's decoration and activity, see Josephus, *A. J.* 15.267–79. I do not know of any art historians working on Roman imperial visual representations of series of conquered peoples who mention this passage. Nevertheless, it gives an important indication of how non-Romans viewed Roman building programs and images of the nations (even if we accept that Josephus is careful in his representation).

121. The Romans themselves are also a nation but stand out as the "lords of the world, nation of the toga" (Virgil, *Aen.* 1.282)—that is, the nation predestined to be associated with civilization and rule over others. See chapter 3.

3. The Fate of the Nations and the Naturalization of Conquest

1. Most of the primary sources are readily available in English translation in the Loeb Classical Library. I have limited this study to the resources that present a picture of Roman imperial ideology that I deemed crucial for a gender-critical re-imagination of Paul.

2. For a thorough examination of how the Romans in the early principate represented their founder(s) in text and space, as well as what that reflected about Roman imperial social order, see Augusto Fraschetti, *The Foundation of Rome,* trans. Marian Hill and Kevin Windle (Edinburgh: Edinburgh University Press, 2002).

3. Such dedication is not restricted to histories but is a common feature of Roman literature of the early imperial age, especially for those authors writing for the express purpose of the imperial court (e.g., Propertius, Horace, Virgil, and Ovid, and at times, Vitruvius and both Plinys). See also the "Priene Inscription," which publicly celebrates the divinely ordained quality of Augustus's life:

> [W]hereas the Providence which has guided our whole existence and which has shown such care and liberality, has brought our life to the peak of perfection in giving to us Augustus Caesar, whom it (Providence) filled with virtue for the welfare of mankind, and who, being sent to us and to our descendants as a Savior (*sōtēr*), has put an end to war and has set all things in order; and whereas, having become visible, Caesar has fulfilled the hopes of all earlier times . . . not only in surpassing all the benefactors who preceded him but also in leaving to his successors no hope of surpassing him; and whereas, finally, that the birthday of the God (i.e., Augustus) has been for the whole world the beginning of the gospel (*euangelion*) concerning him, therefore, let all reckon a new era beginning from the date of his birth, and let his birthday mark the beginning of the new year.

For the text of the inscription, see *Inschriften von Priene*, ed. Hiller von Gaertingen (Berlin: Walter de Gruyter, 1906).

4. Some might take issue with using Dionysius's history for an examination of Roman imperial ideology. His Greekness, his unashamed love of Rome that cancels out his Greekness, and his concentration on an unreachable part of Roman history—archaic history—as his starting point have all been used against his work. I find him valuable precisely because he is a Greek person who has studied at Rome and portrays himself as concluding that the Romans are not only Greeks, but better Greeks than the Greeks by virtue of their having mastered the whole world. This is telling in light of his writing during the Augustan age. Further, his use of rhetoric to present archaic historical events betrays a decision-making process about history. See Matthew Fox, "History and Rhetoric in Dionysius of Halicarnassus," *JRS* 83 (1993): 31–47, and the collected lectures of Emilio Gabba, *Dionysius and the History of Archaic Rome* (Berkeley: University of California Press, 1991).

5. Such a sentiment is challenged by Hill who posits that Dionysius may be telling his Roman story to Romans who were interested in squaring their history with Greekness. He notices considerable overlap with the *Aeneid* that helps to make the case. See H. Hill, "Dionysius of Halicarnassus and the Origins of Rome," *JRS* 51:1–2 (1961): 88–93.

6. Dionysius is no stranger to universal history, as his connections with Polybius are strong.

7. This could be seen as a direct clash with the metanarrative of Israel that posits the one God as the landowner and creator of the cosmos and all of the nations.

8. Ilia/Rhea's particular kind of virginity could itself be suggestive of masculinity, as Vestals took on the performance of rites open only to men, and chastity curbed her own sexual agency. See Mary Beard, "The Sexual Status of Vestal Virgins," *JRS* 70 (1980): 12–27.

9. According to Livy (1.3) and Dionysius (1.76), Amulius, the younger of the two sons of Proca, succeeded to the kingdom of Albans, after forcing Numitor out by beating him. He plotted to deprive Numitor's family of issue, both from fear of suffering punishment for stealing power and also because of his desire never to be dispossessed of his sovereignty. He also killed Aegestus, Numitor's son, and Numitor knew it but pretended to be ignorant. Livy and Dionysius both give genealogies of these

brothers, Livy showing his descent from Aeneas in a purely Roman line and Dionysius showing the descent of all of the Italian tribes from Greek races and Herakles—not, as it might be thought, from barbarians and slaves; see below.

10. Plutarch, *Romulus* 3.3, agrees with the point that Ilia is made to be a Vestal Virgin by Amulius and is discovered to be pregnant but omits any of the details of how that might have happened to her. Here we discover that Ilia was to be put to death for her transgression against the established law for the Vestals but her cousin, the king's daughter Antho, intercedes on her behalf. There is an allusion to divine origin, however, as Plutarch relates that the twin sons are "more than human" in size and beauty.

11. Not only in Dionysius, but in Dio as well (1.5.1), though here it is not rape but mere conception.

12. Ovid, *Fasti* 4.573–77; *Res Gestae* 21.

13. Note, also, that Remus is not named as Ilia's other son.

14. Kellum, "Phallus as Signifier," 170.

15. See Exodus 2:1-4, where Moses is put in a basket, sent up the river, found by the daughter of Pharaoh, and raised in the palace as her own son. He grows up to liberate the Israelites from Egyptian slavery and gives them the law while in the wilderness. Though the two stories are obviously different, the figures of Romulus and Moses can be seen as somehow dialectically opposed to each another: both exposed, both ordained to survive, both lawgivers to their people. However, Moses does not obtain his position through battle and murder as Romulus does, and he does not actually reach the promised land, whereas Romulus tends to the building and violent maintenance of creation (see below). I discuss Paul's interaction with this tradition in chapter 4.

16. I wonder about possible connections between the Ruminalis/fig tree—where Rome's founders were saved from death by the wolf—and Jesus' withering of a similar tree in the Gospels (Mark 11:13–22; Matt 21:18–22; Luke interestingly does not include the story but saves a fig tree from harm in a parable, 13:6-9). Jesus' withering of the fig tree also echoes Psalm 105, a song of liberation from slavery, where the Lord has worked many deeds among the nations, including the withering of the fig trees and vines that leads directly to Israel's exit from Egypt. An examination of such connections, particularly what they could mean in a Roman imperial context, that Jesus (uncharacteristically, some might argue) kills the tree to its roots because it does not bear fruit, is beyond the scope of the present work. But highlighting this allusion here points to more interpretive potential regarding the New Testament in light of Roman imperial ideology.

17. Dionysius is sure to point out that "God was directing him" (1.86.3).

18. Who had "loved them no less than a mother" (Dionysius, 1.87.3), remembering her non-maternal status.

19. See also Ovid, *Fasti* 4.843 and Plutarch, *Romulus* 10.

20. Plutarch ignores the tension between differing accounts, placing blame on Romulus and Celer, and also has Faustulus and his brother Pleistinus dying at the city's wall (*Romulus* 10.2).

21. See also Virgil, *Aeneid* 8.182–279 and Ovid, *Fasti* 1.543–586. Dionysius does not mention the Ara Maxima at this point in his history.

22. "When Romulus had duly attended to the worship of the gods, he called the multitude together and gave them the rules of the law, since nothing else but law could unite them into a single body politic. But these, he was persuaded, would only appear binding in the eyes of a rustic people in case he should invest his own person with majesty, by adopting emblems of authority. He therefore put on a more holy state in every way, and especially by the assumption of twelve lictors" (Livy 1.8).

23. For a summary, see Galinsky, *Augustan Culture*, 204–8.

24. "For when some proposed to confer upon him the name of Romulus, as being, in a manner, a second founder of the city, it was resolved that he should rather be called Augustus, a surname not only new, but of more dignity, because places devoted to religion, and those in which anything is consecrated by augury, are denominated August, either from the word *auctus*, signifying augmentation, or *ab avium gestu, gustuve* from the flight and feeding of birds; as appears from this verse of Ennius: 'When glorious Rome by August augury was built.'" Essentially, both Romulus and Augustus refer

to the founding of Rome, but perhaps Augustus would have meaning for a much wider audience, i.e., those unfamiliar with the Roman origin story.

25. Such allusions are also clear in Ovid's version of the Sabine women story; see below.

26. E.g., as captured prisoners in a triumphal procession; see below.

27. For discussion of the story, including where it appears in literature, on the coin, and in the history of art, see Eva Stehle, "Venus, Cybele and the Sabine Women: The Roman Construction of Female Sexuality," *Helios* 16:2 (1989): 143–64; Norman Bryson, "Two Narratives of Rape in the Visual Arts: Lucretia and the Sabine Women," in *Rape,* ed. Sylvana Tomaselli and Roy Porter (New York and London: Blackwell, 1986), 152–73; G. B. Miles, "The First Roman Marriage and the Theft of the Sabine Women," in *Livy: Reconstructing Early Rome* (Ithaca: Cornell University Press, 1995), 179–219; discussion of the reliefs and their relation to/reflection of Roman imperial ideas about women's roles: Natalie Boymel Kampen, "The Muted Other," and "Reliefs of the Basilica Aemilia: A Redating," *Klio* 73 (1991): 448–58.

28. Robert Brown calls Livy's version of the story a "historical parable on the theme of harmony"; he traces how Livy's account uses the women to show how "Roman greatness was—and continued to be—a function not of strength alone but strength tempered with cooperation and compromise." The Sabine women represent the power of compromise and resultant friendship, which was not just a marriage concept but a political category in the late republic and early empire. See Brown, "Livy's Sabine Women and the Ideal of *Concordia*," *TAPA* 125 (1995): 291–319.

29. The race-mixing inherent in Roman identity from its very beginning is discussed in detail in Dench, *Romulus's Asylum*.

30. Fox argues that rhetorically, this line of deliberation makes Romulus into a great Greek ruler; "History and Rhetoric in Dionysius of Halicarnassus," 35.

31. In this account it is Fortune who has given the women their husbands, and the 683 women (!) are married to an equal number of men, "according to customs of each woman's fatherland" (*kata tous patrious hekastēs ethismous*) (Dionysius, 2.30.6).

32. For example in Cicero, *De re publica* 2.7.12–13, where it is used as an example of early diplomacy as Romulus made an alliance with Tatius, king of the Sabines, "at the intercession of the women who had been abducted."

33. E.g., Susan Treggiari, *Roman Marriage:* iusti coniuges *from the Time of Cicero to the Time of Ulpian* (New York: Oxford/Clarendon, 1991).

34. Kampen, "The Muted Other," 16.

35. Dench, *Romulus's Asylum*, 23.

36. Ovid has the women gather at a temple of Juno and ask for advice. They include Romulus's wife, who makes a speech: "O wives raped alike—for that is a trait we have in common—no longer may we dawdle in our duties to our kin. The battle is set in array, but choose for which side you will pray the gods to intervene: on one side stands your husband with arms and on the other your father: the question is whether you prefer to be widow or an orphan. I will give you a piece of advice both bold and dutiful" (*Fasti* 3.207–12). Upon getting the word, the wives unbind their hair and put on mourning clothes. They kneel on the ground, offering the children in the middle of the battle-scene—their little cries of "grandfather" cause the weapons to fall, the men to clasp hands, and babies to be hoisted up onto shields.

37. Of course, it is not an accident that the *Aeneid* is modeled on Homer's epics and positions the Romans as definitively surpassing the Greeks.

38. Sarah Pomeroy et al., *Women in the Classical World: Image and Text* (New York: Oxford University Press, 1994), 297.

39. Turnus is wearing Pallas's belt as a trophy on his shoulder, perhaps pointing to the later Roman practice of displaying the weapons and armor of the vanquished.

40. See Yasmin Syed, *Virgil's* Aeneid *and the Roman Self: Subject and Nation in Literary Discourse* (Ann Arbor: University of Michigan Press, 2005).

41. Lynn Roller, *In Search of God the Mother: The Cult of Anatolian Cybele* (Berkeley: University of California Press, 1999), 299–304. When Aeneas arrives in Carthage, he is called "that Paris with his half-male (*semiviro*, a common Roman designation for the Galli priests of Cybele) band" (4.215). Numanus, in a battle scene, degrades Aeneas and his Trojan warriors as "Phrygian women" who should "leave fighting to the men" and go back to their ecstatic rituals (9.617–20). Turnus, before the final battle, speaks of further denigrating his effeminate opponent: "Grant that I may strike down his body and tear open with my strong hand the breastplate of this Phrygian eunuch, and mess up his hair, curled with a hot iron and wetted with myrrh, in the dust" (12.97–100).

42. For a development of this theme, see Eve Adler, *Vergil's Empire: Political Thought in the* Aeneid (New York: Rowman and Littlefield, 2003), 193–216.

43. For an equation of Lavinium with femaleness and the importance of Lavinia to the narrative as a whole, see Syed, *Virgil's* Aeneid *and the Roman Self*, particularly 136–76.

44. Ibid., 138.

45. The standard work on Cybele's appearance and function is still Martin Vermaseren, *Cybele and Attis* (Leiden: Brill, 1977); however, Roller, *In Search of God the Mother,* does much to advance a more nuanced diachronic portrait of this goddess.

46. Cybele helps her Trojans throughout the *Aeneid*: her light on Mount Ida signals a brighter future for the Trojans (2.693–97); she tells Creusa to remain at Troy (2.788); she averts the Rutulians from Aeneas's ships (9.77–83, 101–22) and her attributes adorn them (10.156–58).

47. Herodotus on Indians, especially as flesh-eaters: 3.99. Pliny on India/ns and Rome: 6.89; 7.99. Strabo names Indians as having "customs opposite ours," or, more precisely, "without customs" (*aetheia*,15.1.66); Roman provenance naturally extends to those who need "customs." C. R. Whittaker has explored Roman iconography of India and Indians, noting that India is personified as being a nation in willing cooperation with the Romans. There is also evidence of a temple complex to Augustus in India. Whittaker asks if such an "Indian Sebasteion" followed the same triumphal iconographic program as that in Aphrodisias. See Rajan Gurukkal and Whittaker, "In Search of Muziris," *Journal of Roman Archaeology* 14 (2001): 333–50; and Whittaker, "'To Reach out to India and Pursue the Dawn': The Roman View of India," *Rome and Its Frontiers*, 144–62.

48. The rape of Lucretia: Livy 1.57.7–59.12. It is Lucretia's chastity, not her availability, that inspires Sextus to go to her. Note the sexual pun put into Sextus's mouth at the moment he awakens sleeping Lucretia: "Holding the woman down with his left hand on her breast, he said, 'Be still, Lucretia! I am Sextus Tarquinius. My sword is in my hand. Utter a sound, and you die!'" (Livy 1.58.2). He uses his "sword" to rape her and leave, excited about his conquest of a noblewoman's honor.

49. Recounted in full in Plutarch, *Camillus*. According to Plutarch and Livy, Camillus was successful in defeating the Veii, whose fortification was quite formidable, by tunneling underground and bringing in troops that way. Plutarch relates that they burrowed up into the city near the temple of Juno. Camillus, after sacking the city, resolved that he would bring Juno back to Rome and after making a sacrifice to her, negotiated with the image of the goddess for that to come to pass. She agreed to go with the Romans and take a place among the gods in that city. Called the second founder of Rome, Camillus entered the city in triumph in a four-horse chariot; he also kept too much of the booty from the sack of the Veii for himself, depriving the poor.

50. From what we know, there are seven Roman provinces at this time: Sicily, Sardinia, and Corsica, the two Spains, Gallia Transalpina, and Macedonia.

51. E.g., and as mentioned above, in the *Aeneid* itself the contest for world rule is not between Turnus and Aeneas, but between Rome and Carthage (1.17, 1.21).

52. Smith includes this text amongst those detailing a visual series of nations as a possible literary source for the Aphrodisias Sebasteion's north portico; "*Simulacra Gentium*," 72–73.

53. Aeneas's shield clearly has Achilles's shield of the *Iliad* as its reference point; it depicts more and in a better fashion than that shield. See Hardie, *Cosmos and Imperium,* for discussion.

54. According to Livy, Tullus's further response was to destroy Alba Longa and settle the Albans on the Caelian hill. For the story of Tullus, see Livy 1.22.1–31.6. The successor of peaceful Numa,

Tullus is portrayed in this narrative as even more warlike than Romulus. The two also both die in a cloud.

55. Porsenna: Livy, 2.9.1–14.7; Tacitus, *Histories* 3.72. Cloelia's statue, a "new kind of honor" for a woman: Livy 2.13.6. At *Natural History* 34.139, Pliny reports that an outcome of the resultant peace treaty with Porsenna is that the Romans were to use iron only for agriculture.

56. The Salii make another appearance in 8.286, in the procession in preparation for Aeneas's battle. There they sing songs to the achievements of Hercules and beat their shields. Servius, *Ad. Aen.* 8.285, says that they were bound to Hercules and not Mars. They wore armor and swords and shields, the original of which fell from heaven; copies were made to protect it. See also Dionysius 2.70. The Luperci are believed to have celebrated Romulus and Remus, and the Lupercalia's introduction as a festival celebrating fertility is attributed to Rome's foundation. The name itself denotes the she-wolf. See Ovid, *Fasti* 2.267; Plutarch, *Romulus* 21.

57. Much of Catiline's story is from the perspective of the Romans who did him in, most prominently Cicero. However, it is interesting that part of his problem is his promotion of the concerns of Rome's urban poor and his plan to pass a law canceling debts ("new tables," *tabulae novae*). It is thought that he gathered an army of poor people and Sulla's veterans, as well as members of the senatorial and equestrian ranks, to participate in a full-scale overthrow of the Roman government that was to start with the assassination of Cicero. At some point, he sought allegiance from members of the Allobroges, a tribe of Gauls who eventually fought on the same side as Julius Caesar during the Gallic wars, who were in Rome seeking asylum from their governor. They refused to go along with Catiline and exposed the plot to Cicero. Catiline, who was roaming the countryside between Rome and Gaul with his troops in avoidance of conflict, was eventually forced into battle and died along with most of his army. Primary sources include Sallust, *Bellum Catilinae*; Cicero, *In Catilinam, Pro Caelio, Pro Murena, Pro Sulla.*

58. For the logic of the Great Altar, see Kahl, "Reading Galatians and Empire."

59. Discord/Eris is the personification of strife. According to Hesiod, she is a daughter of Nyx and sister of Ares (*Theog.* 225–32). She births toil, pain, battles, bloodshed, ruin, and the like (*Works and Days* 11–26; but see that her golden apple can stir up good ruin or a bad one). Bellona is a Roman goddess of war who was popular with soldiers and had a temple on the Palatine from 296–48 B.C.E. (when it burned). She accompanies Mars in battle and is variously referred to as his sister, wife, and daughter.

60. Descriptions of other peoples take up a lot of space in Greek and Roman literature. It is not my aim to reconstruct a comprehensive history of subject peoples through the whole of the literature for this study.

61. Scott, *Paul and the Nations,* 102–5.

62. Many books and articles have been written on the Age of Augustus. It is not my aim to delineate all of the debates and problems with this particular area of the study of ancient history. One such problem that I side-stepped is whether or not the literature of the Augustan age is pro- or anti-imperial, whether or not it is just propaganda. I do not have the space to consider it; I assume that this literature, like all literature, reflects its immediate socio-historical context, and the immediate socio-historical context of the late republic and early empire involves a coming to terms with the consolidation of world power and domination in the hands of the Romans. The aspect of that context I choose to work on in this project is how Romans perceived their conquest over the nations. For an introduction to the Age of Augustus in text and image, see Galinsky, *Augustan Culture*; Zanker, *The Power of Images*; and Pomeroy et al., *Women in the Classical World*.

63. This title was given by Mommsen, who called it the "queen of inscriptions." The copy I use here is the Loeb version of the "Monumentum Ancyranum," found on the Temple of Roma and Augustus in Ancyra. See also Krenker and Schede, *Der Tempel in Ankara*.

64. According to Dio, Augustus's funeral procession included images of the nations he had acquired; I will discuss it in the next section on processions.

65. Overview of the program, including the *horologium*: Strabo, *Geogr.* 17.805; Pliny, *Nat.* 36.10. Pliny notes the layout at 36.72.

66. Nicolet, *Space, Geography, and Politics*, 16.

67. Agrippa's map is mentioned throughout several geographical source texts, including Mela and Strabo. The bibliography and arguments about the map (including: "It's not a picture, but just a text") are too extensive to be delineated here. Pliny uses it fairly extensively for his own measurements, and describing the object itself at Rome, he calls it "the world to be looked at by the city" (*orbis terrarum urbi spectandus*; *Nat.* 3.17). For discussion of the map in relationship to the Roman Empire and recent bibliography, see Kai Brodersen, *Terra Cognita: Studien zur römischen Raumerfassung* (Hildesheim: Olms, 1995), and Mattern, *Rome and the Enemy*, 49–51.

68. *methērēneumenai hypegraphēsan praxeis te kai dōreai Sebastou theou, has apelipen epi Rōmēs enkecharagmenas chalkais stēlais dusi.*

69. Elaboration: see especially Price, *Rituals and Power: The Roman Imperial Cult in Asia Minor* (New York: Oxford University Press, 1984). Such terms for the emperor are discussed in New Testament studies with increasing frequency; see the classic treatments in Horsley, *Paul and Empire*.

70. Nicolet, *Space, Geography, and Politics*, 19.

71. Velleius 2.73 gives a description of Sextus: he "was a young man without education, barbarous in speech, vigorous in initiative . . . in loyalty (*fide*) a marked contrast to his father, the freedman of his own freedman and the slave of his own slaves, envying those in high places only to obey those in the lowest." Having been recalled from Spain by the senate, he seized Sicily (legendary as a site of slave revolts) and "admitting into his army slaves and runaways, he had raised his legions to their full complement. He supported himself and his army on plunder, and through the agency of Menas and Menecrates, his father's freedmen, who were in charge of his fleet, he infested the seas by predatory and piratical expeditions; nor was he ashamed to infest with piracy and its atrocities the sea which had been freed from it by his father's arms and leadership." Caesar, according to Velleius, quickly put a stop to this. Note that what Augustus claims to have stopped is a revolt of a slave army, a counter-legion to the proper Roman forces. Such a statement, when linked with the next one in this section about the allegiance of the provinces, amounts to a reaffirmation of Augustus's strength and loyalty, as well as a warning to those who would try to resist.

72. I discuss barbarians as nations, as well as nations below.

73. Of course, the Romans' massive military failure of 9 C.E. in the Teutoburg Forest is not mentioned here. Brunt and Nicolet posit this lack, as well as the absence of failure generally, as evidence for a dating of circa 2 B.C.E. for the *Res Gestae*. I submit it also signifies an imperial tendency to repress failure in order to overemphasize and naturalize an ideology of military success; the Romans did not represent themselves, visually or otherwise, as losers.

74. Primary sources on Ethiopia and Arabia as the ends of the earth are extensive. Diodorus, for example, thoroughly discusses them. Relevant to the passage above are the statements that Arabia Felix/"Happy" is rich; the Arabians who are Nabateans being the richest and unconquerable (2.48.1–5), yet are also pirates (3.43.5); Arabia is unconquered by the Persians or Macedonians (making Rome the first to crush them) (2.1.5); that robbers and "barbarous Ethiopians" live there (1.89.1–2; 3.8.1); that Arabia and Ethiopia share gold mines where they join (3.12.1–14); and that Libyan Amazons slay them when others cannot (3.55.4; 19.94.4). Pliny records the expedition of Aelius Gallus into Arabia, describing it as agriculturally especially well appointed; the different nations there are especially war-oriented, and they wear the turban or otherwise keep their unruly hair and their moustaches long. They also are "in equal part engaged in trade or live by brigandage; taken as a whole, they are the richest nations in the world, because vast wealth from Rome and Parthia accumulates in their hands, as they sell the produce they obtain from the sea or their forests and buy nothing in return (*Nat.* 6.32.160–62). Ethiopia is well known as the southern edge of the world, where strange people are thought to live, according to literary accounts as far back as Homer (*Odyssey* 1.23ff., which describes two types of Ethiopians). A sample catalog is given in Pliny, in *Nat.* 5.8.44–45.

75. Herodotus on the Getae: *Hist.* 4.93–96; they are the "noblest of the Thracians" and have a well-developed religio-political system centered on the belief that they cannot die. Salmoxis, their mysterious god, is a former slave from Greece who studied with Pythagoras, headed north, and became divine.

76. ". . . though various sections have occupied the lands adjacent to the coast, in one place the Getae, called by the Romans Dacians, at another the Sarmatae, called by the Greeks Sauromatae, and the section of them called the Wagon-dwellers or Aorsi, at another the base-born Scythians descended from slaves, or else the Cave-dwellers, and then the Alani and Rhoxolani." See also Strabo, *Geogr.* 7.5.1–3; Strabo distinguishes between the Dacians and "Getans" but says they share a language. The Dacians here are also fierce warriors, and having defeated the Celts (*Keltoi*), the Boii, and Taurisci, they often made common cause with the "Scordisi called Galatians (*Galatai*)," who also intermingled with the Illyrians and Thracians. The Dacians were not fully defeated by the Romans until Trajan, the Dacian campaigns of whom spiral around his column in Rome; for a literary representation, see e.g., Dio 68.6, where Trajan makes war against them "for their past deeds." On the dynamics of the Dacians being lumped in with the Scythians, see below.

77. "There was a custom in Hesperian Latium, which the Alban cities always held sacred, as great Rome does now, when they first rouse Mars to battle, whether they prepare to take sad war in their hands to the Getae, the Hyrcanians, or the Arabs, or to march on India's sons pursuing the Dawn, to reclaim their standards from Parthia: there are twin gates of War (so they are named), sanctified by religion, and by dread of fierce Mars: a hundred bars of bronze, and iron's eternal strength, lock them, and Janus the guardian never leaves the threshold. When the final decision of the city fathers is for battle, the Consul himself, dressed in the Quirine toga, folded in the Gabine manner, unbars these groaning doors, himself, and himself invokes the battle: then the rest of the men do so too, and bronze horns breathe their hoarse assent. In this manner then, too, Latinus was bidden to proclaim war on the sons of Aeneas, and to unclose the grim gates." Again, here the geographical focus on war with the nations furthest from Rome "now" (i.e., in Augustus's time) is clear.

78. Pannonia became a province in 9 C.E. and after revolting, was defeated again by Tiberius in 12 C.E. On Aphrodisias, see chapter 2 above; Smith, "*Simulcra Gentium*," and Reynolds, "Further Evidence." Only the base survives for the Dacians. Specific nations in Pannonia are represented: the Andizetii and Piroustae, the latter is the only nation where both a personification (with armor and weapons, representing battle) and base have been found. On the Pannonians: Strabo, *Geogr.* 7.5.3; "her" nations include "the Breuci, the Andizetii, the Ditiones, the Peirustae, the Mazaei, and the Daesitiatae, whose leader is Bato, and also other small nations of less significance which extend as far as Dalmatia and, as one goes south, almost as far as the land of the Ardiaei." Bato the Daesitiatian and another Bato of the Breuci made common cause against the Romans but were defeated; the former executed the latter and surrendered both nations to Rome in 8 C.E. (Dio, 55.29–34; Velleius, 2.114).

79. Nicolet divides these into four categories: (1) Rome, Italy, and fourteen provinces; (2) countries and people defeated, twenty-four in number; (3) rivers, mountain ranges, and seas (four, one, three); and (4) six towns (*Space, Geography, and Politics*, 20). I would tend to agree on a surface level, but also add to these divisions the ideological cleavage between that which is subject to Rome willingly and that which must be forced.

80. See also Appian, *Bell. civ.* 2.101, on Julius Caesar's quadruple triumph after decisive defeats of Scipio's allies in Africa, the Gallic wars, and the Pontic war against Pharnaces. In between, Appian states, Caesar held a triumph over Egypt—where he displayed captives from Egypt alone, as "he took care not to inscribe any Roman names in his triumph, as it would have been unseemly in his eyes and base and inauspicious in those of the Roman people to triumph over fellow citizens."

81. Whittaker, "Sex on the Frontiers," 124–25.

82. Of course, Augustus states in *Res Gestae* 29 that he "compelled" the Parthians to seek friendship and return the most important standards and spoils of all, those deposited in the Temple of Mars Ultor in his Forum. Other returned standards provide the occasion for the building of the Ara Pacis

and are implicated on the Prima Porta Augustus: "from Spain, Gaul, and the Dalmatians, I recovered, after conquering the enemy, many military standards which had been lost by other generals." On Prima Porta Augustus, see chapter 2.

83. The nomadic Scythians are the others *par excellence* of Herodotus (4.2–36, 46–82) and Classical Greek visual representation (e.g., vase-painting). Diodorus includes a creation story about the Scythians that makes them the hybrid offspring of Zeus and a snake-legged goddess: they "lived in very small numbers at the Araks River . . . that they gained for themselves a country in the mountains up to the Caucasus, in the lowland on the coast of the Ocean and the Meot Lake and other territories up to the Tanaïs River. Born in that land from the conjugal union of Zeus and a snake-legged goddess was a son Scyth who gave the name Scythian to the people" (2.43). Known for scalping their enemies, tattooing their bodies, taming horses, working with Amazons, and having androgynous shamans, they mingled with Celts and Thracians and constituted a formidable challenge for many military formations. They are even mentioned once in the New Testament in Col 3:11, as part of a formula similar to, but more expansive than, Galatians 3:28: *hopou ouk eni Hellēn kai Ioudaios, peritomē kai akrobustia, barbaros, Skythēs, doulos, eleutheros, alla [ta] panta kai en pasin Christos* ("where there is no Greek and Jew, circumcision and foreskin, barbarian, Scythian, slave, free, but Christ is all things and in all things").

84. Izates and Helena were persuaded to convert to Judaism by a tradesman named Ananias and "another Jew," respectively. Izates did not undergo circumcision because of his mother Helena's fear that his people would revolt on account of his being too zealous for Judaism, as they "could not bear to be ruled by a Jew" because of the foreignness of their customs. Izates is finally persuaded by Eleazar, a Jewish man from Galilee, though previously he had been told that according to the law of Moses, worship of God is more important than circumcision. When Izates goes to Adiabene to take the throne, he notices that some of his brothers and kinsmen are enslaved and is not pleased—yet, says Josephus, he thought it no political advantage to either free them or kill them. So he sent some of them and their children as hostages to Claudius in Rome and others to Artabanus in Parthia, remembering what had previously happened to them. See Josephus, *A.J.* 20.2.3–4. Helena and Izates also are remembered in Josephus for providing for the poor in Jerusalem and taking the side of the Jews in the war with Rome.

85. See, e.g., Plutarch, *Antony, Caesar, Cicero.*

86. This temple stood on the Capitoline, next to the Temple of Jupiter. A *flamen* of Jupiter performed the ritual associated with her, which involved the right hand. Coins attest to her prominence at Rome. On the Temple of Fides and the personification/goddess, see Gérard Freyburger, "La fides civique," in *Antiquité et Citoyenneté. Actes du Colloque International tenu à Besançon les 3, 4 et 5 novembre 1999*, ed. Stéphane Ratti (Paris, 2002), 341–47.

87. Suna Guven, "Displaying the *Res Gestae* of Augustus: A Monument of Imperial Image for All," *Journal of the Society of Architectural Historians* 57:1 (1998): 30–45; 40. Guven, a Turkish scholar, considers the *Res Gestae*'s ideological function in the spatial context of the Temple of Roma and Augustus in Ancyra.

88. Copies of the inscription have been found at Ancyra, Antioch in Pisidia, and Apollonia. Guven posits that the erection of the inscription actually served to propel these cities into prominence in the Roman world; this could be why there are no known copies from the more established metropolitan centers of Ephesus and Pergamon, even if we know from the sources that the former was among the first to set up a sacred precinct. See Guven, "Displaying the *Res Gestae*," 32. However, if we take Dio 51.20.6 seriously, this inscription may not have been displayed at Ephesus because Augustus "gave permission" for the imperial cult there to be installed for his father Julius Caesar, not himself.

89. Stephen Mitchell, *Anatolia: Land, Men, and Gods in Asia Minor*, vol. 1, rev. ed. (New York: Oxford University Press, 1995), 102, alluding to Dio's statement that, following the victory at Actium, Augustus began to grant permission for such activities in eastern cities.

90. But see Gradel, *Emperor Worship and Roman Religion.*

91. In the western provinces: see Fishwick's *The Imperial Cult in the Latin West,* vols. 1–3, as well as *Subject and Ruler: The Cult of the Ruling Power in Classical Antiquity,* ed. Alastair Small, JRASup 17 (Ann Arbor: University of Michigan Press, 1996).

92. See Zanker, *Power of Images,* as the standard work on the conflation of Roman myth and history in art and architecture to promote Roman imperial ideology.

93. Here I would liken Roman achievement to the *stoicheia tou kosmou* (elemental spirits of the world) to which Paul observes the Galatians are enslaved (Gal 4:3). Such a rewriting of mythology to emphasize the role of the Roman race appears to have been a large part of Augustus's social campaign; the most obvious work to this effect is the *Aeneid.*

94. The complex within the city of Antioch was consciously built in imitation of Rome: it had seven hills within its walls and a Roman style temple. The complex at Antioch, like that at Aphrodisias, combined Doric, Ionic, and Corinthian columns "in a characteristic example of Roman imperial symbolism, uniting the three main architectural orders of the Greek world within a single design" (Guven, "Displaying the *Res Gestae,*" 33).

95. It is not my intention here to give a comprehensive history of the imperial cult in Asia Minor. Others have done that better than I, and New Testament scholars have accepted (somewhat) the idea that the imperial cult is the primary religio-political system operative during the time of the New Testament's textual production, a system which Jews throughout the Roman Empire were known for finding idolatrous. My aim here is simply to situate the *Res Gestae* inscription and other expressions of an ideology of Roman rule over all the nations as central to, and through the spatial and visual context of, the imperial cult. I assume that this context is integral to Galatians. I would add that the imperial cult is inherently and powerfully expressive of gendered hierarchy between Rome and other nations, as Susan Fischler indicates in a recent article ("Imperial Cult: Engendering the Cosmos"). For more information on the imperial cult, see Price, *Rituals and Power,* and his contribution to Horsley, *Paul and Empire*; Zanker, *Power of Images*; and Mitchell, *Anatolia I and II.*

96. *Res Gestae* 12, 25, 26, 28, 29. I am not sure it is clear that only northern Gaul is meant here, except perhaps in reference to the colony of soldiers set up in Gallia Narbonensis (28). Only Spain is mentioned as many times, in the same sections and usually coupled together with Gaul/s. Germany is mentioned only twice as "*Germania*"—the remaining seven times are of German nations: Cimbri (twice in 26, who were subdued), Charydes and Semnones (also in 26, "other *ethnē* of the Germans"), Sugambri, Macromanni, and Suevi (32, as kings sending envoys).

97. It is not my aim to give a comprehensive history of the Celts/Gauls/Galatians and their encounter with Greeks, Pergamenes, or Romans. They are mentioned enough in Roman sources—in fact, we have very few literary representations of them that are not written by "the victors"—that we can reconstruct their status as a consistent threat to Roman rule *and* as willing collaborators. I do discuss several relevant primary sources on the Gauls below. I assume for this project that the Galatians of the New Testament, Paul's Galatians, are a nation under Roman rule and are the historical Gauls who moved east from northern Europe. For a history of the Galatians, which enjoys a much longer bibliography than I list here, see David Magie, *Roman Rule in Asia Minor,* 2 vols., rev. ed. (New York: Arno, 1975); Mitchell, *Anatolia I & II*; and Marzal, "Ubiquitous Barbarians." For a more thorough investigation and linkage of these Galatians to Paul and the New Testament, see Ramsay, *Historical Commentary*; Deissmann, *Light from the Ancient East*; and Kahl, "Reading Galatians and Empire," as well as her forthcoming book on the matter (Fortress Press, 2008). There is also an informative map of the Celts/Gauls and their movement across Europe and into Asia Minor in Grant, *Atlas of Classical History* (New York: Oxford University Press, 1971), 46.

98. For a discussion of the priest list, see Mitchell, *Anatolia I,* 107ff.

99. Mitchell, *Anatolia I,* 113.

100. Guven, "Displaying the *Res Gestae,*" 40.

101. ETHNOUS TRIOUNPEILŌ[N]; Smith, "*Simulacra Gentium,*" 55 and Plate 9.3. The excavation team found that the base had been re-cut and used in the theater.

102. For discussion, see Duncan Fishwick, "The Temple of the Three Gauls," *JRS* 62 (1972): 46–52.

103. He was also not the last emperor to do so. Based on extensive evidence Hadrian was a logical successor both in terms of visual representation of the nations (having issued a coin-series serving as *comparanda* for many earlier personifications of nations and cities, and having set up friendly" personifications of the nations that still exist at Rome's Hadrianeum today) and world-rule itinerary. Pausanias notes that Hadrian installed his *res gestae* as an inscription at his Pantheon in Athens (*Desc. of Greece*, 1.1.5), for example.

104. Nicolet, *Space, Geography, and Politics*, 20.

105. Ibid., 32.

106. See Edwards, "Incorporating the Alien," for an examination of how conquered peoples might have reacted to seeing their art and images of gods displayed, not in their hometowns, but in Rome. The Romans are not the only ones who looked at and responded to the statues and inscriptions that were in the city; see Livy, 25.40.1–3. Underlining Verres's depredations of Rome's subject people, Cicero comments: "and it was then . . . that the allied and foreign nations cast away their last hope of prosperity and happiness for a large number of individuals from Asia and Achaea, who happened to be in Rome serving on deputations at the time, saw in our Forum the revered images of their gods that had been carried away from their own sanctuaries, and recognizing also other statues and works of art, some here and some there, would stand gazing at them, tears flowing from their eyes. What we then heard all these people saying was this, that no-one could doubt the impending ruin of our allies and friends; for there in the Forum of Rome, in the place where once those who had wronged our allies used to be prosecuted and found guilty, now stood, openly displayed, the objects seized from those allies through theft and robbery" (*Verres* 2.1.59).

107. *Cn. Pompeius Magnus imperator bello XXX annorum confecto fusis fugatis occisis in deditionem accpetis hominum centiens viciens semel LXXXIII depressis aut captis navibus DCCCXLVI oppidis castellis MDXXXVIII in fidem receptis terries a Maeotis ad Rubrum mare subactis votum merito Minervae.*

108. Florus is especially reminiscent of the texts discussed here, at the end of a passage describing Pompey as "pursuing the remnants of a rebellious Asia, hurrying through diverse nations and lands (*gentium terrarumque*)" and naming many of the nations he conquered in the process: Armenian, Scythia, Colchians, Iberians (who were pardoned, but gave their children as hostages), Albanians (spared because they sent a golden bed and other gifts), Lebanon and Damascus in Syria (bearing Roman standards through the groves of frankincense), Arabs (ready to carry out orders), Jews (attempted to defend Jerusalem, but Pompey entered the temple and "saw the great secret of that impious nation [*inpiae gentis*] open to view, the heavens beneath a golden vine"; also settling the dispute between Hyrcanus and Aristobulus, putting the latter in prison for wanting to restore his *imperium*). "Thus," writes Florus, "the Roman people, under the leadership of Pompey, traversed the whole of Asia in its widest extent and made what had been the furthest to rule into a central province (*quam extremam imperii habebat provinciam mediam fecit*); for with the exception of the Parthians, who preferred to make a treaty, and the Indians, who as yet knew nothing of us, all Asia between the Red and Caspian Seas and the ocean was possessed, dominated or oppressed by the standards of Pompey." Note that Augustus's list of nations encountered and conquered goes further than Pompey, for example, making contact with the Indians and subduing the Parthians.

109. For more on Pompey, including a comprehensive list of primary sources mentioning his accomplishments, conquests, building projects, etc., see Ulysses K. Vestal, *Imagines Imperatoris ac Monumenta Principis: A Sourcebook for the Building Activity, Iconography, and Monuments Relating to Cn. Pompeius Magnus, 79 BC–AD 1509* (Unpublished Manuscript, 2003).

110. One particular monument of Caesar, controversial to historians, deserves note here. According to Dio, among the honors for his triumphs of 46 B.C.E. "the senate also decreed that his chariot would be dedicated on the Capitolium facing Jupiter and that he would tread on a bronze image of the world (*oikoumenē*), the whole bearing an inscription calling him 'demigod'" (43.14.6).

Later he had the "demigod" erased, but the chariot and *oikoumenē* stood. Nicolet, following Picard and *contra* Vogt, Hölscher, and Michel, states that the image of the *oikoumenē* here is an allegorical personification, a woman's body, and not a globe (*Space, Geography, and Politics*, 39–40). Picard makes this argument partially from the appearance of Tellus under a chariot at the Antonine Altar of Ephesus. *Oikoumene*-as-woman also crowns Augustus on the Gemma Augustea while a foreign woman has her hair pulled below and in an unpublished relief from Aphrodisias, Ge/Gaia/Tellus submits to Roma, sitting beneath her.

111. It is not my intention here to explore in full the etymology, history, or all literary representations of barbarians vis-à-vis Greeks and Romans. For a classic treatment, see Edith Hall, *Inventing the Barbarian*. More recently, see Derek Williams, *Romans and Barbarians: Four Views from the Empire's Edge* (New York: St. Martins Press, 1998).

112. For a full-length exploration of the relationship between ethnography and Roman identity, see Rhiannon Evans, *Forma Orbis* (Ph.D. diss., University of Southern California, 2001); Dench, *Romulus's Asylum,* 37–92, explores ethnographic literature as a means to reconstruct what the Romans thought of themselves and their world.

113. This would certainly seem to be the case with Caesar. See Kuttner, *Dynasty and Empire*, 69–111, for a discussion of Roman encounters with the peoples of the empire as an influence in visual representation.

114. Pliny might seem eccentric, but he is not alone. Roman court-architect Vitruvius, for example, expresses very similar sentiments concerning the natural fitness of the Romans over everyone else and extends such natural fitness to the building of Roman architecture. According to Vitruvius, the superiority of the Romans should be "built in" to their space according to the designs of the gods and nature: "Southern nations (*nationes*) also, owing to the rarity of the atmosphere, with minds rendered acute by the heat, are more readily and swiftly moved to the imagination of expedients; but northern nations (*gentes*) steeped in a thick climate amid reluctant air, are chilled by the damp, and have sluggish minds . . . Hence we need to wonder if warm air renders the human mind more acute, and a cool air impedes. Now while the southern nations (*nationes*) are of acute intelligence and infinite resources, they give way when courage is demanded because their strength is drained away by the sun; but those born in colder regions by their fearless courage are better equipped for the clash of arms, yet by their slowness of mind they rush on without reflection, and through lack of tactics are balked of their purpose. Since, therefore, the disposition of the world is such by nature, and all other nations (*omnes nationes*) differ by their immoderate temperament, it is in the true mean within the space of all the world (*totius orbis terrarum*) and the regions that the Roman people (*populus Romanus*) holds its territories. For in Italy the nations (*gentes*) are exactly tempered in either direction, both in the structure of the body, and by their strength of mind in the matter of endurance and courage. For just as the *stella* Jupiter is tempered by running in the middle between the heat of Mars and the cold of Saturn, in the same manner Italy presents good qualities which are tempered by mixture from either side both north and south, and are consequently undefeated (*invictas*). And so, by assembly (*consiliis*), it destroys (*refringit*, also "declothes") the *virtus* of the northern barbarians, by strength, the imaginative south. Thus the divine mind has allotted to the state of Roman people an excellent and temperate region in order to rule the world (*uti orbis terrarum imperii potiretur*). But if regions differing in climate are assigned to different nations so that the natures of those nations (*gentium*) that arise should vary in mind, and in shape and body, we will not hesitate to arrange the methods of our buildings also, to suit the characters of nations and peoples (*nationum gentiumque*), since from Nature herself we have skilled and ready guidance" (*De Arch.* 6.1.9–12).

115. For a full-length treatment see Trevor Murphy, *Pliny the Elder's* Natural History: *The Empire in the Encyclopedia* (New York: Oxford University Press, 2004).

116. Strabo calls this cloak, common to all Galatian nations, the *sagos* (*Geogr.* 4.4.3).

117. Vitruvius attributes this feature of the northern nations to their greater "distance from the world," whereas the southern nations have a shrill voice, and of course, those of Italy (and Greece) have great pitch (*De Arch.* 1.1.7).

118. This is the reason why, according to Livy, they eventually must leave Rome after sacking it. Pliny notes that the northern barbarians are unfit to rule the world because they hail from a climate that is too cold.

119. They do not even inquire as to where their guests have come from until after the meal. Additionally, they "seize any topic for discussion and then challenge each other to single combat, without any regard for their lives; for the belief of Pythagoras prevails among them, that souls are immortal and that after a prescribed number of years they commence upon a new life" (Diodorus, 5.28.5). The meals of the Celts also are not known for the opulence and social decorum typical of the civilized symposium, as they eat off of animal skins on the ground.

120. Also noteworthy, and well beyond the scope of this project, is the characterization of male effeminacy as a symbol of excess and debauchery in Roman satirical materials. Juvenal's first and second *Satires* are good examples of this. In the context of Rome as a city completely worthy of criticism, the description of the male effeminate (a designation also given to Otho by Juvenal) is a recurring symbol of a system out of bounds or in decline (see also the "man who takes a husband," *Sat.* 2.132). Important to note, however, is the criticism of effeminacy coupled with his lambasting of excessive wealth and problems with women who speak out of line (the most troubling woman of all is the one who comes to dinner and talks of philosophy; see *Sat.* 6), as well as women and men making a lot of noise about their own debauchery and moral ineptitude in the city (the main thrust of *Sat.* 3; it seems as though Juvenal cannot sleep due to all of the noise). Martial's *Epigrams* also make careful mention of men who dress as women, men who wish to be penetrated by other men, men who love fellatio, and eunuch-boys who are the love of emperors, as well as his use of the Gallus as a recurring effeminate character.

Like ethnographic writings, Roman satirical literature of the first century C.E. also equates Galatian with barbarian, but in a slightly different way: the Gallus is a slang term for the eunuch, which comes from the names of the castrated priests of the cult of Cybele and Attis in the province of Galatia. Juvenal's *Satires* (2) and Martial's *Epigrams* make repeated mention of the Gallus in a derogatory manner (2.45 and 47), and one in particular labels the Gauls as beatable. The clothing of the Gauls is also noticeable to Martial, who spends several epigrams describing Gauls as "greasy" (e.g., 6.11), as well as having bright red lower-class cloaks and being lovely to soldiers and boys (14.128 and 129; these are part of a series, the "Apophoreta," a collection of mottoes meant to accompany presents received and taken home at the Saturnalia festival).

121. Strabo says that "all" Celtic nations do this: they do not consider it problematic to send off their own young boys for sex (*Geogr.* 4.4.6), indicating male penetrability and, therefore, femininity.

122. This kind of portrayed sexual transgression is possibly what gets the Galatians put at the top of the list for those who will be eliminated from the earth in the third *Sibylline Oracle.*

123. *hoion to para tois Kantabrois tous andras didonai tais gunaixi proika, to tas thugateras klēronomous apoleipesthai, tous te adelphous hypo toutōn ekdidosthai gynaixin. echei gar tina gynaikokratian. touto d' ou pany politikon.*

124. Amazons are of particular interest as gender transgressors (Diodorus, 2, 4; Pausanias, 14; Strabo, *Geogr.* 11), with *gynaikokratia,* and they are not represented in the Roman period as much as in the Classical and Hellenistic eras. They are a race of women warriors who did all of the work of men, seared their right breast so as to better facilitate weaponry, and had sex with a neighboring tribe of men for the purpose of creating more women only. Alexander reportedly was approached by their queen for the purposes of making a race of super women, as the Amazons were impressed by his military might; she stayed with him for fourteen days. The Amazons were ultimately eradicated and scattered over the land by Greeks and then "neighboring barbarians" whom they had plundered.

125. See Tacitus, *Annals* 14.30ff., a description of women wearing black and with teased hair who weave in and out of the battle lines while Druids perform a spectacle—these "women and fanatics" were burned on the spot by the Romans.

126. Interestingly, one of the primary ways to designate becoming Roman, becoming peaceful, or getting civilization is to change from native barbarian dress to the Roman toga, the clothing of the

law, so to speak. On the Gauls and the process of Romanization, including an analysis of scholarly controversies concerning the making of provincial cultures, see most recently Greg Woolf, *Becoming Roman: The Origins of Provincial Civilization in Gaul* (New York: Cambridge University Press, 1998), especially 1–48, 238–49. Woolf does not discuss the eastern Roman province of Galatia in depth. On "Gallia Togata," see Dench, *Romulus's Asylum*, 275. The primary source on the nations of Gallia Togata, including those who have "disappeared," is Pliny, *Nat.* 3.13.4.

127. "The men of Britain are taller than the Keltoi, and not so yellow-haired, although their bodies are of looser build . . . their customs (*ēthē*) are like the Keltoi, but more simple and barbaric . . . they use chariots in war, like the Keltoi" (4.5.2). The Irish, further away than the Britons, are "more savage than the Britons . . . they count it an honorable thing that, when their fathers die, they eat them" (4.5.4). See also Caesar, *Gallic Wars*, 6.11ff., on the differences between Gauls and Germans; and Tacitus, *Agricola*.

128. Spanish women have barbaric ornaments, according to this very passage in Strabo. Their headgear is elaborate and made of iron, and sometimes they tie their hair around a metal pole that they fasten to their heads. This, according to Strabo, is no ornament at all. They have "the courage of women and men" in common with other barbarians: "these women till the soil, and when they have given birth to a child they put their husbands to bed instead of going to bed themselves and minister to them; and while at work in the fields, often, when they have given birth to a child there, they turn aside to some brook and bathe and swaddle the child" (Strabo, *Geogr.* 3.14.17).

The "contempt for rational living," that is, Roman living, is exemplified by how certain barbarians confront the possibility of having to live under Roman rule: they take their own lives and burn their towns. The Cantabrians fight in battle like Celts and Thracians and, interestingly, have a "contempt" or "rebelliousness" (*aponoia*) because they refuse to be taken as hostages by the Romans: "at the time of the Cantabrian War (i.e., with Augustus in 25 B.C.E.), mothers killed their children before being taken captive, and even a small boy, whose parents and brothers were in fetters as captives of war, gained possession of a sword and at the command of his father, killed them all; and a certain Cantabrian, upon being summoned into the presence of drunken men, threw himself on a pyre" Strabo, *Geogr.* 3.4.17). Their *aponoia* is mentioned again in relation to their attitude toward crucifixion: "when some captive Cantabrians had been nailed to their crosses (i.e., by Augustus, in his war), they proceeded to sing their rule of the ages (*epaiōnizon*). Now such traits as these would indicate a certain savageness" (3.4.18). For a brief discussion of representations of suicide that includes attention to empire and enslaved peoples, see Jared Stark, *The Interpretation of Suicide* (forthcoming).

129. Tacitus, *Germania* 45.9: "Adjacent to the Suiones come the nations (*gentes*) of the Sitones, resembling them in all other respects, and differing only in this, that among them the woman rules (*femina dominatur*): to this extent they have fallen lower not just than freedmen but even than slaves (*in tantum non modo a libertate sed etiam a servitute degenerant*)."

130. Sicily is the site of the famous slave revolts of 170–30 B.C.E. Barbarians figure prominently in the texts describing these revolts. Diodorus, 34 and 35, contains a description of the revolting slaves as barbaric and dangerous; Strabo, *Geogr.* 6.2, has a similar account. Plutarch's *Crassus* describes the war with Spartacus as being planned and conducted partially by slaves in Capua, who were trained for gladiatorial combat and who were mostly Gauls and Thracians (8-11). This legitimates the extreme violence with which the Roman army reacts to the slave uprisings and then continued harsh treatment of slaves through threats of punishment and exile. Varro notices that the Romans' slaves come from many different barbarian nations, including the Galatians, and warns against putting too many slaves of the same nation together, lest they try to revolt: "avoid having too many slaves of the same nation, as this is a fertile source of domestic uprising" (Varro, *Rust.* 1.27). He also notes that the slaves he owns might not be barbarians in their own lands, but under Roman rule they definitely are (1.28).

131. Whittaker, "Sex on the Frontiers," 127. There are several examples *in situ* in Pompeii, but many have been relocated out of context to the famed "secret cabinet" at the Museo Archaeologico Nazionale in Naples. See also John Clarke, *Roman Sex: 100 BC–250 AD* (New York: Abrams, 2003), 95–114.

132. See Anne McClintock, *Imperial Leather: Race, Gender, and Sexuality in the Colonial Conquest* (New York: Routledge, 1995), 232–57. One need not think for too long to notice how the logic of exclusion based on gender and sexual proclivity has played out in historical configurations that have resulted (in the most obvious case) in contemporary gay, lesbian, bisexual, and transgender politics in the United States.

133. Williams, *Roman Homosexuality*, 135.

134. Whittaker, "Sex on the Frontiers," 129.

135. There are actually more accounts in the literature of wartime rape during the Republic; this may be because "the Roman legal definition of rape (*stuprum*) was status dependent and could not be charged for violation of slaves or peregrines and clearly not for the rape of foreign captives who automatically became slaves" (Whittaker, "Sex on the Frontiers," 129). For sources, see Sara Phang, *The Marriage of Roman Soldiers (13 BC–AD 235): Law and Family in the Imperial Army* (Leiden: Brill, 2001); and Williams, *Roman Homosexuality*, 104–7 and 132–37.

136. For a discussion of the speech and Tacitus's overall concern with Britons, see D. J. Mosley, "Calgacus: Clash of Roman and Native," in *Images of Empire*, ed. Loveday Alexander, JSOTSup 122 (Sheffield: Sheffield Academic Press, 1991), 107–21.

137. On an analysis of the control of sexual categories and behavior as obligatory to the creation of respectability in nation- and state-building, see George Mosse, *Nationalism and Sexuality: Respectability and Abnormal Sexuality in Modern Europe* (New York: Howard Fertig, 1985); and Roger N. Lancaster, "That We All Should Turn Queer? Homosexual Stigma in the Making of Manhood and the Breaking of a Revolution in Nicaragua," in *Culture, Society and Sexuality: A Reader*, ed. Richard Parker and Peter Aggleton (London: SCM Press, 2000), 97–116. On hierarchical arrangement of such categories and their use in political debates, see Rubin, "Thinking Sex."

138. It is my general assumption that Josephus should be read not just as a theological resource for ancient Judaism, but in light of the imperial politics that framed his life and writings on both sides, Jewish and Roman. For more on this approach, see especially Schwartz, *Imperialism and Jewish Society*.

139. E.g., Scott, *Paul and the Nations*, 101–4; Tessa Rajak, "Friends, Romans, Subjects: Agrippa II's Speech in Josephus's *Jewish War*," in *Images of Empire*, 122–34.

140. But one of the statements on slavery and freedom notes that the fight against Rome is pointless: "if your objective is to have your revenge for injustice, what good is it to extol freedom? If, on the other hand, it is slavery you find intolerable, to complain of your rulers is superfluous; were they the most considerate of men, slavery would be equally disgraceful" (Josephus, *B. J.* 2.349).

141. *hy gar peira tēs douleias chalepē, kai peritou mēd' arxasthai tautēs ho agōn dikaios; ho d' hapax cheirōtheis, epeita aphistamenos, authadēs doulos estin, ou phileleutheros.*

142. Josephus, *B. J.* 2.356; see Diodorus, 40.1–2, for Pompey's exploits in Jerusalem, culminating in the inscription commemorating dominance over the Jews among all the nations of Asia (discussed above).

143. *ethnē, par' hois prin men oud' oikeios egignōsketo despotēs, nun de trischiliois oplitais hypotassetai, kai tessarakonta nēes makrai tēn prin aplōton kai agrian eirēneuousi thalassan*. The nations of Asia named here: Heniochi, Colchians, Taurians, Bosporans, nations on the Euxine and Lake Maeotis, Bithynia, Cappadocia, the Pamphylian nation (*ethnos*), Lycians, and Cilicians.

144. Josephus has Agrippa give an extended description of the Gauls, who surpass others in land, resources, wealth, and nations subdued: the Gauls "have magnificent natural resources, on the east the Alps, on the north the river Rhine, on the south the chain of the Pyrenees, on the west the ocean. But, though encompassed by such formidable barriers, though swarming with a population of 305

nations (*ethnesin*), possessing, so to speak, in their native land the springs of prosperity and irrigating well the whole world with the overflow of their products, the Gauls are yet content to be treated as a source of revenue to the Romans and to have their own prosperous fortune meted out to them at their hands. And this they tolerate, not through any weakness of mind (*phronēmatōn malakian*) or because they are an ignoble race (*ageneian*), they who fought for eighty years for their freedom, but because they are overawed by the power of Rome and her fortune, which brings her more triumphs than her arms" (Josephus, *B. J.* 2.372–74).

145. A single legion is enough to guard these warriors who have been enslaved (Josephus, *B. J.* 2.376).

146. Josephus is saying here that the Jews understand the payment of Roman tribute to be outrageous and an affront to their freedom, like the Briton Calgacus (see above).

147. "The length of that city is thirty furlongs, its breadth not less than ten; the tribute which she pays to Rome in one month surpasses what you pay in a year; besides money she sends corn to feed Rome for four months; she is protected on all sides from trackless deserts, by seas without ports, by rivers or lagoons. Yet none of these assets proved a match for the fortune of Rome, and two legions stationed in the city curb this far-reaching Egypt and the proud nobility of Macedon" (Josephus, *B. J.* 3.386–88).

148. In this sense, the speech serves not just to map the conquered, but also as a map of the location and numbers of the Roman legions all over the empire.

149. I read the point that Agrippa is making as that the nations are all defeated and the Roman legions are all stationed in their lands, meaning that they also are literally *upon* all the world, i.e., settled on the lands of the inhabited earth to maintain peace. The nations, then, cannot help the Jews as they are, in a sense, under surveillance. This is not to say that the nations did not become Romans, but the larger issue points to Roman military occupation and enslavement of the nations on their own land.

150. The question of God being on the side of Rome in this passage is often discussed. I will not add much to this debate, except a small observation that the Jews' adherence to their customs is used against them here: if they observe the Sabbath, they will be annihilated because of their inactivity; if they do not observe, they are disobeying their God, thereby defeating the whole reason for revolting against the Romans in the first place (Josephus, *B. J.* 2.391–94).

151. "Even the survivors will find no place of refuge, since all dread having the Romans as masters. And the peril does not threaten the ones here alone, but even the ones living in other cities; for there is not a people in the world that does not have a portion of ours (*ou gar estin epi tēs oikoumenēs dēmos ho mē moiran ēmeteran echōn*). All these, if you go to war, will be butchered by your adversaries, and through the folly of a handful of men every city will be filled with murder of Jews" (Josephus, *B. J.* 2.398–400).

152. On emergent Roman universalism, see Hingley, *Globalizing Roman Culture*, 1–13; Katherine Clarke, *Between Geography and History: Hellenistic Constructions of the Roman World* (Oxford: Clarendon, 1999).

153. I am aware that here I switch from describing texts and monuments to describing an event. Actually, as we do not have access to the event itself, I am using literary representation of the event to think about how it was structured and through its repetition and familiar elements, how it could be called a ritual. The triumph, as performance, creates and re-inscribes social order and hierarchy. Ritual studies provides theoretical frameworks for analyzing events like the triumph; see Catherine Bell, *Ritual: Perspectives and Dimensions* (New York: Oxford University Press, 1997); Ron Grimes, *Beginnings in Ritual Studies* (Washington, D.C.: University Press of America, 1982); *Readings in Ritual Studies*, ed. Ron Grimes (Upper Saddle River, N.J.: Prentice Hall, 1996); and Jonathan Z. Smith, *To Take Place: Toward Theory in Ritual* (Chicago: University of Chicago Press, 1987).

154. For a similar exploration of the triumph focused on its mimetic and performative qualities, see Mary Beard, "The Triumph of the Absurd: Roman Street Theatre," in *Rome the Cosmopolis,* ed. Catherine Edwards and Greg Woolf (New York: Cambridge University Press, 2003), 21–43.

155. See Geoffrey S. Sumi, *Ceremony and Power: Performing Politics in Rome between Republic and Empire* (Ann Arbor: University of Michigan Press, 2005), 247–50 and bibliography.

156. For an in-depth treatment of textual accounts of the Roman triumph, see especially H. S. Versnel, *Triumphus: An Inquiry into the Origin, Development and Meaning of the Roman Triumph* (Leiden: Brill, 1970).

157. The triumph is linked to another venerable Roman institution, the games. Like the triumph, the games serve to ritualize and eternalize Roman imperial ideology of world rule: important battles are reenacted using actual members of the defeated. Although examination of the ritualizing practices of the games including their role in public consciousness and the maintenance of gendered social hierarchy might be tangentially relevant for this project, a full-scale examination is outside its bounds presently. Obviously the fate of the nations at the games—as gladiators, workers, victims, and spectators—is important to keep in mind, as is the concrete historical link between crucifixion and the games. For a collection of primary sources in translation, see Anne Mahoney, *Roman Sports and Spectacles: A Sourcebook* (New York: Focus, 2001). The literature on the games also is extensive. See, e.g., K. C. Coleman, "Fatal Charades: Roman Executions Staged as Mythological Enactments," *JRS* 80 (1990): 44–73; *Life, Death, and Entertainment in the Roman Empire,* ed. David Mattingly and David Potter (Ann Arbor: University of Michigan Press, 1999), 171–256; *Gladiators and Caesars: The Power of Spectacle in Ancient Rome,* ed. Eckart Köhne and Cornelia Ewigleben (Berkeley: University of California Press, 2000); Carlin A. Barton, *The Sorrows of the Ancient Romans: The Gladiator and the Monster* (Princeton: Princeton University Press, 1993); and for consideration of the games from the perspective of New Testament studies, the classic Martin Hengel, *Crucifixion* (Philadelphia: Fortress Press, 1977), and Brigitte Kahl's forthcoming book.

158. This particular procession also included a vast sum of money and fifty-two captives from the Galatian nobility.

159. Discussed in Dench, *Romulus's Asylum*, 37 ff.

160. He also had his soldiers gather seashells on the shore to take back to Rome as spoils from the conquest of Ocean.

161. Of these, nine (Egyptians, Dacians, Dardani, Arabians, Ethiopians, Bessi, Rhaetians, and Bosporans) are represented in the reliefs and inscriptions at the Aphrodisias Sebasteion.

162. Account of the triumph: Josephus, *B. J.* 7.131–53. For a discussion, see Mary Beard, "The Triumph of Flavius Josephus," in Boyle and Dominik, *Flavian Rome*, 543–58.

163. They were made to pose in the state in which they had been taken; Josephus describes the floats as being three to four stories high (Josephus, *B. J.* 7.147).

164. Toynbee, *Hadrianic School*, 8.

165. Pliny writes: "[T]he baby is further under the protection of Fascinus, guardian not only of babies but of generals, a god whose worship, part of the Roman religion, is entrusted to the Vestals; hanging under the chariots of generals at their triumphs he defends them as a physician from jealousy" (*Nat.* 28.7.39).

4. Re-Imagining Paul as Apostle to the Conquered

1. For more on the complexity of Paul's identity in Jewish, Greek, and Roman terms, see Richard Wallace and Wynne Williams, *The Three Worlds of Paul of Tarsus* (London: Routledge, 1997).

2. See now, however, Tatha Wiley, *Paul and the Gentile Women: Reframing Galatians* (New York: Continuum, 2005). Wiley takes the new perspective approach (discussed briefly below and in chapter 2 above), where Paul is a Jew who manipulates the tradition of circumcision to render it unnecessary

for Gentiles as a mark of inclusion into the people of Israel. Wiley posits that this maneuver opens Paul's community of Jews and Gentiles in Galatia to women's leadership roles, which may or may not have already been an issue. See also Luise Schottroff, "Law-Free Gentile Christianity: What about the Women?" in *A Feminist Companion to Paul,* ed. Amy-Jill Levine with Marianne Blickenstaff (Cleveland: Pilgrim Press, 2004) for a similar argument. A fascinating examination of the texture of gender and power among Jews and others in Galatia that challenges simple male-female dichotomies is Susan M. (Elli) Elliott's treatment in *Cutting too Close for Comfort,* JSNTSup 248 (Sheffield: Sheffield University Press, 2004), especially her positioning of the castrated *galli*/eunuch priests of Cybele as central to the cultic context of the Galatian communities. Yet connection of these gender issues to Roman imperial power and ideology in both of these recent works is largely missing. Although attention to on-the-ground issues facing real women in antiquity and throughout history is critical for any study purporting to be feminist in methodology and outlook, I maintain that the gendered texture of ideology, and how identities are shaped by power relationships as articulated and naturalized by ruling classes throughout history, are important for understanding the ancient world that produced the New Testament—and, frankly, our own world as well.

3. Acts 9 narrates the sight, blindness, falling down, and getting up as decisive for (S)Paul (Saul/Paul)'s experience on the road to Damascus. Spatially, his consciousness is tied to going down and losing sight and then being raised up and seeing. He falls down due to the light (9:3), then hears the voice while down on the ground (9:4). Jesus tells him to get up (9:6), and he was raised (*ēgrethē*) and though his eyes were opened, he was seeing nothing (*ouden eblepen*); then he was led to Damascus where he saw nothing for three days. Ananias is sent by the Lord through a vision, where he is told that (S)Paul has seen him [in a vision] and will see again at Ananias's touch (9:10–12). He tells the Lord that he has heard about this man's deeds against the saints in Jerusalem), to which the response is ". . . this one is a chosen instrument for me, to carry my name before nations and kings and the sons of Israel, for I will show him how much it is necessary for him to suffer on behalf of my name (*hoti skeuos eklogēs estin moi houtos tou bastasai to onoma mou enōpion ethnōn te kai basileōn huiōn te Israēl egō gar hypodeixō autō hosa dei auton hyper tou onomatos mou pathein*, 9:15–16). (S)Paul's sight, particularly his ability to see differently, is crucial to his overall development as what I am calling the apostle to the conquered. But, as Acts 9:15–16 makes clear, his sight is not just restored, it is a changed line of vision that is accompanied by suffering.

4. Here I concur with Pamela Eisenbaum's definition of what makes traditional perspectives traditional; writing in a pattern of criticism of the new perspective that she calls neotraditionalist, she states: "I regard as neotraditionalist anyone who defends the traditional reading of Paul in light of the new perspective critique. Since the new perspective only emerged in the 1970s, I would regard anyone writing before that time as traditionalist. Many neotraditionalists have acknowledged and even incorporated some of the insights of the new perspective on Paul; some have taken a strong negative stance against it." See Eisenbaum, "A Remedy for Having Been Born a Woman: Jesus, Gentiles, and Genealogy in Romans," *JBL* 123/4 (2004): 671–702; 673 n.4.

5. The introspective or psychological character of religious conversion, for which figures like Paul and Augustine serve as prime examples, is elaborated most famously by psychologist William James in *The Varieties of Religious Experience* (New York: Collier MacMillan, 1961).

6. E.g., James S. Stewart, *A Man in Christ: The Vital Elements of St. Paul's Religion* (New York: Harper, 1935); Michel Bouttier, *Christianity According to Paul,* trans. Frank Clarke (Naperville, Ill.: Allenson, 1966).

7. E.g., in what is arguably the definitive book on conversion in antiquity in the last century: Arthur Darby Nock, *Conversion: The Old and the New in Religion from Alexander the Great to Augustine of Hippo* (Oxford: Oxford University Press, 1933). Although Nock maintains a predominantly Christian and theological view of Paul's conversion, this work defined the study of conversion in the ancient world by theorizing it as a "rare religious experience." What New Testament scholars seem to have forgotten, and what Nock maintained, is that many religious rituals and gatherings in the ancient world were intimately related to the protection of civic order. Participation in such

rituals involved almost a passive acceptance, an adherence to the state as an act of piety. Nock positioned Judaism and Christianity as "prophetic religions" that stimulated conversion as a radical shift in theological orientation and religious life-practice, demanding a more thorough commitment than mere "adherence." This thorough commitment involved an induction of the individual into a more socially marginal position among others who had had similar experiences. However, Nock persisted in figuring conversion as an inward, personal experience, and personal faith as comparatively more central to Christianity than Judaism (but no thoroughgoing comparison to the faith of the state). Importantly, for Nock, it is Acts, and not Paul's own accounts, that matter more in the description of Christian conversion.

For a reframing of conversion in social terms, see Wayne A. Meeks, *The First Urban Christians: The Social World of the Apostle Paul* (New Haven: Yale University Press, 1983). For a thoroughgoing criticism of the psychological approach to religious conversion in the ancient world from a social-scientific perspective, using Paul as a model, see now Zeba Crook, *Reconceptualising Conversion: Patronage, Loyalty, and Conversion in the Religions of the Ancient Mediterranean,* Beihefte zur Zeitschrift für die neutestamentliche Wissenschaft und die Kunde der älteren Kirche 130 (Berlin/New York: Walter de Gruyter, 2004). Although a contribution to the study of conversion in the context of the ancient patronage system, the emperor and the Roman Empire figure here as only one kind of instigator of patron-client relationships among several and not as controlling and shaping the world itself to which Paul responds. Paul is also just a model for this work because his conversion is accessible—thus, Crook is not so interested in reinterpreting what Paul's change is actually about politically and/or theologically. For conversion in antiquity as a sociopolitical, racialized process, see Buell, *Why This New Race,* 158–64.

8. The representations of Paul's conversion are particularly revealing in the history of visual representation. From medieval manuscripts to the Cathedral of Notre Dame to contemporary painting and graphic novels about the Bible, the non-existent horse persistently appears, alternately tossing Paul off its back, trampling him, running away into a nearby pool, and buckling at the light. The horse is actually more consistent than what happens in the sky, what I call the "conversion agent": beams of light through clouds, appearance of the sacred heart of Jesus, rays of fire, the hand of God—all are shown as that which instigates Paul's big fall. Interestingly, when Paul is represented among a group of people traveling together, he seems to be the only one affected by the big, disruptive occurrence in the sky. One could write an entire dissertation on just the visual tradition of Acts 9 and Galatians 1, as well as what such representation means for the category of literacy throughout time. However, it is important to note the appearance of Paul himself in these representations: in many of the most famous pictures, he is represented as a Roman warrior. I discuss this detail below.

9. I find the pattern of highlighting missionary journeys as religiously motivated most telling in the material culture associated with Pauline studies, particularly on maps in Bibles and atlases of ancient history. Maps of the Roman Empire are marked by provincial boundaries, major cities, and expansion lines. There is a separate map tradition for Paul's journeys that focuses on the paths and cities of his missionary work (and, rather amusingly, often includes the abrupt zigzags through the Mediterranean Sea near Sicily to reflect the storms of Acts) rather than on the ideological texture of the Roman imperial terrain he aims to cover. Consequently, the land through which Paul travels is politically neutralized and means something only in the context of a theological mission narrative. I maintain that it does make a difference to think about and see the places Paul visited as distinctly Roman territory and to see them specifically as conquered and colonized places. We know that Paul "thinks in Roman categories, and that in his world-wide mission he has only the empire in view . . . his strategy is orientated to the Roman provinces" (Martin Hengel, "The Pre-Christian Paul," in *Jews among Pagans and Christians in the Roman Empire,* ed. Judith Lieu, John North, and Tessa Rajak [London: Routledge, 1992], 29–52; 31). Paul's desire to go to Spain is but one example (Rom 15:28); Spain is not just territory waiting for Christianity, but is a contested place in the Roman Empire. Spain is represented as full of barbarians, needing civilization "like Gaul," and difficult to subdue in literary texts (e.g., Strabo) and as a conquered nation and province on monuments (e.g., *Res Gestae,*

Prima Porta Augustus). Thus, Paul's political work as extending to the ends of the conquered Roman world, of which Spain constitutes the western border, is underexplored.

10. The effects of the English Bible on colonial politics and expansion are recounted in Alister McGrath, *In the Beginning: The Story of the King James Bible and How It Changed a Nation, a Language, and a Culture* (New York: Anchor, 2002), and less so in Adam Nicholson, *God's Secretaries: The Making of the King James Bible* (New York: HarperCollins, 2003).

11. Anti-Judaism in Pauline studies has been well established by scholars and other interpreters, particularly after the Shoah, and I need not repeat all of that work here. It is sufficient to say that Paul's rhetoric is incomprehensible without sustained attention to the "Hellenistic Jewish" tradition with which he was obviously conversant. It is impossible to understand "Paul the Jew" without understanding, as far as we are able, what Judaism/s might have looked like in his context. Part of the anti-Judaism of Pauline interpretation has been the failure to acknowledge Judaism as part of Paul's world, as well as taking the so-called anti-Jewish and anti-Pharisaic tendencies of the New Testament at face value as a struggle between two different religions—Judaism and Christianity—instead of seeing the major conflicts as intra-Jewish or between different groups that happen to be minorities under Roman rule.

12. Although the new perspective might have catalyzed a paradigm shift regarding how scholars view Paul in light of Jewish law, it is not necessarily the case that conversion to Christianity as such has been sufficiently reworked as a result. E. P. Sanders, in his landmark work, *Paul and Palestinian Judaism* (Philadelphia: Fortress Press, 1977), to which scholars of Paul continue to respond on some level, proposes that Paul relates to a "covenantal nomism" characteristic of Palestinian Judaism, instead of "works-righteousness." In other words, Sanders posits that perhaps first-century Judaism is not as legalistic as New Testament scholars made it out to be, or at least, Paul has a different relationship to the law than medieval and Reformation-era theological perspectives purport. This position has precipitated a vigorous debate about Paul and the law; important contributions include James D. G. Dunn, *Jesus, Paul, and the Law: Studies in Mark and Galatians* (London: SPCK, 1990); Heiki Räisänen, *Paul and the Law* (Tübingen: Mohr Siebeck, 1987); and Peter Thomson, *Paul and the Jewish Law: Halakha in the Letters of the Apostle to the Gentiles* (Assen/Minneapolis: Van Gorcum/Fortress Press, 1990). Although Sanders's reframing of first-century Judaism as a reference point for Paul has sparked new exegetical controversies about the law and Paul's opponents, a core line of inquiry still is centered on why, precisely, Paul "rejected" the "works of the law," apocalyptically departed from Judaism, and spent his time writing a coherent template for Christian theology. Further, the category law as such is generally not interrogated, i.e., there is not just Jewish law but also Roman law with which to contend in Paul's historical context. Paul's Jewishness makes it all the more important to understand how he may or may not draw on Jewishness to negotiate the wider material world in which Jewishness is situated.

13. The title of the essay diagnosing the problems with traditional views of Paul's conversion, "The Apostle Paul and the Introspective Conscience of the West," treats the implications of an increasingly individualistic worldview for Pauline theology and ethics. *Paul Among Jews and Gentiles* (Philadelphia: Fortress Press, 1976), 78–93. Interpreters of Paul who follow Stendahl tend to begin with this essay and then move on to discuss the Jewishness of the apostle to the Gentiles without discussing who the Gentiles are besides non-Jews attracted to Judaism.

14. See James D. G. Dunn, "The New Perspective on Paul," *BJRL* 65 (1983): 95–122, who coined the term *new perspective* for this shift in Pauline studies. For a succinct summary of more recent contributions to the new perspective and provocative applications, see N. T. Wright, *What Saint Paul Really Said* (Grand Rapids: Eerdmans, 1997).

15. See recent Jewish arguments for Paul the Jewish person: Daniel Boyarin, *A Radical Jew: Paul and the Politics of Identity* (Berkeley: University of California Press, 1994); and Mark Nanos, *The Irony of Galatians: Paul's Letter in Its First-Century Context* (Minneapolis: Fortress Press, 2002). For recent concerted efforts by Christians seeking a Jewish Paul as critical to a responsibility regarding New Testament interpretation and theological reflection after the Holocaust, see Calvin Roetzel,

The Letters of Paul: Conversations in Context (3rd ed.; Louisville, Ky.: Westminster/John Knox, 1991), and Tomson, *Paul and the Jewish Law.* Luise Schottroff is also actively involved in positioning Paul as Jewish; in a series of articles and books, she has argued for overcoming Christian anti-Judaism altogether in New Testament studies and includes a re-reading of Paul as thoroughly concerned with Torah and Jewish community formation.

16. What, precisely, the Gentiles are converting *to* is a matter of scholarly debate. Christianity? Judaism? Some kind of Jewish Christianity or Christian Judaism? And, what they are converting *from* is even muddier; it is usually taken for granted that some kind of polytheism will do. Susan M. (Elli) Elliott has done much work to describe the possible Anatolian cultic context that Paul and his Galatian audience negotiates in *Cutting too Close for Comfort.* Whatever the labels, there is some evidence that people became Jewish. What such people should be called—proselytes, converts, God-fearers—is, in my view, still an open question in Paul's first-century context. I will discuss this in relation to circumcision below. See Louis H. Feldman, *Jew and Gentile in the Ancient World: Attitudes and Interactions from Alexander to Justinian* (Princeton: Princeton University Press, 1993); Shaye J. D. Cohen, *The Beginnings of Jewishness: Boundaries, Varieties, Uncertainties* (Berkeley: University of California Press, 1999), 107–238; Daniel Boyarin, *Border Lines: The Partition of Judeo-Christianity* (Philadelphia: University of Pennsylvania Press, 2004). The extraordinary inscription found in Aphrodisias detailing 130 names of Jews and "god-fearers" (*theosebeis*, who constitute 54 of the 130) seems to establish "god-fearer" as group identification, at least in the third century C.E. (when the inscription is dated). There is also evidence of this term in other cities in Asia Minor: Sardis, (Lydian) Philadelphia, Tralles, and Miletus. See Joyce Reynolds and Robert Tannenbaum, *Jews and God-Fearers at Aphrodisias: Greek Inscriptions with Commentary* (London: Society for the Promotion of Roman Studies, 1982). The possibility that Gentile converts are turning away from allegiance to Caesar by joining the group known as Jews, and the wider political implications of such a maneuver, have only recently begun to be discussed in New Testament circles by, for example, Mark Nanos, *The Irony of Galatians,* and Brigitte Kahl, "Reading Galatians and Empire."

17. Paul's view of the law, particularly in contrast to faith, is one of the most written-about topics in Pauline studies; because of space constraints I need not give an exhaustive history here. It is supposed that Paul's new situation enables him to speak to Jews and Gentiles about salvation for both groups through different means: Torah for Jews, Christ for Gentiles. In this sense Paul does not give up Torah but also does not wholeheartedly recommend it for newcomers to his communities. Nor is Paul consistent on the legal instruction he gives his communities; see Tomson, *Paul and the Jewish Law* for specific case-studies of legal discussion. Some maintain that Paul's position toward Torah observance after his conversion experience is that Torah matters for no one, Jew or Gentile, who wants to be saved. In this schema, therefore, Paul proposes no distinction between Jews and Gentiles on a ritual-observance level. See, e.g., Alan Segal, *Paul the Convert: The Apostolate and Apostasy of Saul the Pharisee* (New Haven: Yale University Press, 1992). For a discussion on the contours of this position by scholars drawing on Stendahl's work, and how the position itself can be construed as "equality without difference" between Jews and Gentiles, see Jae Won Lee, *Paul and the Politics of Difference: A Contextual Study of the Jewish-Gentile Difference in Galatians and Romans* (Ph.D. diss., Union Theological Seminary, 2001).

18. The identity of Paul's opponents constitutes an entire cottage industry of its own in New Testament scholarship. The identity of the opponents is methodologically troubling for a number of reasons, not the least of which is that we do not have any materials from the so-called opponents themselves. Additionally, the possibility that Paul is "slandering" opponents just to eliminate anxiety about his own position vis-à-vis his addressees is underappreciated. Yet a reading of Galatians, even one that calls itself a re-imagination, should not proceed without at least a brief consideration of the opponents. Paul's letters, which are not abstract treatises but embedded in concerns of particular communities, are framed as responses to questions or other matters. In 1 and 2 Corinthians, Romans, and Galatians in particular, Paul is clearly presenting his addressees with responses to those who are saying something different than he is, perhaps even contradictory; and perhaps the problem is that

some in Paul's communities accept what the others are saying. Since Paul's rhetoric has been taken at face value as representing a discourse of opposition, his opponents emerge as a category with high stakes in the study of the New Testament. They have alternately been called Judaizers (Baur, Barrett), Gnostics (Lütgert, Bultmann), Divine men (Georgi, referring specifically to "Hellenistic Jews" in Corinth), and Teachers (Martyn). For a summary of the scholarship on Paul's opponents and a bibliography, see *Christianity, Judaism, and other Greco-Roman Cults*, ed. Jacob Neusner (Leiden: Brill, 1975); and Jerry Sumney, *Identifying Paul's Opponents: The Question of Method in 2 Corinthians* (JSNTSup 40; Sheffield: Sheffield Academic Press, 1990). For a slightly alternative view that represents the opponents as a part of Paul's conversations, that we do not have access to, see Roetzel, *The Letters of Paul*. What we can definitely say about the opponents in Galatians—if they really *are* opponents, since Paul says they are "preaching a different gospel which is not another, except there are some troubling you and wanting to turn around the good news of Christ" (Gal 1:7)—is that somehow the Galatians are hearing a message that they must be circumcised in order to participate in the assemblies, which is also linked with following the law. To think and act upon this, according to Paul, makes the Galatians "infantile" (Gal 3:1) in light of what they have experienced with him. I take seriously Paul's charge that the gospel "is not another"; in light of the political demands of Paul's Roman imperial context in Asia Minor—that all peoples are connected through the empire, and should worship the emperor—circumcision as a way out of such worship seems plausible. However, Paul clearly thinks there is more to gain (and more of a risk) if the plurality of the group choosing not to worship the emperor is preserved (Nanos, Kahl). In both cases, Paul and not-Paul, the issue is one of how marginalized people express profound disidentification with the dominant structure's expectations: if all resisters were to become circumcised, in a way it would be playing directly into the Roman structure, policing boundaries between those who play along and those who do not. Not adhering to circumcision, yet associating with the circumcised, demonstrates that resistance to Roman rule is a common cause among the (defeated) nations.

19. Circumcision is usually taken for granted as *the* marker of (ancient) Judaism and in Pauline studies, the idea that Paul does not want the nations to be circumcised, according to Galatians, is used as a proof that he was through with Jewish law, unlike his opponents. However, circumcision is not unique to Jewish males in Paul's first-century context, nor is it exclusively what makes a Jewish man Jewish to a Jewish community. In fact, it is what Greeks and, especially, Romans associated with Jewishness (along with the Sabbath, abstinence from pork, and the sending of money to Jerusalem). See Jonathan Z. Smith, *Imagining Religion: From Babylon to Jonestown* (Chicago: University of Chicago Press, 1982), 1–18; John M.G. Barclay, *Obeying the Truth: A Study of Paul's Ethics in Galatians* (Edinburgh: T&T Clark, 1988); Feldman, *Jew and Gentile*; Boyarin, *A Radical Jew*; Peter Schäfer, *Judeophobia: Attitudes toward the Jews in the Ancient World* (Cambridge: Harvard University Press, 1997); Cohen, *Beginnings of Jewishness*; and Nanos, *Irony of Galatians*. Cohen maintains that "in the first century C.E. in portions of Asia Minor, Syria, Arabia, and perhaps Egypt, circumcision will not have been unusual and certainly not have been a Jewish particularity. There is no certainty that Jewish circumcision looked exactly like Egyptian or Arab circumcision, but we may presume that in these regions circumcision alone was not a distinctive marker of Jewishness" (*Beginnings of Jewishness*, 46). Elliott's work in *Cutting too Close for Comfort* begins to fill out some of the local variations in circumcision (and castration) in Asia Minor, supporting Cohen's position.

20. Cohen, *Beginnings of Jewishness*, 49.

21. Though it is plausible that Jews were not in the habit of lifting their garments for all to see, which prompts an interesting question: how did people know? Cohen, *Beginnings of Jewishness*, 47.

22. Richard Hays, *The Conversion of the Imagination: Paul as an Interpreter of Israel's Scripture* (Grand Rapids: Eerdmans, 2005), 164. Here Hays is speaking of the approach to Paul's use of Israel's scriptures by Craig Evans, who writes of a pattern of "hermeneutics of prophetic criticism" in Paul, congruent with Hays's own view that positions Deuteronomy and Isaiah as Paul's "hermeneutical precursors." See Evans, "Paul and the Hermeneutics of 'True Prophecy': A Study of Romans 9–11" *Biblica* 65 (1984): 560–70.

23. See chapter 1 for a discussion of empire-critical perspectives and how they inform a gender-critical re-imagination. Paul as a Jewish person politically interested in opposing the religion of the Roman Empire is explored most thoroughly in the three Horsley-edited volumes *Paul and Empire, Paul and Politics*, and *Paul and the Roman Imperial Order*. See also Neil Elliott, *Liberating Paul: The Justice of God and the Politics of the Apostle* (Maryknoll, N.Y.: Orbis, 1994). Crossan and Reed build on this work and add rich attention to archaeological remains in *In Search of Paul*.

24. These terms for the emperor as part of the New Testament's contexts are fleshed out in Dieter Georgi, "God Turned Upside Down," in *Paul and Empire*, 148–57.

25. Horsley, "Building an Alternative Society: Introduction," in *Paul and Empire*, 206–14.

26. Horsley has been the most vocal proponent of this idea recently; for a fuller delineation of contemporary issues, see *Religion and Empire*, Facets Series (Minneapolis: Fortress Press, 2004).

27. Elisabeth Schüssler Fiorenza has made this point repeatedly in her work and most succinctly in her response to the October 2004 "New Testament and Roman Empire" conference held at Union Theological Seminary. See Schüssler Fiorenza, "Empire and Christian Testament Studies," *USQR* 59:3–4 (2005): 131–39. In this response, she claims that New Testament research that operates within a "historical paradigm," such as that which takes the Roman Empire seriously, somehow still positions itself as "value-neutral, objective research" (138). In my view, it is theologically-motivated historical work that masquerades as apolitical and value-neutral, and not historical work as such, that should provide much cause for a hermeneutic of deep suspicion. Attention to the historical dynamics of empire in scholarly investigation is far from neutral and objective; in fact, a realignment of primary sources positions the New Testament as a historical counter-narrative to the very same dynamics it has been used to support throughout time. Such an approach should naturally lead us to at least think seriously about a "genealogy of resistance" in biblical interpretation.

28. Buell, *Why This New Race*, for example, is not overtly concerned with the New Testament's visions and constructions of ethnic conflict and formation vis-à-vis that of the Roman Empire. She rightly cites Gal 3:28 four times, without much discussion, as evidence of "Christian Universalism" that claims to overcome race, but in this work there could be more discussion of ethnicity's range of semantic meanings, as well as how ethnicity, through visual and literary representation, is never isolable as a category but is always linked to gender, sexuality, and class.

29. In this pattern of interpretation, the Gentiles are the focus of moral invective that aims to draw boundaries between insiders and outsiders (elites and non-elites, Christians and pagans). Such a view affirms the early Christians as culturally consistent boundary-police. See Jennifer Wright Knust, *Abandoned to Lust: The Politics of Sexual Slander in Early Christianity* (Ph.D. diss., Columbia University, 2001), and Knust, "Paul and the Politics of Virtue and Vice," in *Paul and the Roman Imperial Order*, 155–75.

30. Sze-Kar Wan, "Collection for the Saints as an Anticolonial Act: Implications for Paul's Ethnic Reconstruction," in *Paul and Politics*, 191–215.

31. Martin Goodman argues for the reconnection of worldwide resistance to Roman rule among conquered peoples, not just the Jews of Palestine: "Who can know whether inhabitants of Syria or Cilicia or Greece chose not to rebel because they were happy with their lot or because, after rational consideration of what had happened to people like the Jews, they elected (most of the time) to suffer in silence? . . . Other parts of the empire besides Judea witnessed rumblings of discontent over long periods. It was not only the Jews who evoked horrific retaliation by the imperial state, suffering the deaths of thousands of captives and forcible resettlement. Most important of all, the fact that most provincials at most times (including most Jews) did not rebel may have been a result of fear, not contentment." See Goodman, "Opponents of Rome: Jews and Others," in *Images of Empire*, 222–39; 238–39.

32. E.g., in Agrippa's speech, Josephus, *B.J.* 2.358–87. See chapter 3 for discussion.

33. E.g., Acts 17:16: "And while Paul was waiting for them in Athens, his spirit was aroused, observing that the city was full of idols" (*En de tais Athēnais ekdechomenou autous tou Paulou parōxyneto to pneuma autou en autō theōrountos kateidōlon ousan tēn polin*). For a discussion of how

these images must be taken seriously as a spatial context negotiated by Paul, Peter, and the followers of the way, see Moxnes, " 'He saw that the city was full of idols' (Acts 17:16)."

34. Harl, *Coinage in the Roman Economy*, 3.

35. A letter from Augustus to a Stephanos on behalf of Zoilos, 38–36 B.C.E., inscribed on the Archive wall in the Aphrodisias theater reads: "Caesar to Stephanos, greetings. You know how fond I am of my Zoilos. I have freed his native city and recommended it to Antonius. Since Antonius is absent, take care that no burden fall upon them. This one city I have taken for my own out of [the] whole of Asia (*Mian polin tautēn ex holēs tēs Asias emautō eilēppha*). I want them to be protected as my own townspeople. I shall be watching to see that you carry out my recommendation to the full." Zoilos, a freed slave of Augustus, returned to his city and secured freedom for its inhabitants, for which they were certainly grateful. In another inscription, Zoilos refers to himself as "priest of Aphrodite, savior and benefactor of his fatherland (*sōtēr kai euergetēs tēs patridos*), (for) the temple of Aphrodite." See R. R. R. Smith, *The Monument of C. Julius Zoilos* (Mainz am Rhein: von Zabern, 1993).

36. For a summary of Paul's itinerary according to the sources: Paul Trebilco, "Itineraries, Travel Plans, Journeys, Apostolic Parousia," *DPL* 446–56; for more extensive discussion, see the still-unsurpassed Sir William Ramsay, *St. Paul the Traveler and Roman Citizen* (London: Hodder & Stoughton, 1905).

37. Kahl, "Reading Galatians and Empire," 25ff.

38. Ibid., 26.

39. Crossan and Reed use "Peace through Victory" as the major theme of Roman civilization, in contrast to the "Peace through Justice" of the Pauline Jewish paradigm (which they also call "post-civilization"); *In Search of Paul*, 413.

40. Civilization was not always accomplished violently by the Romans, even if they visually represented it that way. I discuss this in the conclusion to this project.

41. *ēkousate gar tēn emēn anastrophēn pote en tō Ioudaismō, hoti kath' hyperbolēn edikion tēn ekklēsian tou theou kai eporthoun autēn, kai proekopton Ioudaismō hyper pollous synēlikiōras en tō genei mou, perissoterōs zēlōtēs hyparchōn tōn patrikōn mou paradoseōn.*

42. See Martyn, *Galatians*, 154–55, for a recent encapsulation.

43. *diōkō* appears forty-one times in the canonical New Testament. Of those, sixteen are in Paul's letters and six in Acts. Again, this term appears in relationship to what Paul had been doing to the assembly before his consciousness-shift (particularly Gal 1:13, 23; Acts 9:4, 22:4 and 7). He uses this term the most in Galatians (five times: 1:13; 1:23; 4:29; 5:11; 6:12), followed by Romans (four times: 9:30; 9:31; 12:14; 14:19). In these cases Paul describes both what he has done, what has happened to him (e.g., Gal 5:11: "If I still proclaim circumcision, why am I still being persecuted?"), and what his addressees should not do (e.g., Rom 12:14: "Bless those who persecute you, bless and do not curse them").

44. The *BDAG* entry for *portheō* gives very little other information to demonstrate a wider semantic field other than Paul's annihilation of Christian churches.

45. Homer uses the term to describe what men of old did to cities and walls (*Iliad* 4.308), and Odysseus recalls how his comrades "destroyed" the fields of Egypt, "carrying off women and little children" (*ek de gynaikas agon kai nēpia tekna*, *Odyssey* 14.264). Herodotus describes how the Samians, when the Siphnians would not give them money, "destroyed their countryside" (*tous chōrous autōn eportheon, Hist.* 3.58). Diodorus and Strabo use *portheō* to designate what happened to Potidaea at the hands of the Athenians (Diodorus, 12.34) and how the Egyptian kings thought of the Greeks (as "ravagers" [*porthētai*]) and wanted nothing to do with them (Strabo, *Geogr.* 17.1.6). Plutarch describes how, when Sulla was concerned about taking Greece, many barbarian nations gathered against his army yet were more concerned with "ravaging" the lands than facing him directly; thus, they were ruining the place he was about to take for Rome (*Sulla,* 16; 33).

46. Two other examples in Philo stand out concerning annihilation of a people. Regarding the Jews' unwillingness to accept Gaius as a god or demigod, Philo writes that they who were previously "unfortunate" are now "destroyed" (*eporthēsen*), for Gaius regarded the Jews with special suspicion,

as if "they were the only persons who had wishes opposed to his," and who "had been taught in a manner from their swaddling-clothes by their parents, and their teachers and instructors, and even before that by their holy laws, and also by their unwritten maxims and customs, to believe that there was but one God, their father and creator of all the world" (Philo, *Leg.* 114–16). Regarding the interpretation of Moses' burning bush not being consumed as an allegory for when the Jews are being persecuted, their "weakness is their strength," and they will be "saved rather than destroyed, by those who are desirous to destroy your whole race against their will, so that you shall not be overwhelmed by the evils with which they will afflict you, but when your enemies think most surely that they are destroying (*porthousin*) you, then you shall most brilliantly shine out in glory" (Philo, *Mos.* 1.69).

47. The first of the twenty-eight occurrences in Josephus is in relationship to "the ravager Titus Caesar" (*ho porthēsas Kaisar Titos, B. J.* 1.10). The Jews are on the whole not the ravagers, but the ones being ravaged—particularly Jerusalem. See also 1.159, 315; 2.236, 239, 322, 339, 351 (Agrippa's speech), 458; 4.134, 168, 405, 442, 443, 448, 534, 537, 552, 590 (4.442ff. describe Vespasian's march east, ravaging the cities in his path, after hearing that the Gauls had revolted against Nero under Vindex); 5.19, 332, 405, 406, 408 (5.405ff. appear in Josephus's speech to his fellow Jews to consider the virtues of peace under the Romans; similar to Agrippa's speech, in it Josephus says that if God had wanted to punish the Romans for their destruction of the Jews, as he did Assyria, then he would have done so before Titus); 7.26, 44, 425.

48. Whittaker posits that this is at least the case for the Romans (and moderns); see "Sex on the Frontiers," 128; see also Williams, *Roman Homosexuality*, 107–8.

49. Paul never directly calls himself a Roman citizen in his letters; this aspect of his identity is only explicitly found in Acts (16:37–38; 22:25–30). Both times the issue of his citizenship is raised in relation to whether or not it is legal to throw him in prison and in relation to the resultant interaction with Roman authorities, who fear for their error in harming "their own." In Acts 16, Paul does not want he and his fellow prisoners in Philippi, all Roman citizens, to be discharged from prison in secret after they have been publicly beaten; he calls for the magistrates to come and apologize and release them in person, which they do because they heard their prisoners were Romans, and they were afraid (*ephobēthēsan*). Acts 22:25–30 is a clever interaction between Paul, a centurion, and a commander (*chiliarchos*) in Jerusalem. Paul, again imprisoned, is about to be interrogated and beaten; he asks the centurion, as the straps are being laid out, "if a person is a Roman and is uncondemned, is it lawful for you to whip (that one)?" (*ei anthrōpon Rōmaiōn kai akatakriton exestin hymin mastizein*). This question stops the punishment, and the two Roman authority figures determine that Paul did not buy his citizenship but was born with it; in 22:28, Paul responds when the centurion comments that his own citizenship was expensive: "*I* was born that way" (*egō de kai gegennēmai*). This information causes the commander to withdraw from Paul and his examination because he was afraid (*ephobēthē*) that he had bound a Roman citizen; it is this exchange that leads the Roman authorities to convene the Jews and ask them what the issue is with Paul's transgressions. These interactions signify the complex relationship between the Romans, who are in charge of policing the populace, the citizens, and the non-citizen residents; it is clear from Acts that Paul would have been beaten much more severely had he not used citizenship to negotiate with and scare the Roman authorities. Returning to the first sentence of this footnote, that Paul never admits citizenship to his addressees, I wonder if hints of his being strong "in the flesh" indicate not just Paul's Judaism, but also the flesh of the Roman context of citizenship as well; such speculation will be helpful in the future.

50. The binding (literally: *dedemenous*, "having been bound," from *deō*), in the context of capturing and leading bound people, is mentioned three times in Acts 9 referring to what Paul intended to do with members of "the way." Acts 9:2 and 9:21 relate Paul's intention to bind and lead people to Jerusalem (9:2) and to the high priest (9:21). The conversation between Ananias and the Lord concerning Paul also mentions this pattern in Paul's behavior. Ananias asks the Lord, who has told him to go to S(P)aul in Damascus in Judas's house on the "Straight Road." Ananias answers that he has heard of Paul from many people and about the "evil" he was doing to the saints in Jerusalem: "here he has power from the high priests to bind all the ones who call upon your name (*echei exousian para*

tōn archiereōn dēsai pantas tous epikaloumenous to onoma sou)." The Lord tells Ananias to go, that Paul is a "chosen instrument" who will bring his name "before nations and kings and sons of Israel" (*poreuou, hoti skeuos eklogēs estin moi houtos tou bastasai to onoma mou enōpion ethnōn te kai basileōn huiōn te Israēl*). In his Jerusalem speech of Acts 22 that leads to more imprisonment, Paul talks about how he bound men and women and put them in prison (22:4), and how he went to Damascus to bind people and bring them back to Jerusalem for punishment (22:5). Paul is also given a glimpse of the binding that will come upon him as he is staying in Caesarea with Philip's four prophesying daughters, where the prophet Agabus takes his belt and binds himself with it to show Paul what will happen to him in Jerusalem (21:10–12); Paul answers that he is prepared to be bound in Jerusalem and even die there for Jesus (21:13). Soon, Paul is bound himself (23:29), where he has a little exchange about his Roman citizenship with his would-be floggers. Paul himself does not use the language of binding in relationship to his own history of persecution. He does use the term twice to denote marriage, once in reference to a wife's relationship to her husband (Rom 7:2) and once describing the husband's relationship to a wife (1 Cor 7:27).

51. Kahl, "Reading Galatians and Empire," 28. The label "Pre-Damascus" could indicate a conflation of Paul's own statements with the later historical narrative in Acts. Paul does not write that he was on the way to Damascus in Galatians, whereas this is clearly where Luke places him as headed in Acts 9 when his event happens. He was at an indeterminate place, according to Galatians, when he reports that God revealed his son in him. Paul does not tell where he was when this happened, only where he went next: not to consult with "flesh and blood," not "up to Jerusalem to the apostles who were before me," but out into Arabia, arguably an "end of the earth," and then he "returned" to Damascus. So I do not think it is clear, according to Paul's own rhetoric, that he was on his way to Damascus—but it does seem to be the case that he had been there before if he was to "return" there after being in Arabia for a while. If Damascus is the place where he brings his different conceptualization of relationships among the conquered (see below), then I suppose that before he arrives there, according to Galatians, he is a "Pre-Damascus Paul."

52. Kahl, "Reading Galatians and Empire," 29.

53. Ibid., 30. The concept of law in Paul's rhetoric is certainly relevant to this project; however, full discussion is beyond its scope presently. It should suffice to say that, like most concepts that Paul uses in his letters, the term law has a double meaning as both Torah and Roman law. That is to say, like lord and savior and peace and so on, law has a range of references and symbolic weight beyond an exclusively Jewish framework. A "Roman reading" of Paul's commentary on matters related to law is lacking, with the exception of Brigitte Kahl's recent article referenced above and her soon-to-be-published book on the subject. I largely agree with her analysis of a Jewish-Roman meaning to law, which could be extended beyond legal proscriptions to ideology. I would add that it appears to me that the nations are also compelled by (Roman) law to behave in certain ways that the Romans carve out for them after conquest; it also appears that transgression of national behavior might constitute a political difficulty. Also, as I discuss below in relation to the Sarah-Hagar allegory in Gal 4:21–31, it could be the case that Paul presents the Jewish law as enslaved to Roman interests. For more on the shape of the Jewish law under Roman rule (in Palestine), see Schwartz, *Imperialism and Jewish Society*, 17–49. For primary sources in translation concerning multiple aspects of Jewish diasporic interaction with civic authorities, see *The Jews among the Greeks and Romans: A Diasporan Sourcebook*, ed. Margaret Williams (Baltimore: Johns Hopkins University Press, 1998). For a discussion of Roman-Jewish interaction around "law and order," see Erich Gruen, *Diaspora: Jews among Greeks and Romans* (Cambridge: Harvard University Press, 2002), esp. 84–132 and 213–52; and John Barclay, *The Jews in the Mediterranean Diaspora from Alexander to Trajan (323 BCE–117 CE)* (Edinburgh: T&T Clark, 1996).

54. In later, particularly medieval and Renaissance, visual representations of Paul's conversion, two elements are outstanding. First, the horse. This literary lack is frequently seen as another impetus for frustration to teachers of the New Testament, because Paul's horse, absent from the literary text, is omnipresent—which is one factor in the conflation of the Pauline story. The way everyone tells it,

Paul fell off of his horse. The horse endures, most famously in paintings by Caravaggio and Michelangelo. However, there is something else important about Paul's appearance: he is rather consistently cuirassed, cloaked, and armed. This seemingly small detail—maybe we take it for granted?—speaks to the quality of Paul's life as a persecutor on the same level as a Roman military representative. To be sure, there is no way to say definitively that the "historical" Paul was a member of the Roman army. But that historical detail does not matter, as the dress and horse carry symbolic weight in later visual representation; they connect his activity in his former life to a higher position (in the equestrian order) of military domination.

55. The NRSV translation erases the bodily aspect of the womb, the personhood of Paul's mother, and the suggestive image of Christ being "in(side)" him: "God, who had set me apart *before I was born* and called me through his grace, was pleased to reveal his Son *to* me."

56. *hote de eudokēsen [ho theos] ho aphorisas me ek koilias mētros mou kai kalesas dia tēs charitos autou apokalupsai ton hyion autou en emoi hina euangelizōmai auton en tois ethnesin.*

57. For a brief overview of Paul's link to Isaiah, see Scot McKnight, *A Light Among the Gentiles: Jewish Missionary Activity in the Second Temple Period* (Minneapolis: Fortress Press, 1991), 13; 104–6. Hays has repeatedly proposed that Paul knew Deuteronomy and Isaiah intimately; see *Conversion of the Imagination*, 167–68.

58. I will return to the political connotations of idolatry—which as a designation lies beyond worship of images vs. non-images—in chapter 5.

59. See Martyn, *Galatians*, 165–66, for a summary of the view that God reveals Christ to Paul, as in God shows Paul Christ as God's son; see also Beverly Gaventa, "Galatians 1 and 2: Autobiography as Paradigm," *Novum Testamentum* 28 (1986): 309–26.

60. See Martin Hengel, *Crucifixion in the Ancient World and the Folly of the Message of the Cross* (Minneapolis: Fortress Press, 1977).

61. Importantly, in Horsley's three edited works on Paul from the emerging empire-critical perspective, only three essays concentrate on Galatians, and one of them (Schüssler Fiorenza) expressly discusses Gal 3:28, which occupies a special place in the history of interpretation. See Elisabeth Schüssler Fiorenza, "The Praxis of Coequal Discipleship," in *Paul and Empire*, 224–37; Pamela Eisenbaum, "Paul as the New Abraham," in *Paul and Politics*, 139–45; Mark Nanos, "The Inter- and Intra-Jewish Political Context of Paul's Letter to the Galatians," in *Paul and Politics*, 146–59.

62. Martyn, *Galatians*, 568.

63. Concerning the *stigmata* of Gal 6:17, Martyn succinctly summarizes the general feeling of interpreters here when he writes that the marks "reflect the wounds of a soldier sent into the front trenches of God's redemptive and liberating war" (*Galatians*, 568).

64. I have not the space here to fully discuss Paul's (un)manliness in non-canonical sources and can only give a hint of what should be examined further. In the second-century *Acts of Paul* (believed to have been written in Asia Minor), for example, we are given one of the earliest descriptions of Paul's body outside of the New Testament at the beginning of "The Acts of Paul and Thecla": "A man small in size, bald headed, with crooked legs, in a good state of body, with eyebrows meeting, and a rather hooked nose. But full of friendliness, sometimes he seemed like a man, and sometimes he had the face of an angel" (4; see also Tertullian, *Bapt.*). This text is often discussed in the context of early (proto-)Christian asceticism, particularly regarding women's roles and appearance in early Christian communities. In this legend, Thecla hears Paul preaching and decides to change her clothes into those of a man and follow him. The story is full of gendered language about how Thecla negotiates her existence as an unmarried, sexually unattached woman with the appearance of a man, and in some cases centers on her reception by the Roman authorities, including Tryphaena, a relative of the emperor. Thecla's gender performance is well attested; less studied is the contrast between Paul's and Thecla's manliness in this story.

65. Arabia is only mentioned twice in the New Testament, both times in Galatians. I will discuss the other instance in the Sarah-Hagar allegory below. Arabia is also, according to Greek and Roman

geographical literature, a borderland. As such, it is certainly barbarian territory (see chapter 3), where outlandish peoples, animals, and plants dwell.

66. Paul narrates that the Judeans have labeled him with the same terms toward others that he had used himself—persecution (*diōkō*) and ravaging (*portheō*).

67. Jennifer A. Glancy, "Boasting of Beatings (2 Cor 11:23–25)," *JBL* 123:1 (2004): 99–135. Glancy takes seriously the different contexts in which a man's body might be violated in Paul's time and concludes: "many scholars identify Paul's scars as tokens of virtue . . . within a Roman *habitus*, scars that established a man's virtue or virility were typically incurred in battle. Display of war wounds was a common feature of Roman somatic rhetoric. Those habituated to a first-century corporal idiom distinguished between a breast pierced in battle and a back belted by a whip: not every scarred body told a war story. Whippability was a token not of honor, excellence, or virility, but of dishonor, abasement, and servility. In analyzing Paul's boasting of beatings, scholars often cite examples of heroism attested by wounded bodies, although they do not always acknowledge the martial context of those wounds. Scholars have, moreover, passed over the semiotic distinction between a battle-scarred body and a flogged body" (134). On this passage and gender constructs, see also Jennifer Larson, "Paul's Masculinity," *JBL* 123:1 (2004): 85–97. On Paul's "slave" body, see J. Albert Harrill, *Slaves in the New Testament: Literary, Social, and Moral Dimensions* (Minneapolis: Fortress Press, 2006).

68. In addition to the imagery of crucifixion in Galatians, Christ occupies the slave position in Phil 2:6–11, the so-called Christ hymn: "but he poured himself out, taking the shape of a slave, having been born in the likeness of humans, and having been found in appearance as a human, he humbled himself, becoming obedient to the point of death, and death by a cross." This weakness, however, is exalted by God: "therefore God also raised him up and gave him the name above every name, so that in the name of Jesus every knee should bend, of heavenly ones and earthly ones and under-earth ones, and every tongue should confess that Jesus Christ is lord, to the glory of the father." The extra-worldwide dominion of Jesus expressed in the hymn is reminiscent of the universal reach of Caesar predicted in the *Aeneid*; however, the dominion of Jesus comes from a position of punishment and weakness and not military strength.

69. Paul uses the imagery of the triumph himself in 2 Cor 2:14–15: "but thanks to God, the one always leading us in triumph (*thriambeuonti*) in Christ and the fragrance of the knowledge of him manifests through us in every place; because we are an aroma of Christ for God among the ones being saved and among the ones perishing." The nations, here, are both saved and perishing. It has often been assumed by New Testament scholars that in this passage, the people led by God are victorious. As Kreitzer has pointed out using coins and literary sources depicting Roman imperial triumphal imagery, the people being led in triumph are usually those captured in battle and destined for slavery or death. It could be that Paul is turning the phrase around here, and instead of being led in triumph to celebrate Roman victory, God leads a triumph in Christ. But still, the imagery denotes violence and domination. See Kreitzer, *Striking New Images*, 143.

70. 1 Corinthians 7, for example, is the famous "marriage and celibacy chapter" in Paul's rhetoric; I do not have space to discuss it here except to say that Paul's status as a single, presumably celibate man speaks for his non-dominating stance and not necessarily for his self-contained man's-world attitude toward women. I understand celibacy as a political, even queer, stance against naturalized dominant sexual ideologies. See Vincent L. Wimbush, *Paul the Worldly Ascetic;* and *Asceticism,* ed. Vincent L. Wimbush and Richard Valantasis (New York: Oxford University Press, 1995). For a redescription of bodily practices in 1 Corinthians that includes attention to marriage, see Dale Martin, *The Corinthian Body* (New Haven: Yale University Press, 1995). Representatives of the empire-critical perspective have left the political implications of Paul's celibacy virtually untouched; for beginnings of a critique, see Cynthia Briggs Kittridge, "Corinthian Women Prophets and Paul's Argumentation in 1 Corinthians," in *Paul and Politics*, 103–9. For Paul's singleness in the context of Greco-Roman sexuality constructs as a possible queer locus of his self-presentation in Romans, see Stephen Moore, "Sex and the Single Apostle," in *God's Beauty Parlor*, 134–72, particularly 135–46.

71. Paul certainly refers to others as his children, but we mostly take for granted his fatherhood in those relationships (see below). As far as I can tell, Paul does not refer to himself as a father, only to how others are related to him. Mostly it is God who is the father. But still, Paul's rather consistent use of *adelphoi* to address his communities indicates that he thinks of himself not as a dominator, but as someone in horizontal relationship with those with whom he comes into contact and among whom he lives. Of course, he also refers to the Galatians in particular as his children, but this is because he is in birth pains with them as a mother, and not a father at all. For an in depth examination of Paul's kinship terminology, see Reidar Aasgard, *"My Beloved Brothers and Sisters!" Christian Siblingship in Paul* (JSNTSup 265; London: T&T Clark, 2004); see also Caroline Johnson Hodge, *If Sons, Then Heirs: A Study of Kinship and Ethnicity in Paul's Letters* (Ph.D. diss., Brown University, 2002).

72. This is the action Paul uses in connection to Jerusalem in Gal 1:17 (*anēlthon*) and 2:2 (*anebēn*).

73. *all' oude Titos ho syn emoi, Hellēn ōn, ēnankasthē peritmēthēnai.*

74. *oidate de hoti di' astheneian tēs sarkos euēngelisamēn hymin to proteron, kai ton peirasmon hymōn en tē sarki mou ouk exouthenēsate oude exeptysate, alla hōs angelon theou edexasthe me, ōs Christon Iēsoun.*

75. That New Testament scholars have not taken seriously Paul's statement about the Galatians caring for his body is yet another indication that we have not taken seriously the question of who, precisely, the Galatians are (beyond the famous "North-South" debate that I refuse to entertain . . . Paul himself is vague about his addressees, saying only "the assemblies of Galatia" [*tais ekklēsiais tēs Galatias*]). If they are, in fact, the ancient Gauls who represented both a noble yet savage enemy and an ever-present threat to Roman order, then it is not outside the realm of possibility that they would treat their enemies harshly and not just for dogmatic reasons.

76. For a discussion of the "mimesis" pattern in Paul's rhetoric, see Elizabeth Castelli, *Imitating Paul: A Discourse of Power* (Louisville, Ky.: Westminster/John Knox, 1991). Her argument rightly locates Paul's rhetoric as discursively constructing relationships between the apostle and his communities, which are never innocent or not implicated in the maintenance of power dynamics. However, Castelli considers this phrase in Galatians—that does not have the "mimesis" vocabulary, but uses *ginomai*—at the conclusion of her work as a "note." She posits that Gal 4:12 is to be linked to the mimesis pattern where, she theorizes, Paul advocates a unitary Christian discourse that does not have room for difference, only sameness. Castelli certainly supposes that Paul's "discourse of power" operates within a "complex structural and thematic web" (89) that includes attention to the literary and philological context of mimesis in Greco-Roman antiquity. However, she does not necessarily locate Paul's argument within the broader political environment that occasioned Paul's letters. I am not sure, for example, that Paul's recommendation that the Galatians not be circumcised, yet sit at table together with the circumcised in spite of Roman and Jewish inclinations to the contrary, is a clarion call for sameness. In fact, it seems as though Paul's ardent support of difference is what causes a clash between Peter and him in Galatians 2. Further, a Paul who operates at the bottom is not necessarily advocating upward assimilation among those who are different; oneness, exemplified by Gal 3:28, need not always be sameness.

77. E.g., Castelli, *Imitating Paul*, 116–17: "Paul's discourse of mimesis uses rhetoric to rationalize and shore up a particular set of power relations within the early Christian movement. His use of the notion of mimesis, with all of its nuances, reinforces both Paul's own privileged position and the power relations of the early Christian communities as somehow natural . . . Paul's invocation of mimesis indicts the very notion of difference and thereby, constructs the nature of early Christian social relationship: Christians are Christians insofar as they strive for the privileged goal of sameness." It is certainly true that Paul, in the history of interpretation, has a solid profile of quite the domineering patriarch seeking to erase differences into what Castelli calls the "hierarchical economy of sameness." This is especially the case regarding his supposed views on gender and sexuality in relationship to church hierarchies. Schüssler Fiorenza positions Paul as a precursor to what she calls the "New Testament orthodoxy" of the household codes (*In Memory of Her*, 235–36), manipulating

an older, more egalitarian sentiment ("no male and female") but not quite advocating women's participation enough in his letters. Maintaining Paul's impenetrable manliness only contributes to the Paul-as-misogynist characterization. In this project I do not aim to settle the question of what Paul was really thinking about women; I interrogate the gendered imagery he uses as a counter-impression of the imagery of his dominant political environment and begin to think seriously and ask different questions about power relationships in light of such imagery.

78. E.g., Betz, who says that Paul "compares" himself to a mother and dismisses the image as "Gnostic"; *Galatians*, 233–35. Martyn seems to think that the tough-guy Paul is just manly enough to birth a whole people, which requires more suffering than just simple birth pains that mothers endure; *Galatians*, 426–31. Feminist interpretation has all but ignored the image of Paul as a mother, especially in Galatians. For the most extensive discussion, which still only collects the texts and does little to advance a broader thesis on how maternal imagery should change an overall view of Paul, see Beverly Roberts Gaventa, "Our Mother St. Paul: Toward the Recovery of a Neglected Theme," *Princeton Seminary Bulletin* 17 (1996): 29–44. Gaventa calls Paul's maternal imagery "metaphors squared," or twice-removed from possibility (32–33). Most interpreters of Gal 4:19 have referred to Gaventa's work since the publication of this article.

79. Gaventa points out that the image of Paul as a mother is enduring and yet largely forgotten; ibid., 32.

80. In addition to the term for birth pains in Gal 4:19, Paul also uses the language of "begetting" (*gennaō*), i.e., genealogical language characteristic of the father-driven genealogies in Genesis and Matthew. In 1 Cor 4:14–15, he refers to himself as someone who "begot" the Corinthian "children." Even though scholarship leans heavily in the father direction, I do not think it is absolutely clear whether Paul is among the few fathers as opposed to the "guardians," or if he is acting as mother here, thus "overcoming" the father-guardian relationship (*ean gar myrious paidagōgous echēte en Christō all' ou pollous pateras; en gar Christō Iēsou dia tou euangeliou egō hymas egennēsa*). In this passage the Corinthians should imitate him, for which purpose he sent Timothy, "my child, beloved and trustworthy in the Lord" (*Timotheon, hos estin mou teknon agapēton kai piston en kyriō*, 4:16–17). Fatherhood could be supported by the fatherly prerogative of 4:21: "What do you want? Should I come to you with a rod or in love and a spirit of meekness?"—though I submit Paul prefers meekness and not the rod.

81. Gaventa, "Our Mother St. Paul," 44. At the end of the *Acts of Paul*, there is reported a major conflict between Nero and the Christians, called "the army of the king of the ages" (11:2) who will "destroy all of the kingdoms under heaven" (11:2), i.e., the Roman Empire, which itself includes everything under heaven. The army includes three of Nero's chief men, "Barsabas Justus of the flat feet, Orion the Cappadocian, and Festus the Galatian" (11:2). After learning that those closest to him were in this worldwide army, Nero orders a persecution of the "Christians and soldiers of Christ" and imprisons the three men "he greatly loved" (11:2). Nero also had imprisoned Paul and observes that, among prisoners, he was a leader (11:3). Upon this observation, he asks Paul, "Man of the great king, but now my prisoner, why did it seem good to you to come secretly into the empire of the Romans and enlist soldiers from my province?" (11:3). Paul's response to this question prompts Nero to order the burning of all prisoners and Paul's execution: "Caesar, not only from your province do we enlist soldiers, but from the whole world. For this charge has been laid upon us, that no man be excluded who wishes to serve my king. If you also think it good, do him service! For neither riches nor the splendor of this present life will save you, but if you submit and entreat him, you will be saved. For, one day, he will destroy the world with fire" (11:3). Paul is beheaded "according to the law of the Romans" (11:3) at Nero's decree; it is presumably as a Roman citizen that he is afforded this more honorable death than crucifixion or fire. He is portrayed as praying in Hebrew with body facing the east immediately before the execution (11:5), which I take as a signifier of consistent Jewishness. After the execution, Nero is astounded upon hearing about the milk that spurted out of Paul's body, and then Paul appears before the party and calls himself "God's soldier" (11:6). Later, Cestus (a centurion) and Longus (a prefect) approach Paul's tomb to meet Luke and Titus, who turned to flee but

were assured that the soldiers were more interested in cashing in on the promise of life from Paul that they received in prison than killing the "men of God" (11:7). I include this story here because, as I read it, it is a telling portrayal of conflicts between Caesar and Paul. It is not so much Christianity as a religious phenomenon that is offensive to Caesar according to this text, but its military character, drawing of soldiers from all Roman territories and political promise that "all kingdoms under heaven will be destroyed." Nero's persecution is also mentioned by Tacitus (*Ann.* 15.44), where it is clear that those murdered are accused not only of burning the city (see the *Acts of Paul* above) but of "hating the whole of humanity."

82. Most interpreters also focus on the divinely configured heterosexuality implied in God's relationship with Zion as his bride. I do not aim to discuss that relationship here. Phyllis Trible has charted the biblical use of women's wombs, including their use by God as a lover, in "Journey of a Metaphor," in *God and the Rhetoric of Sexuality,* Overtures to Biblical Theology 2 (Philadelphia: Fortress, 1978), 31–59.

83. E.g., Isaiah 3:26, where Zion is sitting on the ground in the sackcloth of mourning. Interpreters have focused on the misogyny of this metaphor and the linkage of idolatry with harlotry. It is less than positive for women's agency, to be sure, but also a reminder of foreign conquest and capture. I believe that this sort of personification of Zion, here as conquered, also signifies the position of the people and city as penetrated and captive to imperial domination. Her appearance should be compared not just with an Israelite "rite of lamentation" (Isa 47:1; Ezek 26:16), but also with the Deuteronomic instructions (21:10–14) for how a woman captured in war is to mourn in her captor's house: she is to shave her head, cut her nails, and remove the garment of captivity. Then she is to mourn her father and mother for one month and after that, she may be possessed by the man as a wife. However, the foreign woman captured in war is not to be enslaved or "sold for money" should the man not want her anymore. For a discussion, see Saul Olyan, "Generating 'Self' and 'Other': The Polarity Israelite/Alien," in *Rites and Rank: Hierarchy in Biblical Representations of Cult* (Princeton: Princeton University Press, 2000), 63–102; 97–98. Zion here could be a personified war captive in mourning, signifying a whole people in captivity.

84. See also 4 Ezra, where Zion, the "mother of us all," is in "deep grief and humiliation" (10:7–8, 45). She was mourning for her dead son, whom she bore "in pain" (10:13). See Luzia Sutter Rehmann, *Geh, frage die Gebärerin! Feministisch befreiungstheologische Untersuchungen zum Gebärmotiv in der Apocalyptik* (Gütersloh: Kaiser Verlagshaus, 1995), 160–213, particularly 186–203. And, of course, Jerusalem and Babylon are both personified in Revelation as bride and whore, respectively; for a gender-critical discussion, see Jorunn Økland, "Why Won't the Heavenly Miss Jerusalem Just Shut Up?" in *Her Master's Tools?*, 311–32. The suffering woman giving birth in Revelation 12 does so to a male son who will "shepherd all the nations with a rod of iron" (*hos mellei poimainein panta ta ethnē en rhabdō sidēra*, Rev 12:5).

85. Here I only mention several canonical First Testament passages using birth pains relative to personifications of cities and lands to denote that Paul is embedded in this tradition much as he is embedded in Genesis; given that I see definitive scriptural echoes, it seems even more unlikely that Paul ever was non-Jewish. Space does not allow me to comment on those other famous First-Testament personifications, those of Wisdom, who is technically also not a city or land. In any case, clearly there are also patterns in Jewish literature contemporary with Paul. Philo's depiction of Jerusalem as the "mother-city" (*mētropolis*) immediately comes to mind (*Flacc.* 46, for example: "For no one country can contain the Jewish nation (*to Ioudaiōn ethnos*), by reason of its populousness, on which account they frequent all the most prosperous and fertile countries of Europe and Asia, whether islands or continents, looking upon their holy city as their mother-city in which is erected the sacred temple of the most high God"). See Sarah Pearce, "Jerusalem as Mother City in the Writings of Philo of Alexandria," in *Negotiating Diaspora*, ed. John Barclay (New York: Continuum, 2004), 19–36. The Nag Hammadi material, particularly the "Thunder, Perfect Mind," also uses gendered personifications to denote (different) corporate power relationships. These should be

considered alongside the personifications in the Hellenistic Greek and, especially, Roman imperial context I discuss in chapters 2 and 3.

86. It is not my goal or prerogative here to fully delineate all of the technical problems discussed in the scholarship on literature like Isaiah. I find it satisfactory for this project to state that Paul is thoroughly aware of the contours of his scriptural tradition. For a succinct overview of the cracks and fissures in Isaiah and what it means for interpretation—particularly regarding the personifications I briefly discuss here—see Susan Ackerman, "Isaiah," in *The Women's Bible Commentary*, 161–68. For Paul as an interpreter of Israel's scripture, see Hays, *Echoes of Scripture in the Letters of Paul* (New Haven: Yale University Press, 1989).

87. Specifically, the Babylonian destruction of Judah and Jerusalem in 587 B.C.E.

88. In addition to Paul personifying herself as a mother in labor in Gal 4:19, s/he echoes the nations collectively in birth pains by designating all of creation as groaning together in Rom 8:22: "We see that all creation groans together and is in birth pains together until now" (*oidamen gar hoti pasa hē ktisis systenazei kai synōdinei achri tou nun*). Paul links this collective pain to the sufferings (*ta pathēmata*) inflicted by the present circumstances in Rom 8:18, which will pale in comparison to the glory about to be revealed by God. Creation (*ktisis*) has been subjected unwillingly to the "slavery of corruption" and longs for the freedom of glory. Romans 8:22 is the only occurrence of *synōdinō* in the New Testament. For a discussion of this term in an apocalyptic context alongside *systenazō*, see Sutter Rehmann, *Geh, frage die Gebärerin!*, 69–119.

89. It is not unproblematic for contemporary women, not to mention a whole Christian tradition of typological interpretation regarding the "suffering servant," that Zion's suffering is redemptive for the world in the "Servant Songs" of Isaiah 42:1–4, 49:1–6, 50:4–9, and 52:13—53:12.

90. For a postcolonial analysis of Micah that places this rhetoric as being from below and exemplary of a hybrid, utopian response to the crisis of political domination, see Erin Runions, *Changing Subjects: Gender, Nation, and Future in Micah,* Playing the Texts 7 (Sheffield: Sheffield Academic Press, 2002).

91. See Daniel Smith-Christopher, "Between Ezra and Isaiah: Exclusion, Transformation, and Inclusion of the 'Foreigner' in Post-Exilic Biblical Theology," in *Ethnicity and the Bible*, ed. Mark Brett (Leiden: Brill, 1996), 117–42. Smith-Christopher advocates a reading of the prophetic inclusion of the foreigners as "a more enlightened way to deal with enemies" than simple destruction (141).

92. "Conceptually, sociologically, and historically, the Jewish experience belongs in this general framework" of exile and restoration. See Shemaryahu Talmon, "'Exile' and 'Restoration' in the Conceptual World of Ancient Judaism," in *Restoration: Old Testament, Jewish, and Christian Perspectives*, ed. James M. Scott (Leiden: Brill, 2001), 108–46; 110.

93. See David Aune and Eric Stewart, "From the Idealized Past to the Imaginary Future: Eschatological Restoration in Jewish Apocalyptic Literature," in *Restoration*, 147–77.

94. I return to the issue of universalism in chapter 5. However, I agree with Scot McKnight when he claims that "God's plan and reign over the whole world and consequent international solidarity [present in Jewish writings of the first few centuries C.E.] . . . have their origin in scripture" (*Light among the Gentiles*, 13), specifically the prophets for Paul. The kind of international solidarity I propose, however, is among the marginalized from a stance of resistance.

95. E.g., Gaventa, "Our Mother St. Paul," 35.

96. I am certainly not the first to suggest that Paul's movement is one of international solidarity from those below, on the underside of history. E.g., Paul figures quite prominently in Nietzsche's denunciation of early Christianity; see Jan Rehmann's summary in "Nietzsche, Paul, and Empire," *USQR* 59:3–4 (2005), 147–61.

97. E.g., David J. A. Clines who, in a recent anthology of essays on New Testament studies and masculinity, tries to dislodge Paul's own manhood from "invisibility" but still comes up with a domineering, manly soldier/father Paul. Galatians 4:19, like much of the letter as a whole, is not a part of his discussion but, interestingly, a whole range of deutero-Pauline literature somehow is a

strong factor in the portrait of Paul as male. Paul is visible as a man in this analysis, and moderns must only choose which ugly man characteristics to notice, like, and dislike. See Clines, "Paul, The Invisible Man," *New Testament Masculinities,* ed. Stephen D. Moore and Janice Capel Anderson (Leiden: Brill, 2004), 181–92.

98. The Romans did seem to take circumcision seriously as a marker for Jewishness. In a well-known passage in Tacitus, the Jews are labeled as having "abominable" customs that date back to antiquity, including their sending money to Jerusalem (not to Rome), their loyalty to one another (not to Rome), their derision of the gods (like Caesar), and circumcision "so they could be recognized by difference" (*Hist.* 5.5.1–2). According to Suetonius, Jews—"registered" and those who tried to conceal their Jewishness—had to pay the *fiscus Judaicus* levied for "reparations" following the war of 66–70 C.E. Those who did not pay were punished further. Circumcision plays a role, as Suetonius recalls how he was present at one point when "a ninety-year-old man was examined by the procurator before a very crowded court to see whether he was circumcised" (Suetonius, *Dom.* 12.2). For a collection of primary sources, see *Greek and Latin Authors on Jews and Judaism, Volumes 1 (From Herodotus to Plutarch)* and *2 (From Tacitus to Simplicius)*, Menahem Stern, ed. and trans. (Jerusalem: Israel Academy of Arts and Sciences, 1980).

99. A compact example of such logic is given in a phrase from the *Satyricon* of Petronius, where some Romans, who are trying to get out of a ship unrecognized, entertain a suggestion that they be disguised by dyeing themselves with ink so as to look like Ethiopian slaves. They reject that suggestion as not good enough, since an adequate disguise requires more than different skin color: "Circumcise us too so we look like Jews, and bore our ears to imitate Arabs, and chalk our faces until Gaul (Gallia) takes us for her own sons" (102.14). Invisibility will be achieved by acquiring stereotypical attributes of foreigners. The Romans mocked the appearances of outsiders, but also had to have carefully studied such appearances in order to represent them visually in public monuments such as those I discuss in chapter 2, and the visual language of ethnic difference must have been common enough to comment on as above. Interestingly, the Romans did not mock the clothing of the Jews in literary representation. For a discussion, see Cohen, *Beginnings of Jewishness,* 30–34. Even if the clothing is not mocked or treated with suspicion, however, the Romans consistently (mis)spoke of the Jews in terms of stereotypical behaviors and customs that demonstrated their abominability.

100. It is unfortunately outside the scope of this project to present a detailed examination of matters related to the common meal for Paul in Galatians or elsewhere in his letters. The meal is a main area of Pauline concern for an encounter between Jews and Gentiles. For a concentrated discussion on table fellowship in Galatians and Romans, see Lee, *Paul and the Politics of Difference,* 94–219. On the social context of the meal in the ancient world, see Matthias Klinghardt, *Gemeinschaftsmahl und Mahlgemeinschaft: Soziologie und Liturgie frühchristlicher Mahlfeiern,* Texte und Arbeiten zum neutestamentlichen Zeitalter 13 (Tübingen: Francke Verlag, 1996); Dennis E. Smith, *From Symposium to Eucharist: The Banquet in the Early Christian World* (Minneapolis: Fortress Press, 2003), especially 173–218, on Pauline meals; Smith and Hal Taussig, *Many Tables: The Eucharist in the New Testament and Liturgy Today* (Philadelphia: Trinity Press International, 1990), 58–66. In *Beginning with the Meal: Social Experimentation and the Performance of Early Christian Identity* (forthcoming, 2008), Taussig proposes an analysis of the common meal as it is performed in early Christian texts and tradition as a "bold social experiment," where visions of alternative relationships were enacted.

101. Again, it is easily possible to conflate the Galatians 2 and Acts 15 accounts of what Paul and the others agree to do, if they ever even had such a meeting. Acts certainly gives a more protracted story that, in the history of interpretation, has been seen as a council. In this story, "some who came down from Judaea" (Acts 15:1) and the Pharisees (Acts 15:5) serve as the dissenting voices requiring circumcision to follow the law of Moses in contrast to Paul and Barnabas's happy reporting of the "turning around" (*epistrophēn*) of the nations. Here it is Peter who self-declares as the chosen apostle to the nations, stating that God has cleansed the hearts of the nations "by faith," thus "he did not differentiate between us and them" (*kai outhen diekrinen metaxy hēmōn te kai autōn tē pistei katharisas tas kardias autōn,* Acts 15:9). Acts also fleshes out the bodily requests of the nations who

want to participate in Israel: they are to abstain from "immorality," stay away from idol meat and blood and strangled things (Acts 15:20, 28), but they are not to be circumcised. For an analysis of the similarities and differences between Acts and Galatians on this matter, see Hal Taussig, "Jerusalem as an Occasion for Conversation: The Intersections of Acts 15 and Galatians 2," *Forum* 4.1 (2001): 89–104.

102. Kahl, "Reading Galatians and Empire," 39.

103. This formula, on its own, enjoys an extraordinarily rich history of interpretation that I do not have the space to reconstruct in its entirety. I hesitate to even discuss Gal 3:28 here, because full consideration requires a much more lengthy presentation of the history of interpretation. I believe that, in contrast to most of the history of interpretation, that this phrase as embedded in Galatians is not a neutralizer of identity constructs or a call for equality, nor is it necessarily modeling nostalgia for primordial oneness; it is a mandate for dominated groups to work together across their differences in the face of larger structural dynamics of oppression. What I can say is that interpretation of this phrase has all but ignored the contours of the Roman Empire or its place among the nations destined to be defeated by Roman rule. I give here only a glimpse at a longer future project.

104. One important aspect of the history of interpretation of Gal 3:28 bears mention: its historicity or Pauline originality, concerning which there is a bi-polar debate. A number of scholars have argued that this phrase is pre-Pauline, or is known before Paul uses it in the context of his letter to the Galatians. Much has been said for the initiatory or baptismal quality of Gal 3:28 to be understood as a performative utterance, giving the participant of a new (usually, Christian) reality. The reunification of male and female is thought to be reminiscent of an early androgyne tradition, preceding Pauline Christianity, popular in some form-critical and *Religionsgeschichte* approaches. For a discussion and bibliography, see Wayne A. Meeks, "The Image of the Androgyne: Some Uses of a Symbol in Earliest Christianity," *Journal of the History of Religions* 13:1 (1974): 165–208; Robert M. Grant, "Neither Male nor Female," *Biblical Research* 37 (1992): 5–14; Dennis Ronald MacDonald, *There is No Male and Female: The Fate of a Dominical Saying in Paul and Gnosticism,* Harvard Dissertations in Religion (Philadelphia: Fortress Press, 1987); Judith Gundry-Volf, "Male and Female in Creation and New Creation: Interpretations of Galatians 3.28c in 1 Corinthians 7," in *To Tell the Mystery: Essays in New Testament Eschatology in Honor of Robert H. Gundry,* ed. Thomas Schmidt and Moises Silva, JSNTSup 100 (Sheffield: Sheffield University Press, 1994); Boyarin, *A Radical Jew*, 180–200; Rosemary Radford Ruether, *Women and Redemption: A Theological History* (Minneapolis: Fortress Press, 1998), 13–44; Donna Wallace, *Androgyny as Salvation* (Ph.D. diss., Claremont Graduate University, 2001); Atushiro Asano, *Community-Identity Construction in Galatians: Exegetical, Socio-Anthropological, and Socio-Historical Studies,* JSNTSup 285 (New York: T&T Clark, 2005), 180–206. Schüssler Fiorenza provides a feminist-critical discussion analyzing the history of interpretation of this Pauline modification; see *In Memory of Her*, 205–41. I do not seek to settle the debate here. In the larger non-idealist framework within which a gender-critical re-imagination is situated, the final version of the text, the one that includes Gal 3:26–28 in the letter, matters. Further, even if such a phrase does not originate with Paul, his quotation does not make him either unimaginative or unintentional about gender constructs. I would tend to see the issue not merely as equality between sexes, but transformation of the circumstances that produce hierarchical gender differences.

105. Schüssler Fiorenza, *In Memory of Her*, 205–42; MacDonald, *No Male and Female*; Sheila Briggs, "Galatians," in *Searching the Scriptures: A Feminist Commentary*, 218–36; Castelli, "Paul on Women and Gender," in *Women and Christian Origins,* ed. Ross Shepard Kraemer and Mary Rose D'Angelo (New York: Oxford, 1999), 221–35. For a more nuanced gender-critical view, see Kahl, "No Longer Male?".

106. Empire-critical interpretations of Galatians are few, yet those few still pay little attention to what significance Gal 3:28 could have in a Roman imperial context. Nanos does not discuss it in his intra-Jewish designation of Paul's rhetoric in Galatians. Wan calls it the "new ethnos" that Paul constructively models where the issue is not Jewishness but "faith in Christ;" see Wan, "Collection

for the Saints," 199. See also Philip Esler, "Group Boundaries and Intergroup Conflict in Galatians: A New Reading of Galatians 5:13—6:10," in *Ethnicity and the Bible*, 215–40.

107. One possibility in this direction can be in thinking more critically—visually and spatially—about Gal 3:26–28 alongside *Gos. Thom.* 22: "Jesus said, when you make the two into one, and when you make the inner like the outer and the outer like the inner, and the upper like the lower, and when you make male and female into one, so that the male will not be male nor the female be female, when you make eyes in place of an eye, a hand in place of a hand, a foot in place of a foot, an image in place of an image, then you will enter [the rulership] (ⲡⲉϫⲉ ⲓ̅ⲏ̅ⲥ̅ ⲛⲁⲩ ϫⲉ ϩⲟⲧⲁⲛ ⲉⲧⲉⲧⲛ̄ϣⲁⲣ̄ ⲡⲥⲛⲁⲩ ⲟⲩⲁ ⲁⲩⲱ ⲉⲧⲉⲧⲛ̄ϣⲁⲣ̄ ⲡⲥⲁ ⲛϩⲟⲩⲛ ⲛ̄ⲑⲉ ⲙ̄ⲡⲥⲁ ⲛⲃⲟⲗ ⲁⲩⲱ ⲡⲥⲁ ⲛⲃⲟⲗ ⲛ̄ⲑⲉ ⲙ̄ⲡⲥⲁ ⲛϩⲟⲩⲛ ⲁⲩⲱ ⲡⲥⲁ ⲛⲧⲡⲉ ⲛ̄ⲑⲉ ⲙ̄ⲡⲥⲁ ⲙⲡⲓ ⲧⲛ̄ ⲁⲩⲱ ϣⲓⲛⲁ ⲉⲧⲉⲧⲛⲁⲉⲓⲣⲉ ⲙ̄ⲫⲟⲟⲩⲧ ⲙⲛ̄ ⲧⲥϩⲓⲙⲉ ⲙ̄ⲡⲓⲟⲩⲁ ⲟⲩⲱⲧ ϫⲉⲕⲁⲁⲥ ⲛⲉ ⲫⲟⲟⲩⲧ ⲣ̄ ϩⲟⲟⲩⲧ ⲛ̄ⲧⲉ ⲧⲥϩⲓⲙⲉ ⲣ̄ ⲥϩⲓⲙⲉ ϩⲟⲧⲁⲛ ⲉⲧⲉⲧⲛ̄ϣⲁⲉⲓⲣⲉ ⲛ̄ϩⲛ̄ⲃⲁⲗ ⲉⲡⲙⲁ ⲛ̄ⲟⲩ̄ⲃⲁⲗ ⲁⲩⲱ ⲟⲩϭⲓϫ ⲉⲡⲙⲁ ⲛ̄ⲛⲟⲩϭⲓϫ ⲁⲩⲱ ⲟⲩⲉⲣⲏⲧⲉ ⲉⲡⲙⲁ ⲛ̄ⲟⲩⲉⲣⲏⲧⲉ ⲟⲩϩⲓⲕⲱⲛ ⲉⲡⲙⲁ ⲛ̄ⲟⲩϩⲓⲕⲱⲛ ⲧⲟⲧⲉ ⲧⲉⲧⲛⲁⲃⲱⲕ ⲉϩⲟⲩⲛ ⲉ[ⲧ]ⲙⲛ̄[ⲧⲉⲣ]ⲟ)." Whether or not Paul and the author(s) of the Gospel of Thomas knew each other should be bracketed for the moment. Spatially, this logion is important: the inner and outer relate to each other in a different way, indicating a permeability of boundaries (e.g., in a building, in group gatherings). Similarly, not only are male and female made into one, but "the male will not be male and the female will not be female," indicating not simple equality but transformation of what makes male and female intelligible in relation to each other. The on the bottom dynamic is bolstered by the statement "when you make the upper like the lower," which does not, as might be expected, have the corollary. In other words, entry into the rulership requires absence of upward mobility, according to Thomas; what is high must be made low. Note also the displacement of images (ⲟⲩϩⲓⲕⲱⲛ ⲉⲡⲙⲁ ⲛ̄ⲟⲩϩⲓⲕⲱⲛ): a different politics of sight ("eyes in place of an eye") is required for this different existence among the lowly.

108. In one of the vision sequences of 4 Ezra, the emperor has wings. The eagle is the "fourth kingdom," i.e., Rome (11:1–9; 12:10–30). The choice of bird is not accidental; the Romans used the eagle to represent their power.

109. The appearance of those who are clothed with Christ in Gal 3:26–28 is a matter of debate. For a thorough investigation of the sources and bibliography, see Jung Hoon Kim, *The Significance of Clothing Imagery in the Pauline Corpus* (London: T&T Clark, 2004). Kim likens being clothed with Christ through baptism to taking the *toga virilis* in the Forum (121–22).

110. Both are the things that matter instead of circumcision and foreskin.

111. *ēthelon de pareinai pros hymas arti kai allaxai tēn phōnēn mou, hoti aporoumai en hymin.*

112. "This thing alone I want to learn from you: did you take the spirit out of works of law or out of hearing by faith? You are so stupid, having started in the spirit are you now being finished in the flesh? Did you suffer so many things in vain? If indeed in vain" (*touto monon thelō mathein aph' hymōn; ex ergōn nomou to pneuma elabete ē ex akoēs pisteōs? houtōs anoētoi este, enarxamenoi pneumati nun sarki epiteleisthe? tosauta epathete eikē? ei ge kai ekē*, Gal 3:2–4).

113. David Petersen, "Genesis and Family Values," *JBL* 124:1 (2005), 5–23. Petersen helpfully extrapolates several Genesis family values according to the text: an expansive view of the family, i.e., that the nations cover the earth after the flood, and Abraham will become a father of many; an interest in longevity, so as to live out the promise to Abraham and his offspring; and non-violent conflict resolution among family members in the interest of *shelom bayit*, "family harmony."

114. The seed of Abraham is also mentioned in Isa 41:8 as being Israel, God's servant: "But you, Israel, I have chosen / Seed of Abraham my friend / You whom I drew from the ends of the earth, and called from its far corners / To whom I said: You are My servant / I chose you, I have not rejected you." Given this status of election by God for Israel, it seems difficult to believe that students of Paul's letters would maintain Abraham as proof that the inheritance is Christian or that Abraham's seed represents an overcoming of Judaism. Further, the seed of Abraham coming from the "ends of the earth" indicates not just coming from far away, but coming from the margins.

115. Brigitte Kahl, "Hagar Between Genesis and Galatians: The Stony Road to Freedom," in *From Prophecy to Testament: The Function of the Old Testament in the New*, ed. Craig A. Evans

(Peabody, Mass.: Hendrickson, 2004). For a different reading of Gal 4:21—5:1 in the context of Anatolian mother-goddess traditions, see Susan M. (Elli) Elliott, "Choose Your Mother, Choose Your Master: Galatians 4:21—5:1 in the Shadow of the Anatolian Mother of the Gods," *JBL* 118 (2000): 661–83.

116. *dyo diathēkai, mia men apo orous Sina es douleian gennōsa, hētis estin Hagar. to de Hagar Sina oros estin en tē Arabia; sustoichei detē nun Ierousalēm, douleuei gar meta tōn teknōn autēs. ē de anō Ierousalēm eleuthera estin, hētis estin mētēr hēmōn.*

117. Karen H. Jobes, "Jerusalem, Our Mother: Metalepsis and Intertextuality in Galatians 4:21–31," *Westminster Theological Journal* 55 (1993): 299–320; 299.

118. David G. Horrell, *Solidarity and Difference: A Contemporary Reading of Paul's Ethics* (New York: Continuum, 2005), 192 n. 78. Horrell, like most interpreters of this passage, places a reading of Galatians in the context of law-observance (Judaism) versus freedom (Christianity).

119. This passage, like Gal 3:28, has a history of interpretation that is too enormous to recount here; it is sufficient to say for now that there has been little variation in the identification of Paul's allegory as a legitimation of, even mandate for, Christian supersession. The two women are always placed in oppositional columns, as if they have no overlap with one another. Martyn summarizes: "Although there have been some variations and a few reservations, one reading has dominated through the centuries, and it can be summarized in six points: (a) The pattern of two oppositional columns is accented. (b) The prepositional phrases by which this polar opposition is largely expressed—'according to the flesh' versus 'according to the Spirit' etc.—are taken to be adjectival identity markers, differentiating from one another two existing peoples. There *is* a people 'according to the flesh,' and there *is* a people 'according to the Spirit.' (c) These two existent peoples are understood to be respectively the Jews and the Christians; the polarity of the passage is thus focused specifically on Judaism and Christianity. (d) Judaism is consequently characterized as the religion of slavery and Christianity as the religion of freedom. (e) Verse 29 is taken to be a reference to the synagogue's mid-first-century persecution of the church. (f) Verse 30 is then read as an affirmation of the resulting supersession—according to God's will—of the synagogue by the church. Henceforth Christians are God's people; Jews are not" (*Galatians*, 450). Martyn is entirely correct concerning the history of interpretation; however, the solution he proposes to the problem—that Sarah and Hagar represent "two Gentile missions"—is still missing a (Roman imperial) context and does not directly address a fuller semantic range of meaning that the women's bodies signify other than religious.

120. The academic study of allegory as a mode of textual interpretation in the ancient and modern contexts is outside the realm of investigation here. In the ancient context, most studies of allegory have been focused on Philo and Origen, two writers most obviously involved in allegorical interpretation. R. P. C. Hanson's classic formulation proposed two schools of allegorical interpretation, "Alexandrian" and "Palestinian," into which all ancient allegorical exegetes can be identified on the basis of style. Hanson, *Allegory and Event: A Study of the Sources and Significance of Origen's Interpretation of Scripture,* rev. ed., ed. Joseph Trigg (Louisville, Ky.: Westminster John Knox, 2002). For a recent introduction to ancient allegory, see David Dawson, *Allegorical Readers and Cultural Revision in Ancient Alexandria* (Berkeley: University of California Press, 1991). Delman L. Coates has brought me up to speed on the study of allegory; his dissertation work seeks to overcome the categories and constrictions proposed by Hanson and Dawson and reorient allegory itself as a strategy employed by the marginalized to navigate "border identities." For an overview, see Coates, "Origen of Alexandria," *USQR* 59:3–4 (2005): 107–12. For a thorough critique of scholarly application of fourth-century allegorical exegesis to Paul's allegory in Galatians, see now Steven Di Mattei, "Paul's Allegory of the Two Covenants (Gal 4:21–31) in Light of First-Century Hellenistic Rhetoric and Jewish Hermeneutics," *NTS* 52:1 (2006): 102–22.

121. In fact, the slave woman as defeated synagogue and the free woman as victorious church has a rich history in Christian textual and visual representation. These two women appear sculpted in similar poses in and on churches, in stained glass, and in illuminated manuscripts. Flanking an entrance to the Cathedral of Notre Dame at Strasbourg (ca. 1250), Ekklesia/Sarah is represented as

draped and cloaked, holding the trophy cup for communion and the war standard of Christianity, the cross. She also wears the crown of Christian victory, unlike the victim Synagoga/Hagar, a woman who is blindfolded and not fancily dressed. She holds a broken lance and looks down in a mourning or submission pose, perhaps at the book of law about to fall out of her hand. In an example from the wooden choir benches of the Erfurt Cathedral in Thuringia, Germany (1400–1410 C.E.), equestrian Sarah impales Hagar, who rides a pig and wears the slave's cap common to representations of Jews in Europe during this time. In some medieval illuminated manuscripts, Ekklesia and Synagoga are standing on either side of a recently crucified Christ. Ekklesia, mounted on a horse on his right, holds up her cup to catch a stream of blood trailing into it from Jesus' side while Synagoga is either crouching under the cross or riding away with head cast down. In others, Jesus, resurrected and robed, takes Ekklesia by the hand while pushing Synagoga out of view. I came across several of this last example at a recent exhibit at the Koninklijke Bibliotheek in The Hague, Netherlands. For a collection of these and more depictions, see Heinz Schreckenberg, *The Jews in Christian Art: An Illustrated History* (New York: Continuum, 1997).

122. These statements also fill out the expansive connotation of the God of Israel and the lack of overcoming the law: "Or is God the God of Jews only? not also of nations? Yes also of nations, since one is the God who will justify the circumcision out of faith and foreskin on account of faith. Therefore do we annul the law through faith? May it never be—rather we confirm the law" (*ē Ioudaiōn ho theos monon? ouchi kai ethnōn? nai kai ethnōn, eiper heis ho theos hos dikaiōsei peritomēn ek pisteōs kai akrobustian dia tēs pisteōs. nomon oun katargoumen dia tēs pisteōs? mē genoito; alla nomon histanomen*).

123. Elizabeth Castelli, "Allegories of Hagar: Reading Galatians 4:21–31 with Postmodern Feminist Eyes," in *The New Literary Criticism and the New Testament,* ed. Elizabeth Struthers Malbon and Edgar McKnight (Sheffield: Sheffield University Press, 1994), 228–50.

124. Di Mattei, drawing on Liddell/Scott, entertains the possibility of "being born *from* Sinai *into* slavery," using the pairing of *apo* with *gennaō* to designate "birth away from someplace"; see "Paul's Allegory of the Two Covenants," 110. Martyn does not support "away from" but "from"—as in "Hagar is from Mount Sinai" or "the 'Hagar covenant' is aligned with that represented by Mount Sinai" (*Galatians*, 436). I propose a more embedded scriptural allusion to an "away from Sinai" translation and logic that can be linked to idolatry. First, directly related to Hagar: Genesis 21:21 notes that Hagar and Ishmael settle in the wilderness of Paran after being assured by an angel that a "great nation" will be made of him. Here Ishmael receives an Egyptian wife from his mother and starts a family. Paran appears later as the place where the Israelites go from Sinai in Numbers 10:11–12. As they are marching troop by troop on the way "out of the mountain of the LORD" (*ek tou orous kyriou*, Num 10:33 LXX) toward the cloud that has settled over Paran, the Israelites begin to complain bitterly to Moses and before God about how hungry they are, reminiscing about how good the food was in Egypt. They keep whining for meat, in particular. This angers Moses, who complains to God: "Did I conceive all these people, did I give birth to them, that you should say to me: 'Carry them in your breast as a nurse carries an infant' to the land that you have promised on oath to their fathers? Where am I to get the meat to give all these people, when they whine before me and say, 'Give us meat to eat!' I cannot carry all these people myself, for it is too much for me. If you would deal thus with me, kill me, I beg you, and let me see no more of my wretchedness!" (Num 11:10–16). God tells Moses to appoint seventy elders to share the burden of the people and then tells Moses to say to all 600,000 of the Israelites regarding the longing for Egypt, signified by desire for meat, "Purify yourselves for tomorrow and you shall eat meat, for you have kept whining before the LORD saying, 'If only we had meat to eat! Indeed, we were better off in Egypt!' The LORD will give you meat and you shall eat. You shall not eat one day, not two, not even five days or ten or twenty, but a whole month, until it comes out of your nostrils and becomes loathsome to you. For you have rejected the LORD who is among you, by whining before him and saying, 'Oh, why did we ever leave Egypt!'" (Num 11:18). The desire to go back to slavery in Egypt for something as gluttonous as meat on the road "away from Mount Sinai" is seen as rejecting the God who brought the Israelites out of oppression. Rejection of God

"away from Mount Sinai" is also the theme of Exodus 32:1–8, the "golden calf" story. When the people see Moses coming down from Mount Sinai they, with Aaron's leadership, melt down their gold and make a calf whom they call "This is your God, O Israel, who brought you out of the land of Egypt!" (Exod 32:4). God tells Moses to hurry, for the people have been quick to turn aside from the path God has made them by declaring the calf their god (Exod 32:8). See also Gal 1:6, where Paul also comments, "I marvel that so quickly you are being turned, *away from* (*apo*) the one who called you in the grace of Christ, *into* (*eis*) a different gospel . . ."—I detect a lament for those turning away from the God of Israel who liberates from slavery, just as in Exod 32:8. Not only is the rejection of the God of Israel linked to the making of the golden calf, but spatially and ideologically, the idolatrous transgression takes place "away from Sinai" and, in each case, the Israelites want to be enslaved to the not-gods and the world order those gods represent—in the case of Numbers 11, just to obtain some fancy meat and garlic! Hagar, then, could be linked to the pattern of turning *away from* Sinai/the God of Israel toward slavery.

125. Many commentators translate and interpret the verb in Gal 4:25, *systoicheō* (its only New Testament appearance is here), as "standing in corresponding column with," positing that we can assume an oppositional column naturally. This analysis draws on Aristotle's comments on Pythagorean opposites: hot/cold, left/right, male/female (*Metaphys.* 1, 5, 986a, 23). As discussed in chapter 2, Aristotle's opposites inform the semiotic diagrams (even if we turn them to represent vertical hierarchy more accurately). However, this term does not necessarily require opposition. In Polybius, for example, the term is used twice to simply denote "standing in line with," as in military formation (*Hist.* 10.23.7) and "similar things" (*Hist.* 13.8.1). For this latter use, see also Diogenes Laertius, *Vit.* 10.76.8 (describing Epicurus's concern for stars and planets and "like things" [*ta systoicha*]). In these cases there is no clear antagonism between "like things" and something else. In Galatians, just because there are two women here, it is not a direct path to dichotomic opposition; such is an invention of Christian anti-Judaism, not to mention Cartesian dualism and, I would argue, patriarchal interests in seeing women destroy one another while vertical hierarchy remains intact. In fact, that both women stand for Jerusalem should lead us to think beyond a clear opposition to one another.

126. That Paul does not quite get it right with the Sarah and Hagar story in Genesis is unfortunately a common area of investigation that I think obscures the specifically Galatian texture of the allegory and its anti-Roman implications. To be sure, one of the more tragic aspects of the Abraham narrative in Genesis is Sarah and Abraham's abuse of Sarah's foreign slave Hagar. Here is where Petersen's non-violence as a mode of conflict resolution is challenged: there is nothing non-violent about Sarah's treatment of Hagar, her handing her over to Abraham for what I suppose could be seen as rape, and how she is then dealt with after the births of the two sons. However, Hagar and Ishmael are not forgotten by God in the story, and she too receives a promise. Interpretation of Paul's allegory has often focused on the absolute rejection of Hagar herself, in Genesis and Galatians. Some feminist scholarship has tried to reconcile this with a call to remember "Jesus' outreach to just such oppressed and forgotten" women (Osiek, "Galatians," 336). The Hagar of Genesis is reclaimed by womanist theologians as the surrogate who "makes a way out of no way" and challenges oppressive power structures, much like contemporary African American women (Williams, *Sisters in the Wilderness*, 15–33). However, these interpretations do not usually mention the Galatian Hagar. I am convinced that, for this passage, it is important to unhinge the individual woman Hagar from the gendered collectivity she represents. Paul indeed even says this is the case: "Hagar=away from Sinai birthing slavery=Mount Sinai in Arabia=Jerusalem now." She is not even Egyptian in Galatians; she is clearly a different Hagar standing for different circumstances. What I am proposing through attention to gendered personifications of lands and peoples, the nations, in visual and literary representation in Paul's context enables a transformation of this individualistic and oppositional characterization of Hagar.

127. Kahl, "Reading Galatians and Empire," 42, Fig. 5.

128. *Euphanthēti, steira hē ou tiktousa, rhēxon kai boēson, hē ouk ōdinousa; hoti polla ta tekna tēs erēmou mallon ē tēs echousēs ton andra* (Gal 4:27 [Isa 54:1]).

129. *kai oikodomēsousin oikias kai autoi enoikēsousin, kai kataphyteusousin ampelōnas kai autoi phagontai ta genēmata autōn; kai ou mē oikodomēsousin kai alloi enoikēsousin, kai ou mē phyteusousin kai alloi phagontai; kata gar tas hēmeras tou xylou tēs zōēs esontai hai ēmerai tou laou mou, ta erga tōn ponōn autōn palaiōsousin. hoi de eklektoi mou ou kopiasousin eis kenon oude teknopoiēsousin eis kataran, hoti sperma ēulogēmenon hypo theou estin, kai ta ekgona autōn met' autōn esontai.*

Index

PAUL IN CRITICAL CONTEXTS

Other Titles in the Series

The Arrogance of Nations
Reading Romans in the Shadow of Empire

Neil Elliott

ISBN 978-0-8006-3844-3

The Politics of Heaven
Women, Gender, and Empire in the Study of Paul

Joseph A. Marchal

ISBN 978-0-8006-6300-1

Christ's Body in Corinth
The Politics of a Metaphor

Yung Suk Kim

ISBN 978-0-8006-6285-1

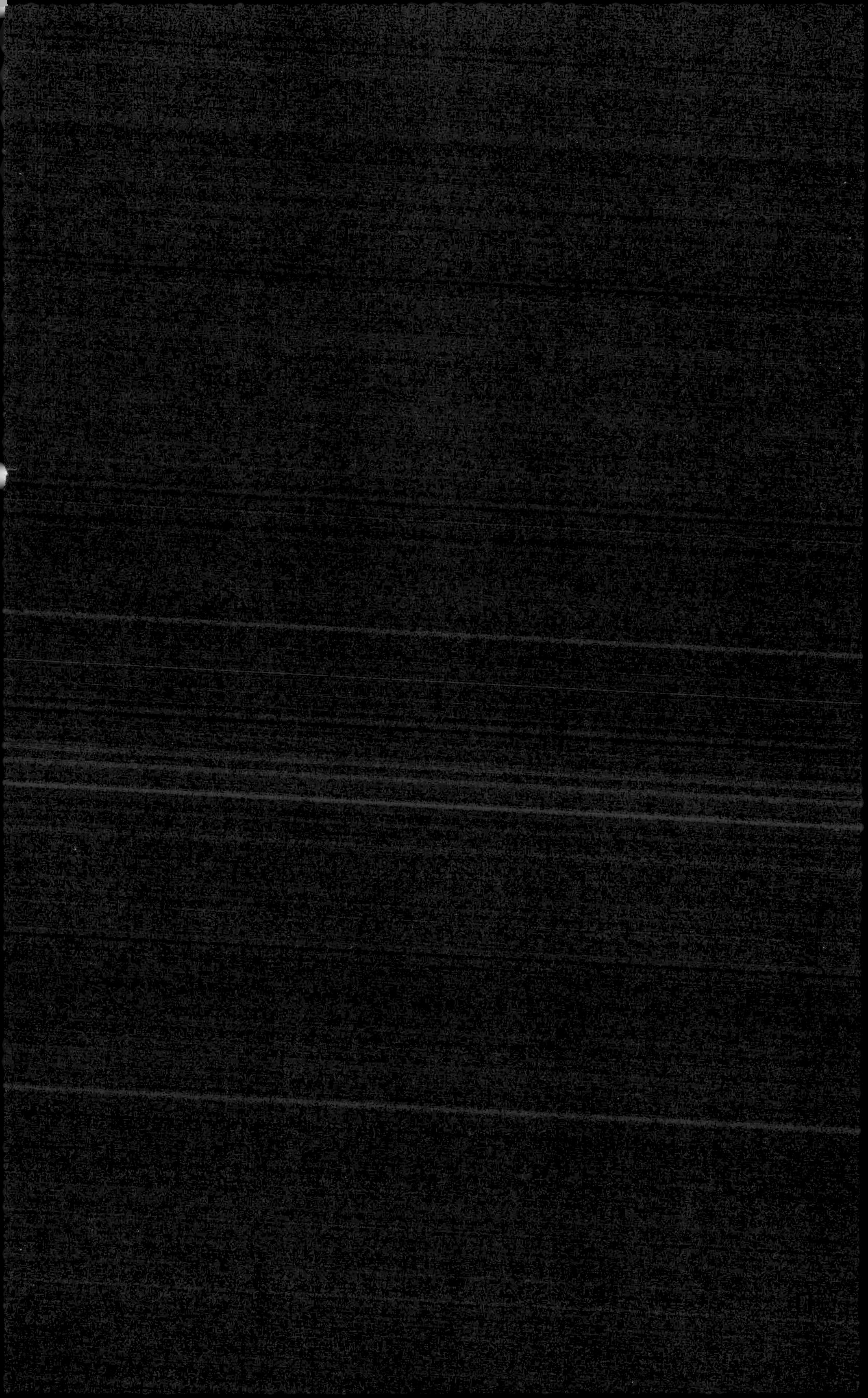